THE CONSUMPTION TAX

THE CONSUMPTION TAX
A Better Alternative?

Edited by
CHARLS E. WALKER
and
MARK A. BLOOMFIELD

The American Council for Capital Formation
Center for Policy Research

BALLINGER PUBLISHING COMPANY
Cambridge, Massachusetts
A Subsidiary of Harper & Row, Publishers, Inc.

International Standard Book Number 0-88730-159-2

Library of Congress Catalog Card Number: 87-17838

Printed in the United States of America

Library of Congress Cataloging-in-Publication Data

The Consumption tax : a better alternative? / edited by Charls E. Walker and Mark A. Bloomfield.
    p.   cm.
   "American Council for Capital Formation—Center for Policy Research."
   Includes index.
   ISBN 0-88730-159-2
   1. Spendings tax—United States. I. Walker, Charls E. (Charls Edward), 1923-   . II. Bloomfield, Mark A. III. American Council for Capital Formation. Center for Policy Research.
HJ5715.U6C658   1987
336.2'71'0973-dc19   87-17838
                                CIP

✳

Contents

v

List of Figures

List of Tables

✳

Preface

The chapters in this book are slightly updated versions of papers presented at a conference titled The Consumption Tax: A Better Alternative? (The discussions that follow the chapters are also updated.) Sponsored by the American Council for Capital Formation Center for Policy Research (CPR) and held in Washington, D.C., in September 1986, the conference assembled prominent academicians, administration and congressional policymakers, fiscal policy experts, business leaders, and members of the financial and economic media to analyze and discuss the fundamental fiscal policy issues and the political realities of an add-on or substitute U.S. consumption tax. These included the economic impact of a national consumption tax upon saving, investment, and economic growth; the international trade consequences; the incidence of such a tax; the regressivity of a consumption tax; the revenue-raising implications; administrative issues; and the politics of a consumption tax.

The Conference was generously underwritten by the following corporations, foundations, and individuals: Aluminum Company of America; American Telephone and Telegraph Company; Amoco Foundation, Inc.; Arthur Andersen & Co.; Baltimore Gas and Electric Company; Chrysler Corporation; Digital Equipment Corporation; E. I. du Pont de Nemours & Company; Enron Corp.; First Maryland Bancorp; Goodyear Tire & Rubber Company; IBM Corporation; Johnson, Lane, Space, Smith & Co., Inc.; William W. Lowry and

Associates; MCI Communications Corporation; Mercantile Bankshares; Meredith Corporation; Mobil Corporation; The John M. Olin Foundation, Inc.; PHH Group; Pfizer, Inc.; Philip Morris Companies Inc.; Potomac Electric Power Company; John and Lolita Renshaw; The Singer Company; Thermo Electron Corporation; Tracor, Inc.; and USF&G Corporation.

The conference and this book represent the work of many individuals. Certainly, as coeditors, our job would not have been possible without the ongoing support of our contributors, the staff of the American Council for Capital Formation Center for Policy Research, and our publisher. We would first like to thank Jack Moseley, chairman, president, and chief executive officer of USF&G Corporation. He graciously and generously served as chairman of the conference and is a director of the American Council for Capital Formation Center for Policy Research (CPR). Special thanks also go to Kate Kiggins, CPR conference publications manager; Margo Thorning, CPR conference director; Ernestine Johnson, CPR assistant conference director; Mari Lee Dunn, CPR vice president; and Carolyn Casagrande, Acquisitions Editor, Ballinger Publishing Company. Our thanks also go to CPR staff members Margaret Burrell, Doreen Kreger, James Rapp, and J. J. Rickerich, without whose efforts neither the conference nor this book would have become reality.

Washington, D.C.   Charls E. Walker
                                                          Mark A. Bloomfield

✳️

Foreword

Charls E. Walker and
Mark A. Bloomfield

Interest in a consumption tax is likely to mount as political and economic pressures build for action on the U.S. budget deficit and the emerging challenge of international competitiveness. Consider the following facts.

First, the United States is a chronically low-saving society, a fact that limits capital formation and long-term growth in the standard of living. Slow capital formation is especially troublesome now, when maximum investment in modern machinery and equipment is necessary if we are to compete with low-wage economies throughout the world. At the same time nearly all our international competitors already rely heavily on consumption taxes with export rebate provisions or, like Japan and Canada, are now considering them. The massive U.S. trade deficit emphasizes the need for a tax system that is less favorable to consumption and more favorable to saving and investment.

Second, the tax rate cuts of the Tax Reform Act of 1986 are paid for, to a large extent, by higher taxes on saving and investment. Lower levels of saving and investment, slower economic growth, less job creation, and a reduced ability to meet the challenge of foreign competition resulting from the 1986 tax changes could help turn attention toward consumption taxes.

Third, the federal deficit is structural; it will not simply go away. Most observers of government fiscal policy are convinced that the deficit cannot be curbed by restraints on spending alone, that sooner or later some tax increase will be needed for deficit reduction. Historically, short of a national emergency, the American public has resisted raising income tax rates; thus the 1986 legislation could lock in lower marginal rates. Since the Tax Reform Act of 1986 uses up the last "easy" and substantial revenue-raiser in the Internal Revenue Code (through repeal of the investment tax credit), the consumption tax option will have to be given strong consideration for deficit reduction in the years ahead.

Fourth, although there is pressure for restraint on aggregate government spending, politicians and public policy analysts recognize the need for stable and adequate financing for basic social welfare programs and a sound defense budget. Politicians also face difficult choices of financing new expensive demands on government ranging from catastrophic health insurance to much greater public support for education to the modernization of our nation's infrastructure. At the same time, many public finance experts ask whether the income tax, alone, is the best and fairest financing tool. For example, both Bob Kuttner of the *New Republic* on the left and Congressman Newt Gingrich on the right have called for a properly constructed consumption tax to help finance Social Security rather than the existing regressive payroll tax. One reason for this agreement may be what Willie Sutton a long time ago discovered about banks. He said: "People rob banks because that's where the money is." For better or worse there may not be much more money to be had from the income tax; and, therefore, a national consumption tax draws increasing attention.

Fifth, the public consistently over the years has preferred consumption over income taxes. A popular president could, with the right campaign, sell consumption taxes to the American people as a means of cutting the federal deficit and fostering U.S. international competitiveness.

If consumption taxes are indeed in the nation's future, as we believe they are and should be, then it behooves the public policy community to help conduct as intensive a dialogue as possible on the pros and cons of such an approach. If a consumption tax is indeed coming, then it should be carefully shaped toward fairness, workability, and economic efficiency.

This book does just that; it evaluates the strengths, identifies the weaknesses, and suggests ways to turn the weaknesses into strengths or at least to mitigate them. As one speaker, Ways and Means Chairman Dan Rostenkowski, told our conference participants: "I'm sure that this is the first inning of the next World Series on Capitol Hill."

PART I

POLITICAL AND ECONOMIC PERSPECTIVES ON A U.S. CONSUMPTION TAX

Chapter 1

A Historical Perspective on Tax Policy

Henry H. Fowler

The question addressed in this book is whether there is a better alternative to the national policy mix that characterizes the current U.S. fiscal and financial nightmare—an alternative that should include a consumption tax. The short answer is yes. The hard truth is that the federal tax system, even after the Tax Reform Act of 1986, will not provide the revenues needed to pay for the adequate performance of the constitutional responsibilities of the national government, as viewed by the people's representatives in the Congress.

A continuing resort to the large-scale deficit financing to make up the difference is unacceptable. A decidedly better alternative is the early enactment of a substantial tax on consumption in the form of a value-added or national sales tax, coupled with continuing constraint on domestic expenditures until the budget approaches balance. A revised Gramm-Rudman-Hollings Act (the Balanced Budget and Emergency Deficit Control Act of 1985) should exclude expenditures for defense and foreign policy. These vital outlays should not be arbitrarily straitjacketed. The existing domestic expenditure entitlements outside the poverty sector should be included under Gramm-Rudman-Hollings.

SETTING THE STAGE

The need for these changes transcends technical tax policy questions or even the larger pursuit of a fairer tax system. The United States is at a crossroads calling for bipartisan conduct of congressional responsibilities and extraordinary teamwork between the Congress and the president.

Four national economic problems need prompt solution. By failing to provide answers, our nation risks succumbing to various ills: recession, inadequate growth due to unsatisfactory productivity and competitiveness, a revival of stagflation or resurgent inflation, permanently excessive unemployment, and a badly weakened national position in the world economy when it, in turn, is limping along under burdensome debt in the developing nations, excessive unemployment and slow growth in Western Europe, and a rising threat of protectionism. The four questions are these:

1. How can the United States sustain a healthy rate of economic growth with an appropriate balance between savings and investment on the one hand and consumption on the other?

2. How can we eliminate the federal budget deficits that have become a cancer on the national economy, diverting huge sums borrowed by government in private capital markets from investment in the private sector, doubling the federal debt in the last five years from that accumulated in the preceding nearly 200 years, and increasing the annual interest on this debt from $83 billion in 1981 to about $142 billion in fiscal 1986?

3. How can the United States support national security and foreign policy requirements, a prime responsibility of the national government, free from the arbitrary and automatic restraints now fixed by the Gramm-Rudman-Hollings Act?

4. How can we reduce the unprecedented deficits in U.S. international balances of trade and payments to levels that will arrest the growth of public and private debt to foreign creditors, reduce recent U.S. dependence on foreign capital, help restore national competitiveness, and halt the drift into a destructive protectionism at home and abroad?

The Tax Reform Act of 1986 makes no contribution to alleviating any of these four national problems—whatever its virtues for tax fairness and its commendable reduction in income tax rates at the margin (always the best method of effective reform to eliminate unfairness and special loopholes). Given the claims by its sponsors that the 1986 Tax Act reflects neutrality between revenue reduction and revenue increases, it clearly does nothing to reduce the intolerable budget deficit, nothing to make possible an adequate financing of national security and foreign policy requirements without exacerbating that deficit, and nothing to reduce the huge imbalance in U.S. trade and payments.

Indeed, its most likely impact on any of the four national problems outlined is its adverse effect on any balance between savings and investment (the supply side) and consumption (the demand side). The 1986 Act makes the national rate of savings and investment, already inadequate compared to other major industrialized nations, even more inadequate. It increases the balance favoring consumption over savings and investment. In so doing, it diminishes the opportunity for domestic industry to increase its productivity and competitiveness by new investment enough to move the U.S. balance of trade toward equilibrium.

Proponents of the Act proudly claim that the legislation will pay for the reduction in individual tax rates, amounting to about $120 billion over the next five years, by tax increases of like amount on business operations. A tax law that repeals the investment tax credit, reduces the claims for depreciation of investment in production facilities, and treats capital gains as ordinary income, among other measures, is bound to result in less savings and investment, particularly in capital intensive industries.

Inadequate increases in productivity and competitiveness and a weakening of both short-term and long-term economic growth will be the inevitable result unless the nation stops turning its back on the accumulated wisdom and experience of the last 25 years.

Congress and the administration must embark on a serious search for a better mix of fiscal, monetary, and trade policies to steer the national economy through the dangerous shoals ahead. One result of such objective reexamination would be the decision to add a national consumption tax to the federal tax system.

A major portion of the revenues resulting from a national consumption tax would help restore fiscal balance between savings and investment and consumption. The effort to return to budgetary equilibrium would assure all concerned that the U.S. government has finally returned to the path of fiscal responsibility.

A minor portion of the revenues of a national consumption tax would make it possible to meet measured necessary increases in the requirements for national security and foreign policy. This could help avoid the arbitrary fiscal consequences of Gramm-Rudman-Hollings Act which are threatening to weaken national security as happened in the 1970s and to damage U.S. association with friends and allies. This development could help assure our allies and convince our potential enemies that the United States is strong enough, wise enough, and consistent enough to be a powerful force for peace, political freedom, and economic stability with development.

The addition to the national tax system of an indirect or consumption tax that can be rebated on goods exported from the United States and imposed as a border tax on goods imported, following the established practice of our principal competitor nations and trading partners, can effect deficit reduction without damaging our trade position. Furthermore, given the level of exchange rates, substitution of a consumption tax for profit or payroll taxes can actually enhance U.S. competitiveness.

A national consumption tax would also provide a measure of insurance against another fiscal policy danger. It would help ensure that no later Congress and administration would be tempted to meet a fiscal crisis calling for large amounts of revenue by increasing income tax to the levels discarded by the Tax Reform Act of 1986.

Of course, a national consumption tax alone will not completely solve the four major national economic problems noted. It must be coupled with continuing restraint on domestic nondefense expenditures, including those entitlements not going to the poverty-stricken, which by law rise with inevitable inflation.

A more efficient national security policy is needed that does not deny essential security requirements arbitrarily for fiscal reasons but assures defense expenditures free from waste or inefficient funding and procurement practices by the Congress and the Pentagon alike.

A monetary policy that nourishes sustained growth without inducing or indulging inflation is essential. We must also have an improved exchange rate and international monetary system that minimizes misalignments such as the United States suffered in the early years of this decade until the Group of Five finance ministers blew the whistle under the leadership of Treasury Secretary James Baker in September 1985.

The successful negotiation of new and improved trade arrangements that provide mutually fair and open competition in world trading markets as well as increasing productivity and competitiveness by U.S. industry is equally essential to a restored equilibrium in the balance of trade.

SOME PERSONAL CONVICTIONS

Sharing Responsibility

In a modern industrialized democracy the business and financial community and related professionals and academicians must bear a heavy responsibility in the world of politics and government. That responsibility is the key factor in the never-ending struggle to sustain healthy economic growth by maintaining an appropriate balance between savings and investment on the one hand and consumption on the other.

Everyone is a consumer of goods and services provided by the private sector and the government. But only a small percentage of the voting population is actively engaged or knowledgeable about the social processes that lead to a healthy production of goods and services by the private sector and jobs for those not supported by the state.

Access to adequate sources of savings and capital for private sector investment to provide goods and services, and hence jobs, is one of the most important of the processes referred to loosely as capital formation. There are many ways in which fiscal policy decisions by those we elect to government can condition this process.

By absorbing, through taxation and borrowing in the private capital markets, an ever larger percentage of personal savings and business profits, government reduces the private sector's access to capital for investment. If the methods of taxation employed are more conducive to consumption of goods and services by taxpayers than to savings and investment, access from that source is reduced. The Tax Reform Act of 1986 represents a sharp shift in public policy toward an imbalance in favor of consumption.

Elimination of millions of individual taxpayers from the tax rolls and a reduction of income tax rates on all individual taxpayers seems a highly commendable decision to the individuals benefited and the members of Congress who seek to enjoy the continuing favor of the voters. What is wrong is that the loss of revenues in consequence of those decisions is being paid for by soaking business income. The personal income being freed for consumption is not being replaced by any tax on consumption.

This shift in tax policy threatens to wipe out much of the gains in creating an appropriate balance between savings and investment and consumption achieved in fits, starts, reversals, and restorations over the last 25 years.

The shift comes against another aspect of fiscal background that makes its consequences even more serious—the existence of continuing annual budget deficits in the neighborhood of $200 billion. The resulting federal borrowing removes these huge amounts from the private capital markets, making them unavailable for investment in the private sector.

It is somewhat ironic to look back at the first conclusion stated in the overview of the 1983 conference of the American Council for Capital Formation Center for Policy Research:

> Capital formation appears to be an idea whose time has come . . . as the members of Congress who participated in the conference indicated, the 1982 experience was not a permanent reversal in the fundamental trend toward tax reform that encourages capital formation and economic growth.[1]

Some Personal Historical Perspective

Like most young people reaching adulthood in the 1930s and 1940s, I had only a superficial impression of the important role fiscal and monetary policy or the federal tax system had come to play in our national life during the 1929–33 worldwide depression, the New Deal, and World War II. Deeper convictions on these subjects began to take form for me in the late 1950s as a result of a three-year stint as a member of the National Commission on Money and Credit, followed by nearly eight years in the U.S. Treasury Department beginning in January 1961.

Even as late as 1960, the nation had not shaken the legacy of war-induced individual income taxes ranging from 20 percent to 91 percent and corporate taxes up to 52 percent. These tax rates were a factor contributing to three recessions in the 1960s and an average rate of economic growth over the eight years from 1953 to 1960 of 2.2 percent.

I remember hearing in the late 1950s a leading executive in the steel industry gloomily predict a decline in the steel industry because, in part, of excessive taxation. This observation and others like it became very personal to me in early 1961. President John Kennedy and Treasury Secretary Douglas Dillon asked me to serve as Dillon's general deputy (as the undersecretary of the Treasury was then called).

For the next nearly three and one-half years in that office much of my life was devoted to working within the Treasury and the administration and with the Congress and its committees on the formation and enactment of the granddaddy of supply-side tax programs. It consisted of three parts: (1) putting into law President Kennedy's unusual campaign commitment to institute a strange fiscal species called the investment tax credit; (2) starting an administrative process called depreciation reform in the Treasury with the blessing of the Joint Committee on Internal Revenue, which shortened the lives of business facilities for tax purposes as a measure complementing the investment tax credit; and (3) enacting President Kennedy's tax program, which became the Kennedy-Johnson Tax Reduction Act of 1964. This law provided, over a two-year period, a 20 percent reduction in both individual and corporate taxes. The bottom bracket for individuals was lowered from 20 percent to 14 percent and the top bracket from 91 percent to 70 percent. The top corporate rate was reduced from 52 percent to 48 percent. The Treasury sought even lower rates. President Kennedy's recommendation that the percentage of long-term capital gains to be treated as ordinary income be lowered from 50 percent to 30 percent (which would have made the top rate of this tax 20 percent) failed to gain acceptance.

What were the results? There can always be differences of opinion about cause and effect. Suffice it to say, however, that for the entire eight years from 1961 through 1968 (the Kennedy-Johnson years) there was sustained economic growth (32 quarters without recession) averaging 4.8 percent per year; with unemployment averaging 4.1 percent for the 1961-68 years; increasing real disposable income 4.8 percent per year with consumer prices averaging increases of a little over 2 percent and budget deficits averaging $7.5 billion per year.

Many factors contributed to this most successful period for the U.S. economy since World War II. But a fiscal policy that sought to balance savings and investment with consumption created an environment conducive to the overall result.

During my tenure as treasury secretary from April 1, 1965 to December 1968, inflationary pressures, largely a consequence of the Vietnam conflict, threatened the permanence and survivability of this fiscal policy. The investment tax credit was temporarily suspended in late 1966 to avoid a credit crunch but fully restored in the late spring of 1967. By that time, a budget deficit of $8.6 billion in fiscal 1967 threatened to expand in fiscal 1968. In August 1967 President Johnson sought the enactment of a temporary 10 percent surtax on both individual and corporate income taxes.

An extended effort involving three sets of hearings before the House Ways and Means Committee failed to result in a reported bill including the surtax. It remained for the Senate Finance Committee to report and the Senate to enact a bill combining the surtax and expenditure control in the spring of 1968.

With a $25 billion budget deficit looming for the fiscal year ending June 30, 1968, final action was taken by the Congress in early June 1968, an election year, after the 10-month struggle. It was called the Revenue and Expenditure Control Act of 1968. It imposed the temporary 10 percent surtax and mandated a $6 billion reduction in expenditures for the new fiscal year beginning July 1 which had been included earlier in the January budget submission. That bill resulted in a surplus in the federal budget for the ensuing fiscal year (July 1, 1968 to June 30, 1969), which incidentally was the last budget surplus registered to the present date.

It was the voluntary efforts of numerous business and financial leaders and their professional associates, acting collectively in an organized fashion, that made possible the passage of the Revenue Act of 1962, the Tax Reduction Act of 1964, and the Revenue and Expenditure Control Act of 1968. It was that experience which gave rise to my conviction earlier stated about the especial responsibility of the business and financial community for a balanced fiscal policy.

It was not long after my departure from the Treasury in December 1968 that the fiscal policy based on a *balance* between savings and investment and consumption and a hot pursuit of a balanced budget was dislodged in the Congress. In the Revenue Act of 1969, in a search for loopholes to close, the investment tax credit was "permanently" removed (until its reenactment in April 1971), the tax on long-term capital gains was substantially increased, and the holding period in which an investment must be held in order to qualify its profits as a long-term capital gains was extended.

In the summer of 1969, when these proposals were pending, all I could do in a busy private life as a general partner in an investment banking firm was to write a long and strong letter to one of my favorite senators, decrying the proposals referred to as reversing a national policy as old as the nation and as recent as the last major revision of our permanent tax structure in the 1960s.

My failure here as a lonely private citizen was equaled by a similar lack of success in upholding fiscal responsibility and a search for a balanced budget in the Congress. I managed to deliver a long lecture in 1970 urging that a definitive congressional budgetary process be put in place to fill the void that had existed for over a century when responsibility for fiscal policy in the Congress was divided between the committees in each house that determine taxing and borrowing and those that determine appropriations. Somehow I thought a process that fastened firmly on each member of Congress the responsibility for voting for or against fiscal responsibility in the voting of an annual budget might be the answer.

Hence, I took heart and applauded the valiant and praiseworthy efforts of those who put through the Budget Act of 1974. But, alas, the decade of the 1970s saw the average rate of federal budget deficits increase to around $30 billion a year.

In 1978 an opportunity was presented to turn the tide once again for saving and investment. After the House of Representatives acted to lower the top rate on long-term capital gains to 35 percent (from various levels ranging up to 49 percent depending on the particular situation of the individual taxpayer), a movement developed in the Senate Finance Committee to resurrect the rejected John F. Kennedy recommendation of 1963 to tax only 30 percent of a long-term capital gain as ordinary income rather than the traditional 50 percent, making the top rate of tax 20 percent.

I lent myself happily to the effort. The public part of my activities is set forth in my statement and testimony before the Senate Finance Committee on August 22, 1978.[2]

The long deferred John Kennedy proposal was adopted overwhelmingly by the Senate Finance Committee and the Senate. In conference the difference between the House and Senate version was split by agreement on a provision taxing only 40 percent of a long-term capital gain as ordinary income, making the top rate 28 percent.

It was further reduced in 1981 as a part of Economic Recovery Tax Act (ERTA) to the current top rate of 20 percent as a consequence of the reduction of the top rate on ordinary income to 50 percent.

Yet, here we are again with the Tax Reform Act of 1986 wiping out a preferential tax treatment of long-term capital gains, thereby pushing the top rate back up to 28 percent.

The momentum toward a tax policy shift favoring capital formation, savings and investment, perceptible in 1978, as just recounted, was further reflected in extensive hearings before the House Ways and Means Committee and the Senate Finance Committee in the summer of 1980. It was the strongest theme of a bipartisan conference sponsored by the Joint Economic Committee, after the election, in December 1980.[3]

This momentum and theme was reflected primarily in the so-called 10-5-3 proposal for depreciation of certain business assets and the adoption of ERTA.

Unfortunately, the provisions most conducive to business capital formation were conjoined to a series of developments—a large reduction in personal income taxes, a rapidly expanding defense budget, swelling entitlement programs, and the recession of 1981-82—which gave rise to a rapidly escalating federal budget deficit. The fruits of that unhappy marriage have proved unfortunate for the balance between capital formation, savings and investment, and consumption. The individual taxpayer, not surprisingly, won out, and the shift *to* consumption and away from a policy favoring capital formation was reflected in Tax Equity and Fiscal Responsibility Act (TEFRA) of 1982 and now in the anti-capital formation features of Tax Reform Act of 1986.

This last shift presents a bitter challenge to the business and financial communities and those in public service who believe in sustained and healthy economic growth accompanied by increased productivity and competitiveness in the industrial sector of the economy. In my judgment this balance is not likely to be restored until and unless a national consumption tax is added to the system and the existing budget deficit is moved substantially toward balance and equilibrium.

The Greatest Threat

Persistent and increasing resort to deficit financing is currently the most potentially damaging internal weakness in our national economy. It has a serious potential for limiting the access of the private business sector to the capital needed from the pool of national savings for investment *on reasonable terms* to engender growth and productivity.

It can contribute to a damaging inflation when conjoined to an unsustainable economic boom, or even bursts of excessive consumption, or speculation based on private borrowing, or even a desire of politicians to inflate their way out of deficits when the medicine of fiscal responsibility is too bitter or unpopular to take.

It is conducive, under some circumstances, to high interest rates that can lead to a recession or stagflation or exchange rate misalignments resulting from increased foreign capital flows to take advantage of attractive interest rates. It can weaken the national will to provide adequately for national security and foreign policy requirements when deficit retrenchment becomes a pressing necessity and the restraint of domestic spending is politically unattractive. It can lead to an unduly restrictive or rigid monetary policy when fiscal policy is not carrying its share of the burden of unwelcome restraint. In view of these unwelcome by-products of deficit financing, it is important to put in historical perspective what has been happening to our federal budget in recent years and what needs to be done about it.

A healthy resistance to indulging increasing budget deficits provided by the business and financial communities and various elements in the Congress and the administration led to commitments to control expenditures as a condition to both tax reduction in the 1964 Act and a temporary tax increase in the Revenue and Expenditure Control Act of 1968. This fiscal discipline held the average annual budget deficit to about $7.6 billion per year in the 1960s. It is reasonable to suggest that balance or equilibrium might have been achieved after the 1964 Tax Reduction Act if the drain of Vietnam War expenditures had not escalated.

The average annual deficit for the fiscal years 1970–1979 was around $30 billion. In the fiscal years 1980–1986, the average escalated to over $200 billion per year. At the end of 1985, federal expenditures equaled 24.6 percent of gross national product while receipts equaled only 19.2 percent. The resulting budget deficit amounted to 5.4 percent of GNP, compared with a deficit of only 0.7 percent in 1979. This dangerous trend prompted a limited activist reaction from the private citizenry, even those long since retired from public life.

Because the deficit trend in the 1970s was accompanied by an inflationary surge (averaging around 8 percent for the decade, but reaching 13 percent in 1979 and breaking at 18 percent in 1980), a small private group called the Committee to Fight Inflation was organized in early 1980 under the leadership of Arthur Burns. I have served as a vice chairman and co-chairman of the committee, which was thoroughly bipartisan in its makeup. When organized, it included four former secretaries of the Treasury, two former chairmen of the Federal Reserve Board, a former chairman of the Council of Economic Advisers, a former undersecretary of the Treasury, and four former members of Congress who had been high-ranking members of the congressional committees concerned with economic and financial affairs.

In its initial report in early 1980, this committee recommended a revision of the budget process that would make it much more difficult for the Congress to authorize budget deficits. The committee so acted because of its conviction that deficit financing was conducive to inflation. The committee's proposal would require: "A balanced budget unless a deficit is authorized by something more than a simple majority—say, two-thirds of each house of Congress."

By 1982 the budget and its projections revealed a deficit outlook of alarming proportions. Despite assurances that the economy would grow out of the deficits as a result of the tax reduction in the Economic Recovery Tax Act of 1981 and expenditure reductions to be enacted, the developing deficit began to arouse ever broader concern at home and abroad.

In May 1982 I became a founding member of the Bipartisan Budget Appeal, joining with former Secretaries of the Treasury Douglas Dillon, John B. Connally, William E. Simon, and W. Michael Blumenthal and led by former Secretary of Commerce Peter G. Peterson. We went public via full-page advertisements in the *New York Times*, the *Wall Street Journal*, and the *Washington Post*. These public statements analyzed the stubborn deficit problem the nation faced, its long-term structural character, and the need for decisive action over a three-year period, proposing "Principles to Guide Action" and a "Three-Part Program for Action—Entitlements, Defense and Taxes."

In subsequent statements published once or twice a year through 1985, we were publicly joined by over 600 former public officials, economists of prominence, and heads of major corporations, commercial banks, investment banks, law firms, accounting firms, universities, foundations, and other organizations. In a special appeal to all candidates for federal office on September 10, 1984, the Bipartisan Budget Appeal Group was joined by some 32 important trade associations representing a broad spectrum of the private sector to make up a Bipartisan Budget Coalition. The "Principles to Guide Action" had this to say on that date:

> *Focus on Investment and Savings.* The objective should be to increase savings and investment. Massive deficits rob the future by depleting savings and absorbing capital needed to build productive jobs, strengthen international competitiveness, provide for home ownership, and generate real income growth and a higher standard of living for all Americans. Cutting deficits by measures that would at the same time reduce savings and investment would make no long-term sense.

In its espousals of its specific program to implement a budget deficit program, the Bipartisan Budget Appeal has made its position clear on both the essentiality of an addition to the national tax revenue base to meet the budget deficit problem and the nature of that addition.

The September 1984 statement declared:

> Any serious program to deal with the deficit will have to address each element of the three-part program [entitlements, defense, and taxes]. . . . Once spending cuts of the type and magnitude described above are assured, any revenue measures needed to reach the deficit reduction goal should mainly rely on consumption oriented taxes in order to avoid weakening incentives to work, save and invest.

There have been some significant developments since the Bipartisan Budget Appeal raised its flag in mid-1982.

First, it has become clear that a large *structural* budget deficit resulted from the massive tax reductions of the Economic Recovery Tax Act of 1981 together with much higher defense expenditures of the 1980s being added to the built-in deficit of the 1970s. It also has become clear that this structural deficit cannot be overcome without increasing revenues and reining in some nondefense expenditures, particularly entitlements going to the population sector above the poverty level. In 1984, the year with the fastest growth in GNP in some years, the deficit dropped by only 1.6 percent.

Second, the structural budget deficit is now viewed as the No. 1 domestic economic problem by a majority of Americans, as well as an obstacle to progress through improved international economic cooperation.

Third, the enactment of the Gramm-Rudman-Hollings Act has added desirable and compelling discipline for future budgetary processes.

Fourth, it appears unlikely that the congressional budgetary processes can comply with the Gramm-Rudman-Hollings Act, now the law of the land, without undermining and weakening the president's national security and foreign policy position.

Fifth, the polls have established the fact that, if additional revenues are necessary to deal adequately with the structural budget deficit and discharge properly the constitutional responsibilities of the national government, the American taxpayer would prefer a consumption tax to any other form of increase.

It is my strong conviction that a national consumption tax is a necessary part of a better alternative to the current handling of our national budget deficit.

National Security

The arbitrary bind on national security and foreign policy in which the nation finds itself as a result of the structural budget deficit and the rigid and undiscriminating discipline of the Gramm-Rudman-Hollings Act should be promptly adjusted. The early enactment of a national consumption tax and modification of the Gramm-Rudman-Hollings Act to exempt national defense and foreign policy expenditures from its sequestration process is a better alternative.

Without this adjustment the efforts of the president and his ministers through appropriate national security and foreign policy activities to maintain peace, stability, and international economic cooperation with our friends and allies will be dangerously weakened. As a co-chairman of the Committee on the Present Danger (CPD) and the Bretton Woods Committee, I share a deep personal concern with many of my colleagues on this score.

The Committee on the Present Danger was organized on November 11, 1976 as a small nonpartisan, nonprofit, and independent group of citizens in private life. It was premised on the shared belief that the principal threat to our nation, to world peace, and to the cause of freedom is the Soviet drive for dominance based upon an unparalleled military build-up. This belief grew out of the fact, among others, that for more than a decade (prior to 1976), the Soviet Union has been enlarging and improving both its strategic and its conventional military forces far more rapidly than the United States and its allies. In the Policy Statement of the Committee on the Present Danger, endorsed at the time of its organization by its 141 founding members, it was pointed out that

> as a percentage of Gross National Product, U.S. defense spending is lower than at any time in twenty-five years. For the U.S. to be free, secure, and influential, higher levels of spending are now required for our ready land, sea, and air forces, our strategic deterrent, and, above all, the continuing modernization of those forces through research and development.

Having watched with dismay the waning financial support of our government for its defense effort in the 1970s in sharp contrast to a seemingly successful effort of the Soviet Union to achieve military superiority, the committee has welcomed a resurgence of U.S. military strength and preparedness in the 1980s.

Yet despite this increase, the outlook is discouraging. In October 1978 the Committee published the first of its detailed studies of the U.S.–Soviet military balance, "Is America Becoming No. 2?" To the question posed in the title, the CPD answered yes, assuming that existing trends continued, this country could soon rank second to the Soviet Union in overall military strength and preparedness. The second study, published in 1982, concluded that America had indeed become No. 2. The third CPD study of the military balance was published in December 1984. Despite the increased U.S. effort in the early 1980s, the CPD stated that not only did the United States remain in second place, but in fact had lost ground since the 1982 study. In the CPD's judgment, based on the most careful research, a significant step-up in U.S. military spending was necessary if further ground was not to be lost.

Unfortunately, just the opposite has occurred. Two years ago defense outlays for 1987 were projected to be $349 billion, whereas the latest House budget shows defense at $286 billion for 1987—an extraordinary shortfall of $63 billion. The administration requested $320 billion in budget authority for national defense in fiscal year 1987. The budget resolution recently approved by the U.S. Senate calls for only $301 billion and the House is bringing in an even lower figure.

The result is that the defense budget has borne and is bearing a disproportionate share of the efforts to meet the Gramm-Rudman-Hollings budget deficit targets.

When a persistent structural deficit and the appropriate national decision to reduce it, now embodied in the Gramm-Rudman-Hollings Act, are conjoined to an unwillingness to raise taxes or cut nondefense spending, the defense program is the main victim. Let us look at the record.

In February 1985 President Reagan submitted a budget asking for $1.8 trillion of defense expenditures for the five fiscal years 1986–1990. Subsequent cuts by Congress and the automatic cuts imposed by Gramm-Rudman-Hollings have already reduced the programmed expenditures for those years to $1.5 trillion, or by one-sixth. The budget resolutions now being considered in the Congress would cut defense expenditures even further. Meanwhile, nondefense expenditures excluding interest on the federal debt have been raised by about $300 billion, or about 10 percent over President Reagan's budget for 1986–1990.

The current outlook is for the military balance to shift further against the United States and in favor of the Soviets.

Apart from the physical consequences in relative strength, the psychological and political consequences of this perceptible trend toward relative weakness is damaging. It gives a wrong signal to our allies, whom we are urging to increase their economic and financial commitment to conventional military strength. It gives the wrong signal to the Soviets, with whom the president and his ministers are trying assiduously to negotiate treaties for arms reduction and control. Why would they conclude meaningful agreements for the reduction and control of arms as long as political and economic developments in the United States work to fortify and improve their relative advantage?

If national security is not to be dangerously impaired or the structural budget deficit further enlarged, significant increases in federal revenues must be assured. Given the indexation of individual income tax rates, such additional revenues cannot be obtained from that source, as was frequently the case in the past, through automatic increases due to inflation and bracket creep. Adequate funding for increased national defense in face of the structural budget deficit can be assured only if there is a new source of federal revenues—a national consumption tax.

A comparable situation exists with reference to our foreign policy. A full, detailed, and thoroughly frightening picture of this aspect of our current fiscal problem was presented at a press briefing on August 11, 1986 by the Honorable John C. Whitehead, deputy secretary of state, on the foreign affairs budget. These were his opening words:

> We face a national security crisis. Proposed congressional cuts in the international affairs budget will seriously jeopardize our national security interests and global foreign policy objectives. The ability of the United States to main-

tain its leadership role in the world; to provide for its national security; and to support the cause of freedom, democracy, and economic development is at stake.[4]

I commend for consideration the detailed factual analysis of this alarming statement as it concerns various activities of the Department of State and the U.S. Information Agency. For my own part, I should like to develop the particular situation of which I have immediate firsthand knowledge—the U.S. fiscal crisis and the multilateral financial institutions that are and have been cornerstones of U.S. foreign economic policy since World War II.

In addition to conducting bilateral aid and related activities in friendly countries who need and welcome our help, the United States is the leading member of the group of industrialized democracies that after World War II formalized and organized international economic cooperation to promote Free World trade, financial stability and growth, and Third World development. To accomplish their objective, they established the International Monetary Fund and the World Bank. These multilateral institutions are called the Bretton Woods organizations, named for the spot in New Hampshire where in 1944 the preliminary plans for their structures were negotiated. In the late 1950s and 1960s, regional development banks of the same multilateral character were organized for Latin America, Asia, and Africa in which the nonregional industrial nations participate.

Currently, I serve with Charls Walker as co-chairman of the Bretton Woods Committee, a private, nonpartisan, nonprofit organization established in early 1985 to develop greater support and understanding of the importance of the Bretton Woods organizations and the regional development banks to U.S. foreign policy. We share the views of President Reagan and many former presidents, ex-secretaries of the treasury and state departments, as well as Secretary Baker and Secretary Shultz, distinguished former public servants in the Congress and the administration, many business and financial leaders, and many civic and nonprofit leaders of the importance of these organizations and their effective functioning to world peace, development, and freedom.

They will need increasing resources if they are to perform their key roles in overcoming the international debt crisis and the recent economic retrogression affecting much of the Third World and improving the working of the international monetary system so important to the trade and growth of all the member nations.

The convergence of this need for additional resources with the structural budget deficit problem and Gramm-Rudman-Hollings approach to its solution creates a unique problem for U.S. participation in this important multilateral framework.

As the leading member and a principal stockholder, but with a minority voting position, the inability of the United States to play its normal role in the needed increases in capital and resources is a real threat to the entire international economic framework. The other members scale increases in their financial participation to that of the United States. The leverage factor results in about four or five dollars being made available to the multilateral banks for every dollar of the U.S. capital subscription. In fact, much of the U.S. and other members' commitments involves only a minor capital outlay since the far greater proportion of the commitment is to participate in the guarantee of a bond obligation of the multilateral bank issued in a private capital market should the World Bank and other regional development banks be unable to meet their obligations, a most unlikely event. It is only to finance loans to the poorer countries through the so-called soft loan window that requires any substantial cash outlay from a member country.

The end result of this arrangement is that an inability or unwillingness of the principal "stockholder" to shoulder its share of the task of increasing the resources available to the institution is a major curtailment of the banks' ability to function effectively.

Given the importance of the present budgetary bind to the adequate functioning of the national security and foreign policy arrangements of the United States, it seems the better part of valor (and wisdom) to carve out a procedure for special treatment of these parts of the national budget even in a time of budgetary stringency.

The Balance of Trade

A national consumption tax could make a significant contribution to reducing the mounting deficit in our international trade deficit for several reasons. The first, already developed, is that the additional revenues would make room for restoring some of the tax incentives to our system most conducive to increasing productivity and competitiveness through increased investment. The second is that a national consumption tax, which under the rules and practices of the General Agreement on Tariffs and Trade (GATT) can be rebated on exports and imposed on imports, could eliminate or reduce a major competitive disadvantage afflicting U.S. manufacturers.

More needs to be observed on this second reason.

Most of our major industrial competitor nations and trading partners employ a value-added tax or some other indirect tax which qualifies under the GATT for border tax treatment. Several additional ones, including Canada and Japan, are said to be considering a value-added tax.

I was first attracted to this fiscal option in 1967 when, as secretary of the Treasury and chairman of the Cabinet Committee on Balance of Payments, we treated that financial factor as a deadly serious matter. It appeared that our then favorable trade balance, a highly important element in the overall balance of payments, was on a declining path. The national effort during the early 1960s to bring back to equilibrium or surplus the U.S. balance of payments deficits in the late 1950s, amounting to around $4 billion per year, was threatened with failure.

Faced with a projected balance-of-payments deficit increasing from $1.4 billion in 1966 to $3.5 billion in 1967, the Cabinet Committee was formulating a report and new program.

Although it developed that indirect taxes such as the value-added tax or turnover tax played a much larger role in the tax systems of our European competitors than in our own system, my advocacy of a countering measure in the new 1968 Balance of Payments program failed because my colleagues favored other options to deal with the imminent problem.

Suffice it to say that the report and the new program released on New Year's Day 1968 on a nationwide telecast by President Johnson was successful in producing a small balance-of-payments surplus in 1968, the first surplus since 1957, but it did not include any value-added or other consumption tax.

But in the years that followed, our balance of trade turned increasingly unfavorable. Looking back now from a current balance-of-payments annual deficit of around $150 billion in which our trade deficit is said to be running at a $170 billion a year rate, it seems timely to bring this topic up again for the reason stated above.

As a matter of fact, the topic was considered in 1969 and 1970 by President Nixon's Task Force on Business Taxation, which submitted its report in September 1970. I had the privilege of serving on that task force which addressed the long-range goals for business tax policy, concentrating on the role of business taxes in promoting economic growth, full employment, and a strong competitive economy. The task force focused its examination on the value-added tax, capital cost recovery, and taxation of foreign income. Its conclusions on the value-added tax were as follows:

> After a detailed study of the subject, the task force concluded, with two members dissenting, to recommend against the adoption of the value-added tax system as a substitution, in whole or in part, for one or more of the exist-

ing federal taxes. One member, who concurs generally with the recommendations, considers the border tax adjustments employed by European nations to be so discriminatory against United States trade that he might favor a partial substitution of the value-added tax for corporate income tax unless a satisfactory international arrangement is reached permitting the United States to make border adjustments for a limited portion of its corporation taxes. *All members of the task force agreed that, should the need ever arise for substantial additional federal revenue, the government should turn to the value-added tax or some other form of indirect taxation rather than to increase the already high rates of the corporate and individual income taxes.* [Emphasis added].[5]

I was the member referred to as favoring a partial substitution unless satisfactory arrangements to eliminate the adverse effect in the U.S. competitive position of the existing situation could be worked out. The two dissenting members (Dan Throop Smith and Norman Ture) on the adverse recommendation to a substitution in whole or in part of a value-added tax for the corporate income tax based their position, in part, on the foreign trade advantage of a value-added tax. A statement of one of those dissenters (Smith of the Graduate School of Business at Stanford University) was prophetic:

The use of a value-added tax would improve our international competitive position. In recent years we have lost our strongly favorable balance of trade. The deterioration has been caused by many developments here and abroad. Border taxes in Europe and elsewhere are by no means the dominant factor, but they are substantial and will grow in importance as more and more countries adopt and increase their reliance on value-added taxes. We cannot afford to remain in a position where we are unable to overcome the foreign border tax barriers to our exports or to counter at our own border the tax rebates given to foreign exporters seeking to penetrate our domestic markets. This issue is not one of protecting domestic profit margins, important though that is to assure a dynamic economy. It is the fundamental one of protecting jobs and the vitality of those of our industries which are subject to international competition both at home and abroad. Our traditional tax structure has placed us at a competitive disadvantage. We can no longer refuse to face this fact. A change would not be made to secure an international advantage. It would be to restore neutrality by overcoming a disadvantage into which we have fallen.[6]

There is a tendency on the part of some to deny any validity to the claim that the present situation puts the U.S. producer at a competitive disadvantage. I have tried very hard but failed to understand their position. It seems to boil down to the lawyer's *ipse dixit*, or "it is so because I say it is so."

There is one difficult counterargument to those of us who urge resort to a national consumption tax for additional revenue because of its tendency toward harmonization of our tax system with that of our principal trading competitor nations, thereby diminishing their competitive advantage we face in trying to diminish our trade deficit. It is that there are many other contributing causes to the increasing U.S. trade deficit—a general decline in our national competitiveness, the misalignment of exchange rates, unfair competitive practices in other nations, inadequate rates of growth or imports in some of our principal trading partners or debtor nations, excessive wage and credit costs at home. The answer is to agree that these other factors need to be tackled too, but that is no reason for not tackling the one in question.

CONCLUSION

One major advantage of a national consumption tax for the purposes outlined is that it could raise an extraordinary amount of revenue. The International Economic Policy Association had this to say on this score in December 1985:

> A five percent VAT with an exemption for food and clothing would have raised $87.9 billion in 1984. With no exceptions, it would have raised $117.1 billion. One type of proposed VAT is called a tax on business transaction (TBT). It amounts to a VAT that is levied on every step of production, but not on retail sales. According to the leading proponent of such a tax, Charls Walker, the TBT would raise $90 billion in 1986 and $150 billion by 1992.

Against the setting of major national economic problems I have described and the question of a turn to a national consumption tax as a better alternative to the present U.S. policy mix, I offer the following conclusions:

1. The leadership of Congress and the administration should embark on an intensive bipartisan search for a better mix of fiscal, monetary, and trade policies to meet the four national economic problems outlined in this chapter.

2. Those with the ultimate political responsibility under our system of governance should determine the techniques for the conduct of this search—for example, a commission such as was employed several years ago in dealing with the Social Security gridlock, extensive legislative hearings, informal meetings between the principals and their representatives, or a combination.

3. All measures, including methods of increasing revenues should be on the table for consideration, including a national consumption tax. Estimates of the amounts of revenues needed and areas of exemption to relieve hardship on the poor resulting from the proposed measures should be explored.

4. Operation of the Gramm-Rudman-Hollings Act should be examined to make it more effective and yet more compatible with our national security and foreign policy requirements.

NOTES

1. Charls E. Walker and Mark A. Bloomfield, *New Directions in Federal Tax Policy for the 1980s*, American Council for Capital Formation Center for Policy Research (Cambridge, Mass.: Ballinger, 1983), pp. xvii, xviii.

2. See Part 2 of Hearings before the Committee on Finance, U.S. Senate, 95th Congress, 2nd Session, on H.R. 13511, pp. 445–473.

3. See "The Economy of 1981; A Bipartisan Look," Proceedings of a Congressional Economic Conference, December 10, 1980, 97th Congress, 1st Session, Joint Committee Print.

4. The Foreign Affairs Budget, U.S. Department of State, Bureau of Public Affairs-Current Policy No. 860.

5. *Report of the President's Task Force on Business Taxation*, September 1970, pp. 1, 2.

6. Ibid., p. 72.

Chapter 2

A View from the Ways and Means Committee

Dan Rostenkowski

Let me say straight away, that I oppose a broad-based federal consumption tax. There are better, if not faster, ways to raise revenue. There are better ways to form capital. There are better ways to promote competitiveness abroad. And there are certainly better ways to earn the taxpayer's confidence in government.

I agreed to [prepare this chapter] for fear that consumption taxes would be measured and judged by scholars alone. I am not an economist. I'm a politician who stands to bear ultimate responsibility for any new tax system. I have a healthy skepticism for economic forecasting, particularly after watching all the hoopla at the launching of supply-side economics. And I am very leary of simple, seductive tonics, like 10-10-10 and 10-5-3 depreciation schedules, that promise far more economic and social cures than they deliver.

I am also a politician who faces an electorate every two years. I listen to young couples who believe that universal health care is on the way, or to small businessmen who expect to gain from Enterprise Zones, or to parents counting on tuition tax credits. Washington is a place where populist ideas come easily, a city that can quickly produce a wrench to fix something that ain't even broke.

Congress spent the better part of two years, 1985 and 1986, renovating the income tax code, bringing it back from decades of decay—two years of rewiring and replumbing a structure so badly patched and jerryrigged by economic do-gooders like myself that, inside the Beltway, they said the job would never be done. They bet on those who were out to protect the status quo—and for good reason—because there were days when tax reform had no pulse.

We succeeded only because we never forgot that the ultimate measure of tax policy, on Capitol Hill and along Main Street, is fairness. It is the single promise that generated what tentative public support the president was able to generate. It wasn't low tax rates or larger paychecks that brought working men and women behind tax reform. It was fairness: knowing they were not subsidizing a loophole for the guy down the street or the corporation across town. It is this new sense of fairness that I hope will lower the wall of cynicism that has grown between Washington and those who pay for Washington.

Add to fairness the fact that Americans believe that a tax system should rest on the ability to pay, and that a citizen's tax burden should rise as his income rises. These are fundamentals that have been tested and challenged over the years and found durable. They are part of our national creed.

Now comes the notion that this country will set those tenets aside for a new faith that preaches that economic growth, not fairness, must be the quest of national tax policy—from one day to the next. It is a consumption tax that is now the best route to more investment and savings, and the proper response to deficit reduction.

There is a certain transparency, if not downright cynicism, to the argument that what is past is not prologue but simply past. Forget that we have just undone most of the code's worst abuses (along with the excesses of the 1981 Act) and used the revenue from a broader tax base to do what economists and corporate leaders have been asking in the name of free enterprise—lower marginal rates and a level playing field. Forget the appeal for stability and the chance to live with a tax code for more than a year at a time.

Now that Tax Reform Act of 1986 is law, the same cynics would have Congress and the American public consider essentially doing away with the income tax and putting in its place a consumption tax that promises to be less visible and therefore less painful to pay. It is that kind of deceit from Washington that my constituents on the northwest side of Chicago have come to know and curse.

The same arguments now used to support a value-added tax (VAT) were used to sell the Economic Recovery Tax Act of 1981 (ERTA) at the outset of the Reagan administration. The same dire forecasts that damned the old code and promised a new world with lower rates and greater economic incentives, like safe-harbor leasing, now echo forward.

You would think that we would learn that economic forecasters can't see around corners. But they are at it again, the same ones who

promised that ERTA would lead to an explosion of capital investment, personal savings, and a balanced budget. Remember the White
House economic theorem that we could grow our way out of the
deficit? They were the ones who scoffed at us early doubters, the
ones who minimized the rate of deficit with wonderful formulas
about its ratio to the overall size of the economy.

And now many of the same cynics are back again with their radar
sets that can bend to the earth's curvature and reach well over the
horizon. And what do they see emerging from the latest tax reform
bill with fewer dodges and lower rates? Doom.

Suddenly, the lowest corporate rate since 1941 is going to retard
investment and place a drag on capital formation. The axiom that
lower taxes and less tax distortion between economic sectors are a
boon to international competitiveness is now outdated. No other
city in the world rivals Washington for economic revisionism. For
every round hole there's a square peg that neatly fits.

I don't doubt that a good stiff VAT would take care of our deficit.
I am not a schooled economist able to predict the side effects that
would emerge. But I am enough of a politician to predict that, at
best, a true VAT proposal would emerge from Congress looking like
a lace doily. If you think today's relatively progressive income tax
system is full of holes and inequities, imagine the alterations awaiting
a national sales tax. Exemptions for food, shelter, medical treatment,
and education are just openers. The long line of appeal begins to
stretch down Capitol Hill from there. Then consider the fundamental
opposition of state and local governments, which view sales taxes
as their jurisdictional prerogatives, or the potential inflationary impact, or administrative problems.

I have long voiced my fear of deficits. The early Reagan calculus
that we could double military spending, cut taxes, and balance the
budget made good slogans but little sense. His mission to resist any
further tax increases to draw down the deficit makes even less.

Everyone knows we will need a tax increase to reduce the deficit. There I would agree with proponents of consumption taxes. But
the increase in revenue should come through higher progressive rates
on income—not by a low, regressive tax on need.

If we failed in the campaign for income tax reform, then my opposition to consumption taxes would not be so strong. A consumption
tax is the tax of last resort. It is the flag of surrender, the admission
that we did not have the courage to take open and direct action
against abuse and inequity.

But we did not fail. And in the process, we have drawn into the
system thousands of taxpayers who have been paying little or noth-

ing on huge incomes. We have reduced the brackets, but we have increased the system's equity. No longer will we suffer giant disparities between individuals or corporations with the same incomes. We are now much more confident that an increase in tax rates will fall reasonably evenly up and down the income scale.

President Reagan's opposition notwithstanding, this country is not unwilling to pay higher taxes, as long as they are fair. The millions of people who are drawing weekly paychecks and trying to raise a family understand the danger of mounting fiscal and trade deficits. They know that cutting domestic spending alone is not a reasonable response—that ultimately, tax increases must come.

But to ask this nation to pay an additional tax that is neither practical nor fair is bad economics and lousy politics. If we need more money for government, then let's go through the front door and collect it from those who can pay—not through the back from those who can't.

I just hope in the days and months ahead that the debate over consumption taxes doesn't dwell so much on the potential benefits for certain sectors of the economy as it does on the essential measure of all tax policy.

And that's fairness.

Chapter 3

An Industrialist Looks at the Consumption Tax

Charles W. Parry

I have never really thought of myself as an "industrialist." Perhaps the term has too many Marxist connotations. My self-image is one of business. And even more to the point, it is one of basic materials. For 99 years now, we at Alcoa have been digging ore out of the ground, refining it, and producing aluminum and aluminum products.

It sounds rather simple, but it is not. And the complexity of modern times comes not so much from alterations to the methodology of the aluminum business, but from changes in the world external to it.

Naturally my own experience has largely shaped my views of the world, including the world of taxation. That is not to say that I am unable to understand the views of others—the retailer or the seller of financial services. It is just that my roots are in basic materials, and my views often reflect that fact.

There is little consensus within the business community on the subject of taxes, except perhaps to wish they'd go away. That wish, though, is nothing more than an expression of frustration. I don't know *anyone* in business who does not expect to pay some taxes. And it is the differences between expectations that have made the 1986 debate over taxes so interesting.

My personal view is that yes, the income tax should be simplified, and yes, the income tax should be more fair. But the cooking of this particular stew is not quite so simple. A testament to its complexity is in the fact that the Tax Reform Bill ran to some 1,500 pages—certainly not a simplified code. And if business takes its predicted

$120 billion hit, how can many of us believe it is fair. Fairness, obviously, is in the eye of the beholder.

A cursory reading of the public opinion polls is interesting. Americans are not against the current income tax laws; they are against high taxes. That sentiment, of course, is reflected by many in business. But, the average American, to a surprising degree, accepts his and her citizenship and pays the tax.

My disappointment with the tax reform process is that it fails to address the single most important economic problem of all, the federal deficit. That view is shared by most in the business community, and by a high percentage of all Americans.

The data supporting that conclusion are confusing to many, and to some are even contradictory. But how much evidence does one need to confirm a point of view that comes so easily from experience? The vast majority of Americans have no difficulty at all in thinking that government should obey the same budgetary restraints that they themselves observe in their day-to-day dealings. Despite the complexity of government, most people really *do* believe that you can't go on spending more than you earn for very long. Certainly that same attitude is shared widely in business. Bankruptcy has not yet become the only alternative to spending.

Our frustration is heightened by the growing realization that political realities actually *preclude* the Congress from addressing the deficit problem through the mechanism of the income tax. It is increasingly clear that all of the blood has been sucked from that particular turnip. And so it is becoming clear within the business community that the time to consider alternative methods of eliminating the deficit is now.

Please note that I would require all revenues from alternative taxes be applied to reducing the deficit. Whether there is a need to expand government programs and revenues beyond the deficit question is quite another debate.

The deficit, however, is certainly a large enough problem by itself. Consider, for example, what the Congress could do with the billions that come right off the top of federal revenues to pay the interest on the deficit. The range of possibilities in the area of social services to the truly needy is huge. Block grants to cities, revenue sharing, the national park system, or even a further reduction in tax rates come to mind as choices one might make.

Think, as I often do, of the monetary impact of a series of balanced federal budgets. I am in an industry that is going through its greatest change in a century. As we move from a business that was national to one that is global, we are also suffering from the disease that has afflicted all basic materials—declining consumption in the developed economies.

Unlike many other basic industries, the U.S. aluminum industry has responded to this change rather well, I think. We are international in our mindsets, even though the United States is by far the largest market for our products. We have done a reasonably good job at staying on top of technology. We are competitive except in basic metal production, which reflects to a large extent noncompetitive labor costs and electricity prices in the United States. Our productivity record is outstanding compared to other basic materials.

Yet following the recession of 1981 and 1982, most U.S. aluminum companies were unable to take advantage of exceedingly strong demand. The fundamental reason was the effect of the federal deficit. It is a fact that I know in my bones. The deficit brought high interest rates, which in turn attracted foreign investment, which in turn strengthened the dollar. The ultimate impact, in the aluminum business, was that the deficit provided a cost reduction of 20 percent or more to non-U.S. competitors who paid their bills in weaker currencies.

I relate that experience because it has helped shape the views of this particular industrialist on the subject of taxes. But those views, contrary to popular perception, are not those of someone focused solely on his own problems.

I have no question that the federal deficit is our most serious economic problem and that it must be dealt with. I have also come to the view that political realities will prevent drastic alteration of the Tax Reform Act of 1986. There are two other realities. One is that federal spending, even with Gramm-Rudman, cannot be reduced to the extent necessary to cut the deficit. The other is that economic activity over the next several years is highly unlikely to increase federal revenues to any great extent.

CONSIDERING THE ALTERNATIVES

It seems clear that we must move to a consumption tax of some kind. I've developed a solid rationale for the need for a consumption tax, although I should point out that they are my views and don't necessarily represent those of any group with which I am associated.

I have no problem with one of the forms of consumption tax that has been proposed—a national sales tax. It is well understood, its mechanisms are relatively simple, and it is a powerful revenue-raising tool. The question of regressivity is rather easily dealt with, and the fact that the collection burden falls on retailers is counterbalanced by their familiarity with the process in most states. To me, this is the simplest, and therefore one of the best alternatives.

Another proposed consumption tax is the value-added tax (VAT). This is an intriguing option from the point of view of one involved in international trade. Since the rules of the General Agreement on Tariffs and Trade (GATT) allow the taxing of imports and the deduction of exports, a VAT goes a long way in leveling out the famous playing field of international trade.

A VAT has some drawbacks, either real or perceived, however. One is that the United States is not terribly familiar with it. Another is that depending how it is applied, it can be an administrative burden. But it seems to me that a VAT, especially if it is separately stated, is worthy of consideration.

A third option is the business transfer tax (BTT). The BTT is also intriguing. As a tax on net business receipts, it has the potential of raising a huge amount of revenue, depending on how it is constructed. It is also attractive because it spreads the impact over all of business, and it is attractive from the standpoint of reducing the cost of capital to business.

The BTT also has drawbacks. Of real concern to me is the fact that it is likely to be hidden from the consumer. But even that concern is not serious enough to preclude it from being considered.

CRITERIA FOR A CONSUMPTION TAX

These three tax types are the primary candidates for a national consumption tax. The various proposals for taxes on energy seem to have major flaws or are politically unrealistic. But I feel that all should be considered for discussion, just as I feel we should consider excise taxes.

There are several things that should be kept in mind as we debate consumption taxes. Again, these are considerations that involve the concerns of a businessperson.

First, any consumption tax should be dedicated to deficit reduction. As that process occurs, there will be time to debate the questions surrounding the temporary nature of the tax, or the application of revenues to additional programs.

Second, any consumption tax discussions must keep in mind its likely favorable impact on our trade balance.

Third, any consumption tax must be broad based, so as to be applied across the entire spectrum of taxpayers. As the nation continues its transition from a manufacturing to a service economy, a selective tax that would artificially hasten the change would create economic problems greater than the one it is intended to solve.

Fourth, as the debate continues to unfold, we will need to keep in mind the concept that ultimately people, not businesses, pay taxes. The potential in changing individual behavior so that investment is encouraged over consumption is compelling.

I find a growing willingness to discuss and debate the issue of a consumption tax. I know that, as always, there will be differing views within the business community. Hammering out those differences will be extremely difficult, but thoughtful debate is essential, for we need all the understanding we can get.

Chapter 4

The Federal Budget Context

Rudolph G. Penner

This chapter describes the deficit outlook under current policy and discusses some of the obvious pressures to increase spending in the federal budget, as well as some of the equally obvious pressures to reduce spending. With those factors in mind, you, the reader, can decide for yourself the extent to which a new tax source might be required either to cut the deficit below that implied by current policy or to finance new spending programs.

Whether there should be a new tax source is ultimately a decision about how big government should be and how big the deficit should be. In turn, those are issues that involve distribution of income and the allocation of resources. Moreover, although they are questions for this generation, how they are answered will affect future generations. In short, they involve profound ideological and value judgments of a kind that the Congressional Budget Office (CBO) is not allowed to make.

In laying the groundwork for a discussion of these issues, however, it is important to determine first how big is big. That is to say, if we are talking about reducing a deficit in the future with a new tax source, what could a consumption tax accomplish in this respect?

In 1985 total personal consumption in the economy was $2.6 trillion. The government could not tax all of that, of course, because some of it is imputed—rent on houses, for example—and some of it is money spent abroad during travel, and so forth. The practical tax base for, say, a value-added tax would be more like $2.3 trillion. Excluded might be such things as housing, medical care, education, as well as those items that are hard to tax practically, such as financial services. The point is that there is a reasonable but narrower base that would reduce the regressivity of such a tax and make it more practical. That base would amount to about $1.4 trillion.

Economists generally agree that if there is going to be a consumption tax of some kind, it should not be a small one. It would be too hard to administer and the compliance costs too high. It would not be worth the trouble, for example, to consider a 1 percent or 2 percent tax.

Some economists would argue that even a 5 percent tax is too low. But let us assume it anyway. Moreover, assume that the tax was to be implemented on January 1, 1988. If applied to the widest practical base, the tax would bring in about $113 billion in 1989, growing to about $129 billion in 1991, according to CBO's economic assumptions. If we were to use the narrower base, the tax would bring in about $67 billion in 1988 or $77 billion in 1991.

Any discussion of the budget outlook these days involves one word more than any other. It is not a four-letter word, however tempted we may be to use one. It is only half as bad. It's a two-letter word "if." *If* all of our economic and technical assumptions come true, and *if* there is no pressure to raise spending, the deficit situation today appears very much better than it did two years ago. Given the latest estimates, *if* the economy were to have a little more than 3 percent real growth between now and 1991, the deficit would decline from about $224 billion in fiscal year 1986 to the low $180 billion range in the fiscal year 1987 and to less than $100 billion by 1991.

There was a time when getting below $100 billion would not have been considered a major triumph. That it is now considered to be quite impressive shows how standards have changed. Of course, the $100 billion figure does not take into account the policy targets implied by Gramm-Rudman-Hollings (the Balanced Budget and Emergency Deficit Control Act of 1985). If (that important word again) we can actually get the deficit down to the $144 to $154 billion range in 1987, and if that movement reflects true, lasting policy changes as opposed to selling assets or using the temporary bulge from the tax bill, and if we can assume slightly over 3 percent economic growth, then further deficit reductions would be relatively easy going and, in fact, downhill from there. Such progress is possible at that point because permanent changes in either the spending or tax side would have a cumulative effect. In other words, a real bonus would result from reducing the national debt and the interest payments on it, which tend to compound through time.

Unfortunately, the events of 1986 illustrate the hazards of relying on long-term budget projections. Early in the year, we at CBO believed that in fiscal year 1986 this country would experience the first in a long series of deficit reductions. By the end of the year, it became apparent that 1986 would see the breaking of yet another deficit record.

A brief review of the year's events is useful if only to show what can go wrong with deficit estimates. Indeed, it illustrates Murphy's law, that whatever can go wrong will. For fiscal policymakers, there is an important corollary—namely, that even if something does go well in the economy, it is bound to be bad for the budget.

In this category goes the drop in oil prices. Although that drop is good news in the long run, the equally surprising and related fall in inflation hurt revenues in 1986 much more than it allowed reduced spending. There was also some shortfall in real economic growth compared with the CBO's February forecast. It was a less important cause, however, of the deteriorating budget situation than the fall in inflation.

The other good news that turned out to be bad for the budget was the bumper agricultural crops, much of which the government has to buy. Indeed, agricultural spending has become the real growth item in the federal budget. It has risen about 24 percent a year since 1980 and by some $18 billion alone between 1984 and 1986.

Those are the sort of things that can go wrong with budget estimates. Given those dangers, it is important to review the "ifs" that were behind my earlier projection that the deficit would improve over time. I said it depended crucially on the assumption that the economy would grow more than 3 percent. On the surface, that assumption seems quite reasonable for the long run.

The average gross domestic product growth since 1948 has been about 3.2 percent. There is now a lot of room for growth in our economy: unemployment is high by historical standards, capacity utilization is very low, and the process of growth should be facilitated by lower oil prices and lower interest rates. But a scenario for continuing economic expansion depends to a large degree on a number of events, two of which deserve highlighting.

First, the trade balance has to start responding to the fall in exchange rates. We keep thinking it will any minute, but trade statistics have been very disappointing in that regard. Second, productivity has to improve for the long run. One reason productivity is so important is that, given the demography in the 1980s and 1990s, the labor force will grow much more slowly than it did in the previous, postwar period, when the United States had over 3 percent growth.

Productivity growth in the 1980s, although better than the 1970s, has been very disappointing—far below what many analysts anticipated. We thought it would move more toward the postwar average rate of growth.

There are obviously other risks to the economy, but those are the main ones. The question becomes: What direction will public policy take? The answer is another important "if."

CBO's deficit projections are not really forecasts; they are merely statements of the implications of current law. The Congress can do anything it wants. The definition of current policy or current law assumes that appropriations for all discretionary programs remain constant in real terms—that is, adjusted for inflation. The projections earlier in this chapter, for example, also make that assumption for defense spending, which is now about 28 percent of the budget. In fact, the radical change in defense policy is largely responsible for the improved budget outlook these days. Certainly in 1986 the defense budget was cut in real terms. In 1987 the appropriation actions indicate that defense spending will not grow much in real terms, but, of course, any international crisis could turn that around.

Demographic trends will also increase pressure to spend more on programs for both ends of the age distribution. At one extreme, we are witnessing a relatively new phenomenon. Not only has the over-65 age group been growing in size more rapidly than the rest of the population, but now, within that group, we see an explosion in the over-80 population. The aging are aging, and that is a very important fact for public policy.

It is creating a demand for long-term care that is not currently covered by Medicare. We do cover such care with Medicaid; in fact, Medicaid is rapidly becoming an old people's program. But because most people do not think that is what Medicaid was intended for, there is pressure to change the system. Whether such change will require federal dollars or private dollars, the pressure for increased spending is clearly there.

At the other end of the age distribution, the high rate of illegitimate births and the high divorce rate are adding enormously to the number of single-parent families in the economy, a disproportionate number of whom are living in poverty. As a result, a great deal of pressure is being placed on welfare budgets at both state and national levels. We have adjusted to that added cost so far by reducing real benefits, but how long we can continue to do that is another question.

Those are just a couple of reasons why the budget could grow in the future. Another is the possibility that spending could fall as a result of the disciplining pressure imposed by the Balanced Budget Act (Gramm-Rudman-Hollings). That pressure led to the passage of a budget resolution that would bring deficits considerably below those implied by current policy.

If all elements of the budget resolution were implemented (and some have already been), the 1987 deficit would be cut by some $23 billion compared with current policy; for 1989 it would be cut by $43 billion. Under the resolution, defense would actually be cut a bit in real terms, and revenues would increase by a modest amount. What would continue with a vengeance is the stringency in the nondefense discretionary part of the budget that has already lowered its share of gross national product to the levels of the early 1960s.

One of the more important and fascinating components of this decrease in nondefense discretionary spending is that a lot of the cutting has come in the area of assistance to state and local governments. Since the late 1970s, grants have been diminishing. There has really been a quiet revolution in our fiscal relationships, which has played a role in halting the growth of state and local spending relative to GNP.

Unfortunately, the deficit reductions implied by the budget resolution are not sufficient to hit the Balanced Budget Act's targets. Clearly, a lot more has to be done.

CBO's estimates are averaged with those of the Office of Management and Budget (OMB), which has been more optimistic than CBO in assessing the prospects for the 1987 deficit. The deficit used for Balanced Budget Act purposes is defined somewhat differently than the deficits I have been discussing.

With the passage of this law, we have now succeeded in making the budget process as complicated as the tax laws. Rather than get into all of those complexities here, I will give you the bottom line as both OMB and CBO see it.

While the Tax Reform Act of 1986 has an $11 billion dollar revenue bulge in fiscal year 1987, which will help meet the deficit targets in the Balanced Budget Act, it also contains large revenue losses in fiscal year 1988 and 1989. Therefore, depending on the Tax Reform Act to solve the Balanced Budget Act problem would result in serious problems in FY 1988 and FY 1989. Some analysts argue that the problem would not be so terrible. They claim that the economy is in such an uncertain state right now that it might be easier to handle deficit reduction in the future.

The counterargument is, of course, that if the Congress is perceived to be putting off the problem, it could have an adverse psychological effect on capital markets. Ultimately, the Congress will have to wend its way between those two very real risks.

Another problem is that both the administration and the Congress want to increase the deficit in a number of areas. For example, they want to pay the Social Security cost of living adjustment (COLA), which according to law, should not be paid if inflation has been less than 3 percent. Both the administration and a wide range of legislators want to change that legislation.

The net result of these budget issues will, of course, depend on how OMB and CBO evaluate the various actions that the Congress takes. In terms of saving the $9.4 billion needed, it will depend on the average estimate of OMB and CBO as to how much has actually been cut.

A note in passing: One can fix almost everything with asset sales. We don't keep the government's accounts on a very sensible basis. We use a cash flow approach, and therefore asset sales count as negative spending. (The District of Columbia in 1986 assessed the Washington Monument at $550 million, which is about a million dollars a foot. Perhaps we could sell part of that as a way of reducing the deficit.)

The basic point, however, is that we face an enormous amount of uncertainty about both the economy and public policy. Therefore, whether extra tax revenues will be needed in the future remains a question. And if policymakers decide that a substantially new tax is needed, they must still determine whether it should be a consumption tax or some other kind of tax.

Chapter 5

Canada Considers a Business Transfer Tax

Michael H. Wilson

This chapter was originally to be titled, "Canada Chooses a Business Transfer Tax." That title was based on the expectation that I would be announcing a new Canadian sales tax system early in the summer of 1986. That announcement did not take place, due in great part to events in Washington, D.C.

The reason for the change in Canada's plans is quite simple. When I announced our intention to modernize the Canadian sales tax system in February 1986, it was the latest initiative in a gradual, phased tax reform process commenced one year earlier. Indeed, the Canadian government had already made significant progress on the corporate and personal tax fronts, and we had given notice that further changes were ahead. This multiphased approach was influenced not only by our desire for stability but our uncertainty over American intentions.

Since February 1986, much has happened in the United States. The surprising speed of the U.S. tax reform process has allowed Canada to forge ahead with greater confidence. Now that we have a better knowledge of the international terrain, we can move beyond the overhaul of our antiquated manufacturers' sales tax to a comprehensive and integrated reform of our corporate, personal, *and* sales tax systems. We are speeding up the reform of personal and corporate taxation to match sales tax reform.

TAX REFORM — CANADIAN STYLE

A truly effective tax system must meet a number of fundamental objectives.

- It should provide sufficient revenues to finance government programs (something that politicians often prefer to ignore).
- It must be appropriate for the economic structure of the nation.
- It must reflect the basic values of the society.
- It must maintain the respect of the taxpaying public.

These social and economic objectives are different in each country. And that means tax systems *must* be different—not necessarily better or worse, just different.

In the Canadian situation, at least seven social, political, and economic realities shape the tax reform effort. Some may sound familiar; others are uniquely Canadian.

First, Canada is a huge country with a small population, the equivalent of the population of California in a country with a land mass much larger than the lower 48 states. Obviously, this means the cost per capita of maintaining a modern national infrastructure is significantly higher than in a physically smaller country with a larger population, such as the United States.

Second, Canadians have historically overcome the handicap of a small population by pooling their resources through the state, to create the economies of scale for massive projects such as railroads and hydroelectric facilities, as well as efficient and effective health and educational institutions. This greater reliance on public investment means Canadians face higher taxes in exchange for lower after-tax expenditures on such things as university fees or medical insurance. This, of course, is a different approach than in the United States, where Americans must pay for many of these goods and services out of their after-tax disposable income. In effect, our countries have achieved similar ends through different means.

Third, not only do we use the state to provide certain goods and services, we also use the federal government to redirect resources between regions, thereby ensuring minimum national standards in all parts of the country. In fact, Canadians feel so strongly about this concept of sharing that the principle of equalization is now entrenched in our constitution. And Canadians in wealthier parts of the country have been willing to pay the price for that principle—in the form of higher federal government spending levels and higher federal taxes than otherwise would be the case.

This commitment to regional equality has long posed tremendous challenges for both tax policy and macroeconomic management. Canada contains a number of less prosperous, thinly populated regions with capital-intensive, resource-based economies. These regions surround a more heavily populated central heartland with a diversified economic base. The siren song of less government spending financed by a simple tax system could lead to not-so-simply resolved economic problems for residents in the have-not provinces.

Canada is not only a country of distinct geographic regions, it is a decentralized federal state with a unique distribution of constitutional and taxation powers. This creates a fourth factor in the tax reform equation.

Our provinces have extensive constitutional responsibilities in such areas as health, education, and welfare. The cost of fulfilling these responsibilities requires the provinces to occupy the sales tax field and particularly the income tax field to a far greater extent than American state authorities. This had led to joint occupation of income and sales tax fields and a complex set of federal-provincial fiscal and tax collection arrangements that must influence any federal tax reform proposals.

Fifth, quite apart from the regional economic impact of tax reform, Canada as a whole is a relatively young country with many capital-intensive industries. Our capital requirements will remain large into the foreseeable future. And that means we must ensure a high domestic savings rate.

Canada's capital needs also require us to maintain a liberalized investment environment, which leads to factor number six. Canada maintains one of the most open economies in the world, with a heavy reliance on both exports and imports. Two basic truisms flow from this situation:

1. Corporate and personal tax systems *must* be internationally competitive.
2. The total tax system must neither impede export performance nor accord any favor or penalty on imports.

It is timely to remember during this period of growing trade protectionism that the open nature of both the U.S. and Canadian economies has led not only to massive trade and capital flows between our two countries, but to significant interdependence. Increasingly freer trade has been a major source of economic growth since the Second World War for *both* our countries.

Unfortunately, this interdependence is being ignored by all those who have made the U.S. merchandise trade deficit a current political issue. Those preaching protectionism in both countries would do well to remember some basic but often forgotten facts:

- Much of our two-way trade is in intracorporate flows at different stages of production.

- The United States continues to enjoy a large surplus with Canada in both manufactured products and the entire service account.

- Canadian imports from the United States have grown by 31 percent since 1982, a period when U.S. exports as a whole grew by only 2 percent (in current dollars).

To put it bluntly, the extent of our interdependence means that if one country takes aim at the other, it will probably shoot itself in the foot. That is why the current trade talks between our two countries are so important. It would be tragic if the long-term interests of both our countries are defeated by the short-term political interests of the moment.

But enough of trade politics. Let me return to the seventh factor in the tax policy environment: the large national debt built up by Canada over the past decade. This economic reality, which may sound familiar, cannot be wished away. If governments do not reform fiscal and tax structures in a coordinated fashion, the resulting compounding debt will likely lead to that most unfair tax of all—high inflation.

Since coming into office in 1984, my colleagues and I have worked hard to regain control of government spending. And that effort has produced results. In our first full fiscal year in office, our deficit trend was reversed. The deficit fell in 1985 by 10 percent, and the policies now in place will ensure that this downward trend continues. Underlying the results of 1985 was a significant reduction in federal program spending, the first decline in program spending since the war. We are now well placed to reach our goal of fiscal stability at the turn of the decade.

Taken together, these seven factors not only shape the options for Canadian tax reform, they explain the central role of a modern consumption tax in any effective Canadian tax system. We have been amending Canada's tax system based on these Canadian conditions.

Corporate Taxation

"The Corporate Income Tax System: A Direction for Change" an official document released in 1985 analyzed the problems in Canada's corporate tax structure, and it proposed changes consistent with recent American reforms: a lower rate with a broadened base made possible by the modification or elimination of investment-distorting incentives.

Phase 1 of this process began in February 1986 with the elimination of certain ad hoc inflation adjustments, and the start of a three-year phase-out of the investment tax credit, accompanied by a three-point reduction in statutory rates of tax. Phase 2 will continue this thrust. Such changes will allow Canada to stop the continuing erosion of its corporate tax base through the creative but nonproductive use of preferences; it will ensure that profitable corporations begin to pay a reasonable amount of tax. And it will encourage investment decisions based on economic realities, not tax planning.

Personal Income Taxation

In the realm of personal income taxation, we have already made a number of major changes. Five initiatives stand out.

We have broadened Canada's taxable income base by eliminating a number of tax avoidance and tax deferral techniques, including deferred compensation arrangements, limited partnerships, and income splitting. We started this exercise from a much broader base than the U.S. tax code. For example, Canada has fewer tax shelters and its taxpayers never enjoyed the luxury of interest deductions on personal loans or home mortgages.

We have dramatically changed the taxation of capital gains and taxable dividends. On the one hand, we have begun the phasing-in of a $500,000 lifetime capital gains exemption to encourage entrepreneurship and equity investment. We have increased the tax on eligible Canadian dividends, in part to reflect the relative lack of risk in preferred shares and other debt-substitutes issued by established corporations. And to ensure that wealthy Canadians cannot combine these and other tax preferences to avoid paying tax in any one year, we have created a floor through the introduction of a minimum personal tax.

We have modified the indexation of our tax system and many government expenditure programs, a policy that will allow us to close the growing gap between revenues and expenditures caused by the indexation of both sides of the ledger to the consumer price index. We are determined to go forward with tax and fiscal reform in a coherent and coordinated manner.

We are enhancing the ability of the self-employed and those with inadequate employer-provided pensions to better provide for their retirement. Not only will this help our aging population prepare for retirement, but it will also provide a growing source of savings for future Canadian economic development.

And finally, we have commenced the important process of integrating social transfer programs with tax provisions, so that they result in resources being better targeted to those most in need.

These are five major developments. Further changes can be expected as we move forward with comprehensive tax reform. The goal is to lower marginal rates as far as possible, consistent with Canadian social and economic needs. Ironically, one of the keys to devising such a competitive personal income tax system is the reform of our sales tax regime.

Consumption Taxes

Unlike the United States, Canada has relied for a significant proportion of its revenues on a manufacturers' sales tax for over 60 years. For decades, its deficiencies have been recognized by manufacturers and the tax community and documented by numerous government task forces and commissions. Yet Canadian politicians have studiously ignored the problem, knowing that the general populace hardly knew of its existence. But if it has been a less visible source of revenue for governments, it has also been a silent killer of jobs, particularly with the gradual dismantling of tariff barriers since World War II. And it will become an ever-growing obstacle to economic growth and jobs should the current bilateral and multilateral trade negotiations bear fruit.

Since coming to office, my colleagues and I have been studying this tax to discover its true impact. Let me briefly describe our findings.

Incredibly, Canada's manufacturers' sales tax appears to be the only tax in the world that discriminates against its own producers in favor of foreign competitors. Due to the differing tax base on domestic and foreign goods, the effective rate of tax is, on average, one-third higher on Canadian products. In several cases, the effective tax rate is as much as 70 to 80 percent higher than on competing imports. This fact alone is reason enough for reform. But the situation is worse.

Not only does the tax discriminate between imports and domestic products, it discriminates against similar products made by different manufacturers in a particular industry. We have discovered that the effective tax rate for a class of products can vary by as much as three to four times, depending on the channels of trade. In fact, it appears that there are probably as many effective tax rates under the present system for any given product as there are companies that produce it.

Approximately one-half of the total sales tax collected is derived from tax on business inputs such as transportation equipment, office equipment, and building materials. The tax on these inputs can then result in cascading, as these inputs may be used to produce goods that are subsequently taxed again. The result is not only an increase in the cost of investment in Canada, but an indirect charge on exported goods, estimated at approximately 1 percent of the sales value of exports. That, of course, is a very substantial part of the already narrow profit margins in today's competitive international marketplace.

Canada's federal sales tax also is too narrowly based. Only about one-third of Canadian consumption is subject to tax. Four products—tobacco, alcohol, automobiles and parts, and motor fuels—account for 42 percent of the revenue, though they represent only about 15 percent of all consumer expenditures.

This narrow base, which is continually eroded by ingenious court challenges, has forced tax rates to rise for fiscal purposes. And this combination of a narrow base and high rates has distorted the natural and efficient operations of the economy.

Faced with these facts, my colleagues and I have decided that it is simply irresponsible to let sleeping dogs lie. We have a public duty to fix up this mess. One way would be to eliminate federal sales tax altogether. But that would mean erecting uncompetitive personal and corporate tax structures, a form of economic suicide. That leaves us with a second option: to design a better system. And that is what we plan to do, to broaden the sales tax base and apply one lower rate through a comprehensive sales tax.

We have reviewed the value-added taxes introduced in other countries and have been examining a business transfer tax. This tax, based on total domestic sales less purchases over a specified period, would be applied at each state in the production-marketing chain. It would be a relatively straightforward calculation for both tax payable and for refunds. It would have limited exemptions to preserve simplicity and efficiency. It would prevent cascading. It would treat domestic products and imports equally. It would remove the indirect, hidden tax on exports. And it would be based on books of account already kept by businesses.

A business transfer tax would be more than just a vast improvement over the current sales tax. It will help meet the broader social and economic needs of Canada in a number of ways. It will provide the necessary foundation to enable us to achieve competitive personal and corporate tax structures with lower marginal tax rates in the context of comprehensive reform. It will allow us the flexibility to offset the inherent regressive nature of consumption taxes with a refundable lower income tax credit geared to family status, and to integrate this credit into progressive social tax reform. It will encourage the level of savings necessary to finance future private and public investment. It will give us much more flexibility in managing the Canadian economy and achieving balanced regional impacts. It will help our industries to compete better in domestic and foreign markets. And perhaps most important, it will help us maintain and enhance such distinctive Canadian institutions and values as accessible health care, affordable higher education, regional equality, public broadcasting, and income support for those in need.

So that is tax reform Canadian style, our reasons for pursuing it, and the role of a modern sales tax in that process.

Chapter 6

Economic Growth: Growing Up

George F. Will

It is my somewhat melancholy task to say a little about the politics of taxation and the politics of the budget, which are quite related at this point. I bring no particular expertise to the discussion. What I do bring is what I consider an honorable obsession with the deficit, and I want to talk about tax reform in connection with that, because tax reform strikes me as, among other things, an enormous, interesting, and successful effort to change the subject from what the subject probably ought to be in this country.

It is the case, I think, that we have been given in tax reform a genuinely radical bill for which there is simply zero clamor in the country. If you went to the average American and said, "Given the $200 billion deficits, do you need a personal income tax cut at this point?" he or she would say, "Of course not." But the average American was not asked, and we will come in a moment to why ordinary taxpayers failed to give the kind of response that was looked for. However, a salutary level of fear about the deficit has taken hold in the country. I say salutary, because it does seem to me that, in a democracy, fear does the work of reason. In the 1930s we made fundamental structural changes in the relationship of the citizen to the central government—changes I think, by and large, correct—and we did so not because people sat down and read Keynes but because they were afraid that, if they did not make these changes, they would be consigned to permanent depression. April-May 1940, the British brought Churchill to power, not because they suddenly heard Churchill, but because Hitler was at the Channel ports, and suddenly they had the salutary level of fear.

The United States got these deficits in 1982. It became clear we had a problem and this tax cut was not, as promised, self-financing. We wasted 1982 talking about a constitutional amendment to balance the budget. The theory was that you could outlaw deficits because it worked so well with gin.

In 1983 we solved the deficit problem with the Grace Commission Report. 1984 being an election year, we decided we would solve the deficit problem with economic growth, if we just made enough interesting assumptions: for example, that we had outlawed the business cycle forever, and that we would have a more rapid rate of economic growth than we have ever had before, for a longer period of time than we have ever had before, and in the midst of the boom, interest rates would decline to 2 percent. Given those assumptions, we could grow to a balanced budget.

In 1985 we decided to change the subject, and talk about tax reform and, lo and behold, on the David Brinkley show in August 1986, a senator, whose name charity prevents me from giving you, said the following thing. He said, "Tax reform is going to solve the deficit problem, because people will be unable to keep more of their money and therefore will work harder and therefore will be more productive and therefore the deficit problem is going to go away."

Whether or not that is true, we shall see. What seems to me objectively certain is that the summer and early autumn of 1986 were the most momentous months, the most interesting months in domestic policy, probably in the postwar period, because of the intersection of two extraordinary pieces of legislation, the Gramm-Rudman-Hollings Act, as modified by Congress in the wake of the Supreme Court, and the Tax Reform Act. Combined, they made this a period of maximum government-generated uncertainty in U.S. economic life. The two laws have this in common: They both are, I think, acts of political, cultural despair on the part of Congress, a despair about Congress's ability to make decisions in a town in which there is now a serious, skillful influence industry, gifted at bending public power to its purpose.

I am not going to recite Gramm-Rudman. It is, I think, a disgraceful law, to put it politely. When it was first introduced, I called Senator Rudman, who's a terrific guy, a feisty, amateur boxer, a good guy, and I said, "Senator Rudman, your bill is a disgrace to democracy, a bankruptcy of the Senate, and proof that Americans are not ready for self-government." Senator Rudman said, "Of course. It's just the best we can do."

It is an attempt to expunge the last vestige of mind from government, that is, the weighing of choices and the setting of priorities.

Senator Rudman was in a caucus of Republican senators and he got up to explain the bill. Seated next to him was Senator Dole who is the funniest, the most intentionally funny, senator. Rudman was explaining this bill, and Dole finally walks up to him and says, "Sit down, Senator Rudman, and quit explaining that bill. Some of us are still for it."

But it was a fundamental statement that Congress had lost confidence in its capacity to make choices, and not Congress alone. In his State of the Union address, the president said, "I love Gramm-Rudman, the Strategic Defense Initiative, and the Space Station." You can't have all three.

The president said, "I love Gramm-Rudman, I hate drugs, and I hate espionage." A 10 percent cut, if ordered under Gramm-Rudman, will cause the firing of one in nine FBI agents—no discretion involved, no thought, choice, weighing. It will cause the closing of all the Drug Enforcement Administration offices in overseas countries. Still, it is just a comprehensive statement that we cannot cope with the conflicting pressures and have to take a Gramm-Rudman approach. That is what has happened, essentially, with the approach to tax-cutting.

Now, the tax cut has an interesting history, because the president is for it. The president has been praised for his terrific consistency over the years. That consistency is not discernible to my naked eye in the approach that the president praised in 1981 and the approach that the president praises in 1986, or, for that matter, the approach that Senator Bob Packwood praised until the middle of July 1986.

For 10 years, Bob Packwood has been a good friend of mine, and for 10 years he has explained that he not only favors the use of the tax code for micromanaging the economy and for micromanaging the achievement of social objectives through private resources. Witness, for example, the energy credits and other legislation for which Packwood, more than anyone else, was responsible.

But he also had a hidden agenda—not very hidden really, he was quite candid about it—which was that if you left enough fringe benefits untaxed, used in a variety of ways, tax exemptions to encourage corporations to provide social services, you would find over time the income tax base so eroded that there would be no choice but to go to something like a consumption tax. Good, bad or indifferent, that was the drill until summer 1986, when things changed rather remarkably.

To go back to the history of this bill, remember that the president is the Great Communicator. Everyone says so, so it must be true. I would point out, however, that the president began to be called the

Great Communicator in the summer of 1981 because in 1981 the president gave a speech that earned him the reputation as the Great Communicator. Remember what he said? He looked the country in the eye, and said, "Be brave and endure a tax cut." And the country said, "My God, that boy can talk."

It's a very different approach to taxes today, except in both cases the emphasis is on the cut in individual marginal tax rates, and that is all. Remember what happened? In 1985 the media decided that the issue was arms control and terrorism, the country decided it was the deficit, and the president, with some help from Congress, decided to change the subject and talk about tax reform.

So the president gave a lot of speeches in the spring of 1985 in which he said, "I'm for tax reform to make things fairer and more simple." And ABC conducted a poll, in which they found that 86 percent of the American people were for a fairer tax code. Kind of makes you want to meet the other 14 percent.

He did that in April and May, and over the summer, whatever momentum the president had aroused (and that was precious little) disappeared.

It did not survive Treasury I, Treasury II, or the first tax bill that came out of the House. In fact, the only thing that galvanized public attention was a number. Bob Packwood discovered, with the help of Bill Bradley, something simple enough to arrest the attention of a fundamentally fat, sassy, and inattentive country, and it was the number 27, and it became a kind of fetish. Oh, it changed over time as it grew up to number 28, but still, it was something people could wrap their minds around. And it was that which imparted such momentum as we have. Still, there was no particular clamor for it.

That is why it was mildly safe for Senator Danforth to do what he and a very few others did, which was resist the bill when it came to the floor. Now, Danforth is a very interesting case. We have said it is a miracle that Congress enacted tax reform. Senator Danforth is an ordained Episcopal priest and something of an expert on miracles. He says this does not really fit the criteria, because it was, after all, essentially a bidding war between the two parties for a long time to see who could define the middle class most capaciously and could cut taxes for it most generously while hiding the cost of those most felicitously in business taxes. That is not a miracle; that is just the way things are done.

Jack Danforth himself was willing to cash in the investment tax credit in favor of lower rates. It is not one particular thing that has aggravated Jack. It was, as Jack says, the comprehensive nature, the investment tax credit, the treatment of capital gains, the treatment of depreciation and, most especially in Jack's mind, the treatment of research and development. It is a comprehensive bill, voting against the future as far as Jack is concerned.

Now, that may be right, or it may be wrong. The case for the bill is interestingly political. The prime impetus for this came, I believe it is fair to say, from a reasonably junior Democratic senator from a northeastern industrial state, Bill Bradley, who regarded this less as an economic matter than as a vote for a different and better kind of government, and you can make a good argument for that.

That is, he said the Democratic party, in the pursuit of fairness, must understand that in the nature of the dynamic of politics and of capital and continental countries such as this, decisions made in Washington to allocate wealth and opportunity, either directly or through tax incentives, are most apt to serve the interests of those who can afford the influence industry that exists in Washington.

Therefore, Bradley, representing a significant portion of this party in endorsing this particular approach, a flatter tax, a more simplified tax code, is pulling his party, or trying to pull his party, away from a kind of statism, away from a politicizing of economic decisions. If that occurs he, with the president's help, will have gone a long way toward rescuing the Democratic party from some of its excesses, and that has got this argument about tax reform couched in an interesting way. Now, it is a question of whether or not we use the tax code, as they say, just to raise revenue, or to achieve social objectives.

In October 1964, in the middle of the Goldwater campaign, a recently converted former Democrat, now Republican, gave a speech for Barry Goldwater on television in which he said the following: "The taxing power of government must be used to provide revenues for legitimate government purposes. It must not be used to regulate the economy and bring about social change." So said Ronald Reagan in his speech for Goldwater that launched Reagan's political career.

That formulation, widely popular, has an artificial clarity and is, in fact, fundamentally silly. I do not know how a great country with a complicated industrial economy raises hundreds and hundreds of billions of dollars without having implicit in the way it does it, a social policy. Indeed, there is nothing more striking than the fact that the Reagan administration has sought all along, from day 1, to use changes in the tax code to change behavior and, indeed, to change values in the United States. A perfectly sensible political program, but one that they have flinched from describing accurately.

The Reagan administration has made an attempt, just as much as the Thatcher administration has made an attempt, to use changes in incentives to change the general fundamental energy and entrepreneurial spirit of the people. It is an exercise in changing the temperament of the country. If that is not the use of the tax code not just to raise revenues but to alter behavior and change values in a most ambitious way, I don't know what is.

U.S. policymakers are asked, as we have undertaken this extraordinary change in the tax code, to do so on the basis of fairly clear expectations about the future. I mean, not just revenue projections that come and go in the most evanescent ways, but to have confidence in our ability to project behavioral changes, even changes in the spiritual and moral climate of the country, as a result of this or that tax cut. We are at sea.

It has been said about the development of particular sciences that they are almost never as developed as they think they are, and it is widely and truly said, that until about 1910, the average trip to a doctor did more harm than good, because all doctors had at that point was the capacity to make you comfortable while nature healed or killed you. This was why, in the nineteenth century, what was valued in doctors was the bedside manner; that is exactly what doctors had to contribute.

Until 1950 it was a good bet against the weather bureau to bet that tomorrow's weather would be just like yesterday. If you bet that 365 days a year against the weather forecasters, you would win. And we are approximately at that state today with economic forecasting.

Nevertheless, the two most ideologically confident conservative regimes in the world, the Thatcher and the Reagan governments, have, in a most temperamentally unconservative way, invested more confidence in the capacity of a clear economic ideology to provide a road map to the future.

It is odd that this has happened, in what is the fiftieth anniversary of the publication of Keynes's general theory in 1936. It is very odd how ideas enter politics in our time. Usually they enter rather slowly. Keynes published his book, and there was a slow maturation. Articles appeared in learned journals and seminars and gradually graduate students and their students entered politics and then modified Keynesianism became public policy.

As is well known, that is not how the supply-side approach entered politics. The Democratic party used to be the party of assistant professors; that was its problem. Then in the 1970s, the Republican party began to get ideas. It used to be a party of gruff, florid farm implement dealers from Montana, tough guys who wanted no truck with untested new ideas, or with tested old ideas; they didn't like ideas.

One day an assistant professor drew a curve on a napkin and his dinner companion, a *Wall Street Journal* reporter, read the napkin. The napkin said, "You can have a self-financing tax cut." What a wonderful idea. It's an answer to all problems. It obviates all difficult political choices. You want more money: cut taxes. Yeah, I could do that.

And he put it in the *Wall Street Journal* and a man out in California who was about to become the epicenter of American politics read the *Wall Street Journal* and said, "I like that." What is true of Ronald Reagan is true of any political leader confronted with an idea that enchanting. It is what Cardinal Woolsey said of Henry VIII when he warned "Be very careful of what you put in his head. You'll never get it out."

The problem is that, in 1981, as I recall my ancient history, the argument was that if you tax something you get less of it. Now we are hearing that if you increase the tax burden on capital formation, you are not going to get any less of it. That was either true once and not true now, or vice versa, as they say. It is simply an interesting, uncontrolled experiment that we are making here.

Economics is, like a lot of other things, the science of single instances. We have very little to go on because circumstances are always different than they were 10 years ago. But, in point of fact, if capital formation is affected by tax rates, we are going to have less of it.

It is argued, of course, that even with the new bill, the tax burden on business overall will be below the historic postwar level. That view may be true, but there are two things wrong with it. It is an aggregate picture, whereas the burdens on particular kinds of industries are going to be exceptionally high, especially when you account for Social Security and state and local taxes; furthermore, when we talk about the historic level, we are ignoring historic changes. We are talking about a period 30 years ago when no one thought of Korea and Taiwan as competitors for the United States.

Who would have guessed, in 1950, if someone had said, "There will be a great warrior nation and a great commercial nation, and the former will be a Jewish state and the latter will be Japan." It is a very peculiar transformation of our understanding of the nations with which we are dealing.

It is at least arguable that the best case to be made for the 1986 Tax Reform Act is that it sets us on course for a 1990 Tax Act. Such a fetish has now been made of low individual and marginal tax rates that it will be very hard for any president, of either party, to reverse what has been done.

Second, it seems to me reasonably clear that the burdens placed upon business by this Tax Act have gone about as far as they can go.

Third, and of this I am absolutely confident, we need a tax increase. We have seen under Ronald Reagan, what a serious president does to a country. We have had fundamental questions asked and answered. The president asked the country, "What kind of government do you want?" He didn't get quite the answer he wanted.

That is partly his fault, in two senses. Ronald Reagan is not a government-cutter. He is a government-rearranger. He wanted to take substantial resources across the river to the Pentagon (perfectly sensible, in my judgment). But a lot of Republicans get confused on that subject. They think that is cutting government, because they do not think the Pentagon is part of government. They think it is a private sector initiative run by the Junior League of Arlington or something.

Second, the president not once asked for, because we were going to have this self-financing tax cut, he never sought, and therefore, never got, a mandate for cutting domestic spending.

That is why, in a span of 48 months, he can carry 93 states (in two elections) and then not be able to cut AMTRAK 15 percent. There was no mandate for domestic budget-cutting built in. We've had a rolling referendum on domestic spending for six years, and it is fairly clear the country doesn't want much more government but doesn't want much less.

I will now save you $25 by telling you all there is to read in David Stockman's book. He has one wonderful phrase in there. He says, "The dirty little secret, the dirty little secret of American politics is that 80 percent of all House Republicans and 90 percent of all Senate Republicans have voted for every major expansion of the welfare state in the postwar period."

That was a secret only to David Stockman. Those were recorded votes. It was a clear pattern that there was a clear consensus in the United States that we want a moderate, social democratic welfare state. It costs money, and we are going to have to pay for it.

Given those three factors: that marginal rates have become something of a fetish, that business taxes have been maximized, that we cannot finance the government we are determined to have with the tax base we now have under a revenue-neutral law, the next time around the tax-raising will be driven—regardless of the merits—in the direction of a consumption tax.

Regardless of the merits, it seems to me that is the case. The question is, whether or not this is good for us, and we are certainly going to find out. Dan Rostenkowski (in Chapter 2 of this book) uses what

I call at the Will house "the F word." Every parent must stop his children from using it as soon as they start. It is a four-letter word, and it is repulsive: it is "fair." You can have no tranquility in any house where people are arguing about fairness all the time.

It strikes me that what is fundamentally fair is for one generation to bequeath to another generation a healthier country, and not to bequeath to the next generation the cost of their consumption. Republicans for 30 years have campaigned against Democrats, against Harry Hopkins, frankly, for saying, "Tax, tax, spend, spend, elect, elect." Republicans said, "That's disgusting. It's wicked. We are going to borrow, borrow, spend, spend, elect, elect."

At least Harry Hopkins had in mind to pass the burdens of the current generation's consumption on to someone else in that generation. The Republican plan is to slough the whole thing off on the future.

Those of us who have had small children know that the definition of infantilism is to will the end without willing the means to that end. If you will economic growth, you have to will the means to that. That means accumulation. That means deferred gratification, all the things children have a hard time with.

And it does seem to me the question about getting tax reform is, "What does this do to your children? What does it do about an equitable allocation of the burdens of your own consumption, and the provisions for future consumption?" That, I thought I understood once, was the point of supply-side economics, and I am frankly bound to say that the Tax Reform Act of 1986 looks to me like an attempt to subsidize consumption in a period of $200 billion deficits with yet further profligacy about the accumulation necessary for the future.

Whether or not the corrective that I see coming in the 1990 tax bill will take the direction Charls Walker wishes depends, in part, on who is president. It will be, it seems to me, a sublime irony if the president in 1990 is a Democrat produced by the 1987—1988 recession, produced by the tax act authored in no small measure by the Democratic House. That will certainly be one of the great dialectics of our time, but it is a question to which I have no answers. All I insist upon is that the question I ask is the central question about tax reform, and that there are reasons for doubts about what we are doing with this.

PART II

A U.S. CONSUMPTION TAX
Possibilities and Problems

Chapter 7

Taxation and the Cost of Capital: An International Comparison

B. Douglas Bernheim and
John B. Shoven

The sluggish performance of investment in the United States since the mid-1970s must be considered disappointing. Despite the enactment of various investment incentives at the corporate level, statistics of the Organization for Economic Cooperation and Development (OECD) reveal that gross fixed capital formation as a percentage of gross domestic product (GDP) fell slightly from an average of 18.5 percent between 1971 and 1980 to 17.3 percent between 1981 and 1984. These figures are roughly on a par with those for the United Kingdom (19.2 percent between 1971 and 1980, and 16.7 percent between 1981 and 1984). While the West German experience was significantly better, even its rates of gross investment (22.3 percent and 20.0 percent, respectively) were dwarfed by those for the Japanese economy (32.7 percent and 29.1 percent).

It is extremely difficult to account fully for these differences. In each country, investment depends upon a variety of factors, including the cost of financial capital, the cost of physical capital, the wage rate, the price level, technology, and government regulations, as well as less tangible aspects of the political and social climate. Of these factors, the cost of financial capital has received perhaps the most attention from economists.

Why might the cost of financial capital differ from country to country? There are two possibilities. First, domestic credit condi-

The authors would like to thank Don Fullerton of the U.S. Treasury and Jim Poterba of Massachusetts Institute of Technology for helpful comments.

tions (real required rates of return) may differ. Second, every country has a unique system of capital income taxes. If policymakers wish to provide incentives for capital formation by manipulating the cost of financial capital through effective fiscal and monetary policies, then it is essential to determine the relative importance of these two factors.

The importance of domestic credit conditions depends upon the extent to which one can characterize the U.S. economy as "open." If markets for goods and financial capital were fully integrated, then international flows of resources would equalize real rates of return across countries. All differences in the cost of financial capital would then be attributable to taxation, and other policies could affect this cost only through altering worldwide credit market conditions. However, much evidence now indicates that the U.S. economy is not completely open. Thus the relative importance of capital income taxation and other credit market policies as determinants of the domestic cost of financial capital remains a critical unanswered question, which we address in this chapter.

A central finding of this chapter is that, under prevailing tax systems differences in the cost of capital between countries are largely attributable to differences in domestic credit market conditions, rather than to taxes. Even the effects of the Tax Reform Act of 1986 as well as those of specific provisions such as reinstating the investment tax credit, would be small relative to intercountry variation in real interest rates. Nevertheless, one cannot dismiss taxes as unimportant. In particular, the elimination of taxation on income from capital either at the personal or corporate levels, or both (a consumption tax) would have a profound effect on the cost of capital in the United States relative to other countries. For example, despite the fact that both Japanese real interest rates and cost of capital are approximately 2.5 percentage points below those for the United States, under one plausible scenario the adoption of a consumption tax would eliminate more than 60 percent of the differential between the cost of capital in the United States and Japan.

REAL INTEREST RATES

The cost of capital in any country depends upon both the tax system and prevailing credit conditions. The relative importance of these two factors is the subject of considerable debate. One school of thought holds that international capital markets function extremely well. Proponents of this view argue that free flows of financial capital serve to equalize real rates of return to available investments across countries. It follows that the cost of capital can differ between two countries only if their tax systems differ. The opposing school of thought holds that, despite the removal of capital controls and the opening of international financial markets, financial capital is in some sense imperfectly mobile across national borders.[1] As a result, differences in available real rates of return can persist as disequilibrium phenomena for significant periods of time. Accordingly, it is possible for countries to influence domestic credit conditions through a variety of fiscal and monetary policies. Only an undetermined portion of the differences between the cost of capital in various countries can then be attributed to taxes.

Economists tend to identify these schools of thought with Arnold Harberger and Martin Feldstein, respectively. Both have provided indirect evidence concerning the efficiency of international capital markets. In his analysis of less developed countries, Harberger[2] found that the ratio of different nations' capital stocks to labor forces explained less than one-third of the variation in rates of return to capital but more than 90 percent of the variation in earnings. He concluded that, unlike labor, financial capital must move relatively freely between countries in order to equalize real rates of return. In contrast, Feldstein and Horioka[3] studied OECD countries and found that, country by country, saving differs very little from investment as a fraction of GDP. Furthermore, they showed that saving and investment are highly correlated both across countries and over time within a single country. They concluded that domestically generated financial capital tends to be invested domestically despite the possible availability of greater returns on foreign investments.

Of course, the evidence presented both by Harberger and by Feldstein and Horioka bears only indirectly on the question of whether credit conditions differ significantly from country to country. More recently Mishkin[4] has directly tested the hypothesis that real interest rates are equal across countries. His findings, based upon data from seven OECD countries, strongly refutes this hypothesis, and supports the inference of Feldstein and Horioka.

The bulk of the evidence suggests that, despite the tendency for capital markets to equilibrate in the long run, many domestic policies can affect a country's cost of capital by altering real domestic interest rates. To the extent the cost of capital differs significantly from country to country, it is important to determine whether these differences are due primarily to taxation or to ambient credit conditions. This is the object of the study reported in this chapter. As a first step, we attempt to identify real riskless rates of return in the United States, the United Kingdom, West Germany, and Japan from

1971 to the present. In subsequent sections, we calculate the cost of capital under appropriate interest and inflation rate assumptions for various tax regimes. This second step of our analysis borrows heavily from the methodology developed by King and Fullerton.[5]

The economist attempting to analyze international credit conditions immediately confronts issues of comparability. Ideally, we would like to identify rates of return corresponding to riskless, freely traded securities in each country. The most obvious choice is to use government bonds. In fact, quarterly data is available on three-month (in the case of Japan, two-month) Treasury bills, as well as on long-term (more than five-year) government bonds for each of the four countries under consideration. These instruments have the virtue of being relatively free of most risks, except, of course, for those arising from uncertainty concerning inflation. This property is extremely important for our purposes, since the King-Fullerton methodology makes no explicit allowance for risk, and indeed may produce misleading results when used to derive the cost of capital for risky projects (see Bulow and Summers[6]). Unfortunately, many countries other than the United States have during various periods chosen to fix the rates of return on certain government bonds, rather than allow these rates to be determined by the free market. In spite of this, government bond rates may nevertheless reflect current domestic credit conditions, or, perhaps more important, target credit conditions which the government pursues through various fiscal and monetary policies.

As an alternative to government bond rates, one could use interest rates on private financial instruments. Perhaps the best available data on such rates comes from the Euro deposit markets. Such deposits are denominated in the currency of each country and are issued on the same bank, so that the Euro rates in different currencies have similar default risks. In addition, Euro deposits are freely traded offshore securities and are therefore not subject to domestic capital controls. Unfortunately, these rates do reflect substantial default risk premiums, and are therefore inappropriate for our purposes. Indeed, in a comparison of three-month Eurodollar and U.S. T-bill rates, Mishkin[7] finds that the corresponding premium is not only typically quite large but also varies dramatically (from 1 to 6 percentage points) over time. Following Mishkin, one could subtract this premium from the Euro rate for each country in every period, thereby producing default-free or risk-free interest rates. We are, however, somewhat skeptical about the validity of this procedure.

In practice, our strategy is to use government bond rates. We are relatively unconcerned about the difficulties arising from the possibility that some of these markets may fail to clear, for two reasons.

First, casual inspection of T-bill and long-term bond rate series reveals that these rates move a great deal in every country. Furthermore, these movements appear to reflect domestic credit conditions, in that they exhibit general patterns that are strikingly similar to those described by Mishkin in his analysis of Euro rates (indeed, we strongly suspect that the use of Euro rates would not substantively alter our conclusions). These observations suggest that large deviations from market clearing in government bond markets may actually have been quite rare.

Second, since interest rates fluctuate for a variety of reasons, it is easily possible that historical market clearing rates do not reflect target credit conditions that governments attempt to achieve through fiscal and monetary policies. If these policies are reasonably successful over relatively long periods of time, then, for our purposes, it may be more appropriate to use a target interest rate than a market clearing rate.

Despite the fact that the use of government bond rates probably does not significantly bias our results, it is nevertheless appropriate to determine the likely direction of any bias that might occur. To the extent there is a tendency for international flows of financial capital to equalize rates of return across countries, policies that prevent government bond markets from clearing should cause differences in bond rates to overstate differences in ambient credit conditions. Thus our calculations will tend to understate the importance of taxes in determining differences in the cost of capital between various countries. Since we find that the effects of certain tax reforms on the cost of capital are large relative to intercountry variation in real interest rates, these conclusions are therefore all the more striking.

At best, data on bond markets provide us with information about nominal interest rates. Our exercise requires us to obtain measures of real interest rates. There is, of course, a simple relationship between the real interest rate, $r(t)$ and the nominal interest rate, $i(t)$, at time t:

$$r(t) - i(t) - \pi^e(t) \quad , \tag{7.1}$$

where $\pi^e(t)$ denotes the expected rate of inflation at time t. We refer to this as the *ex ante* real rate of return, in order to emphasize that it is the real return expected at the beginning of each period. Actual, or *ex post* returns may turn out to be quite different. To transform nominal interest rates into real interest rates, we must therefore first resolve two issues. First, what is the appropriate index of inflation? Second, how does one measure expectations concerning the inflation rate?

In the following analysis, we use consumer price indexes to compute inflation rates for each country. This practice is consistent with our view of international capital markets in that we think of domestic investment as being motivated by the desire to receive a return in terms of consumer goods within each country under consideration.

The proper measurement of expectations concerning inflation poses more formidable conceptual difficulties. Since it is ordinarily impossible to observe expectations directly, one must settle for imputations based upon models that describe the formation of investors' beliefs. Of course, this same consideration makes it extremely difficult to compare alternative models. Accordingly, very little is known about the processes through which investors actually form expectations. Our strategy is therefore to present results based upon three very different hypotheses about these processes and search for patterns that are relatively robust with respect to the maintained hypothesis. In this way we avoid attaching undue importance to any particular set of numbers.

Our first hypothesis is that investors form expectations on the basis of the myopic assumption that current inflation rates will persist into the future. For short-term bonds, we use the inflation rate from the preceding quarter: for long-term bonds, we use the average inflation rate over the preceding year. While this hypothesis strikes us as somewhat implausible, we include it in order to represent one rather extreme possibility.

In contrast, our second hypothesis is that investors form expectations rationally, employing all available information. This hypothesis implies that the actual inflation rate in each period t is on average equal to ex ante expectations of inflation during that period, given available information. As a result, the ex post real rate of return in period t, defined as

$$r^*(t) = i(t) - \pi(t) \quad , \tag{7.2}$$

(where $\pi(T)$ is the actual period t inflation rate) is on average equal to the ex ante real rate of return, defined in equation (7.1). However, unlike the ex ante return, the ex post return is directly observable. Thus, if we average the ex post return over some long sample period, we should obtain an accurate estimate of the average ex ante rate during that period. Even for a relatively short sample period, the average ex post is an unbiased estimate of the average ex ante rate.[8]

To form ex post short-term rates, we simply subtract concurrent quarterly inflation rates (rather than lagged rates, as above) from nominal short-term interest rates. Technically, it is proper to compute ex post returns on long-term bonds by taking some average of inflation rates over their maturity periods, and subtracting this from nominal long-term rates. However, since the maturities of our long-term bonds exceed five years, this procedure would force us to truncate our ex post long-term real interest rate series at a relatively early date. We opt instead to average inflation rates over subsequent one-year periods and subtract this amount from current nominal rates. One must bear this in mind when interpreting our ex post long-run real interest rate series.

Our final hypothesis is that investors forecast future inflation rates on the basis of simple statistical models. Accordingly, we analyzed the statistical properties of inflation rate series using quarterly observations on the consumer price index of each country from the first quarter of 1965 to the final quarter of 1983 (in the case of Japan, our CPI series began in the first quarter of 1970). From this analysis, we generated and estimated a simple model of the inflationary process in each country.[9] We then used this model to forecast future inflation rates from each sample period. We imputed a real short-term rate for each period by subtracting the forecasted inflation rate for the subsequent quarter from the current nominal T-bill rate. Similarly, we imputed a real long-term rate for each period by subtracting the average forecasted rate for the subsequent five years from the current long-term bond rate.

We present the results of these calculations in Tables 7–1 to 7–3. Table 7–1 contains average inflation rates, short- and long-term nominal interest rates, and imputed short- and long-term real interest rates for the United States in every year from 1971 to 1982. Unfortunately, we were not able to obtain quarterly data on interest and inflation rates for all countries subsequent to the end of 1983. Since our ex post calculations require data on future inflation rates, we were forced to truncate our series at 1982. Later, we present calculations for 1983 through 1985 based upon annual data.

The general pattern that emerges from Table 7–1 suggests that real interest rates were extremely low, possibly even negative, during the 1970s. Beginning in 1981, inflation rates began to decline rapidly, and real interest rates rose dramatically. As we shall see, high real rates have persisted through 1985. This pattern has been noted previously by Cumby and Mishkin,[10] among others. Since there appears to be some fundamental, systematic difference between the 1970s and 1980s, and since this difference may have altered real interest rate differentials across countries (Mishkin,[11] for example, suggests that real interest rates might respond differently in different countries to changes in inflation), it seems appropriate to provide separate analyses for the two periods.

Table 7-1. U.S. Inflation and Interest Rates, 1971–1982.

Year	Inflation (%)	Nominal Interest Rates (%)		Imputed Short-Term Real Interest Rates (%)			Imputed Long-Term Real Interest Rates (%)		
		Short	Long	Myopic	Ex post	Forecasted	Myopic	Ex post	Forecasted
1971	3.55	4.24	5.71	0.69	0.72	0.16	1.40	2.44	0.08
1972	3.42	4.44	5.65	1.01	0.24	0.68	2.38	-0.61	0.24
1973	8.37	7.06	6.07	-1.32	-2.72	-0.63	-0.19	-4.90	-1.04
1974	12.21	7.41	6.98	-4.80	-3.61	-3.67	-4.00	-2.24	-1.67
1975	7.36	5.83	7.02	-1.53	-0.63	-1.81	-2.19	1.33	-0.16
1976	4.92	4.92	6.47	0.00	-1.00	-0.55	0.78	-0.13	0.33
1977	6.69	5.41	7.10	-1.28	-1.01	-1.37	0.50	-0.42	0.34
1978	8.80	7.68	7.94	-1.12	-2.15	-0.53	0.42	-3.46	0.58
1979	12.87	10.10	8.75	-2.77	-4.23	-1.51	-2.66	-4.82	-0.14
1980	12.64	12.08	11.03	-0.56	0.88	-0.30	-2.54	0.77	1.91
1981	9.37	13.51	12.89	4.14	6.04	4.94	2.63	6.82	5.13
1982	4.53	10.63	12.03	6.09	7.06	5.44	5.96	8.96	5.95

Table 7-2. Imputed Real Interest Rate Differentials, 1971-1982.

Period/Country	Short Term			Long Term		
	Myopic	Ex post	Forecasted	Myopic	Ex post	Forecasted
1971-1982						
United Kingdom	-2.92	-2.83	-2.43	-1.04	-1.07	0.00
West Germany	2.34	2.43	2.47	3.16	2.90	2.60
Japan	-2.76	-2.71	-2.80	-0.23	-0.30	-0.93
1981-1982						
United Kingdom	-2.12	-2.52	-3.36	-3.07	-2.11	-2.78
West Germany	-0.31	-0.84	-0.06	-1.08	-2.37	-0.73
Japan	-2.86	-3.66	-6.15	-0.72	-1.97	-5.02

Table 7-3. Interest Rates and Differentials, 1983-1985.

	Short Term	Long Term
U.S. nominal	8.54	12.04
Imputed U.S. real	5.06	8.56
Differential for United Kingdom	-0.18	-1.60
Differential for West Germany	-1.69	-2.14
Differential for Japan	-1.14	-2.02

In Table 7-2 we exhibit imputed real interest rate differentials between the United States and, respectively, the United Kingdom, West Germany, and Japan. Entries in this table are calculated by subtracting each country's average imputed real rate over some period from the corresponding average imputed real rate for the United States. Thus, the first entry, -2.92, indicates that, from 1971 to 1982, the average real short rate for the United Kingdom, imputed on the assumption of myopic expectations, was 2.92 percentage points lower than the corresponding rate for the United States. As suggested above, we have calculated separate averages for the two years 1981 and 1982.

Table 7-3 contains data on nominal and imputed real rates, as well as differentials, for the years 1983-1985. The reader should recall that these calculations are based upon annual, rather than quarterly data. It is therefore impossible to calculate ex post real interest rates properly, or to forecast future inflation rates on the basis of our estimated statistical models. We obtain these imputed real rates and associated differentials by simply subtracting average yearly inflation rates from average yearly nominal interest rates. For short-term rates, this corresponds exactly to our imputed real rate for quarterly data based upon the assumption of myopia. Unfortunately, the entries for long-term rates are not strictly comparable with our earlier calculations. However, since interest and inflation rates have been relatively stable since the beginning of 1983, this probably makes relatively little difference.

Since we wish to avoid attaching too much importance to any particular set of numbers or method of calculation, our strategy is to search for robust patterns in Tables 7-1 to 7-3, and to select benchmark interest and inflation rate assumptions accordingly. In most cases, calculated differentials are not terribly sensitive to our method of imputing inflationary expectations. The only significant exception to this appears to be long-term real rates imputed on the basis of statistical forecasts for the United Kingdom and West Germany during the 1970s, and for Japan during the 1980s. A much more im-

Table 7-4. Benchmark Cases.

Period/Country	Inflation (%)	Nominal Interest Rate (%)	Real Interest Rate (%)
1970s			
United States	8	10	2
United Kingdom	12	12.25	0.25
West Germany	5	9.75	4.75
Japan	8	8.5	0.5
1980s			
United States	4	9	5
United Kingdom	6.5	10	3.5
West Germany	3.5	7	3.5
Japan	2.5	5	2.5

portant consideration appears to be whether the short- or long-term rate is a better index of the cost of capital. This issue is the subject of considerable controversy among economists. Since we cannot hope to resolve this debate here, we choose the middle ground, opting for some average of short- and long-term interest rate differentials.

In Table 7–4, we present benchmark inflation and interest rate assumptions. Entries in this table are intended to reflect average ambient credit market conditions prevailing in each country during the 1970s and 1980s (actually, we think of 1981 as the dividing line between these two periods). We chose U.S. credit market conditions to approximately equal average U.S. conditions for each period, with the exception of interest rates during the 1970s. Despite the fact that actual real rates for the United States appear to have been slightly negative, we use a real rate of 2 percent. Unfortunately, negative real interest rates wreak havoc with the King-Fullerton methodology employed in the following two sections. In order to preserve historical differentials while assuming a positive real rate in every country, it is therefore necessary to elevate the U.S. rate. Differentials between countries correspond roughly to averages across corresponding rows in Table 7–3 (in this way, we give equal weight to alternative methods of imputation, as well as to short- and long-rates). The general pattern of differentials that emerges from this analysis is as follows. In the 1970s real rates in the United States were well above those in the United Kingdom and Japan but significantly below those in West Germany. In the 1980s real rates rose in the United States, the United Kingdom, and Japan. Nevertheless U.S. rates remained above U.K. and Japanese rates, and in fact now exceed West German rates as well.

In the next section we use the benchmark credit market assumptions to calculate the cost of capital for each country during the 1970s and 1980s. We follow that with an evaluation of the effect of various tax-reform proposals.

COST-OF-CAPITAL CALCULATIONS

The question of ultimate interest in a study such as this is the relative investment incentives in the different countries examined. We approach that question in the same manner that most economists would, namely we calculate the financial cost of capital in each of the four countries. The financial cost of capital is the pre-tax rate of return which must be earned on corporate investments in order to cover the required taxes and offer investors the post-tax return necessary to get them to commit their funds. Clearly, the financial cost depends upon the details of the tax system as well as the level of real interest rates.

The tax system treats different types of investments differently. For instance, the investment tax credit in the United States applied (before the recent reform) to equipment investments but not investments in structures. Equity-financed investment is subject to the corporation income tax, whereas debt-financed investment is not. A good deal of investments flow through tax-exempt pools of money such as pension trust funds, whereas others are made by individual investors or insurance companies. To avoid dealing with the myriad of special treatments for particular investments, we are going to report average figures for the cost of capital in the four countries under consideration, but the underlying calculations still must be done on a disaggregated basis.

It is difficult to compare the taxation of capital income across countries simply because each of the tax codes has many special features. However, the task of making international comparisons of this sort was made significantly easier with the completion in 1984 of a National Bureau of Economic Research project that analyzed capital taxation in the United Kingdom, West Germany, United States, and Sweden within a consistent framework. The results were edited by King and Fullerton.[12] In general, we adopt their framework and methodology for evaluating the effect of the tax system on the financial cost of capital. We do modify one of their key theoretical assumptions, substitute Japan for Sweden in our analysis, and look at more recent tax legislation developments.

The King-Fullerton methodology can be quite easily summarized. They define three rates of return on an investment, p, r, and s. The pre-tax rate of return is represented by the variable p, r represents the after-corporate-tax rate of return, and s represents the post corporate and personal tax rate of return. That is, p is the gross of tax rate of return of the investment, r is the real interest rate, and s is the net return earned by the ultimate investor. The difference between p and s is termed the tax wedge and $p - s)/p$ is the effective marginal tax rate on new investments. For a particular investment, in in a certain industry, financed in a particular manner, by a stated class of investor, one could calculate r and s given p (or, in general, given one of the rates of return one can calculate the other two simply by applying the relevant tax rates). In the King-Fullerton book, emphasis is given to the "fixed" p " case, where it is assumed that all investments earn a certain pre-tax real rate of return (they use 10 percent) and they proceed to calculate the post-tax rate of return s, the tax wedge, and the effective tax rate. They also do some "fixed r " cases where they assume that the real interest rate is 5 percent for all investments and proceed to use the tax code to determine both p and s and the effective tax rates. They make these calculations for 81 different investment projects in each of the four countries and weight them appropriately to get their average figures. The 81 projects result from their examination of three types of assets (machinery, buildings, and inventories), three types of industries (manufacturing, other, and commerce), three sources of financial capital (debt, new equity issues, and retained earnings), and three types of owners (households, tax-exempt institutions, and insurance companies), The three alternatives in each of four categories gives a total of 81 project types.

The King-Fullerton study captures the most important aspects of the taxation of each of their 81 projects. Such features as the taxation of nominal capital gains on a realization basis, the particular form of depreciation allowed for each asset, the investment tax credit, the tax treatment for inventories, and the different corporate tax treatment given in some countries for dividends and retained earnings are all incorporated in their analysis. Their fixed p and fixed r assumptions are probably satisfactory if the primary purpose of the research is to determine the relative effective tax rates on new corporate investments in the different countries, although the calculated rates depend on the level set for the fixed parameter and which of the two (p or r) is taken as given. The fixed p or r assumption is inappropriate for our work. The previous section of this chapter demonstrated that real interest rates are not fixed across countries, although we assume they are constant across industries within a country. Our procedure is to take the real interest rates of the previous section as the value of r for each country, and to determine p and s

for that country given their tax code and their rate of inflation (since none of the tax systems are completely inflation indexed).

One difficulty in computing the cost of capital involves the choice of the appropriate nominal discount rate to apply to future net of tax cash flows and depreciation allowances. For debt-financed investments King and Fullerton use the after corporate tax interest rate, $i(1 - \tau)$ where i is the nominal interest rate and τ is the corporation income tax rate. That is quite standard. The controversial aspect is the appropriate discount rate for equity-financed investments. The problem centers around the fact that the payment of dividends is difficult to explain in the presence of the existing tax code. If there are other means to return cash to equity investors (such as the repurchase of some of the shares outstanding), then it is difficult to explain the use of this relatively costly means of remitting cash. There are several explanations, however, none of which are completely accepted. Two leading theories are that dividends convey a valuable signal to stockholders about the management's perception of future earnings prospects[13] or that the payment of dividends restricts the actions of management in a manner that helps reduce the control problems brought about by the separation of management and ownership.[14]

King and Fullerton implicitly assume that the only way for stockholders to receive cash from their companies is the payment of dividends. This leads them to the view that a dollar after corporate tax is worth less than a dollar on the stock market because dividend taxes would have to be paid to get it to shareholders. This is referred to as the "trapped-equity" hypothesis and it implies that a dollar of retained earnings will be capitalized in the market as one minus the tax rate on dividends over one minus the effective tax rate on accrued capital gains. For the United States this roughly implies that a corporate dollar will be valued at 75 cents. It is this 75 cents, and not the dollar, which must offer investors a yield equivalent to that on debt. This implies that the corporate dollar of retained earnings must have a return of 0.75 times the interest rate in the United States. This is the situation for the vast majority of firms that are not issuing new equity. Firms that are issuing new equity obviously cannot raise money that will immediately be discounted to 75 cents on the dollar by the stock market. New equity money must compete with bonds on a dollar-for-dollar basis, and therefore in models without risk, such as King-Fullerton and ours, the appropriate discount rate for new equity financed cash flows is the full interest rate.

We have chosen to abandon the trapped-equity story. Firms can return cash to shareholders in ways which are taxed more lightly than dividends. For instance, in the United States, firms can buy back their own shares. Nearly equivalently, they can buy the shares of other companies, or buyout all of another company in a cash merger. Last year in the United States, substantially less than half of the cash that corporations paid out to stockholders took the form of dividends and therefore was subject to full personal taxation.[15] The remainder of the cash received resulted in far lighter taxation. In fact, much of the gain resulting from the cash payments in share repurchase situations can be deferred for tax purposes.

We take a fairly traditional view that some fraction of the return to equity is paid out in the form of dividends, perhaps because of the signaling or incentive reasons cited above, and that the remainder of the return is paid out in forms subject to the effective rate of taxation on accrued capital gains (which might be roughly half the rate on realized capital gains due to the deferral possibilities). We take the fraction ultimately paid out as dividends to be observed ratio of dividends to after-tax corporate earnings. For the United States this implies that about 47.5 percent of earnings are paid out as dividends. We assume that the existence of dividends implies that they confer enough additional value to overcome their tax handicap. This means that a corporate dollar will be valued at a dollar, and the appropriate discount rate will take into account that the fraction of earnings paid out in capital gains form carries a tax preference at the personal level relative to debt. All of this means that we use the same discount rate for new shares and retained earnings and that this common rate is below the interest rate (because of the possibility of lightly taxed payouts), but above the rate that King-Fullerton apply to retained earnings because of their trapped money hypothesis. Since retained earnings are a vastly more important source of finance than new equity issues in all of the countries we examine, the net effect is that we apply a higher discount rate to net of tax corporate cash flows and will end up with higher figures for the cost of capital than we would have if we had maintained the King-Fullerton trapped-equity hypothesis.

Other than this fairly major change in assumptions, our procedure is very much the same as the King-Fullerton model. We can only claim to capture a stylized version of each of the tax codes, because we do not include the many industry-specific tax breaks that have recently become evident in the United States in the transition rules for the 1986 Tax Reform Act. Also, the model has only three types of assets, machinery, buildings, and inventories, whereas the tax laws of most countries specify depreciation and investment incentives at a much more disaggregated level. We first examine the

Table 7-5.   Cost of Capital Calculated at the Average Interest and Inflation Rates for the 1970s Using 1980 Tax Codes (%).

	United States	United Kingdom	West Germany	Japan
Cost of capital	2.44	-1.00	4.96	-1.56
Post-tax real rate of return	-0.65	-2.56	1.01	-0.69
Tax wedge for capital	3.09	1.56	3.95	-0.87
Cost of equity capital	4.28	-0.26	6.47	0.85
Post-tax real rate of return on equity	-1.00	-2.49	0.04	-0.84
Tax wedge for equity capital	5.28	2.23	6.43	1.69
Real interest rate	2.00	0.25	4.75	0.50

cost of capital for the United States, United Kingdom, West Germany, and Japan for their 1980 tax codes and for the interest rates and inflation rates shown in Table 7-4 for the 1970s. Rather than devote an enormous amount of time and space to describing the capital taxation in these four countries, we refer the reader to our sources, namely King-Fullerton[16] for the United States, United Kingdom, and West Germany and Shoven and Tachibanaki[17] for Japan. For the United States this predates the Accelerated Cost Recovery System (ACRS). Lifetimes for depreciation purposes are determined according to the Asset Depreciation Range System, although quite accelerated patterns of writeoffs were permitted (for example, double declining balance switching to sum of years digits for equipment). In the United Kingdom expensing was permitted. West Germany effectively eliminates the double taxation of dividends through a dividend credit arrangement and both West Germany and Japan did not and do not tax capital gains on securities.

The results for the cost of capital with the 1980 tax codes and the average interest and inflation rates of the 1970s are shown in Table 7-5. West Germany has both the highest real interest rate and the largest tax wedge between the return on an investment and the return received by an investor. This results in West Germany having the highest cost of capital. The cost of capital figures are an average of the cost of debt-financed investments and the cost of equity funds. However, in a certainty model such as this, we probably understate the cost of debt. In addition to the incremental interest payments and the tax consequences of additional borrowing, further debt issuance may lower a firm's credit rating and thus raise the interest rate it faces on all of its financing. In other words, the firm may face a upward-sloping supply curve for debt, implying that the marginal cost of debt exceeds the interest rate. For this reason, we report separate figures for the cost of equity capital. West Germany also has the highest cost of equity capital and tax wedge for equity capital. The result that Germany is a high capital tax country is completely consistent with the results of the King-Fullerton study and is primarily a consequence of the fact that it has the highest statutory corporate tax rate and relatively inadequate depreciation (for example, buildings are straight-line depreciated over an average of 30 years and machinery has an average depreciation lifetime of 11 years).

The U.S. tax wedge is also very large, being roughly 80 percent as great as West Germany's. Our risk-free cost of capital was 2.4 percent, about 2.5 percentage points less than West Germany's. Since both countries tax capital heavily, most of difference in the cost of capital comes from the higher real interest rates prevailing in West Germany. In both countries the cost of capital is only slightly above the interest rate. However, the cost of equity capital is substantially above the interest rate; in fact, for the U.S. equity capital costs more than twice the real interest rate. Both the United Kingdom and Japan had low (even negative) costs of capital. This is due both to the very low level of real interest rates which prevailed in the 1970s in these countries and to relatively light taxation. In Japan, the post-tax rate of return to investors actually exceeded the pre-tax cost of capital. This is due to the fact that debt finance is subsidized when inflation allows a corporation to deduct nominal rather than real interest payments, and due to the facts that interest income is very lightly taxed at the personal level in Japan and that debt finance is heavily used. The result is qualitatively consistent with the capital income effective tax rate calculations of Shoven and Tachibanaki.[18]

Both the United States and the United Kingdom experienced major changes in their tax codes between 1980 and 1985, and the interest and inflation rate environment changed dramatically throughout the world. For these reasons we have calculated the cost of capital numbers with the 1985 tax laws and the credit market conditions shown in Table 7-4 for the 1980s. In the United States, the major change was the shortening of depreciation lifetimes and a reduction in personal tax rates. In the United Kingdom, there has been a major restructuring of the corporation tax with a reduction in the statutory rate and the substitution of depreciation for the previous practice of expensing. The United Kingdom has moved toward a corporate income tax and away from a corporation cash flow levy.[19]

The effect of the new tax laws and the changed credit market conditions are shown in Table 7-6. Every country except West Germany experienced an increase in the cost of capital, and the United States replaced West Germany as the country with the highest cost of capital. Again, much of this story is determined by real interest rates

Table 7-6. Cost of Capital Calculated at the Average Interest and Inflation Rates for the 1980s Using 1985 Tax Codes (%).

	United States	*United Kingdom*	*West Germany*	*Japan*
Cost of capital	5.48	3.56	4.39	2.76
Post-tax real rate of return	2.24	1.28	0.70	1.80
Tax wedge for capital	3.24	2.28	3.69	0.96
Cost of equity capital	7.03	3.81	5.48	4.22
Post-tax real rate of return on equity	1.89	1.33	0.00	1.71
Tax wedge for equity capital	5.14	2.48	5.48	2.51
Real interest rate	5.00	3.50	3.50	2.50

with the average cost of capital following the movement in real interest rates quite closely. West Germany remained the country with the largest tax wedge, although the United States' tax wedge was now 90 percent as large. They remain the countries with the largest gap between the return on investments and the return seen by the investor. The tax wedge on equity in the United States is rather enormous, with equity costing the firm slightly over 7 percent while the equity investor receives under 2 percent. The cost of equity capital in the United States exceeds the cost of equity capital in Japan by almost 3 percentage points and the cost in the United Kingdom by more than 3 percentage points. The cost is more than 2 percentage points above the real interest rate in the United States (as it was in 1980). The excess of the cost of equity capital above the interest rate reflects the tax penalty of equity, and this penalty is the highest in the United States in both 1980 and in 1985. This primarily reflects the fact that the United States is the only country that does nothing to alleviate the double taxation of dividends and has, by far, the highest tax rate on realized capital gains on equity securities among these countries.

REFORM PROPOSALS

We now turn our attention to the more difficult task of assessing the probable impacts of various tax reform proposals on the U.S. cost of capital. To do so, we must first resolve a conceptually difficult question, how will each reform proposal affect the prevailing rate of interest (ambient credit conditions)? The answer to this question depends upon the manner in which the burden of capital income taxation is shared by owners of capital and other factor inputs. Thus, we must directly confront the issue of *tax incidence*.

It is essential to begin by deriving an appropriate measure of incidence. This requires a bit of notation. As before, let r denote the real rate of interest. Each tax system can be described by a list of policy parameters, which we shall refer to as T. Throughout, we will assume that the prevailing rate of inflation is fixed and unaffected by tax reforms. Calculations such as those performed here define the cost of capital, p, and the after-tax rate of return, s, as function of r and T:

$$p = p(r, T) \quad,$$

$$s = s(r, T) \quad.$$

The tax wedge, w, which measures the total tax burden on capital income, is simply equal to the difference between p and s:

$$w(r, T) = p(r, T) - s(r, T) \quad.$$

Consider two distinct tax systems, T_0 and T_1. Suppose that under T_0, which we shall think of as the status quo, the prevailing interest rate is r_0. If, however, the government changed the tax system to T_1, then the interest rate would move to r_1. We define an incidence parameter, k, which measures the extent to which the owners of capital bear the incremental tax:

$$k = \frac{p(r_1, T_1) - p(r_0, T_0)}{w(r_1, T_1) - w(r_0, T_0)} \quad. \tag{7.3}$$

Note that when $k = 0$, p is insensitive to changes in the tax system. Thus, s moves by the full amount of the incremental tax wedge: owners of capital bear 100 percent of the tax. On the other hand, when $k = 1$, p changes by the full amount of the incremental tax wedge, and s remains fixed. This implies that owners of capital bear none of the tax.

The King-Fullerton methodology simply allows us to compute the cost of capital, after tax rates of return, and tax wedges for specific interest and inflation rate assumptions. Since it is not based on any behavioral model of the economy, it can shed no light on the question of incidence. We can, however, incorporate such considerations by making an assumption about the incidence parameter, and using equation (7.3) to derive the impact of tax reforms on interest rates. That is, if we believe on the basis of other behavioral evidence that capital bears x percent of the capital income tax burden, then we set $k = 1 - x$, and use equation (7.3) as follows. When contemplating a reform from policy T_0 to T_1 given an initial interest rate of r_0, we find the new interest rate by solving equation (7.3) for r_1. Since

$p(.,.)$ and $w(.,.)$ are highly complex, nonlinear functions that are evaluated by computer, this task is computationally complex. In practice, however, one can always obtain a solution to (7.3) through a simple numerical algorithm, which also yields values for p, s, and w.

Throughout the following calculations, we set $k = \frac{1}{2}$, which corresponds to the assumption that capital bears half the burden of incremental taxation. As the reader may well prefer an alternative incidence assumption, we present our results in a way that facilitates informal sensitivity analyses. Specifically, we report the change in the tax wedge, Δw, induced by each reform proposal. Note that one can rewrite equation (7.3) as

$$\Delta p = k\Delta w , \qquad (7.4)$$

(where Δp is the change in the cost of capital). Of course, the value of Δw depends upon k through equation (7.3). However, as an approximation, it is acceptable to take Δw as fixed, and use equation (7.4) directly to compute the effect of tax reform on the cost of capital under alternative assumptions about k. One natural conclusion that follows immediately is that if capital bears the entire burden of incremental taxation ($k = 0$), then tax policy cannot alter the cost of capital.

For purposes of comparison, we also calculate the impact of each reform proposal under the assumption that the real interest rate, r, is fixed. This assumption corresponds to the view that the U.S. economy is completely open, and that U.S. tax policy has a negligible effect on world credit market conditions. While we believe that this view is implausible for the reasons discussed earlier in the section titled Real Interest Rates. Its proponents will find these results to be of particular interest.

We begin our analysis of reforms with the consumption tax. A true consumption tax would entail the elimination of all capital income taxes both at the individual and corporate levels. Thus the U.S. tax wedge described in Table 7–6 would be completely eliminated ($\Delta w = -3.24$). Under our equal incidence assumption ($k = \frac{1}{2}$), the U.S. cost of capital would fall to 3.86 percent, roughly half a percentage point below that of West Germany. This would eliminate about 60 percent of the gap between the cost of capital in the United States and Japan, and 85 percent of the gap between the United States and the United Kingdom. Since the cost of equity capital would also fall to 3.86 percent, equity would become roughly as cheap in the United States as in the United Kingdom and significantly cheaper than in West Germany and Japan despite an initial differential of more than 3.5 percentage points between the United States and

Table 7-7. Consumption Tax.

	Equal Incidence	*Fixed Real Interest Rate*
Cost of capital (%)	3.86	5.00
Post-tax real rate of return (%)	3.86	5.00
Change in tax wedge	-3.24	-3.24
Cost of equity capital (%)	3.86	5.00
Post-tax real rate of return on equity (%)	3.86	5.00
Change in equity tax wedge	-5.14	-5.14
Real rate of interest (%)	3.86	5.00

Table 7-8. Personal Consumption Tax.

	Equal Incidence	*Fixed Real Interest Rate*
Cost of capital (%)	4.70	7.29
Post-tax real rate of return (%)	3.02	5.00
Change in tax wedge	-1.56	-0.95
Cost of equity capital (%)	6.57	9.76
Post-tax real rate of return on equity (%)	3.02	5.00
Change in equity tax wedge	-1.59	-0.36
Real rate of interest (%)	3.02	5.00

Japan in particular. Less dramatic conclusions follow from the assumption that the world real rate of interest is fixed. Specifically, adoption of a consumption tax would lower the cost of capital in the United States by about 0.5 percentage point, closing roughly half of the gap between the United States and West Germany. We summarize these results in Table 7-7.

A less radical proposal is to eliminate taxation of capital income at the personal level, while retaining the corporate income tax intact. We will refer to this as a personal consumption tax. Table 7-8 contains results corresponding to this proposal. Under our equal incidence assumption, the adoption of a personal consumption tax would eliminate roughly 75, 40, and 30 percent of the differences between the cost of capital in the United States and West Germany, the United Kingdom, and Japan, respectively. In contrast, the cost of capital would actually increase sharply under the assumption of a fixed world interest rate (from 5.48 percent to 7.29 percent). Although this may at first appear counterintuitive, the explanation is fairly straightforward. Since we assume that the required rate of return on bonds remains fixed at 5 percent, the cost of debt finance does not change. Currently, personal capital income taxes treat equity more favorably than debt. Elimination of this favorable treatment would cause the required rate of return on equity to rise, thereby raising the overall cost of capital.

We now turn our attention to the effects of the Tax Reform Act of 1986. Our model is, unfortunately, not sufficiently detailed to capture all aspects of the far-reaching changes embraced by this law. While our representation of the tax reform plan is therefore of necessity somewhat stylized, we are nevertheless able to capture most of its central features. In particular, we model its effects on the corporate tax system by reducing the statutory corporate tax rate from 46 percent to 34 percent, and eliminating the investment tax credit. We assume that average marginal personal tax rates including state and local taxes fall from 28.4 to 21 percent on interest, and from 47.5 to 30 percent on dividends. Further, the personal tax on realized capital gains rises from 14 to 26 percent, and tax rates on dividends and interest for insurance companies fall from 38 to 34 percent. Depreciation changes as follows. The average tax life rises from 4.5 years to 6 years for machines, and from 19 to 31.5 years for buildings. Depreciation methods change from 150 percent declining balance switching to straight line, to 200 percent declining balance switching to straight line for machines, and from 175 percent declining balance switching to straight line, to pure straight line for buildings.

We present results in Table 7-9. Under the assumption of equal incidence, the cost of capital rises by slightly less than 0.2 percent. This occurs despite a slight decline in the cost of equity capital and a substantial fall in the real interest rate. For the case of fixed world interest rates, we find that the cost of capital rises by almost two full percentage points.

The Tax Reform Act of 1986 will undoubtedly be unpopular with industry for repealing the investment tax credit. It is relatively easy to determine the effect that this will have on the cost of capital by hypothetically reinstating the ITC, while retaining all other provisions of Tax Reform Act. We present results in Table 7-10. Under the equal incidence assumption, reinstatement of the investment tax credit would cause the cost of capital to fall by approximately 0.3 percentage point. The corresponding decline is substantially larger (0.75 percent) under the fixed world interest rate assumption.

Our central message is clear: The effects of reform proposals that retain our system of capital income taxes essentially intact are likely to be swamped by variation in domestic credit conditions. However, fundamental reform of capital income taxes (such as the adoption of a consumption tax) can produce large changes in the cost of capital relative to differences across countries.

Table 7-9.   Tax Reform Act of 1986.

	Equal Incidence	Fixed Real Interest Rate
Cost of capital (%)	5.66	7.16
Post-tax real rate of return (%)	2.07	3.05
Change in tax wedge	0.35	0.87
Cost of equity capital (%)	6.92	8.61
Post-tax real rate of return on equity (%)	1.93	2.89
Change in equity tax wedge	-0.15	0.68
Real rate of interest (%)	3.75	5.00

Table 7-10.   Tax Reform Act of 1986 with Investment Tax Credit.

	Equal Incidence	Fixed Real Interest Rate
Cost of capital (%)	5.36	6.40
Post-tax real rate of return (%)	2.35	3.05
Change in tax wedge	-0.24	0.11
Cost of equity capital (%)	6.66	7.84
Post-tax real rate of return on equity (%)	2.20	2.89
Change in equity tax wedge	-0.68	-0.19
Real rate of interest (%)	4.10	5.00

CONCLUSIONS

Our analysis suggests that there are large differences between the cost of capital in the United States, the United Kingdom, West Germany, and Japan. Furthermore, prevailing differences are largely attributable to domestic credit conditions, rather than to tax systems. While the Tax Reform Act of 1986 will raise the U.S. cost of capital by a nonnegligible amount, and while a reinstatement of the investment tax credit would more than offset this increase, both effects are relatively minor in comparison to intercountry variation in credit market conditions. Nevertheless, one cannot dismiss taxation as an insignificant determinant of the cost of capital. In particular, the elimination of capital income taxation on either the personal or corporate levels, or both (a consumption tax) would have a profound effect on the cost of capital in the United States relative to other countries.

NOTES

1. While Feldstein and Horioka appear to attribute this imperfection to a failure of real interest rate parity, Frankel has argued more recently that the failure of purchasing power parity is a more plausible culprit. See Martin Feldstein

and Charles Horioka, "Domestic Saving and International Capital Flows," *Economic Journal 90* (1980): 314–29, and Jeffrey A. Frankel, "International Capital Mobility and Crowding-out in the U.S. Economy: Imperfect Integration of Financial Markets or Goods Markets?" in R.W. Hafer, ed., *How Open Is the U.S. Economy?* (Lexington, Mass.: Lexington Books, 1986).

2. Arnold C. Harberger, "Perspectives on Capital and Technology in Less Developed Countries," in M.J. Artis and A.R. Nobay, eds., *Contemporary Economic Analysis* (London: Croom Helm Ltd. 1978).

3. Feldstein and Horioka, "Domestic Saving and International Capital Flows."

4. Frederic S. Mishkin, "The Real Interest Rate: A Multi-Country Empirical Study," *Canadian Journal of Economics 17*(2) (May 1984): 283–311, and "Are Real Interest Rates Equal across Countries?: An Empirical Investigation of International Parity Conditions," *Journal of Finance 39*(5) (December 1984): 1345–57.

5. Mervyn A. King and Don Fullerton, eds., *The Taxation of Income from Capital* (Chicago: National Bureau of Economic Research and University of Chicago Press, 1984).

6. Jeremy I. Bulow and Lawrence H. Summers, "The Taxation of Risky Assets," *Journal of Political Economy 92*(1) (February 1984): 20–39.

7. Mishkin, "The Real Interest Rate."

8. Despite the fact that our first two hypotheses appear to reflect polar assumptions, they will generate virtually identical estimates of the mean ex ante rate of return in any very long sample period. This paradoxical result follows from the observation that, under each hypothesis, one estimates the mean ex ante return by averaging imputed real rates over the sample period. This is equivalent to averaging nominal rates (which are the same for both calculations), and subtracting the mean of the imputed inflation rates. But the imputed inflation rate series for our first hypothesis is merely the lagged inflation rate series for our second hypothesis. Under relatively weak conditions, the averages of these series must converge to the same number in large samples.

9. Specifically, we assumed that inflation rates follow Auto Regressive Moving Average (ARMA) processes. Analysis of the data suggested that a third-order autoregressive, first-order moving average process was appropriate for the United States. Fourth-order autoregressive processes performed well for the United Kingdom and West Germany, while a first-order autoregressive, first-order moving average process appeared appropriate for Japan.

10. Robert E. Cumby and Frederic S. Mishkin, "The International Linkage of Real Interest Rates: The European-U.S. Connection," National Bureau of Economic Research Working Paper No. 1423, 1984.

11. Mishkin, "The Real Interest Rate."

12. King and Fullerton, *The Taxation of Income from Capital.*

13. Merton Miller and Kevin Rock, "Dividend Policy under Asymmetric Information," unpublished manuscript, University of Chicago, 1984.

14. Michael Jensen and William Meckling, "Theory of the Firm: Managerial Behavior, Agency Costs, and Ownership Structures," *Journal of Financial Economics 3* (1976): 305–360.

15. John B. Shoven, "Outline of Research on Share Repurchase on Corporate Restructuring," unpublished paper, Stanford University, 1986.

16. King and Fullerton, *The Taxation of Income from Capital*.

17. John B. Shoven and Toshiaki Tachibanaki, "The Taxation of Income from Capital in Japan," Center for Economic Policy Research Publication No. 60, revised June 1986.

18. Ibid.

19. Nick Morris, "The United Kingdom Tax System," A Brookings Institution Discussion Paper, Washington, D.C., April 1986.

Chapter 8

Income Tax Reform and the Consumption Tax

John H. Makin

The basic idea behind a consumption tax is simple. It is a method of obtaining revenue without taxing saving twice. The income tax taxes saving twice, once when it is included in an income tax base and once as the yield on accumulated savings. To speak of a single saving-tax system (consumption) and a double saving-tax system (income) would be more accurate. *Both* systems tax consumption once; therefore, the distinction between them rests not upon the taxation of consumption but upon whether nonconsumption (saving) is taxed once or twice.

The consumption tax was advocated by Thomas Hobbes in the seventeenth century, on the grounds that a person should be taxed on what he or she uses up (consumes), and not on what he or she does not use up (saves).[1] While forbearance may have been more popular in seventeenth-century England than it is in twentieth-century America, Hobbes's view of life in the state of nature as "solitary, poor, nasty, brutish and short" would probably fail to win many converts to his ideas in any century or nation. On this negative view of life and those living it, Hobbes based his philosophical justification of absolutism, which held that rulers (the English monarchy) ought to have absolute power in order to govern a brutish population. Hobbes's principal work, *Leviathan*, likened government to its title, the name of a monster mentioned in the Bible: "His heart is

Any views expressed are those of the author and not of the American Enterprise Institute, where Dr. Makin is Director of Fiscal Policy Studies.

as firm as a stone; yea as hard as a piece of the nether millstone" (Job 41: 24).

Despite its undemocratic pedigree, the consumption tax has enjoyed a rebirth among a generation of younger economists who have turned its basic tenets into a comprehensive framework from which to develop models that measure gains in economic welfare under a consumption-based tax system (Bradford[2] and Fullerton, Shoven, and Whalley[3] are two prominent examples). Still, the consumption-based tax remains controversial because of its advocates' claims and the equity-versus-efficiency trade-off that surrounds almost every issue of economic policy (see Makin[4]).

As already noted, the proximate objective of a consumption-based tax system is to increase saving by taxing it once rather than twice. More saving means more funds available to finance investment. More investment means a larger and faster growing capital stock and therefore faster economic growth. Faster economic growth means a bigger economic pie to slice.

The consumption tax can also be viewed as a way to exempt from tax the income from investment. The tax system prior to the 1986 Tax Reform Act contained the following elements of a consumption tax: the investment tax credit, accelerated depreciation, lower tax rates for capital gains, tax credits for research and development, expensing of some expenditures on R&D, advertising, and marketing, and the exclusion from tax of contributions to and accumulations in special Individual Retirement Accounts (IRAs), Keogh accounts, or 401k accounts are examples. But these are the very features of the tax system that are altered most frequently, so their ability to achieve a higher rate of saving, capital formation, and growth that depend upon prospective stability of such provisions in the tax code is hampered.

One of the reasons for the frequent changes in tax measures that relate to the taxation of income from capital in an income-based system is the difficulty of accurately measuring it, especially in an environment of volatile inflation rates. In an unindexed tax system, an unusually large jump in inflation, such as occurred during 1977–1981, results in unintended increases and redistributions in the tax burden on income from capital and labor. What follows are ad hoc efforts to correct tax distortions that are crude and can be inaccurate, particularly if inflation slows more rapidly than is expected, as it has during the 1980s.

A consumption-based tax achieves more than single taxation of saving and associated phenomena. It simplifies and stabilizes the tax system by enabling an accurate measure of income from capital that is inflation-proof. A combination of imputing earnings of capital to

Figure 8–1. Net Investment/GNP, 1950–1985.

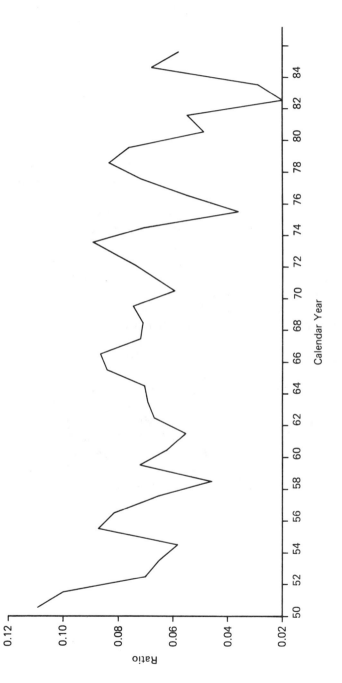

Source: NIPA, BEA, Department of Commerce.

individuals and expensing capital acquisitions insulates the measurement of income from capital from inflation distortions. A low tax rate on a comprehensive expenditure base minimizes distortions across sectors and forms of capital.

A look at performance of the U.S. economy over the past several decades suggests that a consumption tax and its attendant enhancement of capital formation and growth is just what is needed. Average real growth has dropped from about 4 percent in the 1960s to about 3 percent in the 1970s to about 2 percent thus far in the 1980s. And during each succeeding decade, the volatility of growth has increased. Net capital formation as a share of gross national product (see Figure 8-1) has gradually trended downward as well. Private and national saving rates in the United States are about one-half to one-third those in Japan and other major industrial countries.[5]

Yet, despite the close match (apparently at least) between the symptoms displayed by the U.S. economy and the need for a consumption tax prescription, there remains strong resistance to it among politicians and many economists. No major economy employs a comprehensive expenditure-based tax system like that articulated in the *Blueprints for Basic Tax Reform* developed in 1977 by David Bradford and the staff of the Office of Tax Analysis at the U.S. Treasury.[6]

Still, elements of the consumption tax are widespread. France, Italy, the Netherlands, Sweden, the United Kingdom, and West Germany have in place value-added taxes combined with other elements of a tax system which could be said to contribute to a consumption tax system. Even Japan, its high saving rate notwithstanding, is considering a national retail sales tax with the incidence of a consumption tax, to finance lower tax rates on income and to deal with compliance problems. Finally, in the United States, IRA, Keogh, and 401k plans plus investment incentives have introduced elements of a consumption-based tax.

DEBATE ON THE CONSUMPTION TAX

There are two major reasons for strong resistance to a comprehensive consumption- or expenditure-based tax system. The first is a perceived equity problem. Since low-income taxpayers spend—"consume" if you like—a larger share of their incomes than do high-income taxpayers, taxing consumption is seen as unfair. This equity-over-efficiency argument has powerful intuitive, if not logical, appeal and has been successfully employed to argue against a consumption tax, even when the after-tax income of all taxpayers is shown to be higher under a consumption tax. Indeed, according to the well-known Coase theorem, taxpayers having above-average incomes should be willing to make a lump-sum transfer payment to lower income taxpayers in exchange for the option of a comprehensive expenditure-based tax system.

The other major argument against a consumption tax, used to reject any proposed change in the tax system, is the significant transition costs. Taxpayers would be anxious to hide existing assets and then use those assets to make contributions to qualified accounts of the type outlined in *Blueprints* after the consumption tax is adopted. Retirees and prospective retirees would be taxed when they spend savings accumulated for retirement, even though IRA, Keogh, and 401k plans would mitigate such inequities. Still the bulk of accumulations for today's retirees is in more traditional saving vehicles that have already been taxed doubly.

Some might argue that in view of the rapid redistribution of income and assets in favor of the over-65 population, as documented in the Council of Economic Advisers Report to the President 1985, introduction of a consumption tax might perform double duty. It could help to increase saving while taxing away some of the benefits garnered by current Social Security recipients whose prospective receipts are two or three times larger than contributions to the Social Security system. Since this problem, as well as the transition problem related to the switch to a consumption tax, would both gradually disappear with time, a nice coincidence of goals presents itself. Politicians may, however, be reluctant to kill two birds with the consumption tax stone.

There are also equity arguments against a consumption tax concerning younger taxpayers. Since the tax is levied on expenditure, younger households that borrow to finance expenditure in excess of income would find themselves paying a tax on a base that exceeded their total income. Aside from the possibility that an additional incentive for younger Americans to postpone higher levels of consumption would not be a national tragedy, there is always the possibility of introducing some progressivity into a consumption-based tax as a means to cushion the impact on lower income taxpayers, whatever their age might be. As we shall see later in the analysis of consumption tax alternatives, there is unfortunately an equity-efficiency trade-off whereby attempting to retain the degree of progressivity under the current tax system after introduction of a consumption tax reduces the total value of welfare gains available under a consumption tax. Fortunately, however, in most cases it is still possible to increase overall welfare with a consumption tax that maintains the degree of progressivity in the current income-based tax system.

It is important also to recognize that most analyses of an expenditure-based tax system, such as that by Fullerton, Shoven, and Whalley[7] assume a closed economy. More specifically, they assume that all of the saving necessary to finance investment must come from a country's own population. As we have discovered in the United States, a high level of government dissaving coupled with a low private saving rate creates, when investment is stimulated, upward pressure on real interest rates, which in turn attracts saving from abroad to finance the surge in investment engineered at home. Therefore, as long as other countries are willing to foster high saving rates, no compelling need exists to do so here in the United States. This view overlooks the fact that if investment in the United States is financed by foreign funds, then the benefits of saving—an increase in future consumption—will accrue to foreign savers rather that domestic savers. The U.S. economy will have to grow faster in order to provide the means to service a larger accumulation of debt owned by individuals and corporations outside of the United States.

In other words, the United States resembles an affluent but idle family that, wishing to maintain a high level of consumption, gradually sells off claims on its future income, thereby ensuring that subsequent generations will find their standard of living reduced.

REFORMING THE INCOME TAX VERSUS
ADOPTING A CONSUMPTION TAX

Having briefly reviewed some basic points about the consumption tax alternative, we turn now to the actual choice at hand. Since the introduction of the first Treasury plan in November 1984, the primary goal of tax reform has been to reduce the efficiency loss under an income tax system by equalizing the burden on different assets and sectors of the economy while revising the system to levy lower tax rates on a better measure of economic income. A combination of elimination of the investment tax credit, lower statutory tax rates, a reduction in the tax subsidy for the use of debt to acquire owner-occupied housing and capital, and, in the case of the Treasury and the president's plans, a reduction of the double taxation of dividends even out tax burdens across households, assets, and sectors of the economy.

Overall one can say, recalling an analysis by Boskin,[8] that a good deal of attention has been devoted to interasset and intersectoral neutrality while the issue of intertemporal neutrality, that is, elimination of the double taxation on the purchase of future goods (saving), has been neglected. This neglect is largely inherent in selection of income rather than expenditure as the tax base, although it should be noted that the Treasury I plan attempted to reduce intertemporal distortions by indexing interest income and expense so that only real interest income would be taxed and only real expense would be deductible. This attempt proved unsuccessful and illustrated the difficulty of properly measuring income from capital under an income-based tax system. The difficulty in designing appropriate depreciation schemes, particularly in an inflationary setting, is another example of the difficulty of accurately measuring income from capital under an income-based system. The expensing alternative without deductibility of interest expense or without taxation of interest income, unless it is under the expenditure-based tax, is far simpler and more likely to measure accurately income from capital that is to be taxed.

Given that tax reform will probably result in an income tax system with fewer intersectoral distortions and a less progressive tax structure, the need remains to compare such a system with a comprehensive consumption tax system. This amounts to attempting to quantify the relative potential gains of an idealized income-based tax system that achieves intersectoral neutrality and an idealized consumption-based tax system that achieves both intersectoral and intertemporal neutrality.

There are two ways tax reform can improve performance of the economy. The first is to enable maximum production of goods and services from existing resources. The second is to remove impediments to increases in the quantity of productive resources like labor and capital.

In a contemporary setting for advanced economies like the United States, it is important to recognize that tax reform involves a kind of deregulation or disintervention in the workings of the economy. Thus those who argue for tax reform are really expressing confidence in the ability of the marketplace to allocate resources across alternative uses at a certain time. In other words, from an efficiency standpoint lump-sum taxes are optimal since they minimize the effect on the way in which resources are used.

Faced with a given tax system such as the U.S. tax code of the 1980s, a reform effort involves first selecting a tax base—either income or expenditure—and then designing around that base a system that has a minimal effect on economic choices by households and businesses. It is possible to avoid a distortion in the choice between current and future consumption, otherwise known as double taxation of saving, with either an income-based or a consumption-based tax. It is, however, simpler to avoid that distortion by adopting a consumption tax, particularly in the presence of an existing income tax system that not only doubly taxes saving but also taxes both the real and inflationary portion of interest returns by doubly taxing dividends. The discussion of tax reform underway since 1984 makes clear that in addition to choosing between an income and consumption base for the tax system, tax reformers must modify economically ideal textbook versions of income- or consumption-based tax systems to fit political reality.

The broadest lesson to be learned from tax reform efforts in the mid-1980s is that an income-based tax system that preserves the highly favorable treatment of owner-occupied housing under the current system and neglects issues such as indexation of interest income and expense, capital gains, depreciation allowances, and inventoy evaluation can produce only limited efficiency gains that may or may not be accompanied by incentives to increase the stock of capital. Therefore, comparing the 1984–1986 efforts at tax reform such as the Treasury plan (T-1), the president's plan (P-1), the House plan (H-1), or the Senate plan (S-1) with an idealized consumption tax should not be considered a fair comparison of potential gains under reform of an income-based tax system versus a consumption-based tax system. A consumption-based tax reform proposal would very likely also include compromises with political reality that would limit efficiency gains.

Beyond the political constraints on tax reform, it is important to realize the limitations of methods used to evaluate alternative proposals. A major shortcoming of most models is their inability to allow for feedback effects from tax reform to the economy. A good example of such shortcomings arises when the effect of tax reform on interest rates and investment is considered. T-1's indexation of interest income and expense, together with the lower rates present in all tax reform proposals, will necessarily result in a reduction in nominal interest rates in the short run and possibly in a reduction in real interest rates over a longer period of time, to the extent that debt accumulation is reduced. Aggregate demand models such as those employed by major econometric forecasting firms are poorly equipped to capture these effects. General equilibrium models, like the ones developed by Shoven, Fullerton, and Whalley,[9] can capture some of the effect on nominal interest rates, but they impose a given real interest rate that is not allowed to change as the rest of the effects of tax changes work through the economy. This latter feature tends to result in underestimation of the potential gains that may result from indexation of interest income and expense, whereby a major subsidy to debt-financed investment is removed and better balance between debt and equity helps to lower the real interest rate.

Another important consideration is the inability of models to capture the effects of uncertainty on resource allocation and capital accumulation, although Skinner[10] has taken an important step toward measurement of the cost of tax uncertainty. It is one thing to revise the tax system infrequently and nonarbitrarily in order to promote maximum efficiency and encourage saving and capital accumulation. It is another thing to open up the tax code for major surgery nearly every year, as has been the case since 1979, and to pass measures that decisionmakers know are unlikely to survive the next round of tax reform fever.

Frequent comparisons have been made between the U.S. and Japanese tax systems with regard to evaluating which is most conducive to growth and capital formation. Although the evidence on the cost of capital is mixed,[11] there is no doubt that the Japanese tax code is far more stable than the U.S. tax code. That stability, coupled with an absence of discrimination against saving,[12] is probably responsible for some part of the rapid and sustained capital formation in Japan and the longer run planning horizon of typical Japanese businesses.

Another basic element of all the tax reform plans advanced since 1984 is their reduction in marginal tax rates. This feature by itself improves efficiency since, given that distortions are present and given that distortions increase approximately with the square of tax rates, a lowering of tax rates in and of itself helps to mute the distortions built into any tax system. A good example of this effect can be seen in the choice between debt and equity finance. For corporations, the subsidy to debt finance is directly proportional to the marginal tax rate applied to corporate income. If that tax rate is cut from 46 percent to 33 percent, the subsidy to debt finance is reduced proportionately and the debt/equity mix is moved closer to the ratio that would prevail if corporations could choose between the two methods of finance in a tax system where neither was favored nor discriminated against.

The comparison between the economic welfare gains available under income and consumption taxes, beyond the constraints imposed by political reality and the other factors just discussed, depends also on a number of important considerations related to the method of analysis. Typically, proposals are evaluated in a revenue-neutral setting. The way revenue neutrality is maintained is important, however, particularly when evaluating consumption tax alternatives. Revenue neutrality can be maintained by multiplying all marginal tax rates by a constant factor (multiplicative scaling) or by adding the same number of percentage points to all marginal tax rates (additive scaling) or by lump-sum scaling, which simply imposes lump-sum taxes on consumers proportional to their initial income. Consumption tax proposals can be constrained to maintain the distribution of the tax burden under an existing income-tax system, and this also will affect the outcome. It is necessary to make assumptions about substitutability between factors of production, substitutability between corporate and noncorporate sectors, and the response of saving to interest rates.

Ballard, Scholz, and Shoven[13] have shown, for example, that the gains from introducing a flat value-added tax (VAT) in exchange for reductions in personal income tax rates are powerfully affected by the methods used to scale back income tax rates. Not surprisingly, multiplicative replacement, that is, reducing all tax rates at an equal proportion, is superior to the additive method where taxes for lower rate taxpayers are reduced proportionately more. This is an example of the equity-efficiency trade-off that constrains tax reform measures. When a flat-rate VAT of approximately 6.5 percent is imposed and the proceeds used to reduce income taxes with multiplicative scaling, a gain equivalent to about 0.75 percent of the economy's wealth is achieved. That gain is reduced to about 0.5 percent of the economy's wealth when additive scaling is used.

With these considerations in mind, we turn now to evaluation of potential efficiency gains under actual tax reform proposals of recent vintage. It is fair to say that each of the four proposals that emerged in 1984–1986 provides more in terms of efficiency gains, under which better use is made of the existing stock of capital, than in terms of gains related to an increase in the stock of capital. The first step in assessing potential efficiency gains is to compare the impact of a proposal on marginal effective tax rates borne by different forms of capital equipment and different sectors of the economy. The next step is to examine what, if any, the efficiency gains mean in terms of welfare gains for the economy. The scope of welfare gains is best gauged by relating them to the total wealth of the economy. Finally, it is useful to compare prospective welfare gains under actual income-based tax reform proposals with potential gains available under various versions of a consumption-based tax system.

MEASURING THE EFFECTS OF TAX REFORM

The development of so-called large-scale general equilibrium models has increased economists' ability to measure in detail the economic behavior of households and firms and the effects on that behavior of the tax system's many features. Like any new technology, these models are evolving rapidly as their authors attempt to represent accurately the economic effects of changes in the tax system. The discussion that follows should be viewed as a report on results with a new technology that, although still evolutionary, is moving out of the experimental phase into the standard arsenal of tools employed by economists who evaluate the effect of tax policy changes on the economy.

A full description of the methodology employed in this area can be found in *A General Equilibrium Model for Tax Policy Evaluation* by Ballard, Fullerton, Shoven, and Whalley and in *The Taxation of Income from Capital* by King and Fullerton.[14] Further development of the methodology to employ marginal rather than average effective tax rates is found in Fullerton (1985) and in Fullerton and Henderson.[15] Other important applications of the methodology reported by Jorgenson and Kun-Yung Yun.[16]

With regard to the four tax reform proposals advanced in 1984–1986 the broad question is this: What gains can be expected from reforming the income tax in a revenue-neutral manner that leaves the heavily preferential tax treatment of owner-occupied housing largely unaffected? The answer is that to cut tax rates for households and corporations, given that personal income taxes are much larger than corporate income taxes in total, it is necessary to transfer over a period of five years between $100 and $150 billion in taxes from the household sector to the corporate sector. A large part of this transfer comes from rescission of the investment tax credit. What follows will be a look at the effects of these broadly outlined changes on the distribution of tax burdens across different forms of investment and different sectors of the economy.

Table 8–1 compares marginal effective total tax rates under current law with those same rates under T-1, P-1, H-1 and S-1. The marginal effective total tax rate (METR) is the total tax burden, allowing for federal, state, and local taxes and for all special features of the tax system including tax credit and accelerated depreciation allowances, on an extra dollar of investment in different assets such as equipment, structures, or other categories listed in Table 8–1. In short, a change in METR measures the change in investment incentives under alternative tax plans.

The main conclusion that emerges from Table 8–1 is that relative to current law each of the four tax reform plans raises average corporate METR while reducing the degree of difference among METR on alternative forms of investment. Each of the tax reform measures "levels the playing field" in the corporate sector while increasing

Table 8-1. Marginal Effective Total Tax Rates (METR) under Alternative Tax Proposals.[a, b, c]

Corporate Sector Rates	Current Law	T-1	P-1	H-1	S-1
Equipment	-0.183	0.402	0.245	0.412	0.327
Structures	0.379	0.456	0.363	0.409	0.444
Public utilities	0.295	0.435	0.297	0.435	0.403
Inventories	0.416	0.424	0.388	0.398	0.429
Land	0.449	0.448	0.419	0.430	0.452
Overall corporate rate	0.311	0.431	0.344	0.415	0.410
Noncorporate sector tax rate	0.307	0.327	0.310	0.316	0.321
Owner-occupied housing tax rate	0.172	0.217	0.230	0.188	0.201
Overall tax rate	0.263	0.335	0.294	0.306	0.323
Overall cost of capital	0.069	—	0.071	0.072	0.085
Standard deviation	0.0171	—	0.0093	0.0093	0.010
Cost of capital	—	—	0.0093	—	0.014

[a] All figures assume a 5 percent real rate of return and a 4 percent inflation rate.

[b] Figures from current law, T-1, P-1, and H-1 are drawn from Don Fullerton, "The Indexation of Interest, Depreciation, and Capital Gains: A Model of Investment Incentives," AEI Studies in Fiscal Policy Working Paper No. 5, June 1985; and from Yolanda K. Henderson, "Investment Incentives under the Ways and Means Tax Bill," AEI Studies in Fiscal Policy Working Paper No. 6, January 1986.

[c] Figures drawn from Yolanda K. Henderson, "Tax Reform and Investment Incentives: An Update," *Tax Notes*, June 2, 1986. Results are not strictly comparable to those listed in footnote 1 to Table 1, which assumed on average a 5 percent real return for the economy but allowed real return to vary across sectors. S-1 results require a 5 percent return sector by sector.

METR. P-1 provides the smallest increase and P-1 and H-1 give the maximum leveling of the playing field as measured by the standard deviation across sectors of the cost of capital.

This outcome in the corporate sector results from rescission of the investment tax credit, which changes METR on equipment from a *minus* 18.3 percent to a positive range of 24.5 to 41.3 percent, depending on other features of various reform measures. The other major reason for the rise in METR is, somewhat ironically, the reduction in tax rates that reduces the tax advantage from the use of highly leveraged debt finance in a model that assumed a 5 percent real interest rate and 4 percent inflation. Note that these assumptions imply an interest rate of 13.16 percent under current law and a rate over 2 percent lower under the president's plan. Such a sharp drop in interest rates that is due partly to a tax-induced reduction in the incentive to use debt would probably alter the debt/equity mix toward more equity.

In the case of T-1, a fall in the interest rate also reflects the indexation of interest income and expense whereby borrowers can deduct only real interest expense and lenders pay tax only on real interest income. The result of these inflation provisions in T-1 makes tax burdens far less uncertain by reducing their sensitivity to changes in the rate of inflation. The 50 percent dividend-paid deduction coupled with the indexing provisions would probably tilt firms further toward equity finance. The analysis presented in Table 8-1 assumes a fixed debt/equity ratio of one third. In the extreme case of all equity finance, T-1 and P-1 actually reduce the corporate sector METR from 55.3 percent under current law to 49.1 percent and 47.4 percent, respectively. Under H-1, METR for all equity-financed investments is virtually the same as current law (55.7 percent), largely because of its less favorable treatment of depreciation and higher (36 percent versus 33 percent) corporate tax rate. Table 8-2 summarizes sensitivity of METR calculations using alternative assumptions about debt and equity finance under current law, T-1, P-1, and H-1.

The sensitivity of tax burdens on new investments (METR) to changes in the inflation rate has received little attention under current law (save for the important exception of individual bracket indexation enacted in 1981 and effective January 1, 1985) and has been largely neglected in the three reform proposals that followed T-1 of November 1984. In the corporate sector the primary candidates for indexation are interest income and expense, cost basis for capital gains and inventories, and depreciation allowances. Feldstein[17] and others argued convincingly during the late 1970s that

Table 8-2.   Alternative Financing Assumptions.[a]

	Current Law	*T-1*	*P-1*	*H-1*
Corporate sector tax rate				
All debt	-0.275	0.306	.065	.104
All equity	0.553	0.491	.474	.557
Overall tax rate				
All debt	0.106	0.250	.197	.200
All equity	0.334	0.377	.340	.357

[a]METR given 4 percent inflation and a 5 percent real interest rate. Data from Table 5 of Don Fullerton, "The Indexation of Interest, Depreciation and Capital Gains: A Model of Investment Incentives," AEI Studies in Fiscal Policy Working Paper No. 5, June 1985; and from Yolanda K. Henderson, "Investment Incentives under the Ways and Means Tax Bill," AEI Studies in Fiscal Policy Working Paper No. 6, January 1986.

failure to index in these areas created a significant increase in corporate tax burdens. Ad hoc measures to correct for failure to index, including low tax rates on capital gains, investment tax credits, and accelerated depreciation schedules have been the rule. These measures to some extent accomplished their goal, but as Table 8-1 shows, it was at the expense of a very uneven impact across different categories of investment.

Another problem is that such ad hoc measures are enacted and rescinded with great regularity, creating a very uneven pattern in the path of investment spending (see Figure 8-1). Failure to index individual income tax brackets also resulted in a sharp increase in tax burdens of households during the inflationary period of the late 1970s and early 1980s. Uncertainty about future inflation rates combined with uncertainty about enactment and rescission of tax measures designed to compensate ex post for the effect of inflation rates on tax burdens penalizes investment and puts a high premium on projects with quick paybacks. One is again reminded of the contrast in Japan, where a combination of low and stable inflation rates and a less activist approach to tax policy has eliminated this important element of uncertainty and created incentives for more investment and for investments in projects with paybacks over longer periods of time.

A study by Fullerton[18] maps out the sensitivity of METR under current law, T-1 and P-1. The prevalence of indexing provisions under T-1 makes clear the absence of sensitivity of marginal effective tax rates under alternative inflation rates. The president's plan mitigates the sensitivity of METR to changes in the inflation rate while flattening out extreme sensitivity on alternative investments to changes in the inflation rate under the law prior to the 1986 tax reform. Table 8-3, drawn from Henderson,[19] looks at METR on

Table 8-3. Inflation Sensitivity.[a]

	Current Law		Treasury II		Ways and Means	
	No Infl.	*8% Infl.*	*No Infl.*	*8% Infl.*	*No Infl.*	*8% Infl.*
Corporate sector tax rates						
Equipment	-.345	-.069	.273	.180	.318	.458
Structures	.331	.394	.386	.309	.356	.422
Land	.506	.337	.437	.375	.453	.398
Overall corporate rate	.320	.267	.366	.291	.387	.419
Owner-occupied housing	.195	.149	.247	.214	.207	.170

[a]Marginal effective total tax rates in each sector, for the case of a 5 percent real after-tax rate of return. The data for current law and Treasury II are taken from the tax rates underlying Figures 1 and 3 of Don Fullerton's study cited in Table 8-2.

alternative forms of investment, given a zero inflation rate and an 8 percent inflation rate under the law before the tax reform of 1986 and under P-1 and H-1. P-1 indexes the value of inventories for inflation and has a 17.5 percent maximum capital gains tax rate and more general depreciation schedules than H-1. These and other provisions help insulate METR under P-1 from changes in the inflation rate, while under the largely unindexed H-1, corporate tax burdens rise with higher inflation and the advantage to owner-occupied housing is enhanced.

Indexing provisions have thus far not survived the process of rewriting tax reform proposals since the appearance of T-1 in November 1984. Given the high degree of sensitivity in METR in the corporate and noncorporate sectors, and given the dispersion across METR on different forms of investment to changes in the inflation rate, an additional burden on monetary policy arises, to keep the inflation rate low and stable so that it is consistent with the inflationary expectations of investors. Otherwise, a much higher or lower rate of inflation than that expected will alter the returns to given projects in a way that calls for more ex post corrections, such as reenactment of investment tax credits, alteration of depreciation schedules, and special treatment of capital gains. While these measures would partially compensate for the effects of inflation on investment outcomes, they contribute to the atmosphere of tax uncertainty that surely is harmful to the investment climate and to the economy at large.

As was clear from Table 8-1, the four major tax reform proposals since November 1984 have all had a tendency to level the playing field while increasing the level of taxation of new investment. It is interesting to ask what would be the net impact of the beneficial effects of more even taxation across different categories of investment plus the effects of higher METR that tend to reduce investment and therefore create a long-run reduction in the capital stock. Is it possible to achieve a net welfare gain by getting more per unit of capital out of a slightly smaller capital stock?

Fullerton and Henderson[20] have addressed this question for T-1 and P-1 using a latest vintage general equilibrium model developed to take account of the key role of marginal tax rates in affecting investment decisions.

Were a tax reform proposal to increase the average METR for the corporate sector, if greater efficiency due to a more equal distribution of tax burdens across alternative forms of investment increases income, then savings out of the greater production can finance an increase in the overall capital stock. Indeed, Fullerton and Henderson find this outcome likely under both T-1 and P-1 if equity-financed investments are assumed to be funded out of new stock issues rather than out of corporate cash flow. This result stems from the dividend deductibility provisions in both proposals, which reduce the cost of equity-financed investments. The results obtained by Fullerton are also sensitive to the degree of substitutability between alternative forms of capital used in production, the method of production, the degree of substitutability between corporate and noncorporate capital, and the responsiveness of saving to interest rates. Fullerton and Henderson also allow for responsiveness of the labor supply to a change in net-of-tax wages.

Under alternative assumptions about the parameters mentioned above, Fullerton and Henderson find welfare gains ranging from zero to about 1.2 percent of the economy's total wealth under T-1 and from about 0.2 percent to 1.2 percent of total wealth under P-1. Larger welfare gains occur under the view that equity-financed investments involve the issue of new stock rather than the use of retained earnings. In this case, both T-1 and P-1 result in improved resource allocation gains, as well as a long-run increase in the capital stock of about 1 percent.

Although the details of results like those obtained by Fullerton would vary somewhat for alternative plans such as H-1 or S-1, his results are suggestive. Coupled with analysis by Fullerton and Henderson[21] of the potential gains available from tax reform measures that serve only to eliminate different tax burdens across alternative forms of investment and across different sectors of the economy, a general picture emerges of the welfare gains available under politically viable versions of reform of income-based tax systems. The most likely range for welfare gains is 0.5 percent of total economic wealth, or about $600 billion (1984 dollars). These results do not allow for changes in the debt/equity mix, which may result from fewer incentives for corporations to use debt finance that are contained in each of the tax reform proposals. Allowing for slower debt accumulation and some negative effect on real interest rates, which would in turn encourage investment, capital formation and growth, total welfare gains for a generic mid-1980s tax reform measure would probably be about 1 percent of the economy's total wealth, or about $1.2 trillion (1984 dollars). It would take some time to effect changes in methods of production required to achieve these gains, but that fact would not diminish their magnitude as reported here since these numbers are all present discounted values.

A measure that could increase the nation's economic wealth by about 1 percent by changing the way in which the same amount of tax revenue is collected seems worth undertaking. At the same time some hesitation in the face of risks is understandable. The order of magnitude is equivalent to a household with net assets of $100,000 contemplating a change in its business conduct that would increase its net worth by $1,000. These changes might include consolidation of debts, relocation to a house of the same monetary value but better located with regard to work and shopping, or other structural measures which involve uncertainties for perspective modest gain.

It remains to compare the gains just discussed under politically viable revision of the income tax system with gains available under the alternative of a more fundamental reform such as adoption of a consumption-based tax. This comparison is difficult because it is impossible to identify what features of a comprehensive consumption tax would survive were one actually proposed. Revenue neutrality will continue to be assumed, but it is important to remember that we are comparing an idealized consumption tax with realistic, "warts and all" versions of reformed income-based systems that have emerged since November 1984.

COMPARING THE OUTCOME OF INCOME TAX REFORM WITH A CONSUMPTION TAX

The politically viable income tax reform bill is the one that can get through both houses of Congress and be signed by the president. This distinction has been achieved by the Tax Reform Act of 1986 (TRA-86).

TRA-86 is a weaker tax plan than either T-1 or P-1, though it still has enough good features overall to make it marginally worth enacting. The obvious pluses are its lower rates for individuals and corporations, its durable removal of the poor from the tax rolls, and its base broadening. Broadening the base levels out tax burdens across different investments and across different households similar incomes. The lower rates will help to increase incentives to work and save based on economic incentives, and they will also make tax breaks less attractive. The result will be to discourage the use of the tax system for "social goals," thereby reducing tax uncertainty. The costs of such uncertainty are described and measured by Skinner.[22]

The lower rates will help to reduce the $400 billion annual revenue loss to tax expenditures by more than the amount reclaimed by closing loopholes. At a 34 percent rate, corporate deductions are worth only three-quarters of their value under the 46 percent rate that applied before the 1986 tax reform. At a 28 percent rate—the top rate for deductions—deductions for wealthy individuals are worth just over half the value under current law's top rate of 50 percent. These reductions in the incentive to use deductions will mitigate their use and thereby cut revenue losses associated with tax sheltering activities by households and businesses.

The weak points of TRA-86 are the fragility of its intended effects in the face of changing inflation rates, particularly with regard to capital cost provisions, obvious arbitrary exceptions to base broadening and, ironically but most importantly, its failure to provide cuts in marginal tax rates as large as those provided by T-1 and P-1 for taxpayers in the $25,000–$70,000 taxable income range, who pay nearly one-half of all individual income taxes. (See Figure 8–2 and Table 8–4.) For much of that range the statutory marginal rate under TRA-86 at 28 percent is 12 percent higher than the 25 percent rate under T-1 and P-1.

The limitation on rate-cutting of course arises from constraints on base broadening. Continued full deductibility of state and local taxes together with retention of favored tax treatment of owner-occupied housing constrains rate cutting. Taken together these measures cost $300–$350 billion in revenues over five years. Without this massive potential pool of revenue, a large part of the base broadening burden falls upon the corporate sector. While corporate taxes and taxes on capital are not synonymous, a shift from individual to corporate taxes does, holding other things equal, increase the tax burden on capital and depress saving. Of course, lower tax rates per se do reduce the revenue loss from the huge preferences for state and local taxes and owner-occupied housing and all deductions by devaluing them to 28/33 cents on the dollar veruss 50/46. This is part of the genius of achieving tax reform, by lowering rates instead of rais-

Figure 8-2. Taxable Income in 1989.

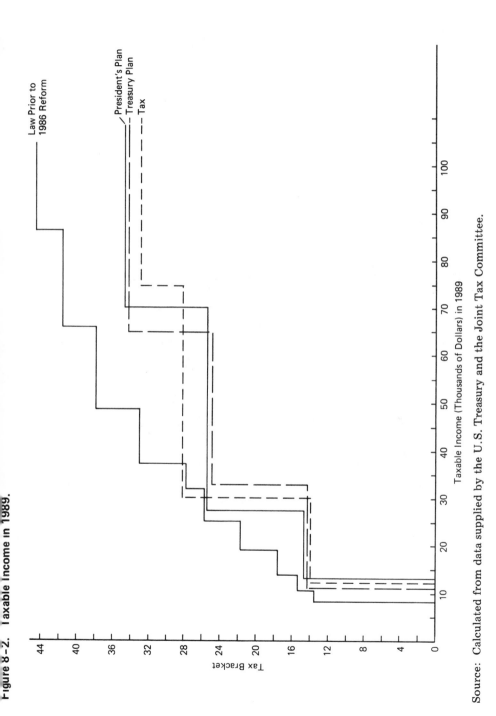

Source: Calculated from data supplied by the U.S. Treasury and the Joint Tax Committee.

Table 8-4. Tax Brackets by Taxable Income (Joint Returns, Family of Four).[a]

Marginal Tax Rate	Current[b]	T-1[c]	P-1[d]	S-1[e]	TRA-86[f]
0	Below $3,670 $3,670-26,540; 11-22%	Below $3,800	Below $4,000	Below $5,000	Below $5,000
15%	n.a.	$3,800-31,800	$4,000-29,000	$5,000-29,300	$5,000-29,750
25%	$26,540-32,260	$31,800-63,800	$29,000-70,000	n.a.	n.a.
27%	n.a.			$29,300-56,000	
28%	$64,740 up; 42-50%				$29,750-71,900
32%				$56,000 or more	
33%					$71,900 or more
35%		$63,800 or more	$70,000 or more		

a For taxable incomes of $115,631-$147,855, the marginal tax rate is 32.4%. Above $147,855 the marginal tax rate is 27%. This group over $147,000 pays about 17% of individual income taxes.

b For 1986 joint returns as estimated in The President's Tax Proposals to the Congress for Fairness, Growth and Simplicity (Washington, D.C.: Government Printing Office), p. 10.

c Tax Reform for Fairness, Simplicity and Economic Growth, Vol. 1 (Washington, D.C.: U.S. Department of the Treasury, November 1984), p. xvi.

d P-1, page 10.

e Joint Committee on Taxation, July 24, 1986.

f Joint Committee on Taxation, August 17, 1986.

ing them as was done in the era when tax reform meant trying—unsuccessfully—to redistribute income through progressive taxation.

TRA-86's shifts from individuals onto corporations of $120 billion in taxes over five years raises the burden on capital in the corporate sector by about 6 percent. But this switch need not have been as burdensome as it is under TRA-86. Virtually the same dollar shift occurs under the president's tax plan, yet the cost of capital and the tax burden on corporate capital rise by less than they do under TRA-86. Although the five-year increase in corporate taxes is $165 billion under the original Treasury plan, there too the cost of capital rises by less than it does under TRA-86, although the overall tax rate on corporate capital rises most under T-1. (See Table 8–1.)

These apparent incongruities emerge because taxes on corporations and taxes on capital are not synonymous. Both corporate and individual taxes are borne by labor and capital, although capital's share is higher for corporations. Both T-1 and P-1 mitigate the burden on capital arising from higher corporate taxes with lower marginal tax rates for individuals, indexation, special treatment of capital gains, and partial deductibility from corporate income of dividends paid. Attention to these details is more important than the simple ratio of taxes collected from corporation to taxes collected from individuals.

General equilibrium analysis employing a methodology developed by Fullerton, Shoven, and Whalley (FSW)[23] to evaluate gains and losses under alternative tax systems provides a comprehensive study of the degree to which such alternatives achieve the objectives of maximum efficiency and growth. The FSW procedure has been employed to estimate gains relative to a standard base case achievable under a consumption tax, Bradley-Gephardt, T-1 and P-1 by Allison, Fullerton, and Makin.[24]

A comparison of T-1 and TRA-86 with a consumption tax using the FSW procedure reveals that TRA-86 yields some gains at low levels of inflation, but those gains are smaller than gains with T-1 and far more sensitive to inflation. Neither T-1 nor TRA-86 yields gains nearly as large as those obtainable with a pure (precompromise) consumption tax. T-1 contains many of the provisions in TRA-86, although the latter's higher marginal rates for many taxpayers, lack of dividend deductibility, limited indexing provisions for income from capital, and higher tax rates on unindexed capital gains all combine to make it likely that T-1 constitutes an upper bound on gains attainable with TRA-86. (See Tables 8–5 and 8–6.)

It is important to remember that when discussing average and marginal tax rates in the context of the FSW general equilibrium

Table 8-5. Marginal Tax Rates.

Income of Consumer Groups (1,000s of 1973 $)	Benchmark (1973)	Treasury Department	TRA-86
0-3	.0100	.0370	.0076
3-4	.0608	.0478	.0472
4-5	.1019	.0869	.0866
5-6	.1228	.0969	.1192
6-7	.1346	.1145	.1311
7-8	.1570	.1267	.1533
8-10	.1813	.1502	.1613
10-12	.2078	.1659	.1822
12-15	.2215	.1846	.1743
15-20	.2618	.2086	.2245
20-25	.2897	.2589	.2431
25+	.4067	.3456	.3064

Table 8-6. Changes in Average Federal Tax Rates.

Income (1,000s of 1973 $)	Treasury Department	TRA-86
0-3	-32.50%	-65.70
3-4	-25.70	-65.70
4-5	-16.60	-49.32
5-6	-14.70	-22.30
6-7	-12.10	-22.30
7-8	-10.80	-22.30
8-10	- 9.10	-11.60
10-12	- 9.18	- 9.80
12-15	- 9.30	- 7.83
15-20	- 9.00	- 8.77
20-25	- 7.40	- 1.96
25+	- 7.25	- 1.87

model, the "rates" refer not to statutory rates under the federal income tax. Rather, the tax rates discussed in this section are those that result from a combination of federal, state, and local tax burdens. Also, corporate tax liabilities are imputed to individuals.

Table 8-7 presents estimates of the present value of total efficiency gains under two income tax reform plans, T-1 and TRA-86, and under the pure consumption tax. Gains are calculated relative to a standardized "benchmark case" calibrated to 1973 data. These are not gains relative to current law since for that case the full data requirements of the general equilibrium model are not met. Therefore, comparisons between the alternatives in Table 8-7 can be made since the figures are all calculated relative to the same (1973) benchmark.

The numbers recorded are model estimates of the present value of equivalent variations from each plan summed across the 12 consumer

Table 8-7. Present Value of Total Gains under Alternative Tax Reforms (*Billions of 1986 $*).[a, b]

Plan	Welfare Gain[c]	
	4% Inflation	*7% Inflation*
Treasury Department	$ 1,094 (0.89)	$ 1,377.8 (1.1)
Tax Reform Act of 1986	$ 450 (0.37)	$ 294.0 (0.24)
Consumption tax	$ 1,822 (1.48)	$ 3,115 (2.50)

[a] These welfare effects are calculated using 0.4 as the elasticity of saving with respect to the interest rate.

[b] In order to separate the welfare effects of the tax reform proposals from revenue impacts, we require real government revenues to remain unchanged from the benchmark. In the results reported, this is achieved by changing all marginal tax rates by the same percentage points.

[c] The numbers in parenthesis represent the gain as a percentage of the present discounted value (using a 4 percent discount rate) of welfare (consumption plus leisure) in the benchmark case.

groups. They measure the amount that could be given to consumers under the old regime such that they would be indifferent to the reform situation. The discount rate used, 4 percent, is the model's average after-tax rate of return to capital in the benchmark. At 4 percent inflation the gains from the adoption of TRA-86 are about 41 percent of those under the original Treasury proposal and about 25 percent of those obtainable with a pure consumption tax. Satisfying the "politically viable" constraint on tax reform is clearly costly.

At a 7 percent inflation rate, the lack of indexing provisions penalizes TRA-86. The indexed Treasury plan and the consumption tax look even better since gains are calculated relative to an unindexed 1973 benchmark case. A rise of the inflation rate by 3 percentage points cuts by one-third the total welfare gain under TRA-86, just over $150 billion. TRA-86 gains are only 21 percent of T-1 gains and just under 10 percent of gains under a pure consumption tax. Since the consumption tax base is calculated as income less the annual change in value of a taxpayer's comprehensive asset account, it is fully indexed and it improves relative to the unindexed 1973 benchmark as inflation rises.

One of the reasons for the difference between outcomes under the three proposals is their different effects on labor supply. All the plans aim to increase the labor supply by decreasing an individual's marginal tax rate. Because the Treasury proposal does not collect as

Table 8-8. Percentage Changes in Labor Supplied in the First Equilibrium Period (4 Percent Inflation).

Income of Consumer Group (1,000s of 1973 $)	Treasury Department	TRA-86	Consumption Tax
0-3	-.139	.004	-.406
3-4	.107	-.170	-.411
4-5	.065	-.206	-.399
5-6	.195	-.387	-.372
6-7	.354	-.506	-.349
7-8	.565	-.640	-.332
8-10	.856	+.537	-.246
10-12	1.304	.895	-.093
12-15	2.275	2.252	.058
15-20	2.789	1.571	.372
20-25	3.076	2.500	.649
25+	4.943	5.431	2.750
Total (weighted average)	2.415	2.004	.557

Table 8-9. Average Effective Capital Tax Rates in the First Equilibrium Period (Industry-Weighted Average).

	Treasury	TRA-86	Consumption Tax
4% inflation	-1.980%	5.079%	- 1.331%
7% inflation	-4.946	6.360	-13.897

much tax from individual income, it is able to offer a rate structure that is more favorable for increased labor supply. Table 8-8 shows that T-1 increases the labor supply by more than TRA-86. T-1 increases the total labor supply by 2.415 percent in the first equilibrium, while TRA-86 provides an increase of 2.004 percent. Both figures assume 4 percent inflation, although the comparison is similar at 7 percent inflation. Labor supply rises overall by less under the consumption tax, and in fact falls for lower income groups since effective tax rates on labor income rise for those groups.

Another reason for the difference between the effects of the proposals is their treatment of capital income. All the tax reform proposals reduce the variance of the average effective capital tax rates across industries. This reduction results in a more efficient allocation of capital among industries and welfare gains. At 7 percent inflation the overall average capital tax rate, however, is 5 percent lower under T-1 than it is under the 1973 benchmark, despite the higher corporate income tax. (See Table 8-9.) This lower rate stems from lower marginal personal tax rates and the indexation of capital gains. TRA-86, which also increases corporate taxes but does not index

Table 8-10. Percentage Changes in Saving in the First Equilibrium Period
(*4 Percent Inflation*).

Income of Consumer Group (1,000s of 1973 $)	Treasury Department	TRA-86	Consumption Tax
0-3	.082	-1.596	7.584
3-4	.649	- .613	12.032
4-5	.986	- .748	17.772
5-6	1.302	-2.208	20.793
6-7	1.526	-2.305	22.676
7-8	1.944	-2.517	26.566
8-10	2.447	-1.870	31.370
10-12	3.249	-1.708	36.686
12-15	4.830	.148	39.824
15-20	5.933	-1.075	49.331
20-25	6.245	- .906	55.824
25+	7.855	2.588	81.423
Total	5.960	.377	58.047

capital gains, produces about a 6.4 percent increase in the average tax rate on capital when inflation is assumed to be 7 percent. At 4 percent inflation, when indexing of capital gains is less important, the average capital tax rate rises 5 percent above the benchmark case under TRA-86.

Since T-1 and a consumption tax result in a higher net rate of return to capital, they induce an increase in saving. Table 8-10 shows saving increasing by about 6 percent under T-1 and by 5.8 percent under the consumption tax. The latter is of course a direct result of removal of a double tax on saving. This increase in saving causes the net return to capital to drop over time. After 50 years it drops to an increase relative to the benchmark of 4.1 percent for T-1 and to a decrease of 25 percent relative to the benchmark for the consumption tax. The lower net rate of return to capital under TRA-86 results, in the first equilibrium period, in a drop in saving by 1.6 percent, leading to a small (0.2 percent) increase in the net return to capital. After 50 years the net return to capital drops slightly, such that the decrease relative to the benchmark is 0.1 percent.

Finally, Tables 8-11 and 8-12 show the static distributional effects of the reform proposals and the consumption tax. Both plans appear regressive relative to the 1973 benchmark in that they increase the after-income tax and transfer income of the higher income individuals relatively more than that of the lower income individuals. The consumption tax appears very regressive, cutting after-tax and transfer income for all but the top income group. Table 8-12, however, with regard to real expanded income which includes the value

Table 8-11. Percentage Changes in Income after Income Tax and Transfers in the First Equilibrium Period (*4 Percent Inflation*).

Income of Consumer Group (1,000s of 1973 $)	Treasury Department	TRA-86	Consumption Tax
0-3	1.005	.701	-3.171
3-4	1.300	1.715	-3.670
4-5	1.410	2.061	-4.170
5-6	1.559	1.231	-4.290
6-7	1.671	1.356	-4.344
7-8	1.887	1.514	-4.428
8-10	2.115	1.872	-4.253
10-12	2.565	2.124	-3.690
12-15	3.546	3.202	-3.106
15-20	4.095	2.920	-1.887
20-25	4.208	2.864	- .620
25+	5.328	4.498	10.982
Total	3.388	2.758	- .445

Table 8-12. Percentage Changes in Expanded Real Income[a] after Income Tax and Transfers in the First Equilibrium Period (*4 Percent Inflation*).

Income of Consumer Group (1,000s of 1973 $)	Treasury Department	TRA-86	Consumption Tax
0-3	-.035	-.191	-1.815
3-4	.233	.616	-1.926
4-5	.198	.760	-2.061
5-6	.318	.224	-1.933
6-7	.286	.275	-1.809
7-8	.318	.391	-1.651
8-10	.356	.103	-1.311
10-12	.507	.061	- .662
12-15	.689	.079	.022
15-20	.976	.158	1.268
20-25	1.069	-.307	2.564
25+	2.679	.067	16.297

[a] Expanded real income includes leisure, valued at the household's net-of-tax wage. Numbers shown are the arithmetic means of the percentage changes to income based on Paashe and Laspeyres price indexes.

of leisure and adjustments for price changes, shows T-1 and the consumption tax still to be clearly regressive but less so than in Table 8-11. TRA-86 with 4 percent inflation is generally progressive relative to the 1973 benchmark. With 7 percent inflation TRA-86 increases after-income tax and transfer income for most income groups but decreases real expanded income for the top half of the income distribution, due to their heavier participation in income from capital.

SUMMARY AND CONCLUSIONS

Comparison of the Treasury proposal and TRA-86 with a well-documented 1973 benchmark provides a useful perspective while omitting some important considerations. Further work could include analysis of other major reform proposals. A full examination of effects of reform proposals on growth and capital formation would benefit from the use of marginal effective tax rates on income from capital. A more recent benchmark data base would enable comparison of reform proposals with more contemporary situations.

Results obtained so far suggest that, as base-broadening or flatter-tax modifications of an income-based tax system, both proposals fall far short of potential economic gains realizable with a consumption-based tax system that fully taxes all economic income but eliminates double taxation of savings. Qualitatively, this conclusion will come as no surprise to most analysts. Perhaps our quantitative result adds some perspective on the difficulty of encouraging adequate saving and capital formation under an income-based system.

The heart of a comparison of T-1, TRA-86, and the consumption tax lies in their effects on taxation of labor and capital. Both T-1 and TRA-86 lower marginal tax rates and increase labor supplies (Tables 8-5 and 8-8). But TRA-86's overall reduction in marginal tax rates is more modest than Treasury's, so that its weighted-average increase in labor supply is smaller, especially at higher inflation rates. A consumption tax falls more heavily on labor income, especially at low income levels, and so modestly increases labor supply only at higher income levels.

The Treasury proposal's indexing provisions and its other features, such as dividend deductibility and inflation adjustment for interest income and expense, combine with its lower statutory corporate and individual rates to reduce average effective tax rates on capital by about 3 percent, relative to the 1973 benchmark. TRA-86, which taxes unindexed capital gains as ordinary income and provides no indexing for interest income, raises the average effective tax rate on capital by about 8 percent at a 7 percent inflation rate and by about 5 percent when inflation falls to a 4 percent rate.

In sum, T-1 realizes more of the gains available under an "ideal" income tax than does TRA-86, largely by virtue of its indexation of capital gains and its larger increase in the labor supply. None of the plans, however, realizes the full potential gains available from fundamental tax reform such as a consumption tax, although it is important to remember that a politically viable consumption tax would likely include protection for low-income individuals that would reduce total gains. It is always possible that in seeking an ideal tax system, we jeopardize the chance for a more modest but acceptable reform. The best can be the enemy of the good. But if further study continues to suggest a wide margin between "the good" and "the best," reexamination of the fundamental choice between an income tax system and a consumption tax system may be necessary.

NOTES

1. Thomas Hobbes, *Leviathan*, part 2 (New York: Dutton, 1924).

2. David F. Bradford, *Blueprints for Basic Tax Reform* (Washington, D.C.: U.S. Department of the Treasury, 1977). Revised ed. published by Tax Analysts, Arlington, Va., 1984.

3. Don Fullerton, John B. Shoven, and John Whalley, "Replacing the U.S. Income Tax with a Progressive Consumption Tax," *Journal of Public Economics 20* (February 1983): 3–23.

4. John H. Makin, ed., *Real Tax Reform: Replacing the Income Tax* (Washington, D.C.: American Enterprise Institute, 1985).

5. John H. Makin, "Savings Rates in Japan and the United States: The Roles of Tax Policy and Other Factors," in F. Gerard Adams and Susan M. Wachter, eds., *Savings and Capital Formation: The Policy Options* (Lexington, Mass.: Lexington Books, 1986). Michael J. Boskin and John B. Roberts, "A Closer Look at Saving Rates in the United States and Japan," American Enterprise Institute *Studies in Fiscal Policy*, Working Paper No. 9, June 1986.

6. Revised 2d ed. published by Tax Analysts, Arlington, Va., 1984.

7. Fullerton, Shoven, and Whalley, "Replacing the U.S. Income Tax with a Progressive Consumption Tax."

8. Michael J. Boskin, "The Impact of the 1981-2 Investment Incentives on Business Fixed Investment" (Washington, D.C.: National Chamber Foundation, 1985).

9. Fullerton, Shoven, and Whalley, "Replacing the U.S. Income Tax with a Progressive Consumption Tax."

10. Jonathan Skinner, "The Welfare Cost of Tax Uncertainty," mimeo, Department of Economics, University of Virginia, May 1986.

11. See Albert Ando and Alan Auerbach, "The Corporate Cost of Capital in Japan and the United States: A Comparison," National Bureau of Economic Research, Working Paper No. 1762, October 1985. John B. Shoven and Toshiaki Tachibanaki, "The Taxation of Income from Capital in Japan," mimeo, Center for Economic Policy Research, Stanford, Calif., September 1985. John H. Makin and John B. Shoven, "Are There Lessons for the United States in the Japanese Tax System?" in *Contemporary Economic Problems*, edited by Phillip Cagan (Washington, D.C.: American Enterprise Institute, 1987).

12. Makin, "Savings Rates in Japan and the United States."

13. Charles Ballard, John Karl Scholz, and John B. Shoven, "The Value-Added Tax: A General Equilibrium Look at Its Efficiency and Incidence," in *The Effects of Taxation on Capital Formation* (Chicago: University of Chicago Press, 1986).

14. Charles L. Ballard, Don Fullerton, John B. Shoven, and John Whalley, *A General Equilibrium Model for Tax Policy Evaluation* (Chicago: University of Chicago Press, 1985). Mervyn A. King and Don Fullerton, eds., *The Taxation of Income from Capital* (Chicago: University of Chicago Press, 1984).

15. Don Fullerton, "The Indexation of Interest, Depreciation, and Capital Gains: A Model of Investment Incentives," American Enterprise Institute *Studies in Fiscal Policy* Working Paper No. 5, June 1985. Don Fullerton and Yolanda K. Henderson, "A Disaggregate Equilibrium Model of the Tax Distortions among Assets, Sectors, and Industries," American Enterprise Institute *Studies in Fiscal Policy* Working Paper No. 7, February 1986, and "The Impact of Fundamental Tax Reform on the Allocation of Resources," American Enterprise Institute *Studies in Fiscal Policy* Working Paper No. 8, April 1986.

16. Dale W. Jorgenson and Kun-Young Yun, "Tax Policy and Capital Allocation," Harvard Institute of Economic Research, Discussion Paper No. 1107, November 1984.

17. Martin Feldstein, *Inflation, Tax Rules and Capital Formation* (Chicago: University of Chicago Press, 1983).

18. Fullerton, "The Indexation of Interest, Depreciation, and Capital Gains."

19. Yolanda K. Henderson, "Investment Incentives under the Ways and Means Tax Bill," American Enterprise Institute *Studies in Fiscal Policy*, Working Paper No. 6, January 1986.

20. Fullerton and Henderson, "The Impact of Fundamental Tax Reform on the Allocation of Resources."

21. Fullerton and Henderson, "A Disaggregate Equilibrium Model of the Tax Distortions among Assets, Sectors, and Industries."

22. Skinner, "The Welfare Cost of Tax Uncertainty."

23. Fullerton, Shoven, and Whalley, "Replacing the U.S. Income Tax with a Progressive Consumption Tax."

24. Michael T. Allison, Don Fullerton, and John Makin, "Tax Reform: A Study of Some Major Proposals," American Enterprise Institute *Studies in Fiscal Policy*, Working Paper No. 2, December 1984 (revised, mimeo, June 1985).

Chapter 9

The Macroeconomics of Tax Reform

Joel L. Prakken

The 1986 Tax Reform Act has been hailed by lawmakers as a landmark effort to shape a tax code that is simpler and fairer than current law and also more conducive to economic growth. The stated rationale behind the tax reform movement is plain enough. The goal of simplicity is met by crafting a code that limits deductions and preferences to those that are available to taxpayers generally. Broadening the tax base promotes fairness by taxing income comparably regardless of its source and enhances economic efficiency by reducing the importance of taxes in the allocation of productive resources. Finally, given a broader tax base, the same stream of revenues can be raised with lower marginal tax rates. Lower rates, it is argued, will unleash previously curbed initiatives to work, save, and invest.

To date, the Tax Reform Act has played to mixed reviews. Macroeconometricians, relying on large-scale structural models, generally conclude that the near-term impact of the Act will be to slow the economy, particularly business fixed investment. Proponents of the Act argue that macro-economic models fail to capture the long-run advantages of tax reform arising from a more efficient allocation of resources. Others less rigorous in their analytics and empiricism seem to take it on faith that lower marginal tax rates are the sure cure for all our economic woes.

I wish to thank Laurence H. Meyer and Chris P. Varvares for their insightful comments and discussion during the preparation of this chapter. Any errors, however, remain mine.

Whichever result proves correct, the chances are good that we have not heard the last of tax reform. If the near-term projections from macroeconomic models prove accurate, pressure may grow to undo those provisions of the bill viewed by many as most damaging: repeal of the investment tax credit (ITC) and the switch to less generous depreciation allowances on structures. Restoration of these provisions would, of course, contribute to larger federal deficits unless offsetting revenue were raised—something likely anyway if Congress and the administration are serious in their intent to meet the deficit targets mandated by the Balanced Budget Act of 1985.

One possible source of revenue is a value-added tax. Popular abroad, the VAT was dismissed in early recommendations by the Treasury as an inviable and administratively expensive alternative to reforming the income tax. There are, however, advantages to the VAT. Because the tax is broadly based, a relatively low rate is capable of raising considerable revenues. Furthermore, a VAT distorts the allocation of resources less than does the income tax with its myriad of implicit subsidies.

This chapter investigates the theoretical underpinnings of the macroeconomics of taxes, and presents econometric evidence on the implications of various tax initiatives for real output, the price level, interest rates, and capital formation. Attention is devoted to the pending tax reform plan and to the value-added tax, which may well represent the next frontier in tax policy. However, the effort is intended as a comprehensive one, as there is missing from the literature a thorough but eclectic treatment of the role of taxes on the macroeconomy.

TAX REFORM AND MACROECONOMICS

Macroeconomic analysis has been eschewed by proponents of tax reform on the grounds that macroeconometric models are not specified to reflect the economic ramifications of changes in the tax code. For example, the Treasury Department had this to say about macroeconomic models in its original recommendations on tax reform:

> It is impossible to predict the precise economic effects of the entire package of Treasury Department proposals on all industries and individuals in the economy. Although many mathematical models of the economy exist, economic science simply is not sufficiently precise to allow accurate prediction of the effects of reforms as pervasive as those proposed by the Treasury Department.[1]

Jane Gravelle concluded that "commercial macroeconomic models are more appropriate for dealing with the transition and not for assessing the long-run economic effects of tax changes."[2] The Council of Economic Advisers (CEA), in evaluating the president's proposals (sometimes referred to as Treasury II) did not use "commercial macroeconomic models . . . primarily because they are not designed to deal with changes in the allocation of capital and other resources, a critical benefit of tax reform."[3]

Yet the CEA's own analysis embarks on discussions of the elasticity of consumption with respect to the after-tax interest rate, the elasticity of labor supply with respect to the after-tax wage, and the responsiveness of capital formation to the cost of capital—parameters all of which play prominent roles in any well-specified macroeconomic model.

Indeed, detractors' resistance to macroeconomic analysis of tax reform breeds, in part, from unfamiliarity with today's macroeconomic model, which bears little resemblance to the income-expenditure or "Keynesian" system pioneered by Klein over 30 years ago. A well-specified model *does* incorporate *estimated* relationships between after-tax relative prices and the trade-offs between work and leisure, saving and consumption, and capital and labor. It *is* constrained in the long run by aggregate supply. Furthermore, macroeconomic models force consideration of the short-run impacts of changes in the tax code, not just the long-run implications. The distinction is important since macroeconomic theory reveals the two to be different not only in magnitude *but also in sign*. A long-run economic benefit bought with short-run sacrifice may not be worthwhile when evaluated in terms of its net present discounted value.

This is not to say that macroeconomic models have no shortcomings when it comes to analyzing changes in the tax code. They do, principal of which is that models are too aggregated to capture *all* the changes in resource allocation that might accompany sweeping reform. But to argue that macroeconomic models contribute little or nothing to the analysis of tax reform is to reveal an ignorance of the current state of macroeconomic theory and modeling.

With these remarks as background, we turn next to the findings. For each of the cases considered, two sets of results are presented. The first "heuristic" set of results is derived from an eclectic theoretical model of the U.S. economy in which taxes are allowed to influence both the supply and demand for goods and services. The full theoretical model is developed and discussed in Appendixes 9A and 9B. The second set of results is the econometric counterpart of the heuristic findings. The econometric results are generated with the Washington University Macroeconomic Model of the United States' Economy, a macroeconometric system consistent in spirit with the theoretical model presented in the appendixes.

CASE 1: THE TAX REFORM ACT OF 1986

The Tax Reform Act passed in 1986 proposes sweeping changes in almost every aspect of the tax code. From a macroeconomic standpoint, the most important of these are the following:

1. Sharp reductions in the federal marginal income tax rate for individuals. Laurence H. Meyer & Associates (LHM&A) estimates that the economy-wide marginal rate (including state and local income tax rates) would fall by about 20 percent, from roughly 30 to 24 percent, with the reduction "blended" in over 1987 and 1988.

2. Repeal of the 60 percent exclusion for personal capital gains income.

3. Reduction of the top marginal corporate income tax rate from 46 to 33 percent, the reduction blended in over 1987 and 1988.

4. Repeal of the investment tax credit retroactive to January 1986.

5. Depreciation of structures according to the straight line schedule, residential buildings over a recovery period of 27.5 years, nonresidential buildings over 31.5 years. Law before the reform allowed structures to be depreciated by the 175 percent declining balance schedule over a recovery period of 19 years.

6. Depreciation of equipment by the 200 percent declining balance schedule. Under previous law, 150 percent declining balance was allowed. Recovery periods would not be fundamentally altered.

7. Revenue neutrality. Households would receive a reduction in their tax burden of $112 billion from 1987 to 1991, while firms would bear an equivalent increase in their tax burden.

Heuristic Results

The heuristic results of the Tax Reform Act of 1986 are summarized in Table 9-1. Column (1), labeled "Impact," shows the changes in variables that would result from the combined impact of the proposed tax changes *at an unchanged pre-tax interest rate.* Thus, for example, the Act would immediately raise the cost of capital by 10.2 percent. Column (2) reports the short-run equilibrium responses derived by assuming that the aggregate price level initially remains unchanged following implementation of the new tax code. Columns (3)-(5) present the long-run equilibrium responses, derived by assuming the aggregate price level to be fully flexible, over a range of values for the elasticity of the labor supply with respect to the after-tax wage.

Table 9-1. Heuristic Estimates for the Tax Reform Act of 1986.

	Impact[a]	Short Run	b = 0	Long Run b = .18	b = .40
Gross output	-8.2	-2.8	-1.0	1.5	5.7
Pre-tax yield	0.0	-1.0	-0.8	-1.8	-3.5
After-tax yield	0.7	-0.0	0.1	-0.6	-1.8
Prices including VAT	0.0	0.0	-0.5	-2.9	-7.0
Prices excluding VAT	0.0	0.0	-0.5	-2.9	-7.0
Real money stock	0.0	0.0	0.5	2.9	7.0
Cost of capital	10.2	4.6	5.9	0.2	-9.1
Pre-tax wage	0.0	0.0	-1.0	-0.0	1.6
After-tax wage	8.6	8.6	7.5	8.5	10.2
Capital stock	0.0	-7.3	-6.9	1.2	14.7
Employment	0.0	-2.8	7.5	1.5	4.1

[a]Impacts are measured as percent changes except for yields, which are measured in percentage points.

In the short run, the Tax Reform Act will generate a near-term decline in output of 2.8 percent. Employment would fall an equivalent amount. The before-tax interest rate would decline by 100 basis points, while the after-tax interest rate would remain about unchanged. Even allowing for the decline in interest rates, the cost of capital would rise by 4.6 percent and investment would fall by 7.3 percent. On balance, the thrust of the Tax Reform Act is unambiguously negative.

In the long run, the macroeconomic impact of the Act depends crucially on the estimate used for the elasticity of labor supply with respect to the after-tax wage. If this elasticity is zero, output would decline even in the long run. If an outsized estimate of 0.4 is assumed, output would ultimately increase by 5.7 percent. For our intermediate estimate of 0.18, the long-run gain in output is 1.5 percent. Since there is considerable professional controversy about the response of the aggregate labor supply to changes in taxes, it is impossible to avoid the conclusion that the 1986 tax reform is a risk from a macroeconomic standpoint. While the short-run losses could be offset by the Federal Reserve, they are sizable and fairly certain, while the long-run benefits are uncertain and may be nonexistent.

Returning again to Table 9-1, for an elasticity of labor supply equal to 0.18, the long-run results are imminently sensible. The pretax interest rate would decline by 180 basis points, while the after-tax yield would drop 60 basis points. Prices would decline 2.9 percent. Despite its initial sharp increase, the cost of capital would ultimately be little changed as a result of the decline in interest rates. The pre-tax wage paid by firms also would be little changed. Nonetheless, labor supply would be up 1.5 percent as a result of an 8.5 percent increase in the after-tax wage. Note that while investment falls in the short run, ultimately it rises.

Econometric Results

Although they shed considerable light on the direction and magnitude of the impacts of the Tax Reform Act of 1986, the heuristic results prove less useful when it comes to assessing the timing of the response of the economy to implementation of the proposed tax code. Answering such questions requires use of a macroeconometric system, and this section reports results generated with the Washington University Macroeconometric Model of the United States Economy, or WUMM for short.

While WUMM is entirely consistent with the heuristic model developed in Appendixes 9A and 9B, it is more sophisticated in several important regards.

1. WUMM disaggregates fixed capital into equipment and structures, each with a respective rental price defined as in equation (9A.1).

2. It explicitly treats business capital as "putty-clay" in nature, so that the equilibrium response of investment to a once-and-for-all change in the cost of capital requires a full depreciation cycle of capital. In the case of equipment, the mean economic life is seven years. The response of investment to changes in rental price is also slowed by a lengthy lag between orders and shipments of capital goods. The slow response of business fixed investment to changes in the cost of capital has the effect of prolonging the initial decline in output associated with the bill.

3. Third, WUMM incorporates other classes of capital, all explained by stock adjustment models incorporating rental prices, that would be influenced either directly or indirectly by the Tax Reform Act of 1986. These include consumers durables, purchases of which would be discouraged by the proposed repeal of the deduction for consumer interest, business inventories, owner-occupied homes, and renter-occupied residential structures. The latter would be subject to stricter depreciation rules. As all these categories of investment also depend on the after-tax interest rate, their inclusion exacerbates the short-run decline in output.

To gauge the macroeconomic impact of the Tax Reform Act of 1986, a "baseline" simulation was first prepared assuming the tax code prior to reform. In this baseline, output grows at slightly below 3 percent per year through 1995, inflation averages about 3.5 percent per year, short-term interest rates are relatively stable, while both the long-term interest rate and the unemployment rate gradually decline. The federal deficit falls from $222 billion in 1986 to $146 billion in 1995, and the trade deficit narrows as well.

Next, a simulation was run in which the provisions of Tax Reform Act were implemented, and this "alternative" compared to the baseline. Before considering the results, however, three important points about the alternative simulation need be discussed.

The first has to do with the assumed response of the monetary authorities. In principle, the Federal Reserve Board could offset the initial decline in output by increasing the real money supply quickly to its long-run equilibrium value. While constructing a simulation based on this assumption would reveal the long-run compositional effects of tax reform, it also would muddy the distinction between monetary and fiscal initiatives during the period of adjustment. For this reason, it is assumed here that the Federal Reserve does not change the rate of growth in the nominal money supply in the wake of tax reform, so that any ensuing increase in the real money stock is attributable entirely to downward adjustment in the price level. The results presented below do *not* constitute a forecast of what will happen under the Tax Reform Act, as I believe the Federal Reserve would not stand idle as the economy weakened.

The second point about the alternative simulation has to do with the assumed revenue effects of the bill. Through 1991, the bill is supposedly revenue-neutral in a "static" sense, a cumulative $112 billion increase in corporate taxes just offset by an equivalent decline in individual taxes. It is not, however, neutral in each of the intervening years, and the implicit year-to-year changes in the average tax rate prove pivotal in determining the near-term response of output. In particular, households would receive roughly a $50 billion dollar tax decrease (relative to current law) in calendar year 1988, but then successively smaller reductions in the ensuing two years. The impact is to spur consumption in 1988 but slow it in 1989 and 1990.

A final point concerns the revenue effects *beyond* 1991. Little if anything is known about this, but some assumptions must be fed into the model. To distinguish between tax reform and changes in the average tax rate, we have assumed that the Tax Reform Act of 1986 is revenue-neutral all the way through 1995. The underlying "static" figures for individual and corporate revenues are presented in Table 9-2. It should be noted that the associated "dynamic" revenue estimates will be quite different from the static ones.

The econometric estimates of the impact of Tax Reform Act are summarized in comparison to the previous law in Table 9-3. They

Table 9-2.   Static Revenue Assumptions for the Tax Reform Act of 1986
($ Billions, Calendar Year).

	Total	Individual	Corporate
1986	3	0	3
1987	26	0	26
1988	-36	-50	14
1989	-11	-31	20
1990	10	-15	25
1991	13	-16	29
1992	9	-17	26
1993	5	-19	24
1994	0	-20	20
1995	5	-21	26
Total	24	-189	213

conform to the predictions of the heuristic model. The initial thrust of the proposed bill is clearly negative. By 1992, real GNP falls 3.1 percent relative to the baseline, and the civilian unemployment rate rises by 2.6 percentage points.

The initial slowdown is centered in business fixed investment as the cost of capital rises sharply. In 1988, the first full year in which all of the relevant provisions of the bill are in effect, the composite rental price of investment jumps by 11.8 percent. Fixed investment immediately starts falling, with expenditures on producers' durable equipment dropping faster than nonresidential construction. The reasons are twofold: (1) the initial rise in the cost of equipment is greater than that for structures, and (2) the lags between changes in the rental price of investment and changes in investment are shorter for equipment. By 1992 the stock of business fixed capital is off by 6 percent.

Personal consumption expenditures, while weakening slightly in 1987, actually rise by 0.2 percent in 1988 even though the overall level of GNP is down. The initial relative strength of consumption is attributable to the very sizable individual tax cut in 1988 (relative to current law), the momentum from which spills over to 1989. However, in 1989 an 1990 consumers' tax reduction is largely reversed (see Table 9-2), with the result that, by 1992, consumption is down as well.

Output reaches its low point in 1993, and thereafter begins rising back toward the baseline. By 1995 GNP is off by 2.5 percent with the result that, over the entire period, the *growth rate* in real output is reduced by about only 0.25 percent annually. The turnaround occurs first in investment, as the gradual decline in the real after-tax interest rate that begins in 1989 works to mitigate the initial rise in

Table 9–3. Econometric Estimates for the Tax Reform Act of 1986.ᵃ

	1986	1987	1988	1989	1990	1991	1992	1993	1994	1995
Real gross national product	-0.06	-0.70	-0.68	-1.06	-1.97	-2.70	-3.14	-3.18	-2.91	-2.50
Personal consumption exp.	-0.03	-0.36	0.20	-0.13	-1.17	-2.20	-3.15	-3.98	-4.71	-5.41
Business fixed investment	-0.42	-3.84	-7.17	-10.19	-13.58	-16.05	-17.34	-16.91	-15.20	-12.97
Producers' durables	-0.53	-4.50	-8.41	-11.73	-15.22	-17.52	-18.71	-18.27	-16.77	-15.11
Nonresidential structures	-0.17	-2.29	-4.33	-6.64	-9.79	-12.61	-14.10	-13.71	-11.52	-7.97
Residential investment	-0.03	-1.89	-1.54	-0.24	-1.58	-2.90	-3.07	-2.32	-1.36	-0.59
As shares of gross national product										
Personal consumption exp.	0.03	0.34	0.89	0.94	0.81	0.51	-0.02	-0.82	-1.86	-2.99
Business fixed investment	-0.36	-3.17	-6.54	-9.23	-11.84	-13.72	-14.66	-14.18	-12.66	-10.74
Producers' durables	-0.47	-3.83	-7.79	-10.79	-13.51	-15.23	-16.08	-15.59	-14.27	-12.94
Nonresidential structures	-0.11	-1.61	-3.68	-5.64	-7.98	-10.18	-11.32	-10.88	-8.87	-5.61
Residential investment	0.03	-1.20	-0.87	0.83	0.40	-0.20	0.07	0.89	1.60	1.96
Civilian unemployment rate (% pts)	0.02	0.30	0.55	0.93	1.48	2.08	2.63	3.00	3.15	3.17
Deflator, GNP	0.01	0.01	-0.06	-0.19	-0.39	-0.69	-1.16	-1.84	-2.76	-3.77
Deflator, net private nonfarm output	-0.00	-0.06	-0.20	-0.39	-0.67	-1.06	-1.59	-2.32	-3.25	-4.26
Pre-tax real bond yield (% pts)	0.00	0.02	-0.02	-0.10	-0.24	-0.42	-0.66	-0.89	-1.12	-1.34
After-tax real bond yield (% pts)	-0.00	0.21	0.28	0.14	-0.00	-0.13	-0.29	-0.44	-0.57	-0.70
Real cost of business fixed capital	6.21	15.20	11.81	11.34	10.69	9.74	8.61	7.57	6.56	5.51
Producers' durables	7.18	14.20	12.57	12.36	12.15	11.78	11.35	10.99	10.64	10.21
Nonresidential structures	3.44	17.90	9.77	8.57	6.77	4.25	1.20	-1.66	-4.32	-6.77
Real business fixed capital stocks	-0.02	-0.31	-1.00	-1.94	-3.15	-4.55	-6.00	-7.30	-8.26	-8.82
Producers' durables	-0.03	-0.54	-1.71	-3.23	-5.08	-7.11	-9.08	-10.77	-11.93	-12.61
Nonresidential structures	-0.00	-0.10	-0.36	-0.75	-1.32	-2.09	-2.97	-3.83	-4.52	-4.91
Personal savings rate (% pts)	-0.01	-0.03	0.81	0.22	-0.05	0.05	0.18	0.41	0.81	1.32
Federal deficit ($ billions, SAAR)	2.64	17.80	-42.58	-22.70	-12.34	-16.70	-26.16	-31.32	-35.38	-41.17

ᵃImpacts are measured as percentage differences from baseline unless otherwise noted.

the rental price of investment. Indeed, by 1995 the composite cost of capital is up only 5.5 percent, compared to an 11.8 percent increase in 1988. Note that the initial increase is more persistent in the case of equipment than is true for structures. The reason is that since structures are relatively long-lived assets, the associated present value of depreciation rises sharply as the interest rate declines.

By 1995 the GNP deflator is off 3.8 percent and the pre-tax real interest rate is down 134 basis points, while the after-tax rate has fallen by 70 basis points. Nonetheless, the long-run adjustment is not nearly complete. Lags between declines in the price level and declines in the long-term real interest rate as well as the putty-clay nature of capital all slow the transition. The only way to hasten it is with offsetting monetary stimulus.

While the Tax Reform Act of 1986 is statistically revenue-neutral as implemented, the induced economic slowdown lowers tax revenues dynamically. Through 1995 the cumulative increase in the federal deficit comes to $208 billion.

THE VALUE-ADDED TAX

Overview

Under a VAT, producers pay a tax on value added, calculated as the difference between sales and purchases (excluding labor) net of the tax. If, for example, prior to the imposition of a 10 percent VAT, a firm purchased $100 of materials to produce $300 worth of widgets sold to consumers, its value added is $200. Under the VAT, the widgetmaker's liability would be 10 percent of $200, or $20.

Ceteris paribus the initial effect of the tax is to raise prices by the percentage amount of the tax. To continue the example, our widgetmaker would, after imposition of the VAT, pay $110 for materials and sell the widgets for $330. The latter figure is sufficient to protect his after-tax income. It covers both the $20 VAT paid by the widgetmaker and the "pass through" of the $10 VAT implicit in the price of materials he himself purchased.

The most widely used method of calculating liabilities under the VAT is the "credit method." Under this scheme, a producer is permitted to subtract value-added tax paid on purchases from tax due on its sales. In the example, if the value-added tax rate (t_ν) is 0.10, the widgetmaker faces a tax on sales of $330(t_\nu/(1 + t_\nu)) = \$30$. The offsetting credit on purchases is $110(t_\nu/(1 + t_\nu)) = \$10$, so that his total liability is $30 - $10 = $20.

There are two ways to grant preferential treatment under the VAT, each with different implications for prices. The first, called "zero rating" absolves the producer from the VAT and also grants a credit for value-added tax paid on purchases. In our example, if widgets are zero-rated, the widgetmaker is not obligated to pay a VAT of $20 and also receives a $10 credit for taxes paid on the purchase of materials. Consequently, the price of widgets need not rise to protect the producer's after-tax income.

The second, called "exempting," only absolves the producer from the VAT. In our example, if widgets are exempted, the widgetmaker is not obligated to pay a VAT of $20, but neither does he receive a credit for taxes paid on the purchase of materials. To protect his after-tax income, the widgetmaker must sell the widgets for $310. The increase in price is, in percentage terms, equal to the tax rate times the proportion of the value of widgets added in the *nonexempt* stages of the production process.

Special Considerations

While the value-added tax seems simple enough in principle, serious consideration of the impacts of a VAT raises many important questions regarding its design and implementation. The most of important of these from the standpoint of a macroeconomic analysis are discussed briefly below. In implementing solutions to the economic and political problems posed by the VAT, we have relied on recommendations made in 1984 by the U.S. Department of Treasury in Volume 3 of *Tax Reform for Fairness, Simplicity, and Economic Growth.*

Consumption-Based VAT. The most widely implemented VAT is "consumption based," allowing the full purchase price of capital assets to be deducted from sales in calulating a firm's "value added." The aggregate tax base corresponds to consumption expenditures, including those by government, unless certain purchases are exempted or zero-rated. The consumption-based VAT is generally favored over other variants because it does not affect *directly* either a producer's desired capital/labor ratio or a household's desired rate of saving. For these reasons, it is the only one considered here.

A general consumption-based VAT leaves relative prices unaltered and so is economically neutral. However, to the extent that some goods are zero-rated or exempted, the value-added tax will alter relative prices and thereby encourage a shift of resources toward the favored items.

Border Adjustments and Net Exports. The Treasury recommends that border adjustments to the VAT be made according to the "destination principle." That is, the tax on a traded good should be levied where that good is consumed rather than where it is produced. This means that sales of exports to foreign purchasers would be zero-rated, while purchases of imports would be subject to the full VAT. Prices of exports initially would remain unchanged, while prices of imports would rise by the percentage amount of the tax. Unless off-setting adjustments were made by foreign governments, the effect would be to encourage our net exports for a given exchange rate.

The Treatment of Government.   Federal agencies bear the burden of the VAT applied to their purchases of goods and services (excluding labor). This does not affect the deficit because the Treasury also collects the corresponding revenues. It does mean that, for a given real level of federal purchases, gross proceeds from the VAT will exceed net proceeds.

However, unless state and local governments are allowed to escape its burden, the VAT involves a transfer of resources to the federal government that almost certainly would raise serious political and perhaps constitutional concerns. For this reason, sales of goods and services to state and local governments (other than labor) likely would be zero-rated, and the price of goods purchased by state and local governments would not rise initially.

Defining the Tax Base.   Perhaps the thorniest issue in defining the appropriate base for the VAT is the treatment of expenditures on housing. In principle, there is no compelling reason why current homeowners should not pay a VAT on their imputed rent. In practice, however, this probably would prove unworkable on three counts. First, there is the difficulty of properly and equitably imputing each homeowner's rent. Second, there would be resistance to including in the tax base imputed consumption not arising directly from a monetary transaction. And third, since they would be treated as firms producing housing services sold to themselves, all home-owners would have to register for the VAT, dramatically increasing its administrative costs.

For all these reasons, the imputed consumption of housing services likely would be exempted from the VAT. Then, to reduce distortion of the tenure-choice decision, and to avoid what otherwise would be viewed by current renters as an injustice, it also would be necessary to exempt rental housing, thereby exempting *all* of consumers' rent and reducing the tax base by a corresponding amount. Some tax on housing would be collected by including in the tax base the value of construction on new housing units as well as the value of additions and alterations of existing units, none of which is included in consumption expenditures as defined in the National Income and Product Accounts. While this solution is imperfect—in part because it generates a one-time transfer of wealth to owners of existing buildings—it is the one suggested by the Treasury Department. Note that because existing housing is exempted (as opposed to zero-rated), initially rents would rise to reflect the VAT paid on purchases for repair and maintenance.

The Treasury Department also recommended that, due to the difficulty or inadvisability of taxing them, medical care, insurance, education, religious, and welfare activities, foreign travel and local transportation be excluded partially or entirely from the tax base. In total, these exclusions would remove roughly 0.33 percent of expenditures on consumer services (as measured in the National Income and Product Accounts) from the tax base, but add back roughly 90 percent of residential investment. In 1986 the corresponding tax base measures $2,473 billion, so that a VAT of 1 percent would raise a net amount of $25 billion.

General Equilibrium Considerations. Statements that a VAT does not affect resource allocation or will raise prices are usually made in the context of partial equilibrium. Thus, for given pre-tax wages and prices, imposition of a VAT does not alter a producer's desired capital/output ratio; for a given pre-tax interest rate, the VAT does not alter a household's saving rate; and, for a given price level net of the VAT, imposition of the tax will tend to raise prices gross of the tax. In general equilibrium, however, imposition of a VAT will alter wages, prices, and interest rates. The general effects are less recognized than the partial effects, even though, from a perspective of macroeconomic policy, the former are the principal concern.

CASE 2: THE "NONACCOMMODATED" VAT

Heuristic Results

In this experiment, a consumption-based VAT of 1 percent is imposed, the proceeds of the rax (roughly $40 billion a year in static terms) used to reduce the federal deficit, and the Federal Reserve leaves the nominal money supply unchanged. The results are presented in Table 9–4.

In the near term, defined as a period during which the price level *net of the tax* does not change, the impact of the VAT is to raise the price *including the tax* by the percentage amount of the tax. This has two distinct impacts. First, the higher purchase price of goods and

Table 9-4. Heuristic Estimates for a 1 Percent VAT, Nonaccommodated.[a]

	Impact	Short Run	Long Run
Gross output	-2.7	-2.4	2.5
Pre-tax yield	0.0	-0.1	-2.3
After-tax yield	0.0	-0.0	-1.6
Prices including VAT	1.0	1.0	-4.0
Prices excluding VAT	0.0	0.0	-5.0
Real money stock	-1.0	-1.0	4.0
Cost of capital	0.0	-0.4	-12.7
Pre-tax wage	0.0	0.0	2.2
After-tax wage	-1.0	-1.0	1.2
Capital stock	0.0	2.0	15.2
Employment	0.0	-2.4	1.2

[a] Impacts are measured as percentage changes except for yields, which are measured in percentage points.

services reduces the real money stock. Second, higher prices initially reduce the level of consumers' disposable income associated with a given level of real GNP. Both these forces push output unambiguously lower, while the interest rate may rise or fall. For the parameter values assumed, the short-term decline in output is 2.4 percent, and the interest rate does decline by a slight 10 basis points.

Whether output rises or falls in the long run depends on the value assumed for the elasticity of labor supply with respect to the real wage. For our estimate of 0.18, the long-run effect of the VAT is to raise output by 2.5 percent. True, labor supply is adversely affected, but the 230 basis point drop in the interest rate encourages enough additional capital ultimately to allow an increase in gross output. Furthermore, even prices including the VAT fall eventually.

The length of the transition from short-run to long-run equilibrium is governed by the rate at which prices excluding the VAT decline after the tax is implemented. The equilibrating process could require considerable time if wage earners, attempting to recoup the initial loss of real income, start a wage-price spiral that leads initially to *increases* in the net price level that forestall the requisite long-run reduction in the real money supply.

Note that in the long run the VAT is neutral with respect to neither the capital/labor ratio nor the consumption/saving decision. The general decline in interest rates (and hence the cost of capital) raises the capital stock by 15.2 percent while the VAT discourages labor supply. The net result is to raise the capital/labor ratio by 15 percent. While the economy-wide ratio of gross saving to output rises, the decline in the interest rate encourages a reduction in the personal saving rate.

Econometric Results

The impacts of the value-added are assessed relative to a baseline that assumes implementation of the Tax Reform Act of 1986. This new baseline was constructed to assure that it is qualitatively similar to the one based on the previous law, discussed earlier, real GNP grows at about 3 percent annually, inflation remains moderate, the long-term interest and the unemployment rate decline gradually, and the federal deficit narrows.

To evaluate the value-added tax econometrically, we begin with a simple experiment in which a VAT is phased in over a period of three years assuming no monetary response, with the goal of raising $40 billion of net revenues *in static terms*. As the economy grows thereafter, so also do the revenues from the VAT, reaching $59 billion in 1995. The cumulative static reduction in the deficit comes to $376 billion.

The implementation of this experiment in WUMM is more complicated than in the heuristic model, principally because in WUMM the base for the VAT is defined as in the section titled "The Value-Added Tax." This is accomplished by zero rating state and local purchases of goods and services (other than labor), exempting roughly 34 percent of consumer services, and assuming that nominal federal purchases of goods and services (other than labor) rise by the percentage amount of the tax. For the defined tax base, a VAT rate of 1.35 percent by 1989 is required. The results of this experiment are summarized relative to the baseline in Table 9-5.

The first point to make is that the nonaccommodated VAT reduces output over the entire period. In 1995 the level of real GNP is off by 2.3 percent, so that the rate of growth in GNP is reduced 0.25 percent annually over the period. By 1995 the unemployment rate is up 2.2 points.

Output is rising relative to the baseline after 1993 but, as was true in the analysis of the Tax Reform Act of 1986, the transition period to the long run evidently is quite lengthy. This fact obfuscates any equilibrium switch from consumption to investment induced by the VAT, since here movements in business fixed investment are dominated by short-run income-induced declines in net investment. However, while the investment reaches a low of –6.35 percent in 1993, consumption continues declining quite rapidly. As a result, from 1990 onward the ratio of investment to consumption is climbing steadily and the personal saving rate also is on the rise.

How prices would behave is one of the most controversial issues surrounding the VAT. The heuristic model suggested that, in the near

Table 9-5.   Econometric Estimates for a 1 Percent VAT, Nonaccommodated.[a]

	1986	1987	1988	1989	1990	1991	1992	1993	1994	1995
Real gross national product	-0.00	-0.17	-0.47	-0.98	-1.50	-1.96	-2.29	-2.46	-2.45	-2.27
Personal consumption exp.	-0.00	-0.18	-0.45	-0.86	-1.29	-1.80	-2.37	-2.98	-3.60	-4.20
Business fixed investment	-0.00	-0.27	-0.93	-2.13	-3.64	-5.04	-5.98	-6.35	-6.11	-5.24
Producers' durables	-0.00	-0.29	-0.99	-2.25	-3.79	-5.15	-6.02	-6.36	-6.17	-5.48
Nonresidential structures	-0.00	-0.22	-0.77	-1.86	-3.30	-4.79	-5.88	-6.31	-5.95	-4.69
Residential investment	-0.00	-0.61	-1.70	-3.41	-5.02	-5.96	-6.00	-5.89	-5.46	-4.60
As shares of gross national product										
Personal consumption exp.	-0.00	-0.01	0.02	0.12	0.22	0.17	-0.08	-0.53	-1.17	-1.98
Business fixed investment	-0.00	-0.11	-0.46	-1.17	-2.18	-3.14	-3.78	-3.98	-3.74	-3.04
Producers' durables	-0.00	-0.13	-0.52	-1.29	-2.33	-3.24	-3.82	-4.00	-3.81	-3.29
Nonresidential structures	0.00	-0.06	-0.30	-0.89	-1.83	-2.88	-3.68	-3.94	-3.58	-2.48
Residential investment	-0.00	-0.44	-1.23	-2.46	-3.57	-4.07	-3.80	-3.51	-3.08	-2.38
Civilian unemployment rate (% pts)	0.00	0.07	0.19	0.44	0.76	1.16	1.54	1.87	2.11	2.24
Deflator, GNP	0.00	0.35	0.84	1.40	1.64	1.69	1.55	1.16	0.53	-0.23
Deflator, net private nonfarm output	0.00	0.05	0.23	0.47	0.65	0.65	0.45	0.02	-0.64	-1.43
Pre-tax real bond yield (% pts)	-0.00	0.06	0.15	0.28	0.35	0.38	0.32	0.19	0.03	-0.16
After-tax real bond yield (% pts)	-0.00	0.05	0.11	0.20	0.25	0.27	0.23	0.15	0.06	-0.06
Real cost of business fixed capital	-0.02	0.35	0.80	1.46	1.88	2.10	1.91	1.43	0.77	-0.02
Producers' durables	-0.01	0.30	0.70	1.33	1.83	2.25	2.38	2.32	2.11	1.78
Nonresidential structures	-0.04	0.47	1.05	1.83	2.02	1.70	0.62	-1.02	-2.85	-4.81
Real business fixed capital stocks	-0.00	-0.02	-0.09	-0.28	-0.62	-1.09	-1.64	-2.21	-2.69	-3.03
Producers' durables	-0.00	-0.03	-0.15	-0.42	-0.91	-1.56	-2.30	-3.00	-3.59	-3.98
Nonresidential structures	-0.00	-0.01	-0.05	-0.15	-0.34	-0.63	-1.00	-1.40	-1.78	-2.06
Personal savings rate (% pts)	0.00	-0.15	-0.30	-0.42	-0.33	-0.22	-0.07	0.16	0.50	0.90
Federal deficit ($ billions, SAAR)	-0.03	8.77	17.94	24.95	19.36	13.89	10.49	7.69	5.88	6.39

[a] Impacts are measured as percentage differences from baseline unless otherwise noted.

term, the price level will rise following implementation of the tax, but that in the long run it would fall unless accommodated by additional monetary growth. To shed light on these issue, two price indexes have been included in the Table 9–5. The first is the GNP deflator, which is gross of the VAT. The second is the implicit deflator for private nonfarm output *net* of indirect business and value-added taxes. The latter measures the price per unit of output received by firms.

The econometric results verify that the initial effect of the VAT is to raise the gross price level. By 1991 the GNP deflator is up 1.7 percent—roughly 1.2 percent for the VAT, and the remaining 0.5 percent because the initial rise in prices triggers a small wage-price spiral. This induced rise in prices is reflected in a 0.65 percent increase in the net price level over the same period. However, rising unemployment eventually reverses the course of prices so that, by 1995, the net price level is down 1.4 percent, and even the GNP deflator, which includes the VAT, has fallen. These results suggest that while the VAT will involve higher prices in the near term, the likelihood of a prolonged bout of inflation is nil.

Since this experiment assumes no monetary accommodation of the VAT, the initial rise in prices leads to a reduction in the real money stock and a concomitant increase in real interest rates. By 1991 the real bond yield has risen nearly 40 basis points, contributing indirectly to the tax's squeeze on aggregate demand by raising the cost of business fixed capital. Note, though, that the magnitude of fluctuations in rental prices are nothing like those under the Tax Reform Act of 1986, precisely because the value-added tax does not directly influence the after-tax relative price of capital.

Finally, while the static cumulative reduction in the deficit attributable to the VAT is $376 billion through 1995, considerable revenues are lost to the induced economic slowdown. As a result, the VAT raises only an additional $114 over the period.

CASE 3: AN "ACCOMMODATED" VAT

Heuristic Results

It is unlikely that the Federal Reserve would stand idle if implementation of the VAT quickly produced an economic slowdown. While the monetary authorities could prevent any near-term reduction in output, a more interesting experiment is one in which the Federal Reserve raises the nominal money supply sufficiently to prevent, in static terms, a decline in the real money supply. Given the dichotomy between money and real activity embedded in the model,

Table 9-6. Heuristic Estimates for a 1 Percent VAT, Monetarily Accommodated.[a]

	Impact	*Short Run*	*Long Run*
Gross output	-2.7	-0.9	2.5
Pre-tax yield	0.0	-0.3	-2.3
After-tax yield	0.0	-0.2	-1.6
Prices including VAT	1.0	1.0	-3.0
Prices excluding VAT	0.0	0.0	-4.0
Real money stock	0.0	0.0	4.0
Cost of capital	0.0	-1.9	-12.7
Pre-tax wage	0.0	0.0	2.2
After-tax wage	-1.0	-1.0	1.2
Capital stock	0.0	2.0	15.2
Employment	0.0	-0.9	0.2

[a] Impacts are measured as percentage changes except for yields, which are measured in percentage points.

monetary "accommodation" does not alter the long-run real implications of imposing the VAT. However, it mitigates the near-term reduction in output and allows an immediate and unambiguous decline in the interest rate. Results from the heuristic model (Table 9-6) suggest that monetary accommodation cuts by more than half the short-run loss in output.

Econometric Results

To investigate the impact of an accommodated VAT, the results of the nonaccommodated case were amended to include a 1.35 percent increase in the nominal money supply phased in over three years coincidentally with the implementation of the value-added tax. This "static" accommodation eliminates the reduction in the real money supply attributable *directly* to the tax, but does not counter the decline that occurs because the VAT induces additional increases in prices and wages.

The heuristic results suggested that, if accommodated, the VAT would result in a smaller short-run loss in output than in the nonaccommodated case, but that the price level would be higher. The econometric results, presented in Table 9-7, support these conclusions. By 1995 real GNP is down 1.36 percent in the accommodated case, compared to 2.3 percent in the nonaccommodated experiment. Without monetary accommodation, the GNP deflator fell slightly by 1995. Here, it is up by 1.42 percent. If one considers only the period 1987-1992, the average annual rate of increase in the GNP deflator is raised nearly 0.5 percent per year.

Table 9-7. Econometric Estimates for a 1 Percent VAT, Monetarily Accommodated.[a]

	1986	1987	1988	1989	1990	1991	1992	1993	1994	1995
Real gross national product	-0.00	-0.03	-0.09	-0.22	-0.43	-0.77	-1.10	-1.31	-1.40	-1.36
Personal consumption exp.	-0.00	-0.09	-0.16	-0.22	-0.25	-0.45	-0.74	-1.07	-1.43	-1.81
Business fixed investment	-0.00	-0.02	-0.01	-0.10	-0.41	-1.11	-1.96	-2.64	-2.95	-2.83
Producers' durables	-0.00	-0.02	-0.01	-0.11	-0.44	-1.19	-2.09	-2.79	-3.11	-3.01
Nonresidential structures	-0.00	-0.01	-0.01	-0.08	-0.32	-0.91	-1.66	-2.27	-2.57	-2.41
Residential investment	-0.00	0.01	0.08	-0.12	-0.73	-1.91	-2.76	-3.14	-3.10	-2.66
As shares of gross national product										
Personal consumption exp.	-0.00	-0.06	-0.07	-0.00	0.18	0.32	0.36	0.24	-0.03	-0.46
Business fixed investment	-0.00	0.01	0.07	0.12	0.02	-0.34	-0.88	-1.34	-1.58	-1.49
Producers' durables	-0.00	0.01	0.07	0.11	-0.01	-0.42	-1.01	-1.50	-1.74	-1.67
Nonresidential structures	0.00	0.02	0.08	0.14	0.11	-0.14	-0.57	-0.97	-1.18	-1.07
Residential investment	-0.00	0.03	0.16	0.10	-0.31	-1.15	-1.69	-1.85	-1.73	-1.32
Civilian unemployment rate (% pts)	0.00	0.02	0.04	0.11	0.21	0.43	0.68	0.93	1.13	1.27
Deflator, GNP	0.00	0.35	0.87	1.53	1.93	2.19	2.28	2.18	1.87	1.42
Deflator, net private nonfarm output	0.00	0.07	0.30	0.66	1.03	1.26	1.32	1.18	0.84	0.37
Pre-tax real bond yield (% pts)	-0.00	-0.02	-0.05	-0.06	-0.01	0.08	0.10	0.08	0.02	-0.08
After-tax real bond yield (% pts)	-0.00	-0.02	-0.05	-0.07	-0.04	0.02	0.03	0.02	-0.01	-0.05
Real cost of business fixed capital	-0.02	-0.14	-0.30	-0.40	-0.15	0.28	0.50	0.47	0.24	-0.10
Producers' durables	-0.01	-0.11	-0.24	-0.31	-0.04	0.39	0.71	0.87	0.87	0.81
Nonresidential structures	-0.04	-0.21	-0.45	-0.67	-0.45	-0.02	-0.06	-0.63	-1.47	-2.53
Real business fixed capital stocks	-0.00	-0.00	-0.00	-0.01	-0.04	-0.14	-0.32	-0.58	-0.87	-1.12
Producers' durables	-0.00	-0.00	-0.00	-0.01	-0.06	-0.21	-0.48	-0.85	-1.24	-1.57
Nonresidential structures	-0.00	-0.00	-0.00	-0.00	-0.02	-0.07	-0.17	-0.32	-0.49	-0.65
Personal savings rate (% pts)	0.00	-0.23	-0.51	-0.88	-1.04	-1.13	-1.16	-1.14	-1.07	-0.94
Federal deficit ($ billions, SAAR)	-0.03	11.65	26.07	42.79	46.59	47.10	47.10	47.64	49.05	52.10

[a] Impacts are measured as percentage differences from baseline unless otherwise noted.

Table 9-8. Heuristic Estimates for Higher Taxes on Capital.[a]

	Impact	*Short Run*	*Long Run*
Gross output	-5.9	-2.0	1.4
Pre-tax yield	0.0	-0.7	-2.0
After-tax yield	0.0	-0.5	-1.4
Prices including VAT	0.0	0.0	-3.1
Prices excluding VAT	0.0	0.0	-3.1
Real money stock	0.0	0.0	3.1
Cost of capital	4.5	0.4	-6.5
Pre-tax wage	0.0	0.0	1.1
After-tax wage	0.0	0.0	1.1
Capital stock	0.0	-2.4	7.9
Employment	0.0	-2.0	1.4

[a] Impacts are measured as percentage changes except for yields, which are measured in percentage points.

Also as expected, real interest rates are lower than in the non-accommodated case, as are the rental prices of investment and hence the capital stock. As the overall economy is stronger, the federal deficit is cumulatively reduced by $368 billion through 1995, compared to only $114 when the VAT is not accommodated monetarily.

CASE 4: RAISING CORPORATE TAXES INSTEAD

Heuristic Results

For an equivalent static increase in revenues, how do the economic impacts of the VAT compare to those associated with higher corporate taxes, particularly those that bear on new capital? To answer this question, an experiment was performed in which corporate income taxes were raised and depreciation lives lengthened sufficiently to raise the same long-run revenue as the 1 percent VAT. The heuristic results are presented in Table 9-8.

In the short run, output declines by 2.3 percent, considerably more than the 0.9 percent drop in the case of the accommodated VAT (compare to Table 9-6). The reason is that an increase in the average income tax rate is more onerous in its near-term effects than an equivalent increase in the VAT. Moreover, the considered changes in corporate taxes initially raise the marginal cost of capital and so foster an additional decline in net investment that does not occur under the VAT. This is a good example of how introduction of a value-added tax, by initially not altering the allocation of resources, can prove less damaging than tampering with the income tax—even in a macroeconomic sense.

In the long run, output rises by 1.9 percent, somewhat less than the 2.5 percent long-run rise under the accommodated VAT. This

Table 9-9. Econometric Estimates for Higher Taxes on Capital.[a]

	1986	1987	1988	1989	1990	1991	1992	1993	1994	1995
Real gross national product	-0.00	-0.11	-0.38	-0.74	-1.05	-1.25	-1.36	-1.39	-1.28	-1.07
Personal consumption exp.	-0.00	-0.02	-0.12	-0.33	-0.58	-0.86	-1.15	-1.44	-1.68	-1.87
Business fixed investment	-0.00	-0.91	-2.76	-4.81	-6.51	-7.37	-7.58	-7.38	-6.71	-5.77
Producers' durables	-0.00	-1.23	-3.62	-6.14	-8.10	-8.96	-9.11	-8.91	-8.30	-7.52
Nonresidential structures	-0.00	-0.17	-0.78	-1.77	-2.84	-3.63	-3.97	-3.77	-2.99	-1.66
Residential investment	-0.00	-0.02	-0.29	-0.88	-1.20	-1.15	-1.12	-1.06	-0.64	-0.04
As shares of gross national product										
Personal consumption exp.	-0.00	0.09	0.26	0.41	0.47	0.39	0.21	-0.05	-0.41	-0.81
Business fixed investment	-0.00	-0.80	-2.39	-4.10	-5.52	-6.20	-6.31	-6.07	-5.50	-4.75
Producers' durables	-0.00	-1.12	-3.26	-5.44	-7.12	-7.81	-7.86	-7.63	-7.11	-6.52
Nonresidential structures	0.00	-0.06	-0.40	-1.04	-1.81	-2.42	-2.64	-2.41	-1.73	-0.60
Residential investment	-0.00	0.09	0.09	-0.14	-0.15	0.10	0.25	0.34	0.64	1.04
Civilian unemployment rate (% pts)	0.00	0.03	0.09	0.24	0.41	0.59	0.74	0.84	0.85	0.78
Deflator, GNP	0.00	0.01	0.04	0.07	0.06	-0.00	-0.13	-0.35	-0.67	-1.03
Deflator, net private nonfarm output	0.00	-0.01	-0.01	-0.03	-0.07	-0.16	-0.31	-0.54	-0.86	-1.21
Pre-tax real bond yield (% pts)	-0.00	-0.01	0.00	-0.02	-0.09	-0.16	-0.23	-0.32	-0.42	-0.52
After-tax real bond yield (% pts)	-0.00	-0.01	0.00	-0.01	-0.07	-0.12	-0.17	-0.23	-0.29	-0.36
Real cost of business fixed capital	-0.02	7.43	6.26	5.95	5.54	5.16	4.80	4.39	3.96	3.45
Producers' durables	-0.01	9.95	7.90	7.59	7.30	7.10	6.92	6.74	6.53	6.23
Nonresidential structures	-0.04	0.81	1.78	1.46	0.69	-0.16	-1.02	-2.07	-2.98	-3.92
Real business fixed capital stocks	-0.00	-0.06	-0.30	-0.74	-1.34	-2.00	-2.63	-3.17	-3.57	-3.80
Producers' durables	-0.00	-0.11	-0.57	-1.38	-2.43	-3.52	-4.49	-5.30	-5.87	-6.22
Nonresidential structures	-0.00	-0.01	-0.04	-0.14	-0.31	-0.54	-0.79	-1.03	-1.22	-1.29
Personal savings rate (% pts)	0.00	-0.01	-0.04	-0.08	-0.11	-0.13	-0.12	-0.06	0.05	0.19
Federal deficit ($ billions, SAAR)	-0.03	0.66	12.37	17.88	14.89	14.71	25.79	25.98	31.30	38.85

[a] Impacts are measured as percentage differences from baseline unless otherwise noted.

difference is explained by the fact that, while the VAT discourages labor supply in the long run, it is also the case that higher corporate taxes discourage capital formation. For the assumed values of the elasticity of labor supply with respect to the after-tax wage and the elasticity of the substitution between capital and labor, the former effect is larger than the latter.

Econometric Results

To implement a similar experiment using WUMM, we assume that Congress decides to (1) keep the 150 percent declining balance depreciation schedule (instead of the proposed 200 percent) for equipment, (2) double the average recovery period for equipment, and (3) lower the marginal corporate tax rate to only 35 percent instead of 33 percent. These initiatives raise approximately the same static revenues through 1995 as the phased-in VAT considered above.

The heuristic results suggested that raising revenue by taxing new capital retards the economy more in the near term than would an equivalent increase in value-added taxes. This contention is born out by the econometric estimates presented in Table 9-9. Through 1991 the higher taxes on capital work to reduce the level GNP by 1.25 percent, or a 0.25 point reduction in the annual rate of economic growth over that period. For the accommodated VAT, the corresponding figures are 0.77 percent and 0.15 percent. The slowdown is concentrated on expenditures on producers' durable equipment, which is off by 9 percent in 1991. This is not surprising, since the effect of the new initiatives is to raise the cost of equipment by nearly 8 percent in 1988 (relative to the Tax Reform Act baseline).

By 1995, however, the higher taxes on capital would reduce GNP by less than the accommodated VAT. This should not be interpreted as a refutation of the long-run heuristic results, but rather as a consequence of differences in the dynamic response of the economy to tax initiatives that are fundamentally different in nature. In particular, under the accommodated VAT there is enough induced inflation so that, by 1995, the real bond rate is nearly 50 basis points higher than in the case of additional tax on capital. Given the lags between interest rates and aggregate demand embedded in WUMM, the result in the latter experiment is to spur output in the mid-1990s.

CASE 5: BUYING INVESTMENT INCENTIVES WITH THE VAT

If near-term projections based on macroeconometric models prove accurate, the economy will decelerate under the Tax Reform Act of

1986 with the slowdown concentrated in investment spending. In that event, Congress may well consider restoring some of the subsidies for investment now scheduled for repeal or curtailment. However, given large prospective federal deficits, it likely could do so only if an offsetting amount of revenues were raised from an alternative source. One possibility would be to pay for the reinstatement of investment incentives by imposing a consumption-based VAT.

Heuristic Results

To investigate this possibility, we consider a scenario in which Congress allows equipment to be depreciated by the 250 percent declining balance schedule over five years and without the half-year convention. In addition, it is assumed that depreciation allowances are indexed to the price level. The effect of these changes is roughly to halve the "impact" increase in the cost of capital that would otherwise occur under the Tax Reform Act of 1986. The revenue lost to these initiatives lowers the average income tax rate. To pay for the investment incentives, a value-added tax of 0.47 percent was imposed and "accommodated" with an equivalent percentage increase in the nominal money supply. Results of the experiment are shown in Table 9–10.

The heuristic model suggests that, in the near-term, buying investment incentives with an accommodated VAT raises output by a little more than 1 percent. The reason is that the negative effect of introducing the VAT is exactly offset by the positive effect of reducing the average income tax rate, allowing the reduction in the marginal rate of taxation on capital to boost output by encouraging net investment. Even in the long run, output would rise, as the addi-

Table 9–10. Heuristic Estimates for Buying Investment Incentives with an Accommodated VAT.[a]

	Impact	*Short Run*	*Long Run*
Gross output	3.0	1.0	1.1
Pre-tax yield	0.0	0.4	0.2
After-tax yield	0.0	0.3	0.2
Prices including VAT	0.5	0.5	-0.3
Prices excluding VAT	0.0	0.0	-0.8
Real money stock	0.0	0.0	0.8
Cost of capital	-4.5	-2.4	-5.8
Pre-tax wage	0.0	0.0	1.0
After-tax wage	0.0	0.0	0.6
Capital stock	0.0	3.4	6.9
Employment	0.0	1.0	0.1

[a] Impacts are measured as percentage changes except for yields, which are measured in percentage points.

Table 9–11. Econometric Estimates for Buying Investment Incentives with an Accommodated VAT.[a]

	1986	1987	1988	1989	1990	1991	1992	1993	1994	1995
Real gross national product	-0.00	0.12	0.36	0.55	0.66	0.69	0.61	0.50	0.32	0.16
Personal consumption exp.	-0.00	0.01	0.09	0.19	0.29	0.41	0.49	0.54	0.53	0.49
Business fixed investment	-0.00	0.99	2.72	4.33	5.43	5.78	5.58	5.12	4.42	3.75
Producers' durables	-0.00	1.18	3.19	4.94	5.99	6.14	5.77	5.26	4.57	4.05
Nonresidential structures	-0.00	0.53	1.65	2.94	4.13	4.93	5.13	4.81	4.06	3.04
Residential investment	-0.00	0.13	0.27	0.28	0.01	-0.41	-0.94	-1.46	-1.98	-2.31
As shares of gross national product										
Personal consumption exp.	-0.00	-0.11	-0.27	-0.37	-0.37	-0.28	-0.12	0.04	0.21	0.33
Business fixed investment	-0.00	0.87	2.36	3.76	4.73	5.06	4.94	4.60	4.09	3.58
Producers' durables	-0.00	1.06	2.83	4.36	5.29	5.42	5.12	4.73	4.24	3.88
Nonresidential structures	0.00	0.41	1.29	2.38	3.45	4.22	4.49	4.29	3.73	2.88
Residential investment	-0.00	0.01	-0.08	-0.28	-0.65	-1.09	-1.55	-1.95	-2.29	-2.46
Civilian unemployment rate (% pts)	0.00	-0.03	-0.12	-0.20	-0.30	-0.37	-0.38	-0.34	-0.24	-0.12
Deflator, GNP	0.00	0.03	0.11	0.22	0.40	0.58	0.79	1.00	1.20	1.32
Deflator, net private nonfarm output	0.00	0.01	0.06	0.16	0.29	0.44	0.62	0.81	0.97	1.07
Pre-tax real bond yield (% pts)	-0.00	0.01	0.03	0.07	0.13	0.23	0.31	0.36	0.42	0.47
After-tax real bond yield (% pts)	-0.00	0.01	0.02	0.05	0.09	0.16	0.21	0.25	0.29	0.32
Real cost of business fixed capital	-0.02	-7.22	-4.70	-4.48	-4.18	-3.71	-3.48	-3.58	-3.50	-3.22
Producers' durables	-0.01	-7.20	-4.73	-4.51	-4.29	-4.01	-3.89	-3.99	-3.98	-3.76
Nonresidential structures	-0.04	-7.27	-4.62	-4.40	-3.86	-2.87	-2.37	-2.46	-2.18	-1.78
Real business fixed capital stocks	-0.00	0.06	0.30	0.72	1.22	1.74	2.20	2.55	2.78	2.89
Producers' durables	-0.00	0.11	0.52	1.19	1.96	2.68	3.25	3.65	3.85	3.92
Nonresidential structures	-0.00	0.02	0.11	0.28	0.53	0.84	1.16	1.46	1.69	1.83
Personal savings rate (% pts)	0.00	0.00	-0.01	-0.00	-0.01	0.00	-0.00	-0.03	-0.06	-0.06
Federal deficit ($ billions, SAAR)	-0.03	1.21	3.78	5.83	6.89	4.84	2.23	-0.39	-3.82	-7.76

[a] Impacts are measured as percentage differences from baseline unless otherwise noted.

tional capital more than offsets the negative impact on aggregate supply of the reduction in the supply of labor attributable to the VAT.

Econometric Evidence

The design of this final experiment is more involved than the
others. First, we introduced into WUMM the proposed changes in
depreciation, running a simulation in which "residual feedback" was
used to force the economy along the same path as in the baseline.
From this was estimated the static revenue loss attributable to the
investment incentives. These figures in turn were used to compute a
path for the VAT rate that recouped statically an equivalent amount
of revenue on a yearly basis. The calculations show that by 1995
the VAT would have to be raised only to 0.4 percent to maintain
revenue neutrality. Finally, to accommodate the VAT, the rate of
growth of in the money supply was upped by roughly 0.03 percentage points per year, and the simulation including all these changes
executed.

The results, presented in Table 9–11, reveal that buying some
additional investment incentives with the VAT would raise output
relative to the Tax Reform Act of 1986—as suggested by the heuristic model. By 1991 the level of real GNP is up nearly 0.7 percent.
Consumption and residential investment as shares of total output
have fallen slightly, while the share of business fixed investment in
GNP is up dramatically. The price level is higher as is the real interest
rate.

After 1991 output begins declining relative to the baseline, again
due to the dynamics implied by the gradual rise in real interest rates.
Nonetheless, the cumulative gain in GNP over the entire period is
$168 billion, roughly 4.6 percent of GNP in 1986, or the equivalent
of one strong year of economic growth. Furthermore, in 1995 the
stock of capital has risen 2.5 percent relative to labor, implying an
increase of labor productivity (and hence real wages) of about 0.7
percent. The gross price level is 1.32 percent higher in 1995, implying that the average annual inflation rate over the period is 0.15 percentage points higher. The combination of lower corporate taxes and
a VAT leaves the cumulative federal deficit little changed.

CONCLUDING COMMENTS

What conclusions can be drawn from such a wide-ranging assortment
of theoretical propositions and empirical results? Most economists
would not take serious issue with the long-run structure of the theoretical model presented in the appendixes. They probably would also

find acceptable its short-run structure and agree that the entire system is useful for analyzing the comparative statics of tax reform.

However, in the "real world," tax policy must also be considered in a dynamic context. In this regard, the most pressing question is how quickly does the macroeconomy move from one long-run equilibrium to another following the fiscal shocks likely to result from the tax initiatives considered here. All econometric results generated with the Washington University Macroeconomic Model presume that the adjustment is slow and that the short-run effects from our heuristic model should not be ignored by policymakers. This leads us to conclude, for example, that, taken by itself, the Tax Reform Act of 1986 will have a detrimental impact on economic performance for many years. This is not to say that the Act should *not* have been passed. Indeed, the heuristic results suggest that its long-run effects are positive. It does mean, however, that the monetary authorities must be prepared to hasten the long-run adjustment by providing additional monetary stimulus.

Unfortunately, theory tells us little about macrodynamics. Instead, dynamic time paths typically are generated by simulating models that incorporate empirical estimates of the lags between changes in policy and changes in the key variables of the model in question. The most important of these, and probably the most difficult to assess accurately is how quickly the nominal price level varies following a change in policy. In the structural econometric models with which we are familiar, this key lag is uniformly long.

Of course, these models are subject to the "Lucas critique"; that is, previously estimated empirical relationships quickly may be rendered useless by sharp, unanticipated shifts in policy. This caveat does not affect conclusions drawn from the heuristic model, which are based on firms' technological constraints (the production function) and households' preferences (or utility function), neither of which change quickly. The same is not necessarily true for the Phillips curve, which is instrumental in governing the behavior of prices during the transition from the short run to the long run and is based on empirical estimates of "inflation expectations."

To summarize the other key finding of this chapter:

1. The Tax Reform Act of 1986 threatens to slow the economy in the near term. While the Act is revenue-neutral for 1987–91, and so does not involve any direct "income" effects, it sharply raises the cost of capital. Unless offset by additional monetary stimulus, this will induce a decline in net investment and temporarily slow economic growth.

2. In the long run, the Tax Reform Act may or may not carry substantial benefits. The precise assessment depends crucially upon how responsive labor supply is to changes in the after-tax wage. Unfortunately, there is little consensus on the value of this key parameter. If the elasticity of labor supply is moderately positive (and we estimate that it is), the tax code would raise output in the long run.

3. By itself, introduction of a consumption-based value-added tax would raise prices and slow the economy in the near term.

4. The short-run adverse consequences of the VAT on the real economy are approximately cut in half if the nominal money supply is raised by the percentage amount of the VAT. Near-term inflation, however, is aggravated.

5. In the long run, the VAT leads to *lower, not higher*, prices net of the tax even if the nominal supply is raised by the percentage amount of the tax. It is even possible that prices including the VAT may fall.

6. The value-added tax does not *directly* influence either the cost of capital or the after-tax rate of return to savers. In general equilibrium, however, it can have important impacts on the allocation of resources by *indirectly* changing the pre-tax interest rate. As a general proposition, the VAT discourages labor supply, lowers the real interest rate and encourages use of capital in the long run.

7. Using the VAT to close the federal deficit will inflict less damage on the real economy than curbing investment incentives to the same end.

8. Using revenues from the VAT to pay for additional investment incentives will raise output in both the short term and the long term.

APPENDIX 9A: TAXES AND THE COST OF CAPITAL

This appendix and the following two develop the theoretical underpinnings of the Washington University Macroeconomic Model of the United States' Economy, the econometric system used to generate the empirical comparisons of the tax proposals under consideration herein. As a point of departure, and because it plays such a pivotal role in tax reform, we consider first the cost of capital.

Much of the controversy surrounding the macroeconomics of tax reform centers on the impact of changes in the tax code on investment spending, particularly business fixed investment. Two questions need be addressed: (1) How sensitive is business fixed investment to changes in the cost of capital? and (2) How do proposed changes in the tax code affect the cost of capital?

The answer to the first of these questions hinges crucially on the value of the elasticity of substitution between capital and labor *e*. The higher *e*, the more investment varies in response to changes in the cost of capital. Estimates of the aggregate elasticity of substitution range from near zero to in excess of one. Generally speaking, researchers have concluded that a unitary value cannot be ruled out statistically. This, of course, corresponds to the case of a Cobb-Douglas production function, which is assumed hereafter.

Regarding the second of these questions: one might think there to be relatively little professional disagreement over how changes in taxes affect the cost of capital. In fact, there are wide disparities in results. For example, Prakken, Meyer, and Varvares conclude that the Tax Reform Act of 1986 would raise the cost of capital by between 8 and 13 percent, depending on the class of investment good under consideration.[4] Bonilla, however, concludes that the same bill would *lower* the cost of capital by 6–14 percent.[5]

The most widely accepted approach to measuring the cost of capital is to derive the *rental price* of investment by assuming that corporate managers, acting on behalf of shareholders and constrained by a neoclassical production function, maximize the value of shareholders' wealth by expanding capacity to the point where the real marginal product of capital equals its real after-tax cost. The latter takes into account the real purchase price of the investment good, the corporate income tax rate, the investment tax credit, rules governing the depreciation of the investment good for tax purposes, the tax "gain" from leveraged financing, the after-tax real financing cost, and the rate of economic depreciation of capital.

The seminal work in this field is that of Jorgenson, who assumed implicitly that all income to shareholders—including capital gains—are taxed equivalently.[6] Consequently, the Jorgensonian rental price does not include personal tax rates. If, however, capital gains are taxed differently than ordinary income, Maloney has shown that the analysis must be expanded to allow for the differential rate of taxation.[7] Then, both the personal income tax rate and the capital gains tax rate appear in the expression for the cost of capital. This subtlety is important given that the Tax Reform Act of 1986 eliminates the preferential treatment afforded capital gains income under the previous tax code.

In the Washington University Macroeconomic Model of the U.S. Economy the cost of capital, derived explicitly from the above considerations by Prakken, Meyer, and Varvares[8] is

$$c = (P_k/P)\{(1 - u - t_c z)(i - q + d) - ilg\}/(1 - t_c) ,$$ (9A.1)

where

P_k = the purchase price of capital
P = the price per unit of output received by firms
u = the investment tax credit
t_c = the marginal corporate income tax rate
z = the present value of depreciation allowances
i = the nominal after-tax discount rate
q = the expected inflation rate
d = the economic depreciation rate
l = the proportion of investment debt-financed
g = the tax gain from leverage

The nominal after-tax discount rate, i, is defined as

$$i = r(1 - t_p)/(1 - t_g) + .035 ,$$ (9A.2)

where r is the nominal pre-tax interest rate, 0.035 is the estimated risk differential between the rate of return on bonds and that on equity, t_p is the marginal personal income tax rate, and t_g is the *effective* marginal tax rate on capital gains. The latter is defined as the statutory marginal tax rate on capital gains discounted by $r(1 - t_p)$ over a period of seven years to allow for the fact that capital gains taxes are paid on a realized basis rather than as they accrue. Note that the discount rate depends on the wedge, $(1 - t_p)/(1 - t_g)$, between the tax rates on ordinary income and capital gains.

The present value of depreciation allowances, z, is determined by statutory rules governing allowable depreciation schedules. For analytical simplicity, we assume below that the "declining balance" schedule is used. In that case,

$$z = d'/(i + d')$$ (9A.3)

where d' is the tax depreciation rate. For example, under the law prior to the tax reform an investment good with a five-year recovery period could be depreciated using the 150 percent declining balance schedule (ignoring both the half-year convention and the allowable switchover to the straight-line schedule). This corresponds to a tax depreciation rate of $1.5/5 = 0.30$. If $i = 0.1$, the corresponding present value of depreciation is 0.75, or 75 cents per dollar invested.

Finally, the gain from leverage is

$$g = 1 - (1 - t_g)(1 - t_c)/(1 - t_p) \qquad (9A.4)$$

which, again, depends on the wedge $(1 - t_p)/(1 - t_c)$. If income and capital gains are taxed equivalently $(t_p = t_g)$ then the gain from leverage is simply t_c. That is, the ability to deduct interest as an operating expense reduces the firm's effective financing cost by rlt_c—a typical result.

Indeed, (9A.4) is nothing more than a generalization of the original Jorgensonian rental price. To see this, assume that all investment is equity-financed $(l = 0)$, that earned income and capital gains are taxed equivalently $(t_p = t_g)$, that there is no risk premium earned by holding equity, and that there is no expected inflation $(q = 0)$. Then (9A.1) collapses to

$$c = (P_k/P)(1 - u - t_c z)(r + d)/(1 - t_c) , \qquad (9A.5)$$

precisely Jorgenson's formulation.

While other measures of the cost of capital can be derived by including in (or omitting from) the analysis other detail about the tax code, this general approach is the most useful for analyzing the impact of taxes on investment incentives. It integrates taxes, both corporate and personal, directly into the theory of investment. Furthermore, it is explicitly consistent with the proposition that corporate managers act in the best interest of shareholders, a theoretical paradigm considerably better than the next best alternative.

Measuring "the" cost of capital empirically is complicated by the existence of many classes of investment goods, both business and household, that differ with regard to purchase price (P_k), tax depreciation rate (d'), eligibility for the investment tax credit (u), and the appropriate leverage ratio (l). However, by formulating weighted averages of these parameters across classes of investment goods it is possible to use (9A.1) to calculate a composite rental price of business fixed investment. In 1985, for example, the average values for the variables used in this calculation are $P_k = 1.01$, $P = 1.052$, $d' = 0.11$, $u = .07$, $l = 0.31$, $t_c = 0.46$, $t_p = 0.30$, $t_g = 0.06$, $r = 11.38$, and $q = 6.77$; the corresponding value of c in 1985 is 0.167, or 16.7 percent per year per dollar invested in business capital.

From this analysis, what can be inferred about the impact of taxes on investment incentives, here defined as the change in c associated with a change in taxes *for a given pre-tax interest rate?* To answer the question, the total derivative of (9A.1) was evaluated in 1985 holding constant the real purchase price of capital. The result is

$$dc = -.29du - .15dd' - .08dt_p + .04dt_g + .04dt_c + .93dr . \quad (9A.6)$$

For an unchanged interest rate ($dr = 0$), several important conclusions can be drawn from expression (9A.6):

1. The investment tax credit is the single most important tax factor influencing the composite cost of business capital. Repeal of the investment tax credit ($du = -0.07$) by itself would raise the cost of capital by roughly 2 percentage points, or 12.2 percent. It does so by directly raising the effective purchase price of investment goods.

2. Reductions in the corporate marginal income tax rate reduce the composite cost of business capital. Lowering the corporate rate from 46 to 33 percent ($dt_c = -0.13$) reduces c by 0.5 percentage points, or 3.1 percent. This calculation suggests that it is not possible to offset the disincentives for investment associated with the repeal of the ITC by lowering the marginal corporate tax rate by the amount mandated by the Tax Reform Act of 1986.

Note also that, in principle, a reduction in the corporate tax rate could actually *raise c*. The reason for this is straightforward. While it is true that a lower corporate tax rate tends to reduce the cost of capital by increasing the after-tax price received by producers per unit of output, two other factors tend to raise it. First, as t_c falls, the tax advantages of leveraged financing decline. Second, the tax advantages of depreciation also fall. The net effect of these influences depends on the values of the parameters used in calculating c. In particular, a disaggregate analysis reveals that the rental price of equipment *rises* modestly as t_c falls, but that the cost of nonresidential structures falls enough to lower the composite measure.

3. The composite cost of business capital falls as the tax depreciation rate rises. For example, our estimate is that the Tax Reform Act of 1986 will raise the tax depreciation rate from 0.21 to 0.26 ($dd' = 0.05$), lowering c by 0.75 percentage points, or 4.5 percent. This would not prove sufficient to offset the impact of repealing the ITC. Again note the differential treatment of equipment and structures. For the former, d' would rise nearly 25 percent. For the latter, it would decline by 60 percent.

4. The composite cost of business capital falls as the personal marginal income tax rate rises. Thus, reducing t_p by 20 percent, from 0.30 to 0.24 ($dt_p = -0.06$), raises c by almost 0.5 percentage points, or 2.8 percent. The principal reason for this is that, *for a given pretax interest rate*, the after-tax discount rate rises as the personal income tax rate falls unless capital gains are taxed as ordinary income. This increases the rental price on two separate counts: by raising the after-tax opportunity cost of tying up funds in capital and by reducing the present value of depreciation allowances. These influences more than offset an associated rise in the gain from leveraged financing.

5. The composite cost of business capital increases with the capital gains tax rate. For example, increasing the effective *statutory* tax rate on capital gains from 12 percent to 24 percent ($dt_g = 0.07$) raises c by 0.3 percentage points, or 0.2 percent. The reason is that an increase in t_g raises the after-tax discount rate sufficiently to offset an associated increase in the gain from leverage.

If one examines the overall ramifications of Tax Reform Act of 1986 on the cost of capital, it is clear that it carries disincentives for business fixed investment, at least as defined here. True, the proposed depreciation rules are, in the aggregate, somewhat more generous than those currently in force, and the corporate tax rate would fall. However, the other three provisions—repeal of the ITC, reduction of the personal income tax rate, and increasing the capital gains tax rate—all tend to raise c. On balance, simultaneous implementation of all the changes considered above raises the composite cost of capital by 10 percent for a given pre-tax interest rate.

It is worth stressing that a general equilibrium analysis does not hold the pre-tax interest rate constant; indeed, under the Tax Reform Act r could fall sufficiently in the long term to guarantee a reduction in the composite cost of business capital. Declines would be even larger for the rental price of household capital, most of which is unaffected by the repeal of the ITC. Yet none of this undermines the conclusion that the 1986 Act will reduce the aggregate capital intensity of production. That is not to say that, in the long term, it will reduce the *level* of production.

6. By way of contrast, a consumption-based value-added tax would not affect the cost of capital for a given pre-tax interest rate. While the purchase price of investment goods (P_k) would rise under a VAT, firms would receive an offsetting tax credit that would maintain the *effective* (after-tax) price unchanged. This does not mean that investment is independent of a value-added tax in general equilibrium. However, the channel through which the VAT would influ-

ence capital formation is an indirect one, via changes in the real interest rate.

APPENDIX 9B: THE COMPLETE MODEL

To assess the impacts of changes in the tax code on general equilibrium it is necessary to present theoretically the complete macroeconomic model of which the cost of capital forms an integral part. The analysis begins by developing a long-run "aggregate supply" schedule dependent on taxes. Next, the same is done for "aggregate demand." Then, for representative values of key parameters, comparative statics are used to analyze both the short-run and the long-run impact on output, interest rates, and prices of various changes in the tax code.

Aggregate Supply

Critics frequently claim that macroeconomic models are flawed in their failure to incorporate a "supply side" in which taxes play an important role. This is not necessarily so. While most models do explain near-term fluctuations in output primarily by changes in aggregate demand, a well-specified system is constrained by aggregate supply in the long run. The discussion of aggregate supply begins with the production function.

The Production Function. Production technology is characterized by a Cobb-Douglas production function in two inputs, capital and labor.

$$X = e^{gt}K^a L^{(1-a)} ,$$ (9B.1)

where

X = real output at time t

K = the net real capital stock at time t

L = labor hours at time t

g = rate of Hicks-neutral disembodied technological advance

a = capital's share in income

The choice of a Cobb-Douglas production function in lieu of the more general C.E.S. formulation was dictated by two considerations: (1) Laurence H. Meyer and Associates estimates that the elasticity of substitution between capital and labor is not significantly different from unity in the long run when proper attention is given to the ex post rigidity of factor proportions; and (2) there is, in our judgment, considerably less controversy surrounding the magnitude of the elasticity of substitution than surrounds either the responsiveness of labor supply to the after-tax real wage or the responsiveness of personal saving to the after-tax real interest rate. The latter two parameters are considered explicitly in the analysis below.

Factor Demands. Given (9B.1), it is a straightforward matter to show that the optimal ratio of labor to output is defined by

$$L = (1 - a)X/w \ . \qquad (9B.2)$$

Here w is the real wage paid by producers for labor, defined as

$$w = W/P \ , \qquad (9B.3)$$

where W is the nominal wage paid by producers and P the price (excluding any VAT) per unit of output received. The corresponding expression for the ratio of capital to output is

$$K = aX/c \ . \qquad (9B.4)$$

The cost of capital, c, is defined by (9A.1). As is conventional in macroeconomic analysis, expressions (9B.2) and (9B.4) are interpreted as the derived demands for labor and capital, respectively.

Factor Supplies. The supply of capital is presumed to be perfectly elastic. This permits the relative price of capital, P_k/P in expression (9A.1), to be set arbitrarily equal to unity for the remainder of the analysis:

$$P_k/P = 1 \ . \qquad (9B.5)$$

The supply of labor is posited to depend upon population (N) and the after-tax real wage received by suppliers of labor, w'.

$$L = N(w')^b \ , \qquad (9B.6)$$

where b is the elasticity of labor supply with respect to the after-tax real wage. At the margin, the after-tax wage received by suppliers of labor is defined as

$$w' = [W(1 - t_p)] / [P(1 + t_v)] = w[(1 - t_p)/(1 + t_v)] \ , \qquad (9B.7)$$

where t_v is the VAT rate. Note that, for labor suppliers, the real wage is valued in terms of the price of output gross of the VAT, since the price paid by consumers includes the tax. The income tax rate also contributes to the "wedge" between the real wage paid by demanders of labor and that received by suppliers. If $b > 0$, the labor supply schedule is upward sloping and a reduction in either the marginal income tax rate or the VAT rate will, ceteris paribus, increase the quantity of labor supplied for a given pre-tax wage. If $b < 0$, the opposite is true. In theory, the sign of b is ambiguous, depending on the relative strengths of the relevant income and substitution effects, and so must be determined empirically.

Factor Market Equilibria. Substituting the supply of capital (9B.5) into the demand for capital (9B.4) yields the following expression for the equilibrium quantity of capital in terms of output and, via the cost of capital, the rate of interest and the various tax parameters.

$$K = aX/c , \qquad (9B.8)$$

where now c is

$$c = [(1 - k - t_c z)(i - q + d) - ilg]/(1 - t_c) . \qquad (9B.9)$$

Combining the supply of labor (9B.6) with the demand for labor (9B.2) to eliminate the real wage paid by producers (w) yields the following expression for the equilibrium quantity of labor in terms of population, output, and the various tax parameters:

$$L = N^{1/(1+b)}[(1 - a)X(1 - t_p)/(1 + t_v)]^{b/(1+b)} \qquad (9B.10)$$

The Aggregate Supply Schedule. A long-run aggregate supply (AS) schedule showing the relationship between output (X) and the interest rate (r) is derived by substituting equations (9B.8–9B.10) for the equilibrium quantities of factor inputs into the production function (9B.1), and solving the resulting expression for output. Considerable expositional simplicity is gained (with no analytical consequence) by expressing the supply schedule as a total differential and assuming that there is neither technological advance ($g = 0$) nor growth in population ($dN/N = 0$). Then

$$dX/X = -[a/(1 - a)][(1 + b)/c]dc - [b/(1 - t_p)]dt_p - [b/(1 + t_v)]dt_v .$$

$$(9B.11)$$

Expression (9B.11) shows that, ceteris paribus, the quantity of output supplied varies inversely with the interest rate via the cost of capital. The reason is that the capital stock (and hence productive capacity) is allowed to vary as changes in the interest rate induce associated changes in the marginal product of capital. Furthermore, taxes affect the AS schedule via both the cost of capital and, if b is nonzero, the supply of labor. This differs from the "textbook" exposition that typically assumes both the stock of capital and the labor force to be fixed at "full employment," thereby denying taxes a role in determining "potential" output in the long run.

Setting capital's share of income to 15 percent, using 0.18 as the elasticity of labor supply with respect to the after-tax real wage, and substituting expression (9A.6) into (9B.11) yields the following empirical estimates of the AS:

$$dX/X = -1.14dr + .036du + .019dd' - .016dt_p$$

$$- .005dt_g - .005dt_c - .018dt_v . \qquad (9B.12)$$

Thus, a 1 percentage point increase in the pre-tax interest rate ($dr = 0.01$) reduces aggregate supply by 1.1 percent and so forth. From (9B.12) it is seen that increases in either the ITC or the tax depreciation rate raise aggregate supply, while increased tax rates on income or capital gains lowers it, as does the imposition of a value-added tax. Of these conclusions, three deserve further attention.

1. In principle, changes in the marginal income tax rate have an ambiguous effect on the AS schedule. On the one hand, as t_p rises, the after-tax wage received by labor falls, tending to reduce labor supply and hence aggregate supply at any pre-tax interest rate, provided that the labor supply curve is upward sloping. On the other hand, as t_p rises so also does the rental price of investment, tending to increase capital and hence aggregate supply. In order for aggregate supply to fall as the marginal personal income tax rises, it must be the case that the response of labor supply to the after-tax real wage is positive and large enough to counter the impact of the higher tax rate on the desired capital stock. Given the parameter values assumed here, this condition is met.

2. Since, as argued in Appendix 9A, the cost of capital may rise or fall with the corporate income tax rate, aggregate supply could rise or fall with t_c. For the parameter values assumed here, it falls.

3. Because the supply of labor depends on the after-tax wage, changes in the VAT rate (t_v) shift the AS schedule at any interest rate, provided that b is not zero. If $b > 0$, so that the labor supply curve is upward sloping (as assumed), an increase in t_v, by reducing the after-tax wage received by labor, leads to a reduction in the quantity of labor supplied and hence in aggregate supply. If $b < 0$, the opposite is true.

Aggregate Demand

As in most macroeconomic analysis, the derivation of aggregate demand starts with an identity that expresses real GNP as the sum of its components:

$$X = C + I + G , \tag{9B.13}$$

where C is consumption demand, I is gross investment demand, and G is government purchases. For simplicity, the economy is considered "closed" so that there are no net exports, government purchases are set exogenously, and I is composed only of business fixed investment.

Investment Demand. In equilibrium, the capital stock is proportional to output:

$$K = aX/c . \tag{9B.14}$$

In steady state (with no growth in population and no technological advance), gross investment demand is composed entirely of depreciation, which in turn is proportional to the equilibrium stock of capital by way of the economic depreciation rate, d. Hence, the long-run demand for investment is written as

$$I = adX/c . \tag{9B.15}$$

That is, gross investment demand varies proportionately with output and in inverse proportion to the cost of capital.

Moving from one steady state to another requires net investment (or disinvestment). Such short-run changes in investment are governed by a "stock adjustment" model that relates changes in the stock of capital to the difference between the equilibrium capital stock and last period's actual stock:

$$dK = f(aX/c - K_{-1}) . \tag{9B.16}$$

Here f is the speed with which the actual stock of capital adjusts toward equilibrium and K_{-1} is the lagged capital stock. Gross investment is the sum of net investment, given by (9B.16), and depreciation. The latter is simply the depreciation rate times the lagged capital stock. Thus the short-run investment function is

$$I = f(aX/c - K_{-1}) + dK_{-1} = daX/c . \tag{9B.17}$$

on the assumption that the speed of adjustment just equals the economic depreciation rate ($f = d$).

Consumption. The discussion of consumption demand begins with a brief review of definitions of national and personal income in the presence of the value-added tax. The VAT likely would be treated as an indirect business tax for accounting purposes. Then, real national income, NI, equals GNP less depreciation less revenues from the value-added tax. If the VAT is consumption-based, so that gross investment is excluded from the tax base, then

$$\text{NI} = X - dK_{-1} - t_\nu(X - I) = (X - I)(1 - t_\nu) + t_\nu dK \ . \qquad (9\text{B}.18)$$

Thus, ceteris paribus, real national income falls with an increase in the VAT. A partial offset does occur if there is net investment, since under a VAT firms effectively receive a credit on the portion of investment goods purchased but not exhausted in production during the period.[9]

If factors of production are owned by households and net investment is financed externally, then personal disposable income, Y, is equal to national income less net income taxes, or

$$Y = (1 - t_y)(1 - t_\nu)[X - dK_{-1} + t_\nu dK/(1 - t_y)] \ , \qquad (9\text{B}.19)$$

where t_y is the average net income tax rate. Expression (9B.19) shows that if there is no net investment, the impact of the value-added tax rate on disposable income (and hence consumption demand) is analytically analogous to that of the average income tax rate. If there is net investment, an allowance must be made for the credit received by firms (and paid out to individuals) under the VAT for capital purchased but not exhausted in current production.

From (9B.18) and (9B.19) follow two important upshots. The first is that a given change in the value-added tax rate raises less real revenue than the same change in the average income tax rate. If a value-added tax of 1 percent were introduced ($dt_\nu = .01$), the average income tax rate tax rate would only have to fall by an amount equal to $-dt_\nu(1 - t_y)(1 - dK/\text{NI}$, or roughly 80 percent of the increase of the VAT rate for current values of t_y ($= .15$) and dK/NI ($= .06$), in order keep real tax receipts unchanged. The second and more important is that *a revenue-neutral combination of a value-added tax and a lower average income tax rate leaves personal disposable income— and hence consumption demand—unchanged for a given level of output.*

Consumption demand rises with real disposable income and also varies with the after-tax interest rate:

$$C/Y = (i')^{-s} \ , \qquad (9\text{B}.20)$$

where i' is the after-tax real interest rate earned on personal saving:

$$i' = r(1 - t_p) - q \ , \tag{9B.21}$$

and s is the elasticity of consumption with respect to the real after-tax interest rate. If $s > 0$, the personal saving rate is positively related to the after-tax interest rate. If $s < 0$ the opposite is true. In theory, the sign of s is ambiguous, depending on the relative strengths of the relevant substitution and income effects.

Substituting (9B.17), (9B.19), and (9B.21) into (9B.20) and rearranging terms yields the short-run consumption function:

$$C = (1 - t_y)(1 - t_p)[(1 + (t_p/(1 - t_p))ad/c)X - dK_{-1}][r(1 - t_p) - q]^{-s} \ . \tag{9B.22}$$

An expression for the long-run consumption function is derived by assuming there is no net investment, and substituting (9B.15), (9B.19), and (9B.21) into (9B.20):

$$C = (1 - t_y)(1 - t_p)(1 - ad/c)[r(1 - t_p) - q]^{-s}X \ . \tag{9B.23}$$

Note that the short-run response of consumption to output is considerably larger than the long-run response. The reason is that, in the near term, fluctuations in gross output generate fluctuations in net investment that are reflected in personal disposable income. In the long run, a change in output generates only a change in replacement investment, which is *not* reflected in disposable income.

The IS Curve. In the short run, the combinations of output and the interest rate for which investment equals saving, commonly referred to as the "IS" curve, is derived by substituting (9B.17) and (9B.22) into the GNP identity (9B.13) and solving for X in terms of r. When expressed as a total differential, the short-run IS curve becomes

$$dX/X = - (I/G)(1/c)[1 + t_p(1 - t_y)C/Y]dc - (C/G)(1 - t_p)(s/i')dr$$
$$+ dG/G - (C/G)[(1/(1 - t_y)]dt_y$$
$$- (C/G)(1 - dK/NI)[1/(1 - t_p)]dt_p + (C/G)(sr/i')dt_p \ . \tag{9B.24}$$

Expression (9B.24) shows variations in output to be related to changes in the interest rate through two channels. One is via changes in the cost of capital, which in turn are inversely related to changes in investment and hence in X. The second is via changes in the after-tax interest rate faced by consumers, which may be positively or negatively related to changes in consumption demand and hence in output. A sufficient condition for the IS curve itself to be negatively sloped is that consumption does not *rise* with the after-tax interest rate ($s > 0$). Note, too, the typical result that an increase in government purchases or a decrease in the average tax rate raises the level of output associated with any interest rate. Finally, the role of the value-added tax rate is analytically similar to that of the average tax rate, again with an allowance for net investment. However, it follows immediately from the earlier discussion of equations (9B.17) and (9B.18) that a revenue neutral swap of a value-added tax for a lower average income tax rate leaves the IS curve stationary.

An empirical estimate of the short-run IS curve is derived by substituting (9A.6) into (9B.23), setting s equal to LHM&A's estimated value of 0.01, and using 1985 values for (C/G), (I/G) and (dK/NI):

$$dX/X = -5.22dr + .109dk + .057dd' + .059dt_p - .014dt_g$$

$$- .014dt_c - .272dt_v - .380dt_y \quad . \tag{9B.25}$$

Thus, a 1 percentage point increase in the pre-tax interest rate ($dr = .01$) reduces aggregate demand by 5.2 percent, and so forth. From (9B.25) it is seen that an increase in the ITC, the tax depreciation rate or the marginal personal tax rate raises aggregate demand. An increase in average income taxes, capital gains taxes or the value-added tax reduce it. Several of these results warrant further discussion.

At any pre-tax interest rate, the after-tax interest rate falls as the personal marginal income tax rate rises and, if $s > 0$, consumption demand strengthens. This increase is reinforced by the fact that, as argued in Appendix 9A, the cost of capital falls as t_p rises so that investment demand increases as well.

For the assumed parameter values, an increase in the corporate income tax rate raises the cost of capital, reducing investment and hence aggregate demand. The same is true for the capital gains tax rate.

Note also that expression (9B.25) reveals that a change in the VAT rate is analytically similar to a change in the *average* income tax rate, and hence does not directly influence the personal saving rate. Nor is there any direct link between the VAT and investment demand, consistent with the oft-stated proposition that, given the pre-tax wage rate and the pre-tax interest rate, a VAT leaves unaltered the optimal capital/output ratio.

The long-run IS curve is derived by substituting (9B.17) and (9B.23) into the GNP identity (9B.13) and solving for X in terms of r. When expressed as a total differential, the long-run IS curve becomes

$$dX/X = - (I/G)(1/c)[1 - (1 - t_y)(1 - t_\nu)C/Y]\,dc$$
$$- (C/G)(1 - t_p)(s/i')\,dr + dG/G - (C/G)[1/(1 - t_y)]\,dt_y$$
$$- (C/G)[1/(1 - t_\nu)]\,dt_\nu + (C/G)(sr/i')\,dt_p \ , \qquad (9B.26)$$

an empirical estimate of which is

$$dX/X = -2.44dr + .021du + .011dd' + .035dt_p - .003dt_g$$
$$- .003dt_c - .323dt_\nu - .380dt_y \ . \qquad (9B.27)$$

The principal difference between (9B.25) and (9B.27) is that the former, by explicitly allowing for net investment, shows output to be much more sensitive in the short run to changes in either the interest rate or any of the tax parameters that influence the cost of capital than is true in the long run.

The Money Market and the LM Curve. A money demand function, derived from standard transactions considerations, relates the demand for nominal money balances to the price faced by consumers transacting for goods and services (with a unitary elasticity), the real quantity of transactions, proxied for by the real value of output, and the rate of interest, which represents the opportunity cost of holding money in lieu of "bonds":

$$M = [P(1 + t_y)]\,X^m r^{-n} \ . \qquad (9B.28)$$

Assuming the nominal money supply to be exogenously set by the Federal Reserve, expression (9B.28) also is a statement of equilibrium in the money market which, when expressed as a total derivative becomes:

$$dM/M = dP/P + dt_\nu/(1 + t_\nu) + m\,(dX/X) - (n/r)dr \ . \qquad (9B.29)$$

For given values of the net price level (P), the VAT rate (t_ν) and the nominal money supply (M), (9B.29) describes the combinations of output and the interest rate consistent with equilibrium in the money market—what is commonly called the "LM" curve. An empirical estimate of the LM curve is derived by introducing estimated values for $m(= .46)$ and $n(= -.14)$, solving (9B.29) in terms of X, expressing the results as a differential and evaluating it at the 1985 level of the interest rate:

$$dX/X = 2.67dr - 2.17(dP/P + dt_v/(1 + t_v) - dM/M) \ . \qquad (9B.30)$$

Thus, a 1 percentage point increase in the interest rate ($dr = .01$) requires a 2.7 percent reduction in output to restore equilibrium to the money market *ceteris paribus*, and so forth.

From (9B.30) it is clear that an increase in the VAT rate, which is equivalent to a reduction in the real money supply, reduces the level of real output consistent with equilibrium in the money market at any interest rate. However, *a VAT accommodated by a corresponding percentage increase in the nominal money supply ($dt_v = dM/M$) will leave the LM curve stationary.*

The Short-Run and the Long-Run

The short-run solution to the complete model presumes that prices are inflexible ($dP/P = 0$) and that changes in investment reflect changes in net investment. In that case, the *short-run* IS curve and the LM curve constitute two equations in two unknowns (dX/X and dr) that can be solved without regard to the AS schedule and hence irrespective of any impact of taxes on aggregate supply.

The long-run solution to the model presumes that prices and wages are fully flexible and that all investment is to replace depreciating capital. In that case, the *long-run* IS curve and the AS schedule constitute two equations in two unknowns (dX/X and dr) that can be solved without reference to the money market. Given that real output and the interest rate are determined in the "real" sector, the only role of the money market in the long run is to determine the price level—the classical "dichotomy."

Much of the confusion surrounding the macroeconomic impact of changes in taxes can be traced to a failure to distinguish carefully short-run and long-run impacts, *which generally are opposite in direction.* As an example, consider Figures 9B–1 and 9B–2, which respectively depict the near-term and long-run impacts of 1 percentage point reduction in the marginal personal tax rate ($dt_p = -.01$).

In Figure 9B–1, initial equilibrium occurs at point A, the intersection of the curves denoted L-M and I-S, drawn here in $r-X$ space. From equation (9B.15), the reduction in t_p raises the cost of capital and thereby shifts the short-run IS curve to the left by .059 percent, to I′-S′; the LM curve is unaffected as prices—and hence the real money supply—remain fixed. Output and the interest rate fall until a short-run equilibrium is established at point B, the intersection of the L-M and I′-S′ curves. The decline in output is accentuated by a reduction in net investment as firms attempt to reduce the capital/output ratio in response to the higher cost of capital.

The magnitude of the near-term reduction in X and r depends on the slopes of the IS and LM curves, the shift in the IS schedule, and the "initial conditions" at the time of the reduction in t_p. Generally speaking, the more inversely sensitive consumption is to the after-tax interest rate, and the higher the elasticity of substitution between capital and labor, the more the IS curve shifts back and the larger the short-run decline in output. For the parameter values assumed here, output falls by 0.2 percent and the interest rate by 8 basis points.

Figure 9B-2 shows the corresponding long-run analysis. Initial equilibrium occurs at point A, the intersection of the long-run IS curve (denoted I-S) and the aggregate supply schedule (A-S).[10] The reduction in personal marginal taxes shifts the IS curve back by 0.035 percent, to I'-S', and the aggregate supply schedule out by 0.016 percent, to A'-S'. Long-run equilibrium is reestablished at point C, the intersection of the I'-S' and A'-S' curves. Output is unambiguously higher, and the interest rate also has fallen. The long-run advantages of lower personal tax rates depend on the slopes and shifts of both the long-run IS curve and the AS schedule, as well as the "initial conditions" at the time of the reduction in t_p. Generally speaking, the larger the (positive) elasticity of labor supply with respect to the after-tax wage and the higher the elasticity of substitution between capital and labor, the larger the long-run gain in output. For the parameter values assumed here, output rises by 6 percent and the interest rate falls by 39 basis points.

The transition from short run to long run is governed by the behavior of prices. With the price level fixed, output is constrained in the near term by aggregate demand, which falls in response to the initial rise in after-tax interest rates. However, in short-run equilibrium (point B) there is an excess supply of output that initiates a decline in prices and a corresponding increase in the real money supply. As the real money stock expands, the interest rate falls further, permitting an increase in output that eventually surpasses the initial decline. The faster the price level adjusts toward its new, lower equilibrium level, the less and shorter lived is the short-run decline in output.

Another crucial factor in the transition is the speed with which investment responds to changes in the cost of capital. In the simple model presented here, firms mechanically move toward equilibrium at a rate that is independent of the reason for the change in the desired capital stock. However, if capital is putty-clay," so that the capital/output ratio cannot be varied ex post in response to a change in the

Figure 9B–1. Short-Run Impact of 1 Point Decline in Marginal Personal Tax Rate.

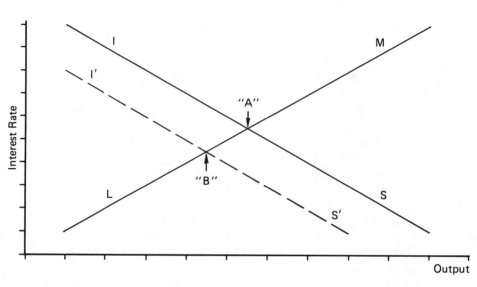

Figure 9B–2. Long-Run Impact of 1 Point Decline in Marginal Personal Tax Rate.

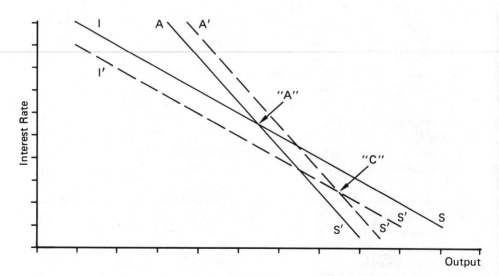

rental price of investment, full adjustment may take *at least* as long as one full depreciation cycle of capital. A conservative estimate puts this at seven years.

The complete model sheds considerable light on the debate over the macroeconomic impacts of changes in the tax code. Strong advocates of tax reform typically assume that consumption is strongly and inversely related to the after-tax interest rate, that labor supply is strongly and positively related to the real after-tax wage, and that the elasticity of substitution between capital and labor is relatively high. Furthermore, they generally focus only on the long run (often without stating so explicitly), claiming that macroeconometricians are either too preoccupied with the near term or that their models do not embody a "supply side" and so cannot be used to address the germane issues.

This position is naive. The specification of a good macroeconometric system is entirely consistent with the long-run solution of the above equations which would be accepted generally as a reasonable representation of the macroeconomy. The key behavioral parameters in such a model are estimated and, in the case of s and b, prove small—not surprising since, as noted earlier, they are theoretically ambiguous in sign.

It is true that macroeconomists consider the short-run effects of tax reform, and worry explicitly about the dynamic time paths of output, interest rates and prices during the transition from the short run to the long run. In the latter regard, the key question is, How long is the long run? In most macroeconomic models, long-run price flexibility is introduced via a Phillips curve that explains deviations of actual inflation from expectations by the gap between the actual and "natural" rates of unemployment. Expected inflation typically is measured adaptively, the adaptive scheme exhibiting strong inertia. Information costs, institutional rigidities, and the modern theory of contracts are used to rationalize the result. With such an equation, full adjustment of prices can require years and is achieved only at the cost of a temporary rise in the unemployment rate.

Proponents of tax reform reject this approach to macroeconomic dynamics, arguing instead that the real interest rate would move quickly to its long-run equilibrium value, preventing an initial rise in the cost of capital and so sparing us any transitional economic pain. While these issues cannot be settled here in full, three observations seem pertinent.

First, given the logic of the model, to argue that the interest rate moves quickly to long-run equilibrium is to argue that the price level does so as well or else the money market is out of equilibrium. As

Figure 9B-3. Rental Price of Producer Durables.

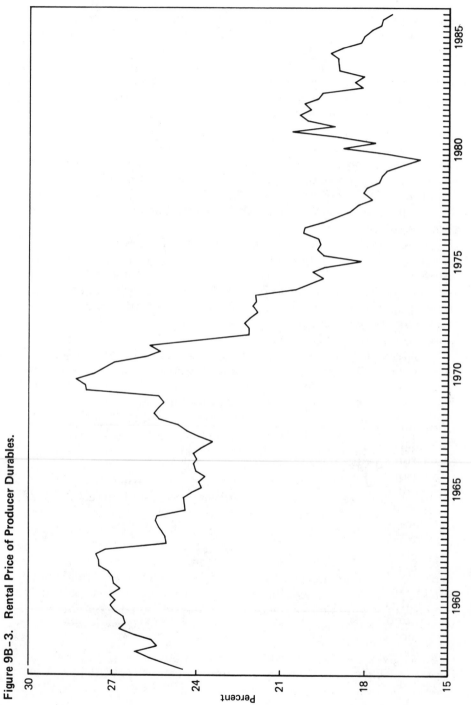

Source: Laurence H. Meyer and Associates.

suggested in the chapter, full adjustment to the pending reform bill requires a 3 percent decline in prices—a huge drop for a short period of time not dominated by other deflationary surprises.

Second, our experience is that the Phillips curve—specified to allow for inflation shocks emanating from the farm and energy sectors and properly adjusted for changes in demographics and in the underlying rate of technological advance—has proved remarkably robust in explaining inflation since World War II. Recall that this period witnessed the introduction of the investment tax credit, major changes in depreciation rules, and allowable recovery periods for depreciable assets and sharp reductions in taxes in both 1964 and under the Economic Recovery Tax Act.

Finally, empirical evidence belies the assertion that the interest rate moves quickly to offset the impact on the cost of capital of sharp changes in the tax code. This is clearly evident in Figure 9B-3, which depicts the rental price of producers' durable equipment since 1950. Important changes in taxes, including the temporary repeal of the investment tax credit in 1969, the shortening of recovery periods in 1972, and the introduction of the Accelerated Cost Recovery System in 1982 all are easily discernible. Indeed, if this were not the case, how could changes in taxes have any long-run impact on saving and investment?

APPENDIX 9C: THE VALUE-ADDED TAX

The model developed in Appendix B yields considerable insight into the macro implications of the VAT in both the short run and the long run. To see this, consider a simple experiment in which a consumption-based VAT of 1 percent is imposed ($dt_v = .01$), the proceeds of the tax (roughly $40 billion a year in static terms) used to reduce the federal deficit, and the Federal Reserve leaves the nominal money supply unchanged ($dM/M = 0$). The short-run and long-run responses are depicted graphically in Figures 9B-4 and 9B-5, respectively.

Consider first the short-run results. Initial equilibrium occurs at point A, the intersection of the short-run IS curve, marked $I'-S'$, and the LM curve denoted $L'-M'$, drawn here in $r-X$ space. In the near term, defined as a period during which the price level *net of the tax* does not change, the impact of the VAT is to raise the price *including the tax* by the percentage amount of the tax. This has two distinct impacts in the model. First, because an increase in the purchase price of goods and services is tantamount to a reduction in the real

Figure 9B–4.   Short-Run Impact of 1 Percent VAT.

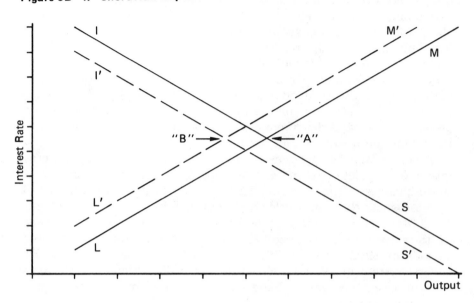

Figure 9B–5.   Long-Run Impact of 1 Percent VAT.

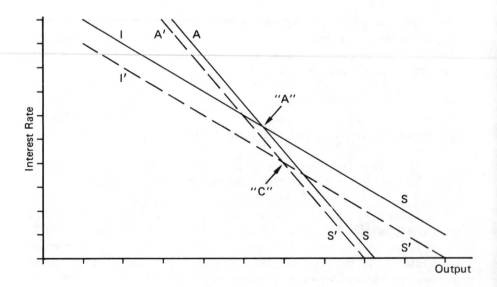

money stock, the LM curve shifts leftward to L'-M'. Second, higher prices initially reduce the level of consumers' disposable income associated with a given level of real GNP. This shifts the IS curve leftward to I'-S'. A new short-run equilibrium occurs at point B, the intersection of I'-S' and L'-M', with output unambiguously lower. The interest rate may rise or fall. For the parameter values introduced earlier, the short-term decline in output is 2.5 percent, and the interest rate does decline by a slight 10 basis point (see Table 9B-4).

The long-run results may be contrary to the short-term ones. In Figure 9B-5, initial equilibrium again occurs at point A, the intersection of I-S and A-S. Imposition of the VAT shifts the long-run IS schedule leftward to I'-S' by undermining consumers' real disposable income. The aggregate supply schedule also shifts leftward (to A'-S') if the elasticity of labor supply with respect to the after-tax wage (*b*) is positive. Whether output rises or fall depends on the value of *b*. For our estimate of 0.18, the long-run effect of the VAT is to raise output (point C). True, labor supply is adversely affected, but the 230 basis point drop in the interest rate encourages enough additional capital ultimately to allow an increase in *X*. Furthermore, even prices including the VAT fall eventually.

Again, the length of the transition from short-run to long-run equilibrium is governed by the rate at which prices excluding the VAT decline after the tax is implemented. The equilibrating process could require considerable time if wage earners, attempting to recoup the initial loss of real income, start a wage-price spiral that leads initially to *increases* in the net price level that forestall the requisite long-run reduction in the real money supply.

NOTES

1. U.S. Department of the Treasury, *Tax Reform for Fairness, Simplicity and Economic Growth, Volume 1* (Washington, D.C.: U.S. Treasury Office of Tax Analysis November 1984), p. 43.

2. Jane G. Gravelle, "Assessing Structural Tax Revision with Macroeconomic Models: The Treasury Tax Proposals and the Allocation of Capital," Congressional Research Service, March 1985, p. 2.

3. Council of Economic Advisers, "The Economic Case for Tax Reform," September 1985, p. 1.

4. Joel L. Prakken, Laurence H. Meyer, and Chris P. Varvares, "The Senate Finance Committee Proposal for Tax Reform: A Macroeconomic Analysis," Center for the Study of American Business, May 1986.

5. Carlos E. Bonilla, "Packwood II and the Cost of Capital," Institute for the Research on the Economics of Taxation, June 1985.

6. Dale Jorgenson, "The Theory of Investment Behavior" in *Determinants of Investment Behavior* (National Bureau of Economic Research, 1967).

7. Kevin J. Maloney, "Inflation, Taxes and the Productive Capacity of the U.S. Economy," Ph.D. Dissertation, Washington University, 1983.

8. Joel L. Prakken, Laurence H. Meyer, and Chris P. Varvares, "The Treasury Department's November 1984 Tax Reform Proposal: Implications for Capital Formation," Laurence H. Meyer and Associates, December 1984.

9. An interesting implication of this is that, since perhaps 20 percent of investment represents net additions to the capital stock, *nominal* national income would rise following implementation of the VAT, the increase being recorded as corporate profits before tax. Thus, for no change in real economic activity, the VAT would raise revenue not only directly but also via the corporate income tax. This would not occur if the VAT allowed only depreciation (rather than gross purchases) of capital to be excluded from the tax base.

10. Note that the aggregate supply schedule cuts the long-run IS curve from above in $r-X$ space. While this is empirically the case, it is also required if, in the long run, prices are viewed as moving to clear the market for output and the model is to satisfy the normal stability conditions.

Discussants:

THE CONSUMPTION TAX ALTERNATIVE

Dave Durenberger

I have many questions about the overall impact that the Tax Reform Act of 1986 will have on the economy. I am sure many people fear that loss of the investment tax credit will continue the erosion of America's industrial competitiveness. There seems little doubt that repeal of the credit will increase the cost of capital to American companies, especially the hard-hit industrial sector of the economy. But when we consider the pros and cons of the tax bill, it is important to remember that tax policy is but one factor to weigh in comparing costs of capital.

John Shoven's chapter makes it eminently clear that two other factors—interest rates and inflation—play a much larger role in determining costs of capital than tax policy. Indeed, I am reminded of a study done by Arthur Andersen last year which showed that if tax policy is used as the sole measure of the cost of capital, Japan would have the highest cost of capital and Luxembourg and Belgium would have the lowest capital costs.

Thus in the debate over our nation's competitiveness in the international marketplace, too often we on the Senate Finance Committee focus too much of our attention on such matters as the investment tax credit and accelerated depreciation, and too little on monetary policy and exchange rates. That's why Senator Jack Danforth's drumbeat for a stronger congressional role in trade policy is an unwelcome intrusion into tax policy discussions.

The greatest danger to our industrial competitiveness comes from the ballooning federal deficit and the concomitant impact it has on interest rates, exchange rates, and inflation—all of which have a substantial bearing on the cost of capital in the United States. Furthermore, it should not go unnoticed that the precipitous decline in our industrial competitiveness vis-à-vis the Japanese, the Koreans, and the

This discussant refers to Chapters 7, 8, and 9.

Taiwanese, coincided with huge ERTA tax subsidies and their concomitant hemorrhaging of the federal deficit.

I think 1986 will be remembered as a turning point in the federal
government's philosophy of taxation and the role it plays in direct-
ing the resources and priorities of the nation's economy, and inevitably the world economy. It is my view that the lower rates and base
broadening encompassed in the bill reflects a renewed confidence in
the decisionmaking power of U.S. citizens and a diminished reliance
on a government that substitutes its priorities for those of the
governed.

Its philosophical underpinnings are those of consumer choice, the
principle involved in the 1980s revolution in health care financing,
economic deregulation, and now education.

While the 1986 tax reform may contribute to greater taxpayer
equities, it has done nothing to alleviate the budget monster that en-
dangers the economic wealth and security of our nation's economy
and the generational equity of its citizens. I only hope Joel Prakken
is wrong in predicting that by 1995 GNP growth will be reduced by
3.1 percent, unemployment will rise 2.6 percent and the budget deficit will increase by $208 billion. If he is right, the 97 senators who
voted for the bill have made a devastating mistake.

I think we have learned some important lessons this year in trying
to achieve the twin goals of cutting the deficit and reforming the income tax. I think 1986 will prove to be the last year that we can find
enough "fat" to cut in federal spending in order to achieve deficit
reduction. We are about at the point where what is left in spending is
nearly all muscle.

And in the process of overhauling the income tax, from Treasury I
all the way through to the House-Senate conference, I think we have
found out just how far we can broaden the income tax base without
incurring the unforgivable wrath of our individual and corporate constituents. There are certain "untouchables" outside the base: home
mortgage interest, inside build-up on life insurance, tax-free health
insurance, state and local income and property taxes, and incentives
for oil and gas investment.

We have broadened the base about as far as politically possible,
and I think it would be unwise for Congress to begin another round
of income tax "reform" in the next few years. After a while, I think
the public will become even more cynical (if that is possible) about
what we in Washington do when we promise to reform the tax system every two years.

Moreover, I believe business could not stand the shock of another
round of tax reform, unless we promised to keep rates low and rein-

stitute the investment tax credit. Of course, under the current income tax system, that is just not affordable; you cannot have a top rate of 34 percent on business and still retain the investment tax credit.

Thus we face a quandary in the next few years. If we cannot squeeze much more out of the income tax base, and we cannot find much more to cut in the budget, how are we going to meet our Gramm-Rudman targets?

There is an early warning sign from Texas as to what is likely to be in store for Congress and the president in the next two years as the budget and tax battle really turns serious.

Texas Governor Mark White realizes that he is going to have to raise taxes to meet the state's $3.5 billion budget shortfall. Legislators continue to balk at a politically unpopular sales tax increase and continue to try to find ways to get revenue from spending cuts. But the news from Texas is, there is just not enough to cut to cover the red ink. The result is a deadlock that, in the words of the lieutenant governor, will lead to "bounced state checks and a nosedive in the state's credit rating that may take more than a decade to recover from."

If the Congress and the president heed the warning signs from Texas, we will inevitably have to face up to our budgetary responsibilities and look at the tax side of the budget ledger. We could put a surtax on the income tax. We did it to finance the Vietnam War and it might be possible to justify as a necessary measure to fight the budget war.

However, I think a surtax would be unwise because it would, in many ways, negate the encouragement to saving and capital formation which result from the lower tax rates included in the Tax Reform Act of 1986. And it would add to the public's cynicism about the promise of tax reform.

It would thus appear that the only viable option we have to solve the budget deficit mess is to phase in a consumption tax, either in the form of a value-added tax or a business transfer tax (BTT) as proposed by Senator William Roth. As you know, there is great reluctance on Capitol Hill to go down the consumption tax route.

We all remember what happened to Al Ullman when he first raised the idea of a VAT. And the president and many of my colleagues in the Senate oppose the idea because they fear that its revenue potential is so large that it will reduce our budget cutting discipline and become an easy vehicle to finance new social spending programs.

I share the president's and my colleagues' concern that a VAT or BTT would undiscipline Congress. And I would note that many of the European countries that have adopted VATs spend a larger percentage of their budgets on social expenditures. Yet, I believe the consumption tax alternative is inevitable and that we can protect against any attempts to inch up the VAT rate a point or two to pay for questionable spending programs.

A consumption tax cannot be tried as an experiment with a low rate of 1 or 2 percent either to pay for the budget deficit or, as some would suggest, to pay for restoration of an investment tax credit. In 1984 the U.S. Treasury estimated that if a VAT were adopted, the Internal Revenue Service would have to hire 20,000 additional employees and that the cost to the Treasury would be $700 million a year. And that does not include the additional hundreds of millions or billions in compliance costs for business.

If we are serious about adopting some form of consumption tax, the public and the business community will have to be thoroughly convinced that the benefits of the VAT outweigh its costs. Some estimates, based on political realities as to the consumption tax base, suggest that such a tax could raise $25 billion for each percentage point of tax. Thus if we adopt a 7 percent VAT, in theory we could raise $175 billion a year. Depending on how Congress chooses to "spend" that money will determine whether the VAT or any other type of consumption tax can pass political muster with the public.

In my view, at least $75 billion of that money must be earmarked by Congress to reduce the deficit. That would send a clear and unmistakable signal to the business community and our trading partners that the United States is committed to ending its federal deficit. With that commitment, I believe the course of the economy would be headed in one direction—upward; and the direction of interest rates would head in the other direction.

Of the remaining $100 billion, $60 billion could be used to entirely eliminate the 2.9 percent Hospital Insurance (Medicare) portion of Federal Insurance Contributions Act (FICA) payroll deductions. We are headed for a crisis in the willingness of a declining base of workers to finance the health failures and prolonged lives of a growing number of the elderly. Unless we begin to consider alternatives for Medicare financing, such as a consumption tax, we are faced with inevitably raising the most regressive and unfair tax on labor, which already is set to drain up to $8,000 per worker per year in 1989.

The remaining $40 billion could be used to eliminate all federal excise taxes. By eliminating federal excise taxes, state governments would no longer have to compete for excise tax revenues with the federal government. This is especially important for the state governments since the decision recently to end deductibility of sales taxes, coupled with the adoption of a federal VAT, will make it extremely difficult for states to raise revenues from sales taxes.

The federal government has been increasingly imposing mandates on state governments, while concurrently cutting federal aid to the states. The Tax Reform Act of 1986 will make it extremely difficult for states to issue tax-exempt bonds to finance badly needed infrastructure improvements. Under these circumstances, it would be a welcome relief to the states to be able to make greater use of excise taxes.

These are just a few of the ways that a consumption tax could be used to alleviate the stresses on the payroll tax and on state and local governments. The list of alternative uses of consumption tax revenue is endless. We could lower income tax rates further, eliminate the corporate tax entirely, end the taxation of savings, restore genuine long-term capital gains. But the key point is that a major portion of the revenues *must* be used for deficit reduction. In fact, my constituents at home have indicated their preference that we repay the principal on the U.S. debt held by foreign investors. That will be an extraordinarily difficult task. But when one considers that a single Japanese securities firm—Nomura Securities—is responsible for financing nearly one-third of the U.S. national debt, I think the answer is clear. We must extinguish the national debt.

Nearly 20 percent of the fiscal 1987 trillion dollar budget is dedicated to paying interest on the debt. Fifty-five percent of the income tax is needed to pay the national debt. The deficit was responsible for the soaring dollar that destroyed many of our export markets and is a prime factor in the trade deficit that appears to get worse each month.

I think the public recognizes the inevitability of some new taxes to close the deficit. There is a growing awareness that the debt we are accumulating today is going to cause a shock to the living standards of our children and our children's children. It is not unlike the situation we see in Latin America where poorly managed governments, having piled up extraordinary debts in the 1970s, are now paying for such excesses with lower living standards and extreme inflation. That is the legacy we will leave to our children, if we do not address the deficit soon.

It is clear to me that there is a price the economy will pay in adopting a consumption tax. Joel Prakken suggests that U.S. gross national product would be reduced and civilian unemployment would rise in the first 10 years. I would hope that an accommodative monetary policy would ease the burden that would be associated with introduction of a consumption tax. However, I think we face no choice. We either begin to pay now for our excessive consumption or face a future that promises less growth, higher unemployment, and a lower standard of living for our children.

THE IMPACT OF TAX POLICY ON SAVINGS

Lawrence H. Summers

It was said that World War I was going to be the war to end all wars. But it was not so. And it was originally hoped that the Tax Reform Act of 1986 would be the tax law to end all tax law, or at least to staunch the flood of new tax legislation. But it will not be. Even before the technical corrections to the 1986 Act were legislated, attention was turning toward the next tax reform effort. Losing lobbyists were already urging their discouraged clients to "wait till next year." Tax reform debates, like large budget deficits, lie ahead of us for as far as the eye can see.

Regular changes in the tax law may not be welcomed by many people. But we public finance economists can see their virtues. They reveal that congressmen as well as economists are prone to vacillation. They give us a host of natural experiments to study. And, most important, they ensure that our predictions regarding previous tax bills can never be checked out. Perhaps buoyed by this knowledge, Drs. Prakken, Makin, and Bernheim and Shoven examine a number of aspects of past and prospective tax policies. Each of the analyses is carefully conceived and executed. My comments today will take up the issues raised by each chapter as I consider the current tax reform agenda.

Before taking on any of the papers specifically, I want to highlight one economic relationship that is central to an understanding of our current economic difficulties. It is one of the few projections that all economists accept—because it is an accounting identity. This fundamental economic relationship holds that net exports, the nation's trade balance, is just equal to the difference between national saving and investment. The inflow of capital to the United States is just equal to the difference between national saving and investment. When, as has been the case in recent years, investment exceeds savings, we must borrow from abroad.

It is a truism that the balance of payments must balance. The mirror image of our rising capital account surplus as funds flow in to

This discussant refers to Chapters 7, 8, and 9.

the country must arithmetically be a current account deficit. We must export less than we import. The economic mechanism here is simple. Capital inflows raise the demand for dollars, increasing the exchange rate. This in turn makes American producers of tradeable goods less competitive on world markets.

The savings-investment identity I have just explained has an immediate and obvious consequence. The only way in which we can raise both investment and international competitiveness simultaneously is to increase national savings. There is no alternative. Without changes in national saving, increases in investment must be financed from abroad and so must come at the expense of improvements in our trade balance. Reductions in the flow of funds from abroad that bring the dollar down and improve the U.S. balance of trade will necessarily lead to higher interest rates and reduced investment. Seen in this light, the clear priority for economic policy in the next few years is to raise the national savings rate.

Only Chapter 7, by Bernheim and Shoven, takes up the crucial question of the interaction of the U.S. economy with the rest of the world. Bernheim and Shoven's approach is to examine differences in the cost of capital across countries and relate them to international differentials in tax rules. While their analysis is skillful and is in a number of ways an improvement over earlier work in this area by Fullerton and King, I do think they pass too lightly over one aspect of the problem. As they stress, real interest rates are not equated everywhere, but then why should they be? An American considering whether to borrow money here or in Germany is not concerned just with the difference in interest rates, he is also concerned with prospective exchange rate movements; that is, if the dollar depreciates, paying off his German loan will turn out to be more expensive than he had planned. International capital markets should equalize not real rates of return but, rather, real rates adjusted for anticipated changes in exchange rates.

This condition has the consequence that differences induced by monetary policy in the cost of capital between countries are very unlikely to be permanent. Increases in the real interest rates brought about by monetary policy will cause a temporary increase in exchange rates as capital flows in. But, capital inflow into a country with a high real interest rate will be limited by the expectation of eventual exchange rate decline. The policy implication is that monetary policy cannot permanently change a country's cost of capital. Any differences it can create in the short run will be offset by unsustainable movements in the exchange rate.

It is because of the inherently transitory effect of monetary policy that tax measures affecting saving and investment are such important tools of economic policy. Balanced increases in both saving and investment can promote a substantial lowering of the cost of capital and lead to rapid growth. Unbalanced policies like those pursued in the United States in recent years, where investment has been strongly encouraged but savings have been reduced through the government deficit, lead to considerable capital inflows and reductions in competitiveness. The key to successful policies in support of capital formation is that they be balanced in promoting both saving and investment.

American policy as embodied in the Tax Reform Act of 1986 does go in the direction of bringing investment and savings back into balance. Unfortunately, it moves toward balance in the wrong way—by dragging down investment rather than increasing savings. The major policy error in the 1986 Act is the abolition of the investment tax credit and scaling back of depreciation in allowances.

This is likely to have significant adverse consequences for economic growth over the next two decades. The adverse impact of reduced investment incentives will far exceed the rather speculative neutrality benefits stressed by proponents of tax reform.

The Tax Reform Act of 1986 will increase total corporate tax liabilities by about $125 billion for 1987 through 1991. This represents an increase of about one-fourth in corporate tax liabilities. But this figure substantially understates the adverse impact that the Act will have on investment. The Tax Reform Act would raise much more in corporate revenues but for the fact that the corporate rate is reduced from 46 to 34 percent. This rate reduction has the primary effect of reducing the tax rates on the profits that firms will earn in coming years on investments that they have made in the past. Even the most zealous supply-sider must acknowledge that reductions in the tax rate on old capital can not create more of it. On the other hand the revenue-raising features of the Act, especially the abolition of the investment tax credit and changes in depreciation rules will have their primary effect on new investment, where incentives have potent effects.

In this important sense, the 1986 Tax Reform Act is perverse. It simultaneously reduces the tax rate on old capital while raising it on new capital. Tilting the playing field toward yesterday in this way is favored by entrenched firms now reaping the benefit of past investments. They will receive windfall gains as their tax rate falls and the tax burden on potential competitors is increased. However, the arguments made on public policy grounds by those favoring reductions in investment incentives do not stand up under close scrutiny.

The combination of reduced investment incentives and a reduced corporate tax rate embodied in the 1986 Act is often defended on grounds of neutrality. It is suggested that the law before reform somehow favored capital-intensive industries and that this favoritism will be undone by tax reform. This is a fundamental misconception. Investments in intangibles—research and development, advertising, marketing, or goodwill—all receive the ultimate in accelerated depreciation, expensing. Although these outlays yield a stream of benefits over time, just like capital investments, firms are permitted to write them off in the year they are undertaken. For example, the large expenditures incurred by Coca-Cola in developing and marketing New Coke can all be expensed. In contrast, outlays on physical capital are necessarily amortized over time. The resulting tax bias toward intangible investment has until now been partially mitigated by the investment tax credit and accelerated depreciation. It will be exacerbated by the Tax Reform Act of 1986, which scales back these investment incentives.

It is often argued that investment incentives should be scaled back because they do not work. This is not a fair reading of recent history. We have lived through a period of unprecedented high real interest rates, large federal deficits, and increasing foreign competition. Almost any observer asked to predict the consequence of this combination for investment would have foreseen an unprecedented degree of crowding out. Yet, at least until recently, business fixed investment has proven remarkably robust during the current recovery and has actually proven stronger than would be predicted from normal cyclical relationships. Indeed the share of gross business fixed investment in GNP reached its postwar high in 1985. The strength of business investment reflects many factors. But most economists agree that the tax incentives enacted in 1981 deserve at least some of the credit.

No one can accurately predict the consequences of the tax bill for business investment decisions. But some suggestive estimates are possible. The Tax Reform Act of 1986 would have the effect of raising the cost of capital by at least 10 percent. In the long run this will lead to a reduction of between 10 and 15 percent in the stock of plant and equipment. This in turn will translate into a reduction of at least 3 percent in the economy's potential output. Beyond the direct effect of reduced capital accumulation, it is likely that reductions in capital investment will slow the rate of technical progress in the economy, thereby reducing our growth rate. This indirect effect could easily reduce real GNP in 1996 by another 2 or 3 percent. Combining these two effects, a reasonable estimate is that the Tax Reform Act would reduce real GNP in 1996 by up to 5 percent.

While reducing investment is one way to bring investment and savings into balance and thereby enhance our international competitiveness, it has the highly undesirable side effect of reducing economic growth. The better way of bringing savings and investment into balance is through increases in savings. Here the major necessary step is a reduction in federal deficits. There is also a limited role for tax measures directed at encouraging private savings. It is from this perspective, the pressing need for more national savings, that I want to comment on Chapters 8 and 9.

Chapter 8, by John Makin, is directed at a rather academic question: Would we be better off with an ideal, politically untainted consumption tax than with the reformed income tax produced by the Congress? Makin answers this question affirmatively and concludes that a pure consumption tax would be a powerful revenue raiser. I have little doubt that both these conclusions are correct. But they do not have much relevance for policy.

Within this decade or even this century, we are very unlikely to see anything like the pure consumption tax that Makin envisions. Such a radical reform will surely not be legislated soon after the sweeping changes so recently enacted. Politics would surely impinge on any consumption tax proposal prior to its enactment to the point where it would no longer have many of the virtues that Makin applauds. And, as the tax lawyers remind us, the transition to a pure consumption tax would be hideously complex if it could be managed at all.

Makin's chapter is useful, however, in highlighting how far we are from an ideal tax system. The problems with the current tax system that he identifies should be remedied when the time comes, as it soon will, to raise revenues. One important area where a consumption tax would have substantial benefits is in the choice of financial structure. It would substantially reduce the incentive to use debt finance, because interest would no longer be deductible. But progress in this direction could be made under the income tax by tightening the limits on interest deductibility. The 1986 Act makes some progress in this direction, though some of its provisions, such as the increased taxation of capital gains, actually work in the direction of increasing incentive to use debt finance.

Only Chapter 9, by Joel Prakken examines the policy-relevant question of the implications of alternative ways of raising revenues to reduce the federal deficit. Prakken's econometric analysis is skillfully carried out and his chapter provides a useful framework for thinking about the short-run consequences of tax policy. My judgment about the effect of a small value-added tax (VAT) are similar to his. Perhaps that is why I liked this chapter. The inflation point he emphasized is an important one. A VAT that raises prices is very much like a self-imposed supply shock to the economy. Its implementation will lead to high prices or less growth in the short run just as did the supply shocks of the 1970s. My own research suggests that Britain's movement from income taxation toward value-added taxation in 1979 contributed to their stagflation woes.

As Prakken notes, the use of monetary policy to cushion the adverse effects of VAT on growth runs the risk of enhancing its inflationary impact. Its inflationary consequences are an important drawback of a VAT, but they represent a one-time cost and not a permanent one. The benefit of a VAT, in terms of greater capital formation and economic efficiency are permanent and so must be given greater weight than its one-time effect on inflation.

As I have already made clear, my judgment is that the crucial tax priority for the next several years should be increasing national savings by reducing government borrowing. Given the amount by which government spending has already been cut, I suspect that this will require tax increases if government borrowing is to be curtailed. A tax increase is the feasible way to generate the extra savings necessary to avoid a harsh choice between reduced competitiveness and real investment. The VAT or some similar consumption tax is one way of raising revenue. It would be much better for Congress to enact the VAT than to permit a $200 billion deficit to persist. Certainly, if a VAT is enacted, some of the profits should be directed to increasing investment incentives. But before undertaking a national commitment to a value-added tax, we need to consider all the alternatives carefully.

❋ Chapter 10

The Consumption Tax and International Competitiveness

Gary Hufbauer

Imagine, if you will: In 1990, the system of corporate income taxation is swept away and replaced with a uniform value-added tax. The rough dimensions of the new system appear in Table 10-1. For this exercise, I assume that the Tax Reform Act of 1986 increases prospective 1990 corporate tax revenue to $160 billion (by comparison with $130 billion under the pre-1986 law). I also assume that the alternative value-added tax would yield $160 billion, and that the VAT is levied on a base of about 70 percent of gross national product. Hence, the contemplated VAT rate is 4 percent and the corporate income tax is eliminated.[1]

Practical observers will say that elimination of the corporate income tax is just not realistic or that the foremost challenge is reduction of the budget deficit. Table 10-1, therefore, includes two additional scenarios: Replace half the corporate tax with a 2 percent VAT; or use a 4 percent VAT to curb the federal budget deficit.

What difference would these various tax scenarios make for the international competitive posture of the United States? A casual survey of the world economy shows that taxes are not the dominant part of the competitiveness picture, even among industrial countries. Some small countries, such as Sweden and Switzerland, display quite different tax systems—one burdensome, the other not—yet both nations have performed well. Conversely, some large countries, such

John Banks and Sabra Purtill, both graduate students at the School of Foreign Service, Georgetown University, assisted in writing this chapter.

Table 10-1. Comparison between the Corporate Tax System and the Hypothetical VAT System. (*Estimates for 1990, $ Billions*).

	Corporate Tax under Tax Reform Act of 1986	*4% VAT Replaces Corporate Tax*	*2% VAT Replaces Half Corporate Tax*	*4% VAT Used to Balance Budget*
Gross national product	5,600	5,600	5,600	5,600
Assumed base for VAT	—	4,000	4,000	4,000
Corporate income tax	160	—	80	160
Value-added tax amount	—	160	80	160
VAT rate	—	4.0%	2.0%	4.0%

Sources: Value Line Investment Survey, *Selection and Opinion*, New York, August 29, 1986.

as the Federal Republic of Germany and the United Kingdom, exhibit broadly similar tax systems, yet these nations have performed very differently. Such comparisons suggest caution in relating economic performance to tax structure.

And, indeed, economists have much to be cautious about. Many economists were surprised by the triumph of a super-Keynesian budget and a Mundellian monetary-fiscal mix, all traveling under the label of Reaganomics. Some economists were surprised by the failure of supply-side policies to raise the private savings rate or to reduce the public deficit.

In the spirit of humility, I do not claim to prove anything about the relationship between tax structure and competitivenss. I only claim to put forward arguments that the connection is not trivial.

At bottom, the international competitiveness of an economy is determined by its productivity compared to other economies. The tax structure affects productivity, and hence international competitiveness, through three important channels: (1) The level of corporate profitability, (2) The cost of capital, (3) The balance of trade in goods and services.

THE TAX STRUCTURE AND CORPORATE PROFITABILITY

Corporate profitability is vital to international competitiveness because corporate profits provide both the incentive for expanding capacity and the means of acquiring new capital assets. Corporate profitability reflects many features of the economy, including the

Table 10-2. Corporate Income Taxes as a Percentage of Gross Domestic Product.

	1965	1983
Canada	3.9	2.5
France	1.8	1.9
Germany	2.5	1.9
Italy	1.9	3.8
Japan	4.1	5.4
United Kingdom	2.2	4.1
United States	4.2	1.6

Source: Organization for Economic Cooperation and Development, *Revenue Statistics of Member Countries 1965-1984* (Paris: OECD, 1985, table 12).

tax regime. Among the seven major industrial powers, three countries—Canada, West Germany, and the United States—have conspicuously cut corporate taxation as a percentage of GNP since 1965 (see Table 10-2). On the other hand, three countries—Italy, Japan, and the United Kingdom—have increased the corporate tax burden over the past two decades.

In recent decades, U.S. corporate income taxes have claimed only a small percentage of U.S. GNP. Over the period 1965 to 1985, taxes on corporate income averaged 2.7 percent of GNP, while individual and Social Security taxes averaged 8.4 percent and 5.2 percent, respectively. Moreover, corporate tax revenues have steadily declined as a percentage of GNP. In 1965 corporate taxes stood at 3.8 percent of GNP; by 1985 they had declined to 1.6 percent.[2]

The Tax Reform Act of 1986 promises to reverse the progress made in reducing corporate taxation. It seems likely that U.S. corporate income taxes will rise to about 2.9 percent of GNP in 1990. This escalation will generate about $120 billion of new revenue over the years 1987-1991, and will pay for an almost equal reduction of personal taxes. Higher corporate taxes are the combined result of four major changes: repeal of the investment tax credit; a decrease in depreciation benefits; a minimum corporate tax that overrides an array of surviving deductions; and a lower corporate tax rate (a statutory rate of 34 percent, compared to the pre-1986 rate of 46 percent).

In terms of international competitiveness, the Tax Reform Act of 1986 will have three effects: one good, two bad. The good effect is the harmonization of tax rates across industries and types of assets. The bad effects are lower corporate profitability and a higher cost of capital.

Table 10-3. Marginal Effective Tax Rates by Industry under Pre-1986 Law and the Tax Reform Act of 1986 (%).

Input-Output Sector	Sector Description	Pre-1986 Law	Tax Reform Act of 1986[a]
1	Livestock and products	22.1	31.8
2	Other agricultural products	22.1	31.8
3	Forestry/fishery products	15.8	36.7
4	Agricultural/forest/fishery service	15.8	36.7
5	Iron/corollary mining	4.4	30.8
6	Nonferrous metal mining	4.4	30.8
7	Coal mining	5.3	32.8
8	Crude petroleum/natural gas	10.7	17.9
9	Stone mining and quarrying	6.1	32.6
10	Chemical mineral mining	6.1	32.6
11	New construction	15.5	34.5
12	Maintenance construction	15.5	34.5
13	Ordinance and accessories	22.7	34.8
14	Food and kindred products	16.9	33.4
15	Tobacco manufactures	23.1	34.5
16	Fabrics and thread mills	14.5	33.6
17	Miscellaneous textile goods	14.5	33.6
18	Apparel	28.5	35.0
19	Miscellaneous textile products	28.5	35.0
20	Lumber and wood products	11.2	33.7
21	Wood containers	11.2	33.7
22	Household furniture	23.8	34.2
23	Other furniture	23.8	34.2
24	Paper and allied products	8.2	32.6
25	Paperboard containers	8.2	32.6
26	Printing and publishing	11.7	34.3
27	Chemicals and products	11.9	32.1
28	Plastics and synthetics	11.9	32.1
29	Drugs	11.9	32.1
30	Paints, allied products	11.9	32.1
31	Petroleum refining	16.2	32.8
32	Rubber and miscellaneous plastic	13.3	34.4
33	Leather tanning/finishing	28.5	34.8
34	Footwear and leather products	28.5	34.8
35	Glass and glass products	9.8	35.2
36	Stone and clay wear	9.8	35.2
37	Primary iron/steel manufacturing	10.3	33.1
38	Primary nonferrous manufacturing	10.3	33.1
39	Metal containers	16.0	34.8
40	Heating, plumbing products	16.0	34.8
41	Screw machine products	16.0	34.8
42	Other fabricated metal	16.0	34.8
43	Engines and turbines	18.0	35.5
44	Farm and garden machinery	18.0	35.5
45	Construction/mining machinery	18.0	35.5

Table 10-3. continued

Input-Output Sector	Sector Description	Pre-1986 Law	Tax Reform Act of 1986[a]
46	Materials handling machinery	18.0	35.5
47	Metalworking machinery	18.0	35.5
48	Special industry machinery	18.0	35.5
49	General machinery	18.0	35.5
50	Misc. machinery, not electric	18.0	35.5
51	Office/computing machines	17.6	34.1
52	Service industries machinery	17.6	34.1
53	Electric equipment	17.6	34.1
54	Household appliances	17.6	34.1
55	Electric lighting equipment	17.6	34.1
56	Radio and TV equipment	17.6	34.1
57	Electronic components	17.6	34.1
58	Miscellaneous electrical machinery	17.6	34.1
59	Motor vehicles and equipment	22.6	34.5
60	Aircraft and parts	22.6	34.5
61	Other transportation equipment	22.6	34.5
62	Scientific instruments	19.6	35.1
63	Optical equipment	19.6	35.1
64	Miscellaneous manufacturing	22.7	34.8
65	Transportation/warehousing	2.1	35.9
66	Communications	4.2	32.9
67	Radio and TV broadcasting	9.1	33.8
68	Utilities services	11.2	31.0
69	Wholesale and retail trade	27.5	33.6
70	Finance and insurance	14.9	36.1
71	Real estate and rental	35.1	34.0
72	Hotels, personal services	26.0	38.5
73	Business services	3.7	37.5
74	Eating/drinking places	26.0	38.7
75	Automobile repair/service	1.6	35.4
76	Amusements	12.4	34.8
77	Medical and educational services	15.1	35.9

Source: U.S. International Trade Commission, *Effects of Proposed Tax Reforms on the International Competitiveness of U.S. Industries,* USITC Publication 1832, Washington, D.C., April 1986, table 4.

[a] The figures for the Tax Reform Act of 1986 reflect estimates made for the House bill, H.R. 3838.

Harmonization of Tax Rates

One result of the Tax Reform Act of 1986 is to narrow greatly the dispersion of effective corporate tax rates both across industries and across types of assets. This is shown by Tables 10-3 and 10-4.

Table 10-3 summarizes results from an International Trade Commission study that estimated marginal effective tax rates for 77 industries. Under pre-1986 law, the average marginal effective rate was

16.0 percent, but the rates ranged from a low of 1.6 percent to a high of 35.1 percent. Under the Tax Reform Act of 1986, which closely followed the House bill (H.R. 3838), the average marginal effective rate was raised to 34 percent, but the dispersion of rates was substantially narrowed. Rates for nearly all sectors now range between 30 percent and 39 percent. The coefficient of variation (the standard deviation divided by the mean) of tax rates by industry was reduced from 0.43 under pre-1986 law to about 0.07 by the Tax Reform Act of 1986.

Much the same story of compressed variation in tax rates is told by type of asset. Table 10-4 indicates that, under pre-1986 law, effective rates ranged from 1 percent to 45 percent. Under the Tax Reform Act of 1986, nearly all rates fall within the range of 27 percent to 43 percent. The coefficient of variation of tax rates by asset type is accordingly reduced from 1.26 to 0.19.

Historically, one argument for a VAT has been to improve tax harmonization among industries and types of assets and thereby to improve the efficiency of resource allocation.[3] However, the Tax Reform Act of 1986 has largely achieved the harmonization of corporate taxes. Thus, on grounds of resource efficiency, not much further case can be made for shifting to the VAT.

Reduction of Corporate Profitability

On grounds of corporate profitability, however, a strong case can be made for the VAT. The case depends upon assumptions about the incidence of taxation. There is not much debate about the incidence of a value added tax: most observers agree that the VAT is passed on to consumers in higher product prices,[4] both because the VAT is uniform from company to company, and because it is closely identified with each unit sold.

However, the incidence of corporate taxation is an old, almost theological, debate. Briefly, one school maintains that corporate income taxes are absorbed in after-tax corporate profits; therefore, corporate taxes are ultimately borne by the shareholders. Another school asserts that corporate taxes are promptly passed along to purchasers of corporate goods and services; therefore, the corporation merely acts as a tax collector from the general public.

In academic fashion, I agree with both schools, but I give each its turn. In the short run, changes in the corporate income tax are absorbed in after-tax profits; in the long-run, changes in the corporate income tax are reflected in product prices as capital enters or leaves the corporate sector.[5] In the short run, corporate income tax changes are not reflected in product prices because tax payments are highly

Table 10-4. Average Effective Tax Rates by Asset Type under Current Law and the Tax Reform Act of 1986 (%).

Asset Type	Pre-1986 Tax Law	Tax Reform Act of 1986[a]
Equipment		
Autos	2	43
Office/computing equipment	2	38
Aircraft	2	43
Trucks, buses, and trailers	2	37
Construction machinery	2	30
Mining and oilfield machinery	2	39
Service industry machinery	2	36
Tractors	2	39
Instruments	7	40
Other equipment	2	40
General industrial equipment	7	38
Metal working machinery	1	36
Electric transmission equipment	20	43
Communications equipment	1	27
Other electrical equipment	1	36
Furniture and fixtures	1	35
Special industrial equipment	1	34
Agricultural equipment	1	33
Fabricated metal products	14	32
Engines and turbines	28	42
Ships and boats	1	37
Railroad equipment	22	32
Structures		
Mining/oil and gas	11	8
Other	45	42
Industrial structures	41	39
Public utility structures	24	34
Commercial structures	38	36
Farm structures	38	36

Source: Jane G. Cravelle, "Effective Tax Rates in the Major Tax Revision Plans: Updated Tables Including the Senate Finance Committee Proposal," Congressional Research Service, Library of Congress, Report 86-691E, Washington, D.C., May 16, 1986, table 1.
[a]The figures for the Tax Reform Act of 1986 reflect estimates made for the House bill, H.R. 3838.

variable from year to year and from company to company. A company that attempted to build these fluctuations into its price structure would find itself out of kilter with its competitors and customers.[6] On the other hand, the corporate sector must compete with the noncorporate sector for resources, including capital. Therefore, over a sustained period, corporate sector prices must rise to the point where average after-tax rates of return on heavily taxed investments in corporate equity equal after-tax rates of return on lightly taxed investmsnts outside the corporate sector (principally capital invested in real estate).[7]

Such considerations persuade me that abolition of the corporate income tax would provide a short-term boost to corporate profitability. Improved profitability would be eroded little, if at all, by the value-added tax, since the VAT would be largely passed along in higher product prices.

Based on these assumptions about short-term tax incidence, Table 10-5 presents a scenario of corporate profitability under different tax regimes. By comparison with the base case projection, the Tax Reform Act of 1986 portends a decrease in corporate profitability from 13.6 percent to 12.0 percent (the percentages refer to after-tax earnings divided by total assets), and a drop in domestic savings by about $14 billion.

By contrast, the substitution of a 4 percent VAT for the entire corporate income tax would increase profitability to 20.7 percent, a substantially higher figure than achieved in recent years. At the same time, domestic savings would increase by about $61 billion, or by somewhat more than 1 percent of GNP in 1990. The substitution of a 2 percent VAT for half the corporate tax would increase profitability to 16.3 percent and would raise domestic savings by about $23 billion

Extraordinary profitability would not last. In the long run, higher corporate profitability would attract capital to the corporate sector from the rest of economy, principally from the real estate sector, and from foreign sources. With more capital resources, corporate output would expand, and corporate profitability would return to more normal levels.[8]

Total eradication of the corporate tax, coupled with a 4 percent VAT, might enlarge corporate output in the early 1990s, by about $160 billion.[9] Partial elimination of the corporate tax, coupled with a 2 percent VAT, might enlarge corporate output by $80 billion. The U.S. corporate sector serves as the cutting edge of international competition; expansion of corporate output would therefore provide an enduring international payoff from a total or partial switch to the VAT. Corporate expansion would enable U.S. goods and services both to capture new markets abroad and to recapture old markets at home.

By contrast with these scenarios, a 4 percent VAT used to balance the budget (see the last column of Table 10-5) would not improve corporate profitability, nor would it prompt an expansion of corporate sector output. The virtues of a balanced budget would instead show up in larger domestic savings, lower interest rates and lower inflation rates.

Table 10-5. Corporate Profitability and Corporate Savings under Alternative Tax Regimes (Estimates for 1990, $ Billions).

	Base Case Pre-1986 Tax Law	Tax Reform Act of 1986	4% VAT Replaces Corporate Tax	2% VAT Replaces Half Corporate Tax	4% VAT Used to Balance Budget
Gross national product	5,600	5,600	5,600	5,600	5,600
Corporate profits before tax	380	380	380	380	380
Corporate income tax	130	160	—	80	160
Value-added tax	—	—	160	80	160
Corporate profits after tax	250	220	380	300	220
Corporate profits as percentage of total capital	13.6%	12.0%	20.7%	16.3%	12.0%
Dividends paid (50% of corporate profits)	125	110	190	150	110
Retained corporate profits	125	110	190	150	110
Corporate depreciation allowances, as stated for financial purposes	190	190	190	190	190
Gross corporate savings	315	300	380	340	300
Change in gross corporate savings by comparison with the base year	—	-15	65	25	-15
Change in personal savings by comparison with the base case [a]	—	1	-4	-2	-9
Change in government savings by comparison with the base case	—	—	—	—	160
Net change in domestic savings by comparison with the base case	—	-14	61	23	136

Sources: Value Line Investment Survey, *Selection and Opinion*, New York, January 31, 1986, February 21, 1986, and August 29, 1986. *Wall Street Journal*, "Senate, House Tax Bills Remain Apart on Top Rates, Fate of Some Deductions," June 25, 1986. *Economic Report of the President*, Washington, D.C., February 1986.

[a] Calculated assuming a 6 percent personal savings rate and a change in personal disposable income equal to the sum of the changes in the individual income tax, the VAT, and dividends paid.

TAX STRUCTURE AND THE COST OF CAPITAL

The second element in the international competitive equation is the cost of capital. Peter Drucker, surveying the world economy, reached an important conclusion:

> The cost of capital will thus become increasingly important in international competition. And this is where, in the last ten years, the United States has become the highest-cost country—and Japan the lowest. A reversal of the U.S. policy of high interest rates and costly equity capital should thus be a priority for American decision makers. This demands that reduction of the government deficit, rather than high interest rates, becomes the first defense against inflation.[10]

According to Drucker, direct labor costs will become increasingly irrelevant as automation renders them an ever smaller part of the total cost of manufactured goods. Drucker further believes that raw material costs will continue their post-1980 decline, owing both to material-saving technology and to abundant supplies. Drucker concludes that capital costs will ultimately distinguish one industrial competitor from another.

Capital costs are influenced not only by direct outlays for plant and equipment, but also by the taxation of capital earnings, depreciation allowances, and other features of the economic environment. The standard Hall-Jorgenson formula for the cost of capital contains five main elements: [11]

1. The monetary outlay for the capital asset, either physical assets or a body of knowledge
2. The cost of raising financial capital
3. The rate of economic depreciation experienced by the capital asset
4. The rate of taxation of corporate profits
5. The investment tax credit and the present value of depreciation allowances permitted for tax purposes

A simple version of the formula for the cost of capital is

$$c(1 - t) = q(r + d - p)(1 - k - tz) . \qquad (10.1)$$

In formula (10.1):

c = the user cost of capital, namely the amount of money which, if received as an annual taxable rent, represents the minimum compensation necessary to make it worthwhile to hold the capital asset, taking into account the tax aspects and other features of asset ownership.

t = the marginal corporate tax rate (i.e. the statutory rate).

q = the price of the capital asset.

r = the corporate discount rate, which reflects the average cost of raising debt and equity capital.

d = the rate of economic depreciation of the capital asset.

p = the rate of price inflation applicable to the capital asset.

k = the investment tax credit, expressed as a percentage of the price of the capital asset.

z = the present value of depreciation allowances permitted for tax purposes, expressed as a percentage of the price of the capital asset (in a present-value calculation, future-year depreciation allowances are discounted by the corporate discount rate).

Table 10-6 summarizes the cost of capital for a hypothetical basket of capital goods under various tax scenarios. By comparison with pre-1986 law, the Tax Reform Act of 1986 raised the cost of the hypothetical basket of capital goods from $0.209 to $0.244 per year per dollar of assets. This translates into an increase of about 16.7 percent. By comparison, the combined effect of the Economic Recovery Tax Act of 1981 (ERTA) and the Tax Equity and Fiscal Responsibility Act of 1982 (TEFRA) was to reduce the cost of capital by about 7.3 percent.[12] In other words, the 1986 Act more than offsets the desirable features of President Reagan's earlier tax initiatives.

Based on Boskin's methodology, the adverse impact of the Tax Reform Act of 1986 on investment outlays may be estimated at about $255 billion, or about 9 percent of projected gross nonresidential fixed investment over the period 1987 to 1991.[13] Assuming that the adverse impact is spread over five years, this works out to a reduction in investment of about $51 billion per year.

If the corporate income tax in the Tax Reform Act of 1986 were replaced by the VAT, the cost of capital would drop significantly. For the hypothetical basket of capital goods, the average cost would drop from $0.244 per year per dollar of assets to $0.204, or by about 16.4 percent. Based on Boskin's methodology—which by extrapolation suggests that a 1 percent decline in the cost of capital in 1990 would stimulate investment by about $4.4 billion annually over five years—additional investment may be estimated at about $72 billion per year starting in 1991.[14]

How does the 4 percent VAT and elimination of the corporate tax compare with other policies designed to lower the cost of capital?

Table 10-6. Cost-of-Capital Estimates for Hypothetical Basket of Capital Goods in 1990 under Alternative Tax Scenarios.[a]

	Base Case Pre-1986 Tax Law	Tax Reform Act of 1986	4% VAT Replaces All the Corporate Tax	2% VAT Replaces Half the Corporate Tax	4% VAT Used to Balance Budget
Assumed parameter values					
t = corporate tax rate	0.46	0.34	—	0.17	0.34
q = price of capital asset	$1.00	$1.00	$1.00	$1.00	$1.00
r = corporate discount rate[b]	0.126	0.139	0.139	0.139	0.075
d = rate of economic depreciation[c]	0.105	0.105	0.105	0.105	0.105
p = rate of price inflation for capital assets	0.04	0.04	0.04	0.04	0.00
k = investment tax credit[d]	0.077	—	—	—	—
z = present value of depreciation allowances[e]	0.724	0.618	—	0.618	0.765
Calculated cost of capital, per year per dollar of assets	0.209	0.244	0.204	0.220	0.202

Sources: Joel L. Prakken, "The Macroeconomics of Tax Reform," this volume, and parameters supplied to the author by Prakken. Also see Council of Economic Advisers, "The Economic Case for Tax Reform," Washington, D.C., September 1985.

a. The hypothetical basket of capital goods consists of 67 percent equipment and 23 percent structures.

b. The corporate discount rates reported here reflect several assumptions:

1. The rate of interest on corporate bonds is 10 percent, and the rate of inflation is 4 percent.
2. The risk adjusted real after-tax return to asset holders is the same for both shares and bonds.
3. The Tax Reform Act of 1986 reduced the personal tax rate of the median asset holder from 30 percent to 24 percent, and the capital gains exclusion from 60 percent to zero percent.
4. As a consequence of the change in tax rules, the effective tax rate on capital gains (taking into account an average holding period of 10 years) was increased by the Tax Reform Act of 1986 from 6.1 percent to 11.5 percent.
5. The ratio of debt to equity is 41 percent.
6. As a consequence of a balanced budget and the elimination of inflation, the corporate discount rate would drop to 7.5 percent.

c. The rate of economic depreciation reported here reflects a rate of 0.129 on equipment and 0.057 on structures.

d. The investment tax credit, before the Tax Reform Act of 1986, was 0.10 on equipment and 0.03 on structures (public utilities).

e. The present value of depreciation allowances, before the Tax Reform Act of 1986, assuming a corporate discount rate of 12.6 percent, was 0.82 for equipment and 0.53 for structures. After the Tax Reform Act, assuming the corporate discount rate was raised to 13.9 percent, the present value was 0.77 for equipment and 0.31 for structures.

One alternative is a 2 percent VAT coupled with elimination of half the corporate tax. Assuming that corporate taxation is reduced by cutting the statutory rate in half, to 17 percent, the cost of capital would fall from $0.244 (under the Tax Reform Act of 1986) to $0.220.[15] Based on Boskin's methodology, additional investment may be estimated at $43 billion per year starting in 1991.

What about a much smaller fiscal deficit financed by a 4 percent VAT? In common with many observers, Peter Drucker asserts that international differences in capital costs mirror international differences in government budget policies. The argument is familiar: With a higher deficit, higher interest rates are required both to elicit greater savings (from domestic and foreign sources) and to crowd out domestic investment. Higher interest rates, in turn, push up the cost of capital by raising the corporate discount rate.

Suppose that the United States enacts a balanced budget and that a "dream scenario" ensues: Inflation drops to zero; interest rates fall dramatically; and the discount rate applied by corporations to their capital projects dive to 7.5 percent. What would all this do to the cost of capital? The calculations in Table 10-6 suggest that this "dream scenario" would reduce the cost of capital to about $0.202 per year per dollar of assets—in other words, to about the same level as elimination of the corporate income tax.

Unfortunately, there are reasons to be suspicious about this "dream scenario." In the first place, among industrial countries, the connection between nominal interest rates and government deficits, after taking inflation into account, is not particularly robust. This is shown by equation (10.2):

$$\text{INT} = 6.26 + 0.58 \, (\text{DFL}) + 0.16 \, (\text{DEF/GNP}) \qquad R\text{-squared} = 0.61.$$
$$\phantom{\text{INT} = 6.26 + } (0.70) \, (0.08) \qquad\quad (0.12)$$

$$(10.2)$$

In formula (10.2) and, later, formula (10.3):

INT   = the nominal rate of interest on short-term high-quality debt instruments, expressed as an annual percentage return. Note: Short-term rates rather than long-term rates are used as the dependent variable because year-to year changes in inflation have a more direct impact on short rates. Long rates reflect not only year-to-year changes in inflation but also expected inflation over the time horizon of the debt investment.[16]

DFL   = the GNP deflator. [17]

DEF/GNP = the combined (federal and subfederal) budget deficit or surplus expressed as a percentage of GNP. For purposes of this equation, a budget deficit has a positive sign and a budget surplus has a negative sign. [18]

CA/GNP = the current account deficit expressed as a percentage of GNP. For purposes of this equation, a current account deficit has a positive sign and a current account surplus has a negative sign.[19]

The figures in parentheses below the coefficients are standard errors of estimates.

Equation (10.2) was estimated using annual data over the period 1978-1985 for the seven major industrial countries: Canada, France, West Germany, Italy, Japan, United Kingdom, and the United States. The regression coefficients indicate that a zero rate of inflation and a zero budget deficit are associated with a 6.26 percent short-term interest rate. Thereafter, the interest rate rises by 0.58 percent for each 1.00 percentage point rise in the GNP deflator, and by only 0.16 percent for each 1.00 percentage point rise in the government budget deficit (expressed as a percentage of GNP). The impact of higher budget deficits on short-term interest rates is both small and statistically weak. Equation (10.2) suggests that slashing the budget deficit by 4 percentage points would reduce the short-term interest rate by little over 0.5 percent. To the extent that the discount rate applied by corporations to their capital projects reflects the short-term interest rate, the conclusion must be drawn that slashing the budget deficit would exert only a modest impact on the cost of capital.

In some industrial countries (such as Japan and Canada) private thrift regularly offsets government profligacy. This suggests that only when government deficits absorb more than the surplus between private savings and private investment is upward pressure put on interest rates. Only then must capital be pulled from abroad, and it is the act of pulling capital from abroad that drives interest rates higher. According to this argument, the correctly specified relationship is between the interest rate and the current account deficit, again taking inflation into account:

$$INT = 6.88 + 0.59 \, (DFL) + 0.54 \, (CA/GNP) \qquad R\text{-squared} = 0.64.$$
$$(0.64) \ (0.07) \qquad\quad (0.23)$$

$$(10.3)$$

Equation (10.3) is certainly more robust than equation (10.2). A 1.00 percentage point increase in the current account deficit is associated with a 0.54 percentage point increase in the short-term rate. Equation (10.3) would support the notion of a strong linkage between budget deficits and interest rates if bigger budget deficits were mirrored in bigger current account deficits. Unfortunately, the connection between budget deficits and current account deficits is weaker than commonly supposed. Several large-scale macroeconomic models reported by Shafiqul Islam indicate that a sustained decrease in the budget deficit equal to 1.0 percent of U.S. GNP would reduce the current account deficit by between 0.0 and 0.5 percent of GNP.[20] These models suggest that reducing the budget deficit by 4.0 percent of GNP might reduce the current account deficit by no more than 2.0 percent of GNP, with a resulting fall in short-term rates of only 1.0 percent—not enough to produce a dramatic decline in corporate discount rates.

Out of this exercise, three main conclusions can be drawn:

- The Tax Reform Act of 1986 will hurt the international competitive position of the United States by raising the cost of capital.

- Replacement of the corporate income tax by a VAT would sharply reduce the cost of capital.

- A balanced budget, if it eliminated inflation, led to a zero current account position, and prompted a dramatic fall in the corporate discount rate, would sharply reduce the cost of capital. However, it seems unlikely that a balanced budget would yield this sort of dream scenario.

TAX STRUCTURE AND THE TRADE BALANCE

The third element in the international competitive equation is the balance of trade in goods and services (more precisely the current account balance).[21] Mere mention of the trade balance requires some explanation, since prevailing academic opinion holds, first, that the trade balance says little or nothing about competitiveness and, second, that tax structure makes little or no difference to the trade balance.

My own view is that the trade balance gauges the nation's overall ability to meet foreign competition. A current account surplus that exceeds net long-term capital outflows proclaims a competitive exchange rate; conversely a current account deficit that exceeds net long-term capital inflows betrays an overvalued exchange rate.[22] I do not subscribe to the view that any trade balance is satisfactory simply because it can be financed by short-term capital flows.

Turning to the connection between the trade balance and the tax structure, it is useful to begin with an overview of the border tax adjustment question. Within the framework of the world economy, all taxes can be classified either as "source" taxes or as "destination" taxes. The distinction depends on who pays the tax—the producer (exporter) or the purchaser (importer). Historically, income taxes have been considered source taxes, while excise, sales, and value-added taxes have been considered destination taxes. Under the terms of the General Agreement on Tariffs and Trade (GATT),[23] destination taxes can be removed at the border on exports and imposed at the border on imports—hence the term "border tax adjustment."

The ability to adjust destination taxes at the border is not simply a matter of GATT rules. As a practical matter, it is difficult to trace the impact of corporate income taxes (or personal income taxes) to particular products. Any border adjustment for corporate taxes would necessarily require complicated and disputatious schedular estimates; by contrast, sales and value added taxes are easily traced to individual products.

If the corporate income tax is replaced with a VAT, many businessmen believe that export prices would fall, and that domestic goods would become more competitive with imports; hence the U.S. trade balance would improve. According to this analysis, U.S. goods and services would decline in price relative to foreign goods and services, for two reasons: first, because the VAT, which is considered a destination tax, can be adjusted at the border while the corporate income tax cannot be adjusted; second, because, the total or partial elimination of the corporate income tax would eventually result in lower prices for goods and services produced by the corporate sector.

Contrary to this line of analysis espoused by business, many scholars believe that a switch from the corporate income tax to the VAT would make no difference to the trade balance or, indeed, might even make the trade balance worse:

> the conclusion of the analysis is that the issue of international trade is not of major importance in designing a tax structure.[24]

> I want to argue that switching from income tax to VAT will not produce a net advantage to the U.S. through the balance of trade. There are good arguments for VAT, but balance of trade is not one of them.[25]

> The introduction of a [VAT] would have little direct effect on trade but would probably induce capital movements that would worsen the competitive position of United States companies.[26]

The argument that there is no connection, or even a perverse connection, between the tax structure and the trade balance rests on three propositions.

Proposition 1. The balance of trade is determined by the net volume of international capital flows. Net capital inflows compensate for any deficiency between domestic savings and domestic investment; conversely net capital outflows absorb any excess between domestic savings and domestic investment. Tax structure makes little difference to aggregate domestic savings. Hence, so the argument goes, tax structure makes little difference to the balance of trade.

Proposition 2. Proposition 1 is not affected by the presence or absence of border tax adjustments. Border tax adjustments, if put in place, will be quickly offset by exchange rate movements.

Proposition 3. If a value-added tax improves corporate profitability, more capital will be attracted to the United States from foreign firms and less capital will be sent abroad by U.S. firms. As a result, net capital inflows will expand and the balance of trade will worsen. In other words, a conflict exists between international competitiveness measured in terms of the balance of trade and international competitiveness measured in terms of corporate profitability.

According to the analysis embodied in these propositions, it makes little difference to the balance of trade whether or not the VAT is adjusted at the border. Indeed, it hardly makes a difference to the balance of trade if a VAT system, adjusted at the border, is substituted for the corporate income tax, not adjusted at the border. The key assumption in this analysis is that net capital flows are either determined independently of the tax structure, or that improved corporate profitability following the introduction of VAT would attract capital to the United States. Any improvement in the trade balance resulting from the price effects of a changed tax structure would thus be offset, or more than offset, by the impact of capital flows on the exchange rate.

This line of reasoning is open to challenge. It contains a basic weakness: the assumption that tax structure makes no difference to long-run domestic savings. In my view, the value-added tax, substituted for the corporate income tax could, in the long run, enlarge domestic savings and thereby ratify an improved trade balance. My story explores the short-run effects before turning to the long-run effects.

Before embarking on the argument, I must stress that the whole debate has the character of a minor academic squabble. At most, the argument is whether traded goods made in the United States would become more competitive on world markets by the amount of the

VAT, say 4 percent. Under a regime of floating exchange rates, a 4 percent move in the relative price of traded goods can easily occur within a month. Indeed, a scowl from Federal Reserve Chairman Paul Volcker can move exchange rates almost that much! Whether the VAT alters trade competitiveness by 1 percent, 2 percent, or 4 percent is, therefore, not a matter of decisive importance.

The Short Run: Larger Savings and Higher Investment

Continuing the earlier analysis, I assume that reduction of the corporate income tax improves corporate profitability in the short run. I also assume that the VAT is adjusted at the border, meaning that the VAT is imposed on imports and rebated on exports. These assumptions imply that the total or partial switch from corporate income tax to VAT leaves export prices expressed in dollars unchanged, at least until there is a response in corporate sector output. Moreover, prices of imports and competing domestic goods both rise by the amount of the VAT. All in all, then, there is no change either in export price relations or in import price relations that would alter the trade balance.

Recall, however, that higher corporate profitability translates into larger domestic savings, by about $75 billion annually from the position after the Tax Reform Act of 1986, if the corporate tax is entirely replaced with a 4 percent VAT; or by about $37 billion annually, if the corporate tax is half replaced with a 2 percent VAT (see Table 10-5). Meanwhile, a lower cost of capital will stimulate corporate investment in the United States. According to the estimates cited earlier, total or partial elimination of the corporate income tax would stimulate business investment by between $72 billion and $43 billion per year over five years, beginning in 1991. Combining larger domestic savings with higher business investment gives the following scenarios:

	4% VAT Replaces Corporate Tax	*2% VAT Replaces Half Corporate Tax*
Larger domestic savings (mainly business savings)	$75 billion	$37 billion
Minus: higher business investment	-$72 billion	-$43 billion
Equals: Excess domestic savings seeking to replace foreign capital inflows; or shortfall in domestic savings attracting larger capital inflows	$3 billion	-$5 billion

These scenarios suggest that using the VAT to replace all or part of the corporate tax could place upward pressure on the net demand for funds from foreign sources. This pressure might be invisible in the turbulence surrounding the overall savings-investment balance. But to the extent that tax forces enhance the net demand for funds from foreign sources, the exchange rate would appreciate, and the balance of trade would correspondingly weaken.

Aaron argues that improved corporate profitability would attract a rush of foreign capital[27] and greatly accelerate the pace of business investment beyond the estimates based on cost-of-capital calculations. That scenario would further worsen the trade balance in the short run. By the same token, it would hasten the emergence of a new long-run equilibrium.

The Long Run: Greater Corporate Output and Sustained Improvement in the Balance of Trade

After a period of exceptional corporate profitability and high corporate investment, life would settle down. Corporate profitability and investment might well approach pre-VAT levels. But corporate sector output would be cheaper, relative to noncorporate output, than before the change in tax structure. The reason is that the corporate income tax selectively raises the price of corporate sector goods and services, whereas the VAT evenly raises the price of all goods and services.

What story can be told for the trade balance? The long-run impact can be examined from two perspectives: first, from the trade perspective and, second, from the savings-investment perspective. A plausible account requires that the two perspectives be consistent.

Consistency requires that two relations be respected. To begin with, total sources of savings must equal total uses of savings:

$$PS + BS + FS = PI + GD . \tag{10.4}$$

In equation (10.4):

PS = personal savings.
BS = gross business savings (including depreciation allowances).
FS = the net inflow of capital from abroad (net foreign savings), which, by definition, equals the current account deficit.
PI = gross private investment (residential, nonresidential, and inventories).
GD = the combined budget deficit of federal and subfederal governments.

Meanwhile, net imports must reflect price competitiveness on international markets, among other variables. At the same time, net imports must equal the net inflow of foreign capital:

$$(M - X) = f(Pd, Pw, e) = \text{FS} \qquad (10.5)$$

In equation (10.5):

M = net imports of goods and services.
X = net exports of goods and services.
f = a functional relationship.
Pd = the domestic price level of traded goods, in domestic currency units.
Pw = the world price level of traded goods, in foreign currency units.
e = the trade-weighted exchange rate between domestic currency units and foreign currency units.

One consistent view that reconciles equations (10.4) and (10.5) is the view offered by Gravelle, Brannon, and Aaron: the balance of trade, $(M - X)$, is dictated by the net inflow of foreign capital, FS. The exchange rate, e, must therefore adjust to offset any changes in the price terms, Pd and Pw.

Another consistent view holds that net inflows of foreign capital will adjust to the trade balance as domestic savings expand or contract. The paragraphs below sketch this view. Note that we are considering the period *after* the surge of corporate investment has passed.

First, suppose that traded goods and services made in the United States improve in price compared to goods and services made abroad by the full extent of the VAT adjusted at the border, some 4 percent. Suppose further—contrary to Gravelle, Brannon, and Aaron— that there is no offsetting change in the trade-weighted exchange rate. What would this mean in terms of the balance of trade? According to estimates by Marris, each 1 percent depreciation in the trade-weighted dollar exchange rate in 1990 would, after three years, produce an improvement in the trade balance of about $6 billion.[28] By extension, the prospective improvement in the trade balance from a 4 percent shift in relative prices owing to the new tax structure would be about $24 billion.

Now consider the savings-investment perspective. Permanently higher domestic savings are needed to staunch the demand for foreign capital and to ratify the hypothesized improvement in trade performance. Contrary to Gravelle, Brannon, and Aaron, there are three mechanisms by which higher domestic savings might be realized.

In the first place, the improved trade balance would stimulate domestic economic activity and domestic savings through the old-fashioned Keynesian multiplier. The level of domestic savings would rise on account of a larger national income. For example, with an income multiplier of 2.5,[29] an initial $24 billion improvement in the current account would stimulate a gain in GNP of about $60 billion. This amounts to little more than 1 percent of prospective 1990 GNP and could certainly be accommodated by slack in the American economy. If the marginal domestic savings propensity is 0.25 (representing government savings plus household savings plus business savings), then additional domestic savings on account of greater economic activity would reach about $15 billion ($60 billion × 0.25 = $15 billion).

In the second place, corporate sector output is probably associated with a higher savings rate than noncorporate sector output, owing to the age and income characteristics of corporate shareholders. Suppose that savings attributable to corporate output are just 3 percentage points greater than savings attributable to noncorporate sector output. With a shift in the composition of output by $160 billion, the improved savings propensity could add about $5 billion of additional savings to the national economy.

In the third place, it is possible that capital profitability would not entirely return to pre-VAT levels. Suppose that returns on assets increased a bare 0.2 percent; suppose further that total privately held capital assets are twice GNP,[30] or about $11,400 billion in 1990; and suppose that savings on capital income are 20 percentage points higher than savings on wage and salary income. On these assumptions, savings would increase by almost $5 billion.

On the basis of these three mechanisms, it is possible to envisage an increase in domestic savings, flowing from the change in tax structure, of at least $24 billion. In other words, it is possible to envisage new savings that would curb the inflow of foreign capital and ratify the postulated improvement in the trade balance. The point of this exercise is not to defend particular numbers, but rather to suggest that, in the long run, larger domestic savings can indeed accommodate an improved trade balance.

CONCLUSIONS

In this chapter, I have identified three insignia of international competitiveness: the level of corporate profitability, the cost of capital, and the balance of trade. A case can be made that the VAT, *substituted* for the corporate income tax, would improve U.S. competitiveness measured by the first two indicators; the balance of trade, however, gives a mixed picture.

Total or partial replacement of the corporate income tax with the VAT would surely improve corporate profitability, at least in the short run. It would also cut the cost of capital, by at least as much as ERTA and TEFRA combined. Both features would enhance the international competitiveness of the U.S. economy. In the long run, higher profits would inspire larger investment and expanded corporate output relative to the noncorporate sector. The altered composition of national output represents a significant payoff from adopting the VAT.

The balance of trade presents a mixed picture. In the short run, introduction of the VAT would cause little change in the price of traded goods relative to nontraded goods. However, in the short run, the VAT might worsen the domestic balance between savings and investment. In the long run, however, a more competitive price structure for traded goods could be ratified by a permanent increase in domestic savings. In that case, the United States would enjoy an improved balance of trade.

NOTES

1. A close cousin of the VAT is the business transfer tax (BTT). The BTT is a tax levied on net business receipts, defined as receipts from the sale of goods and services minus current expenses and capital expenditures. One popular proposal is to allow the BTT to be used as a credit against liability for Federal Insurance Contributions Act (FICA) payroll taxes. In other words, a firm could deduct BTT payments from its FICA taxes (a BTT of about 4 percent would virtually offset FICA liability). In the same spirit, a BTT could be used as a deduction against corporate income tax liability.

2. All the figures in this paragraph are from Congressional Budget Office, *The Economic and Budget Outlook: Fiscal Years 1987–1991* (Washington, D.C.: CBO, February 1986), table D-4, p. 140.

3. An example will illustrate the gains that can be realized through tax harmonization. If after-tax rates of return are equalized at 10.0 percent in two industries, and if the 10.0 percent rate prevails both before and after tax reform, and if, through tax harmonization, $100 million of capital assets are shifted from industry A with a previous 1 percent tax rate to industry B with a previous 36 percent tax rate, then the annual economic gains will be $5.5 million. This is calculated as $100 million $\times$ [(10.0%)/(1.00 − .36) − (10.0%)/(1.00 − .01)].

4. For qualifications to this consensus view, see Alan A. Tait, "The Value-Added Tax: Revenue, Inflation, and the Foreign Trade Balance," International Monetary Fund, Provisional Papers in Public Economics No. 86-2, Washington, D.C., February 1986.

5. This view of corporate income tax incidence was popularized by Harberger. A recent statement appears in Arnold C. Harberger, "The State of the Corporate Income Tax: Who Pays It? Should It Be Replaced?," in Charls E. Walker and Mark A. Bloomfield, eds., *New Directions in Federal Tax Policy for the 1980s*, American Council for Capital Formation Center for Policy Research (Cambridge, Mass.: Ballinger, 1984), ch. 8.

6. The corporate tax is highly variable for two reasons: first, because operating margins are highly variable, and second, because corporate tax rates on those margins vary from company to company. The Tax Reform Act of 1986 may substantially reduce the variation in tax rates between companies, but it will have little effect on the variation in pre-tax profit margins.

7. For an analysis of the gentle taxation of real estate income under the pre-1986 law, see Roger Gordon, James Hines, and Lawrence Summers, "Notes on the Tax Treatment of Structures," National Bureau of Economic Research, Working Paper No. 1896, 1986. Under the Tax Reform Act of 1986, real estate income is subject to higher taxation, but it is still preferentially taxed by comparison with corporate income.

8. Following Harberger's analysis, the intermediate impact of abolishing corporate taxation would be a general rise in the rate of after-tax returns on capital throughout the economy. If savings from domestic and foreign sources are responsive to higher returns, corporate profitability would eventually return to levels prevailing before the corporate income tax was eliminated.

9. This calculation assumes that a 1 percent decrease in the relative price of corporate sector goods and services prompts a 1 percent increase in their volume.

10. Peter F. Drucker, "The Changed World Economy," *Foreign Affairs* (Spring 1986): 781.

11. Robert E. Hall and Dale W. Jorgenson, "Tax Policy and Investment Behavior," *American Economic Review 57* (June 1967): 391–414.

12. See Michael J. Boskin, *The Impact of the 1981–82 Investment Incentives on Business Fixed Investment* (Washington, D.C.: National Chamber Foundation, 1985), table 3.

13. According to Boskin, ibid., a 7.3 percent reduction in the cost of capital enhanced the rate of net investment by $17.5 billion annually over 5 years beginning in 1983. This amounts to $2.4 billion per 1.0 percent cut in the cost of capital. Note that the level of nonresidential fixed investment in 1983 was $357 billion and that it is estimated at $458 billion in 1986. (See Value Line Investment Survey, *Selection and Opinion*, August 29, 1986, p. 907.) By extrapolation, therefore, a 1.0 percent reduction in the cost of capital in 1986 might stimulate a $3.08 billion increase in net investment annually over the succeeding 5 years: ($2.4 billion) × ($458/$357) equals $3.08 billion per year per 1.0 percent cut in the cost of capital.

Multiplying $3.08 billion by 16.7 indicates a drop in investment of $51 billion per year, or $255 billion over 5 years. According to the Value Line Investment Survey, ibid., nonresidential fixed investment between 1987 and 1991 inclusive will total about $2,800 billion. The drop of $255 billion amounts to about 9 percent of $2,800 billion.

14. See Boskin, *The Impact of the 1981–82 Investment Incentives*, table 3, and note 13 above. Note that the level of nonresidential fixed investment in

1983 was $357 billion and that it is projected to reach $653 billion in 1991. (See Value Line Investment Survey, *Selection and Opinion*, August 29, 1986, p. 907.) By extrapolation, therefore, a 1.0 percent reduction in the cost of capital in 1990 might stimulate a $4.38 billion increase in net investment annually over the succeeding 5 years: ($2.4 billion) × ($653/$357) equals $4.38 billion per year per 1.0 percent cut in the cost of capital.

15. For cost of capital calculations, it makes a great deal of difference how the corporate tax is reduced. Generally, for a given revenue loss, larger depreciation allowances exert a greater impact in cutting the cost of capital than a lower corporate tax rate.

16. Data sources: Salomon Brothers, Inc. *International Bond and Money Market Performance 1978–85*, New York, July 1986; International Monetary Fund, *International Financial Statistics*, New York, July 1986.

17. Data source: International Monetary Fund, *International Financial Statistics*, Washington, D.C., July 1986.

18. Data sources: Vito Tanzi, "The Deficit Experience in Industrial Countries," in Phillip Cagan, ed., *Essays in Contemporary Economic Problems, 1985: The Economy in Deficit* (Washington, D.C.: American Enterprise Institute, 1985); Organisation for Economic Cooperation and Development, *Economic Outlook*, no. 38 (Paris: OECD, 1985).

19. Data sources: Organisation for Economic Cooperation and Development, *Economic Outlook: Historical Statistics* (Paris: OECD, 1984); Morgan Guaranty Trust Company, *Morgan International Data*, New York, June 1986.

20. Shafiqul Islam, "Fiscal Policy and the Dollar: A Post-Plaza Perspective," Federal Reserve Bank of New York, Research Paper No. 8607, May 1986. Also see Gary Hufbauer, "Floating Exchange Rates, Trade Deficits, and Budget Deficits," Statement before the U.S. Senate Committee on Finance, Subcommittee on Trade, Hearings on the Role of Floating Exchange Rates in The International Trading System, Washington, D.C., April 23, 1985.

21. More precisely still, the current account balance in goods and nonfactor services. International payments for factor services (interest, dividends, and royalties) reflect asset positions inherited from the past, not current competition in the goods and services markets.

22. See John Williamson, *The Exchange Rate System*, Policy Analyses in International Economics 5 (Washington, D.C.: Institute for International Economics, June 1985).

23. The rules are spelled out in the 1979 GATT Agreement on Interpretation and Application of Articles VI, XVI, and XXIII (The GATT Subsidies Code), Geneva, 1979.

24. Jane G. Gravelle, "Effective Tax Rates in the Major Tax Revision Plans: Updated Tables Including the Senate Finance Committee Proposals," Library of Congress, Congressional Research Service, Report No. 86–691E, Washington, D.C., May 16, 1986.

25. Gerard M. Brannon, "Does VAT Provide a Balance of Trade Advantage?" *Tax Notes* (March 31, 1986).

26. Henry J. Aaron, "How a VAT Would Hurt our Exports," *The New York Times*, March 3, 1986.

27. Ibid.

28. Stephen Marris, *Deficits and the Dollar: The World Economy at Risk*, Policy Analyses in International Economics 14, Institute for International Economics, Washington, D.C., December 1985, pp. 86 and 274. The estimate of about $6 billion per 1 percent depreciation in 1990 is based on my assumption that exports of goods and nonfactor services will be about $400 billion and that imports of goods and nonfactor services will be about $500 billion. Against these base levels, 1 percent depreciation enlarges the value of exports (after three years) by about $4.8 billion (1.19 percent) and diminishes the value of imports (after three years) by about $1.3 billion (0.25 percent).

29. Marris, ibid., pp. 271–272.

30. Based on data reported in U.S. Bureau of the Census, *Statistical Abstract of the United States: 1986* (Washington, D.C.: 1985), p. 462.

ADDITIONAL BIBLIOGRAPHY

Ballentine, J. Gregory, *Effective Corporate Tax Rates: Their Level and Dispersion across Industries* (Washington, D.C.: National Chamber Foundation, 1986).

Boskin, Michael J., and William G. Gale, "New Results on the Effects of Tax Policy on the International Location of Investment," National Bureau of Economic Research, Working Paper No. 1862, March 1986.

Carlson, George N., *Value Added Tax: European Experience and Lessons for the United States* (Washington, D.C.: U.S. Treasury Office of Tax Analysis, October 1980).

Carlson, George N., Gary C. Hufbauer, and M.B. Krauss, "Destination Principle Border Tax Adjustments for the Corporate Income and Social Security Taxes: An Analysis of Sectoral Effects," Annual Conference for the National Tax Association-Tax Institute of America, Papers and Proceedings, 1976.

Council of Economic Advisers, "The Economic Case for Tax Reform," Washington, D.C., September 1985.

de Seve Economics, "Effect of the President's Tax Plan on Investment Incentives," Report Prepared for the Coalition for Jobs, Growth and International Competitiveness, Washington, D.C., September 26, 1985.

Gravelle, Jane G., "Effects of the 1981 Depreciation Revisions on the Taxation of Income from Business Capital," *National Tax Journal* (March 1982).

_____ , "International Tax Competition: Does It Make a Difference For Tax Policy?" *National Tax Journal* (September 1986).

Hartman, David G., "Tax Policy and Foreign Direct Investment in the United States," *National Tax Journal* (December 1984).

Hendershott, Patric K., "Tax Reform and the Slope of the Playing Field," National Bureau of Economic Research, Working Paper No. 1909, April 1986.

Horst, Thomas, and Gary Hufbauer, "International Tax Issues: Aspects of Basic Income Tax Reform," in Charls E. Walker, and Mark A. Bloomfield, eds., *New Directions in Federal Tax Policy for the 1980s* (Cambridge, Mass.: Ballinger, 1984).

King, Melvin A., and Don Fullerton, eds., *The Taxation of Income from Capital: A Comparative Study of the U.S., U.K., Sweden, and West Germany* (Chicago: The University of Chicago Press, 1984).

Kravis, Irving B., and Robert E. Lipsey, "The Assessment of National Price Levels," National Bureau of Economic Research, Working Paper No. 1912, May 1986.

Makin, John, Norman Ornstein, and Eugene Steuerle, "The Economics and Politics of Tax Reform," American Enterprise Institute, Washington, D.C., June 1986.

Makin, John, ed., "Real Tax Reform: Replacing the Income Tax," American Enterprise Institute, Washington, D.C., 1985.

Mann, Catherine L., "Price, Profit Margins, and Exchange Rates," *Federal Reserve Bulletin* (June 1986).

Marris, Stephen, *Deficits and the Dollar: The World Economy at Risk*, Policy Analyses in International Economics 14, Institute for International Economics, Washington, D.C., December 1985.

Mutti, John, "International Implications of the Treasury Tax Reform Proposal," *Tax Notes* (April 29, 1985).

Mutti, John, and Harry Grubert, "Corporate and Personal Taxation of Capital Income in an Open Economy," *OTA Papers*, Office of Tax Analysis, U.S. Department of the Treasury, March 1984.

_____ , "The Taxation of Capital Income in an Open Economy: The Importance of Resident-Nonresident Tax Treatment," *Journal of Public Economics 27* (1985).

_____ , "The Domestic International Sales Corporation and Its Effects," in Robert E. Baldwin and Anne O. Krueger, eds., *The Structure and Evolution of Recent U.S. Trade Policy*, National Bureau of Economic Research (Chicago: University of Chicago Press, 1984).

Prakken, Joel L., Lawrence H. Meyer, and Chris P. Vavares, "The Senate Finance Committee Proposal for Tax Reform: A Macroeconomic Analysis," Center for the Study of American Business, St. Louis, Mo., May 23, 1986.

Reynolds, Alan, "Some International Comparisons of Supply Side Tax Policy," *The Cato Journal* (Fall 1985).

Sinai, Allen, Gary Leahey, and Edward Friedman, "'Tax Reform' and the U.S. Business Sector," Shearson Lehman Brothers, Economic Studies Series, New York. July 1985.

Tolley, George S., and William B. Shear, "International Comparison of Tax Rates and Their Effects on National Income," in John W. Kendrick, ed., *International Comparisons of Productivity and Causes of the Slowdown* (Washington, D.C.: American Enterprise Institute, 1984).

U.S. Department of the Treasury, *Tax Reform for Fairness, Simplicity and Growth: Value Added Tax*, Vol. 3 (Washington, D.C.: Office of the Secretary, November 1984).

U.S. International Trade Commission, *Effects of Proposed Tax Reforms on the International Competitiveness of U.S. Industries*, Publication No. 1832 (Washington, D.C.: USITC, April 1986).

U.S. Senate, *Tax Reform Act of 1986*, Report of the Committee on Finance to Accompany H.R. 3838 (Washington, D.C.: May 19, 1986).

Wall Street Journal, "Dollar Is Down but Exports Are Barely Up," July 14, 1986.

Discussants:

THE IMPACT OF A VALUE-ADDED TAX
ON U.S. COMPETITIVENESS

Henry J. Aaron

Tax analysts are belatedly paying attention to the effects of tax policy on international economic relations. In Chapter 10 Gary Hufbauer adds to this welcome and important new literature by presenting his views on the effects of introducing a value-added tax.

Actually, he discusses two quite different proposals. One is the replacement of the corporation income tax by a VAT, what I shall refer to henceforth as the "Hufbauer swap." He concludes that such a swap would substantially increase the profitability of U.S. corporations, increase corporate saving, and improve the U.S. trade balance. The Hufbauer swap would change tax structure, but not fiscal policy.

The second proposal is to use a VAT to close the deficit. Such a policy would change tax structure, although less dramatically than would the Hufbauer swap (a new tax would be added, but no old tax would be terminated); more important, it would change fiscal policy. Thus, its effects would be a compound of those resulting from a change in tax structure and of those resulting from a significantly more restrictive fiscal policy.

Both the politics and the economics of these two proposals are radically different. The difference in economics and politics becomes transparent once one recognizes that a VAT of the consumption type over each person's lifetime is approximately equivalent to a tax on labor income. The Hufbauer swap is thus simply a proposal to replace a tax on capital income with one on labor income. The fact that a VAT is equivalent to a tax on labor may at least partially explain why in his proposal of a VAT (which he calls a business transfer tax), Senator William Roth would use part of the proceeds to offset payroll taxes. Because the two proposals that Hufbauer examines are so different from each other, I shall discuss them separately.

The Value-Added Tax as a Revenue-raiser

Hufbauer estimates that introducing a VAT to cut the deficit would increase national saving. His estimates suggest that the overall effect would be almost equal to the net revenue from the tax. The increase in saving is somewhat less than the net revenue because the reduction in government dissaving is partly offset by small drops in household and business saving. His estimate assumes that the introduction of a VAT as a new tax would not change saving propensities. Hence, private saving would decline, but solely because of reduced real private disposable incomes. I think that this assumption is a reasonable one and that the estimated effect on national saving is plausible.

Hufbauer spends almost no time dilating on the virtues of a reduced deficit for U.S. competitiveness. The one direct comment is, rather curious. He writes: "The virtues of a balanced budget would . . . show up in lower interest rates and lower inflation rates." Striking by its absence from this list is any effect of reduced budget deficits on the value of the dollar. It appears that Hufbauer has no strong opinion on whether a massive reduction in the federal deficit would lead to an appreciation or to a depreciation of the dollar.

The reason for this curious omission comes a few pages later. Hufbauer presents some regressions that he claims show that the size of budget deficits is not closely correlated with interest rates and that higher budget deficits are not closely correlated with higher current account deficits.

Given the nature of these regressions, I would have been staggered had Hufbauer found any consistent relationship. The problem is that there is no reason in theory to expect increases in budget deficits to be related in any systematic way to changes in either interest rates or current account deficits. Budget deficits can rise because of domestic growth slows, which would tend to cause the current account to swing toward surplus. Or they can rise because the government undertakes stimulative fiscal policies that would tend to cause the current account to swing toward deficit. Thus, the fact that Hufbauer's regressions find no consistent relationship proves nothing.

If the U.S. deficit were eliminated by a change in fiscal policy and the federal government stopped draining more than 4 percent of GNP from capital markets, I suspect that few economic analysts would doubt both that U.S. interest rates would fall and that this drop in interest rates would lead to, or even be preceded by, a decline in the value of the U.S. dollar. And, I am sure, no analyst doubts that a drop in the value of the dollar would improve U.S. competitiveness.

A few words on the politics of the introduction of a VAT as a source of additional revenue is in order. Political forecasting is treacherous, as those of us know quite well who sagely predicted that tax reform stood no chance of surviving all the political gauntlets it had to run. But, I think it safe to say that President Reagan is not going to decide at this late date that a $150 billion tax increase, the proposal Professor Hufbauer examines, is just what the United States needs. Nor is a Congress, bruised by its debate over tax reform and relieved that it has ended without disaster, likely to pine to take up a major tax bill soon again. In short, a VAT is an academic curiosity in the United States, at least until January 20, 1989.

President Reagan's successor may view a VAT quite differently. If deficits confound current projects and remain close to $200 billion, a VAT may seem an attractive way to save a new administration from four or eight years of budgetary paralysis. And, if the Japanese should decide to adopt a VAT, it might become so chic as to be irresistible.

Swapping a Value-Added Tax for the Corporation Income Tax

Hufbauer's proposal to replace all or part of the corporation income tax with a VAT elicited from me two reactions. The first was a powerful sense of déjà vu, as the swap is identical to one suggested 25 years ago by the Committee for Economic Development on which I wrote my first journal article. The second was that Professor Hufbauer had made some qualitatively legitimate points but had grossly exaggerated their quantitative significance.

As I stated earlier, numerous analysts have shown that a VAT of the consumption type, indeed any consumption tax, is equivalent to a wage tax. Thus, if we want to be honest, the Hufbauer swap involves the replacement of a tax on capital with a tax on labor. We should be aware that to repeal the corporation income tax would bestow a windfall gain to all owners of capital goods in existence at the time of the swap. The net income from all such assets would rise by the value of the tax liability that had been removed. Furthermore, because this capital already exists, removing taxes on it cannot improve economic efficiency. But imposing new taxes to make up the revenues that repeal of the corporation income tax would necessitate would impose excess burdens. What this means is that, even if Congress decided to enact the Hufbauer swap, they would—and *should*—be under strong pressure to retain some tax on old capital. (Why repeal taxes on existing capital that impose no excess burden and replace them with taxes that do impose such burdens?) Thus, even if Congress agreed to shift tax burdens massively from capital to labor, the corporation income tax would be phased out gradually. And that means that the desirable effects that Professor Hufbauer anticipates would be deferred.

But the more fundamental question is whether and when those beneficial effects would occur. Several of them would. First, some increase in private saving might well occur, although the imperceptible response of private saving to the 1981 tax act should instill caution. Second, some drop in the cost of capital should eventually occur, and that development should improve the competitiveness of relatively capital-intensive industries. (Incidentally, no such improvement would occur if the estimates of the user cost of capital that Professor Hufbauer presents in Table 10-6 are correct. He indicates there that the user cost of capital would be higher after repeal of the corporation income tax than it is under current law.) However, for reasons I shall now present, the gains would be much smaller than Professor Hufbauer suggests, and they would be preceded by an extended period during which U.S. competitiveness would be reduced, not increased.

To explore why, I shall examine the effects of the Hufbauer swap in two stages. First, I shall confine my attention to the current account, as if all capital movements were accommodating and as if no changes in domestic saving occurred. Next, I shall examine the likely effects of the Hufbauer swap on saving and international capital movements.

Effects on Current Account

Despite its demonstrable unimportance, many people talk as if the replacement of other taxes with a VAT would improve the U.S. current account, even if no changes in saving or in international capital movements occurred. (Professor Hufbauer does not make this mistake.)

The erroneous reasoning proceeds as follows. Income taxes of all kinds are not rebateable at the border under the General Agreement on Tariffs and Trade (GATT), but value-added taxes are. It might appear, therefore, that replacing the corporation income tax with a VAT will improve the competitiveness of U.S. producers. Exporters will gain, it is alleged, because they will be trading a tax they cannot deduct for one they can deduct. Importers will gain, it is suggested, because their foreign competition will start having to pay taxes they are now spared.

This argument is clearly wrong. By itself, imposing a VAT will have no effect *through the current account* on competitive advantage. A VAT will increase commodity prices, but the rebate at the border will undo this effect for exports. The final market price of imports will be increased by the amount of the VAT, but so, of course, will be the price of import-competing domestic goods.

The fact that the VAT is neutral in its effects on international competitive advantage through the current account means that any competitive advantage must come from repeal of the corporation income tax.

In a world of flexible exchange rates, the removal of the corporation income tax, indeed any tax change, must be competitively neutral in the aggregate *if attention is confined to the current account.* Flexible exchange rates guarantee current account balance if international capital movements did nothing more than accommodate to trade flows. Companies that gain more than average from repeal of the corporation income tax would find their international competitiveness improved. Companies that gain less would find their international competitiveness worsened. That is all that one can say, *if one ignores the effects of tax policy on capital account.*

Effects on Capital Account

My argument so far suggests that *all of the effect* that taxes have on competitiveness of U.S. companies must come through their effects on capital account. And those effects depend on at least three types of behavior: domestic saving, investment by U.S. firms, and the relative demand for U.S. and foreign assets.

Most of us would agree that the Hufbauer swap would tend to increase domestic saving (because of the increase in after-tax rates of return, given the capital stock at the time of the swap), increase investment demand by U.S. firms (because of the reduction in the user cost of capital resulting from repeal of the corporation income tax), and increase the relative attractiveness of United States over foreign assets (because the after-tax rate of return on U.S. corporate capital would have increased while that of foreign capital would not have changed).

Because we know from national income identities that

$$I(d) + I(f) = S(h) + S(b) + S(g) \ ,$$

where $I(d)$ and $I(f)$ are domestic and net foreign investment, respectively, and $S(h)$, $S(b)$, and $S(g)$ are, respectively, household, business, and government saving and because, by assumption, government saving is unchanged, the assumption that U.S. producers "become more competitive" (in other words, that $I(f)$ increases) is equivalent to asserting that

$$dI(d) < dS(h) + dS(b) \ ,$$

where, as customary, d means "change in. . . . " In other words, the competitive position of U.S. firms will improve provided that the Hufbauer swap increases domestic investment less than it increases domestic private saving. This condition will be satisfied if and only if U.S. net capital exports increase or net capital imports decrease.

Hufbauer asserts that this is exactly what will happen, and he gives some estimates to back up the contention. Saving, he estimates, will rise $60 billion per year, investment will rise $30 billion per year, leaving $30 billion to flow overseas and in the process to reduce the value of the dollar, thereby helping U.S. producers to win or win back foreign markets.

Are these estimates believable? The answer, I am afraid, is that they are not. In fact, they are not even close. I would like to explain why.

To start with the change in saving, Hufbauer reports that corporations retain just over 55 percent of after-tax profits in 1986. He assumes that if the corporation income tax is repealed, they will continue to retain just over 55 percent of profits. If they do so, corporate saving will rise by just over $60 billion.

This estimate implies that with the repeal of the double taxation of corporate dividends and, presumably, with the full taxation of capital gains provided in the 1986 tax reform bill, corporate dividend-paying behavior will not change. Does anyone doubt that the pressures on corporations to increase the proportion of net profits paid out as dividends would rise and that retention rates would fall?

It also implies that household saving will be unaffected by the sharp increase in corporate saving that Hufbauer predicts. This implication also flies in the face of abundant research that household saving is negatively correlated with business saving. The purest expression of this negative relationship is Denison's law, which holds that private saving is roughly constant, so that changes in business saving are roughly offset by equal and opposite changes in household saving. Even if one rejects Denison's law in its pure form, numerous other analysts have documented that households take corporation saving into account in planning their own saving.

In short, Hufbauer's estimate of the effect of the tax swap on saving is many fold too high.

Moving now to Hufbauer's estimate that investment will rise by about $30 billion per year, I would like to be able to comment on that estimate. Unfortunately, Hufbauer provides no explanation whatsoever of how that estimate was derived. Table 10–6 reports that the user cost of capital would be higher if there were a value-added tax, but no corporation income tax, than it is under current law, a situation that could arise only if the effective rate of corporation income tax were negative (which it is not) or if interest rates rose when the corporation income tax was repealed (which they would not if saving rose as much as Hufbauer suggests). In any event, why investment would be higher than under current law *if* the user cost of capital is increased is a puzzle that will require great ingenuity to solve.

An Alternative View

Rather than comment further on Hufbauer's numbers, which I believe are inadequately supported and implausible, I want to suggest a sequence of events that would follow the repeal or substantial reduction of the corporation income tax and the imposition of a VAT to make up the revenue.

First, and foremost, the attractiveness of U.S. corporate assets would increase, both for U.S. and foreign investors. Both U.S. and foreign residents would tend to sell off foreign assets to acquire U.S. assets. In short, there would be a significant increase in relative demand for U.S. assets. The size of outstanding stock of assets dwarfs the annual flow of savings. Even a small shift of preferences on the part of U.S. and foreign owners of capital between U.S. assets, which total several trillion dollars, and foreign assets, which are even larger, would cause large movements in the ownership of capital that would cause the value of the dollar to appreciate sufficiently to produce balancing current account flows—in other words, to an increased deficit on current account. This situation would persist for several years.

Eventually, after the adjustment of portfolios and the location of real capital to the changed tax situation was complete, capital flows would come to a halt, and the value of the dollar would fall. At that point, the United States would be obliged indefinitely to pay returns on the increased net holdings of U.S. assets by foreigners. To make these payments, the United States would have to run a larger current account surplus (or a smaller deficit) than would otherwise have been necessary and the value of the U.S. dollar would have to be lower than it otherwise would have been to make these flows occur. In short, only after adjustments of portfolios and of the real capital stock would the improvement in U.S. competitiveness that Professor Hufbauer forecasts actually occur. While that adjustment is occurring, U.S. competitiveness would be reduced.

To be sure, if U.S. saving increases in response to the change in tax structure, the effects that I have just sketched will be mitigated. But analysis that is based exclusively on annual income flows and takes no account of shifts in stocks of assets is simply incapable of dealing with the consequences of a major shift in capital income taxation. For this reason, I do not think that Professor Hufbauer's estimates are even close to an accurate portrayal of the effects on U.S. competitiveness of replacing the corporation income tax with a value-added tax.

THE INTERNATIONAL TRADE ISSUES

Harvey E. Bale, Jr.

One hears much today of the argument that the huge U.S. trade deficit is attributable to the lack of an "administration trade policy," meaning insufficient action by the administration to deal with foreign subsidies and other unfair trade practices. This absurd assertion is made notwithstanding the important gains of the administration since 1985 in addressing a wide range of foreign unfair trade practices and the overvalued dollar.

The argument about the trade deficit's relation to U.S. trade policy has led to a real possibility that the Congress will pass seriously flawed trade legislation. The trade bill that passed the House in 1986 (H.R. 4800) contains a key provision based on this absurd argument. West Germany, Japan, and Taiwan are called on to reduce or eliminate unfair trade practices that contribute to their large trade surpluses with the United States or face potential unilateral U.S. actions (quotas and tariffs) to reduce the surpluses by 10 percent per year. This piece of demagogic legislation is akin to treating a battlefield wound with a hand grenade.

The plain fact is that the U.S. trade and current account deficits continue to grow *in spite of* a strong and aggressive U.S. trade policy. Instead, our trade deficit and our basic international competitiveness have more to do with our domestic economic policy—our spending and tax policies. The president's efforts to get major spending reductions would have substantial favorable effects not only on our budget deficit, but also on our trade deficit. Regarding tax policies, we have nearly passed a major tax reform package that should serve to increase our economy's efficiency in the longer term. Thus, the discussion of an entirely new tax system is one about possible future options.

Sharing Gary Hufbauer's spirit of humility, I will not venture so far as to "claim to *prove* anything about the relationship between tax structure and competitiveness." Also, I share Hufbauer's belief that a case can be made for the existence of some significant relationship between the two. Perhaps, the most significant connection between taxes and competitiveness is through the impact of tax policy on national savings and investment.

As Hufbauer has argued, the Tax Reform Act of 1986 will undoubtedly increase overall corporate efficiency in the long term by more nearly equalizing tax burdens across sectors and types of investment. However, as the new tax code will increase the tax burden on corporations by more than $20 billion per year, we may see a reduced level of overall corporate profitability over the next several years.

Lower overall corporate profitability means reduced corporate savings. Corporations have historically made the largest contributions to the domestic stock of capital in this country (Table 10-7). In 1985 corporate saving was $566 billion, or 81 percent of total gross private saving of $695 billion. (Corporate saving exceeded gross domestic saving—$554 billion in 1985—because of government dissaving of $140.1 billion.) Thus, changes in corporate profitability can have dramatic effects on the level of gross domestic saving.

Moreover, if gross domestic saving falls, our trade and current account deficits can only worsen. The gap between gross domestic saving and gross domestic investment has increased dramatically in recent years (Table 10-8). In 1982 investment exceeded saving by only 0.03 percent of GDP. By the first quarter of 1986, that gap had increased to 3.6 percent of GDP. Foreign investors have increased their holding of dollars, forcing up the price of the dollar. As the dollar has appreciated, U.S. goods have become less price competitive, and the ultimate result has been trade and current account deficits of magnitudes previously unimaginable.

The sizable U.S. current account deficit is, as it must be, financed by substantial net foreign capital inflows. The amount of required foreign financing and the current account is equivalent to, or a mirror image of, the gap between domestic saving and domestic private investment shown in Table 10-8. Table 10-9 breaks out the components of savings/investment/current-account gaps, showing that in 1983, 1984, and 1985 gross domestic private (corporate and personal) saving was sufficient to finance private investment; however, the $100+ billion combined federal, state, and local government deficits in these years made the difference in creating the domestic savings gap that translates in the foreign accounts into a large current account deficit.

Table 10-7. Gross Domestic Product and Saving in Current Dollars ($ Billions).

	Gross Domestic Product	Total Saving	Gross Private Saving	Personal	Corporate	Government	Federal	State and Local
1980	2,586.4	405.9	435.4	110.2	325.2	-30.7	-61.2	30.6
1981	2,907.5	477.5	504.7	130.2	374.5	-28.2	-60.0	31.7
1982	3,114.8	446.4	557.1	153.9	403.2	-110.8	-145.9	35.1
1983	3,350.9	469.8	600.6	133.2	468.4	-130.8	-179.4	48.6
1984	3,726.7	584.5	693.0	172.5	520.5	-108.5	-172.9	64.4
1985	3,947.7	554.9	695.0	129.0	566.0	-140.1	-199.3	59.2
1986(1)[a]	4,080.3	580.0	725.9	126.3	599.6	-145.9	-210.5	64.9
Saving as a Percentage of GDP								
1980	100.0	15.7	16.8	4.3	12.6	-1.2	-2.4	1.2
1981	100.0	16.4	17.4	4.5	12.9	-1.0	-2.1	1.1
1982	100.0	14.3	17.9	5.0	12.9	-3.6	-4.7	1.1
1983	100.0	14.0	17.9	4.0	14.0	-3.9	-5.4	1.5
1984	100.0	15.7	18.6	4.6	14.0	-2.9	-4.6	1.7
1985	100.0	14.1	17.6	3.3	14.3	-3.5	-5.0	1.5
1986(1)[a]	100.0	14.2	17.8	3.1	14.7	-3.6	-5.2	1.6

Sources: *Survey of Current Business*, Department of Commerce and U.S. Trade Representative.
[a] 1986 figures annualized from the first quarter.

Table 10-8.   Growth of the Saving-Investment Gap, 1980-1986.

	Gross Domestic Saving		Gross Domestic Investment		Gap	
	$ billions	% GDP	$ billions	% GDP	$ billions	% GDP
1980	405.9	15.7	401.9	15.5	+4.0	0.2
1981	477.5	16.4	471.5	16.2	+6.0	0.2
1982	446.4	14.3	447.3	14.4	-0.9	0.0
1983	469.8	14.0	501.9	15.0	-32.1	-1.0
1984	584.5	15.7	674.0	18.1	-89.5	-2.4
1985	554.9	14.1	669.3	17.6	-114.4	-2.9
1986[a]	580.0	14.2	726.3	17.6	-146.3	-3.6

Source: *Survey of Current Business*, Department of Commerce and USTR.
[a]1986 figures annualized from the first quarter.

Using Hufbauer's calculations, corporate profits in 1990 would fall from $220 billion under current law to $190 billion under the Tax Reform Act of 1986. In turn, gross corporate saving would fall from $313 billion to $296 billion. Thus, in the absence of dramatic cuts in government spending or private investment, the gap between domestic saving and domestic investment would increase, and the current account deficit would worsen. (This scenario assumes that foreigners will continue to desire to increase their holdings of U.S. assets. Persistent, huge current account deficits could, however, lead to a loss of confidence in the worth of these assets and lead to an extreme credit crunch and very high interest rates.)

We are already approaching a near-crisis political atmosphere surrounding the issue of the trade deficit. Politicians are under increasing pressure to take action to decrease imports and increase exports. Import-surcharge proposals and the Gephardt amendment of the House-passed trade bill (mentioned above) epitomize this approach. Supporters of an import surcharge claim that the surcharge would raise substantial revenue, increase the price of imported goods, and cause domestic consumption to switch from imported goods to domestic goods. Imports would fall, and the trade balance would improve.

In effect, some Democrats, labor officials, and business leaders have proposed a partial value-added tax, applicable only to imports. The trade "benefits" of the surcharge would come through its revenue-raising effect as well as the surcharge's effect in raising the relative price of imports. Increased government revenue, if not offset by increased spending, would decrease the government deficit and its drain on gross domestic saving. As the federal deficit falls, gross domestic saving rises, reducing the gap between domestic savings and

Table 10-9. The Relationship between the Foreign Balance, Domestic Saving, and Investment ($ *Billions*).

	T	+	S	=	NFI	=	PS	–	GB	–	PI	+	SD
1980	-19.6	+	21.1	=	+1.5	=	+435.4	–	30.7	–	401.9	+	-0.9
1981	-23.7	+	29.0	=	+5.3	=	+504.7	–	28.2	–	471.5	+	0.3
1982	-33.3	+	25.7	=	-7.6	=	+557.1	–	110.8	–	447.3	+	-6.6
1983	-63.2	+	19.7	=	-43.5	=	+600.6	–	130.8	–	501.9	+	-11.4
1984	-111.5	+	6.3	=	-105.2	=	+693.0	–	108.5	–	674.0	+	-15.7
1985	-121.7	+	6.3	=	-115.4	=	+695.0	–	140.1	–	669.3	+	-1.0

Key: T = balance on trade in goods.

S = balance in services, interest, and transfers.

NFI = net foreign investment (= the current account).

PS = gross private domestic saving, made up of corporate saving plus household saving.

GB = net government borrowing, consisting of the budget balances of the federal government and state and local governments.

PI = gross private domestic investment.

SD = statistical discrepancy.

domestic investment. Real interest rates fall, capital inflows decline in response to lowered returns, and the dollar depreciates further. Imports become even more expensive, U.S. exports become cheaper abroad, and the trade balance settles at a level to accommodate the new, lower level of capital inflows.

Unfortunately, a "temporary" three-year import surcharge, as it has been proposed, does not address the fundamental disequilibria driving the current account imbalance. If federal spending has not been reduced, the deficit will return to its previous levels once the surcharge is removed. The deficit may even worsen if the government begins to spend these additional revenues. A temporary import surcharge can at best postpone the need to address the domestic saving-investment imbalance.

This leaves aside the serious and negative international trade ramifications of a surcharge. There is a provision in the GATT allowing for import surcharges to be imposed to rectify serious balance-of-payments disequilibria. However, this provision is meant to apply chiefly in a world of fixed exchange rates, where an import surcharge could offset the effects of an artificially overvalued currency. In a floating exchange rate regime, an import surcharge is much less defensible and would be perceived as a protectionist move. An import surcharge would be seen as a U.S. repudiation of the commitments embodied in the GATT and movement toward closing U.S. markets to international trade. The end result would be retaliation against U.S. exports.

The Gephardt amendment contained in the 1986 House-passed trade bill attempts to address the trade deficit in a similar manner, by targetting countries which have large trade surpluses with the United States and forcing them to reduce their exports or increase their imports. Although bilateral actions of this sort could have some effect on the bilateral balances, they would have no effect at all on the overall deficit (unless some revenue is raised through tariffs or surcharges, and used to reduce the federal deficit). If imports from Japan or West Germany were restricted, we would import more from other markets.

Basically, we cannot reduce the U.S. trade deficit without closing the gap between domestic saving and investment. We are utterly dependent on foreign capital inflows to finance domestic investment and consumption.

Despite the clear negative implications of an import surcharge (or partial VAT), or country-selective measures such as the Gephardt amendment, the pressures for measures will grow as our trade and current account deficits grow or persist. Again, the problem is not

U.S. trade policy. Rather, it is one of generating greater domestic savings relative to domestic investment. This requires either or both: the *reduction of federal government dissaving* and the *increase in private saving.*

Clearly, achieving the maximum possible reductions in our federal budget *expenditures* needs to be the top priority. The problem with raising any tax revenues on top of existing taxes—whether as income or consumption taxes—is that the hard choices about expenditure reduction can thus be avoided. The additional revenues, in effect, could finance the expenditures that "cannot" be cut.

In any case, it is extremely difficult to see how U.S. trade policy (or the type of "agreement" that the G-5 reached concerning exchange rates) can be effective in the light of the enormous savings shortfall that exists in this country. As a means to correct this, the option of a VAT to replace some or all income taxes is far superior to the import surcharges that have been suggested and debated in the Congress.

While it would apply a new tax to imports, it would be "GATT legal," since the tax would also apply to similar goods produced in the United States. A problem with another proposal before the Congress, for a business transfer tax (BTT) to be credited against Federal Insurance Contributions Act (FICA) payments, is the issue of GATT legality. A BTT added to imports at the border would not offset any taxes paid by the foreign producer, while a BTT paid by domestic producers would be credited against payment of FICA taxes. A BTT credited against FICA payments would amount to a tax only on imports, since the producer of the imported good would bear the full burden of the tax, while domestic producers would essentially pay no additional tax via the BTT credit against the direct FICA tax.

If a VAT were substituted for the corporate income tax in a revenue-neutral way, we could see two possible beneficial effects on the U.S. trade-competitiveness position.

First, in the short run, such a shift could increase the level of domestic saving if (using Hufbauer's assumption) corporate savings are not passed on in lower domestic prices. Raising this level of saving would improve the current account.

Second, over the longer run, when lower corporate income taxes may be largely passed through in the form of lower prices (using Hufbauer's assumption about longer term incidence), the prices of domestically produced goods would have tended to fall in relation to imports. This eliminates the positive savings effect that arises in the short term; but, if the present tax reform proposal realizes expected

Table 10-10.   Value-Added Tax Rates for Selected Countries.

	Food and Other Goods[a]	Normal Goods	Luxury Goods
Austria	10	20	32
Belgium	6	19	25–32
Denmark	22	22	22
France	5.5–7	18.6	33.3
West Germany	7	14	14
Ireland	Goods = 35	Services = 23	—
Italy	2	18	38
Luxembourg	3–6	12	12
Netherlands	0–5	19	19
Norway	20	20	20
Sweden	19	19	19
United Kingdom	0	15	15

Source: Deloitte Haskins & Sells.

[a] In many countries, some items are taxed at a lower rate for reasons of social policy. These items may include food, pharmaceuticals and medical services, and other essentials.

substantial efficiency gains, which in turn are translated into higher personal incomes and saving, and if it were supplemented by a VAT substitute for corporate income taxes to restore corporate profitability, then the domestic level of saving in the longer term could still significantly increase.

Because GATT rules allow rebates of indirect taxes (while they forbid direct-tax rebates) at the border, many in Congress and industry perceive other VAT countries taking a "free ride" at the expense of the United States. VAT rates vary across many industrial countries and among types of goods, and in some cases may be as high as 35 percent (Table 10-10). The degree to which the tax structure affects the price competitiveness of traded goods is uncertain. If all countries have similar and uniform tax structures, theoretically there should be no net effect of them on price competitiveness. But when tax structures differ, as between the United States and many of our trading partners (Table 10-11), it is unclear to what extent border adjustments affect the trade balance, or are offset by exchange rate movements.

We in the administration may have a greater political problem for our ongoing free-trade negotiations with Canada if that country moves to a full or partial VAT system now under consideration. Many in industry already believe the Canadians have an "unfair" competitive advantage in an "undervalued" Canadian dollar. I do not believe the Canadian dollar is undervalued; but this perception would be further fostered by a Canadian VAT or BTT.

Table 10-11. Central Government Indirect Tax Revenue as a Percentage of Total Tax Revenue: Selected OECD Countries, 1980-1984.

	1980	*1981*	*1982*	*1983*	*1984*
United States	5.1	6.4	5.4	5.6	n.a.
Canada	24.4	27.1	25.5	23.5	23.6
Japan	13.0	13.3	12.8	11.9	12.6
France	31.1	30.7	30.2	28.5	29.2
West Germany	23.7	23.4	22.8	23.1	23.0
Greece	46.2	47.1	45.9	47.1	42.3
Ireland	41.2	42.2	42.7	42.6	n.a.
Italy	28.5	26.3	25.5	25.7	26.3
Netherlands	23.0	22.3	21.5	21.5	22.6
Norway	33.6	34.4	34.6	34.8	34.9
Portugal	47.8	45.8	n.a.	n.a.	n.a.
Spain	19.7	20.7	21.4	n.a.	n.a.
Sweden	26.7	27.9	28.3	29.3	31.1
Switzerland	20.0	19.7	19.3	19.3	19.0
United Kingdom	33.4	32.8	31.7	31.1	31.1
Australia	25.2	24.2	24.8	26.5	26.4

Source: OECD, *National Accounts.*

Debates over incidence, pass-through, border adjustments, and other price issues may be of little real importance in the end. Without an increase in the level of gross domestic saving relative to gross domestic investment, a policy directed at improving the trade balance through the relative price mechanism will be frustrated. And, by corollary, any policy that affects the level of saving or investment, either closing or widening the gap, will have a direct and lasting effect on the trade deficit.

The impact of the VAT on the international competitiveness of the United States, through the VAT's effects on savings, deserves greater study, building in the papers by Hufbauer and others presented at this conference. A VAT's impact on our competitiveness and long-term growth would be more beneficial than any future substantial increases in individual income and particularly, corporate profit taxes.

A CONGRESSIONAL PERSPECTIVE ON COMPETITIVENESS

Max Baucus

For the rest of this century, the United States will be struggling to improve its international competitiveness. In time, this struggle will drive most public policy decisions, whether about education policy, labor policy, or tax policy.

International Competitiveness

Proponents of a value-added tax for the United States have always argued that a VAT will enhance America's international competitiveness. In the past, this argument wasn't taken seriously. International competitiveness did not seem very important. After all, when Congress passed the 1954 tax code, Americans produced 60 percent of the annual world output of goods and services and owned 26 of the world's top 30 corporations. We led the pack and could afford to make tax policy decisions as if we existed in splendid isolation from the rest of the world. Even in 1977, when Al Ullman proposed his infamous Tax Restructuring Act, the unified trade account showed an $8 billion surplus.

Well, the world isn't changing. It has *changed*. Instead of producing 60 percent of the annual world output of goods and services, we produce 26 percent. Instead of owning 26 of the top 30 corporations, we own 15. And instead of having a trade surplus, we have a $140 billion deficit. Exports have fallen, and we import 50 percent of our steel, 33 percent of our lumber, 31 percent of our textiles, and 30 percent of our cars.

These are not just abstract statistics. They translate into lost jobs and a lower standard of living. The median income of the average American family is now the same as it was in 1965.

The days of splendid isolation are over. We can no longer afford to take U.S. economic superiority for granted.

As a result, we have to make many changes. Eliminating unfair foreign trading practices, as mentioned by Dan Rostenkowski in Chapter 2 and by Harvey Bale in the preceding discussion, is important. So is stabilizing the value of the dollar.

But the problem runs much deeper than that. Since 1960, U.S. productivity has grown at an annual rate of 2.7 percent. Britain's has grown at a rate of 3.6 percent. Japan's has grown at a whopping 8 percent. Every major foreign competitor has increased its productivity faster than we have. *Every* one.

Unless we reverse this trend, all the trade laws in the world won't maintain our competitive edge or our relative standard of living.

In the end, we have to *produce* our way out of the trade deficit by improving the "inputs" into our economy—the cost of capital, education and training, and management skills.

The VAT and Competitiveness

The tax system plays an important role. It affects virtually every aspect of the economy. And it has a particularly important effect on the cost of capital. As technology improves, labor costs become a smaller proportion of total costs, and the cost of capital becomes a more important factor in international competition. At this point, our cost of capital is twice as high as Japan's and significantly higher than any of our major competitors'. The tax reform bill may drive it even higher.

If we want a tax system that is designed for international competition, we need to address this problem.

Dr. Hufbauer's chapter explains how this can be done. It is an excellent analysis, and I agree with his conclusions. By replacing the corporate income tax with a value-added tax, we would improve our international competitiveness. We could impose the tax on imports and rebate it on exports, without running afoul of the GATT tax subsidy provisions. Some economists argue that exchange rate adjustments would offset this effect, but I do not have much faith in exchange rate theories after the unpredictable fluctuations we have seen in the 1980s.

In addition, Hufbauer shows that replacing the corporate tax with a 4 percent VAT would increase corporate profits, increase personal savings, and reduce the cost of capital. Overall, that would stimulate as much as $50 billion/year worth of new investment.

We also should consider imposing a VAT to reduce the budget deficit, as Lester Thurow has suggested. The budget deficit is an important cause of our trade deficit. It offsets all of the personal savings in this country, forcing us to rely excessively on foreign capital. At this point in the budget process, the easy spending cuts and revenue base broadeners have already been enacted. From the perspective of international competitiveness, a VAT may be preferable to continued budget deficits. This deserves further study.

The Political Dimension

Congress is unlikely to enact a VAT in the near future. At this point, the Congress of the United States is no more likely to replace the corporate income tax with a value-added tax than the next session of the Montana legislature is to outlaw fly fishing.

As an institution, Congress tends not to lead, but to follow the mood of the American people. And the American people are not in the mood for a national consumption tax. Consumers are not likely to support a tax on consumption just because it will increase corporate profits. They are suspicious that those profits will be frittered away on tinker-toy mergers rather than plowed back into new equipment and better jobs. They saw what happened after the Economic Recovery Tax Act of 1981. And they know that the decline in corporate taxes has not been accompanied by an increase in U.S. competitiveness. The tax reform debate demonstrated this in spades. The one argument that was consistently well received was the argument that we should raise corporate taxes.

Given such skepticism, we can only persuade the American people to support a VAT if we persuade them that their standard of living will rise. And that kind of persuading will require American business leaders to demonstrate that they can look beyond short-term profit margins and come up with creative solutions to get their companies moving.

Conclusion

That is no easy task. And it won't happen overnight. But we are not running a 100-yard dash. We are running a marathon. We have gotten off to a slow start, but there is plenty of time to establish a steady, winning pace.

There is good evidence that a VAT will improve U.S. international competitiveness. But it will take time to convince the American people that improving the nation's international competitiveness means improving our standard of living. And it will take time to refine the analysis of the VAT and just how it should work. Professor Hufbauer's chapter is an important contribution to both of these efforts.

Chapter 11

The Value-Added Tax
as a "Money Machine"

J. A. Stockfisch

SOME FISCAL THEORY

Large federal deficits raise a question of whether new taxes should be introduced. A value-added tax (VAT) is a possibility that has acquired much attention in recent years. One reason is its adoption by many West European countries.[1] Some critics believe, however, that increased tax revenues encourage increased government spending and that a VAT too easily raises additional revenue. For example, Charles McLure states "if foreign experience is any guide, introduction of a VAT would facilitate growth of the relative size of the federal government, whether VAT was initially introduced to raise additional revenue or only as a substitute for existing taxes."[2] Hence, some skeptics regard a VAT as a potential "money machine" that will only feed more spending rather than help reduce deficits.

The idea that a tax increase, whether it be from a VAT or any other tax, leads to increased government spending is at odds with a more "orthodox" view that there is no connection between a particular tax and either the total level of government spending or total tax revenues raised. This idea is an implication of the concept of "functional finance," advanced by Abba Lerner[3] and others, which asserts that the function of taxes levied by a central government is to *constrain* private spending and to avert inflation, given ability of the

This paper does not necessarily represent the views of the Rand Corporation or any of its government contractors.

government to raise unlimited funds from a central bank. (Yes there is a "money machine"; but it is the central bank, not any particular tax.) An important implication of the functional finance viewpoint is that elected policymakers are less constrained than many believe. If so, tax increases (as well as expenditure reductions) are feasible ways to reduce a deficit.

The functional finance model thus claims there is no functional relationship between taxing and spending. It recognizes that one part of the government (or Congress) appropriates funds and specifies entitlement programs, and another part determines the tax laws which, in conjunction with general economic conditions, determine government revenues. Deficits or surpluses invariably result. The Treasury takes care of these, or "picks up the pieces," so to speak, by its debt operations. It also follows that a deficit is not a policy instrument; rather, it is a residual. The relevant nonspending fiscal policy instruments are taxes, and debt operations, including open market operations of the central bank.

It is obvious that the functional finance model rests upon a system of highly developed secondary security markets, as well as a central bank. Hence Treasury debt operations and central bank open-market operations are essential parts of the system. In this setting, sale of Treasury debt to private investors performs the same function as do taxes. Specifically, they induce people to surrender dollars in exchange for interest-bearing assets. Since Treasury debt purchasers would otherwise have spent on privately created assets, Treasury debt sales are deflationary. But from the private sector's side of things, some private investment is "crowded out." Thus the functional finance approach to fiscal economics is relevant to the subject of this conference, namely, concern that deficits adversely affect capital formation.

It should be nevertheless acknowledged that the functional finance model as stated here draws criticism from several directions. The argument that introduction of a VAT by increasing tax revenues increases government spending is a version of the assertion that taxes and spending are somehow functionally related. The "supply-side" experiment undertaken by the present administration may be viewed as the obverse of the idea that tax increases lead to spending increases; specifically, tax reductions lead to expenditure reductions.[4]

Private investment "crowding out" of Treasury debt operations as an aspect of the functional finance model draws a criticism from two widely divergent quarters. First, there are Keynesians (most of whom would accept the functional finance view about taxes), who would nevertheless reject the idea that Treasury debt sales to private investors have strong if any "crowding-out" effects. In strict Keynesian (income-expenditure) models, any deficit, whether "financed" by new money or by debt sales to the private sector, is expansionary. Debate over this issue has been a prominent part of macroeconomics.[5]

The second (and implicit) rejection of the functional finance model is evident in the revival of David Ricardo's argument by Robert Barro that deficits and sale of government debt change nothing because the additional government debt implies additional future taxes to pay interest on the debt (if not to retire the debt as well).[6] Barro draws upon two arguments to support this position. First, he asserts that future tax payments necessary to service the debt are "capitalized." Hence, the effect of additional government debt on people's net worth or "wealth" is zero. Second, if people are motivated to acquire wealth—say for the welfare of future generations— they will save and buy "real assets," and not be "fooled" by pieces of paper issued by the Treasury.

Capitalization of future taxes is thus a necessary feature of Barro's implicit attack on the functional finance model. Unfortunately, Barro does not derive his tax-capitalization assertion from any model or theory of capital or capitalization rate determination. Nor does he consider the possibility that some taxes might be capitalized and others might not. For example when Ricardo wrote on taxation, war finance necessitated by Napoleon caused Britain's increased debt. As Ricardo and other classical economists viewed the world, any "surplus" adequate to finance a war had to come from the only place where a surplus was available, namely, from the land-owning class and hence from land rents. A good theoretical case can be made that special taxes on land rents are capitalized. But whether more general taxes are capitalized is a point upon which Barro and his followers are silent.

Thus the theoretical underpinnings of the functional finance model, although open to challenge in certain aspects and contexts (for example, the nineteenth-century gold standard), remains fairly robust. It asserts separability with respect to major sets of central government fiscal actions. It imposes minimal a priori constraints on any model attempting to explain the financial behavior and actions of sovereign governments. It suggests that deficits should not be surprising; but it further implies that deficits are not inherent in the nature of things. Moreover, it suggests that both tax increases and spending reductions reduce the need to sell Treasury debt. This last idea is not universally accepted, however, especially with respect to the possible introduction of a new revenue source, like a value-added tax. As indicated above, some students have argued that introduction of a VAT in many West European countries led to increased spending. This assertion suggests that some of the available evidence be examined.

SOME EVIDENCE: TAX TRENDS

Since 1970, 12 member countries of the Organization for Economic Cooperation and Development (OECD) have introduced value-added taxes. Twelve other OECD countries did not.

Available OECD national accounting data permit making comparisons for the 24 OECD member countries. These data provide annual series for the years 1964–1981 for gross domestic product (GDP), total direct and indirect taxes, and social security taxes. Data are also published, for most of those countries, on total government spending, government saving (that is, deficits and surpluses) and, for a few of these countries, detailed breakdowns of spending.[7] In this section we examine tax trends as between these sets of (VAT and non-VAT) countries.[8] In the next section, attention is directed to government spending and saving behavior.

Table 11-1 treats the tax behavior of these countries. It presents "growth ratios" designed to capture the point of whether taxes increased more in VAT countries after the introduction of VAT than in non-VAT countries. In this table a growth ratio is the annual rate of growth in a country's total tax collections divided by the annual rate of growth in its GDP. Thus, for Austria during the period 1964–1973, total tax revenues (excluding social security taxes) grew at an annual compound rate of 10.51 percent, while its GDP grew 9.51 percent. Division of the first figure by the second gives the 1.105 ratio, shown in the first column of Table 11-1. When this ratio is greater than unity, taxes (and, likely, the relative size of government) grew at a faster rate than did the economy as a whole.

Table 11-1 shows "Before" and "After" columns. In the case of countries with a VAT, these refer to subperiods before and after the country imposed its VAT. The year in parentheses immediately after the country is the year in which a country introduced its VAT. Thus, in the case of Austria, during the period 1974–1981, total tax revenue grew 8.37 percent a year while GDP grew 7.89 percent. The 1.061 ratio in the "After" column is the ratio of those growth rates. For the 12 countries without a VAT, the "Before" and "After" subperiods are taken to be 1964–1971, 1972–1981, on the assumption that 1971 represents the median year in which the VAT countries imposed their respective VATs.

Table 11-1. Tax to Gross Domestic Product Growth Ratios for Countries with and without Value-Added Taxes (VAT), 1964–1981, before and after Imposition of VAT.

	Total Taxes (Excluding Social Security)/GDP		Total Taxes (Including Social Security)/GDP	
VAT Countries	Before	After	Before	After
Austria (1973)	1.105	1.061	1.120	1.193
Belgium (1971)	1.306	1.286	1.301	1.247
Denmark (1967)	1.482	1.234	1.486	1.101
France (1968)	0.900	1.023	1.018	1.124
Germany (1968)	1.031	1.049	1.180	1.171
Ireland (1972)	1.278	1.066	1.308	1.107
Italy (1973)	0.878	1.282	0.993	1.179
Luxembourg (1970)	1.239	1.487	1.202	1.512
Netherlands (1969)	1.167	1.043	1.300	1.094
Norway (1970)	1.247	1.102	1.386	1.067
Sweden (1969)	1.424	1.075	1.533	1.202
United Kingdom (1973)	1.188	1.050	1.193	1.038
Average	1.187	1.146	1.252	1.169
Non-VAT Countries	*1964–71*	*1972–81*	*1964–71*	*1972–81*
Australia[a]	1.150	1.170	1.150	1.170
Canada	1.324	0.953	1.374	0.976
Finland	1.183	1.053	1.221	1.036
Greece	1.193	1.059	1.205	1.113
Iceland	1.120	0.901[b]	1.034	0.908[c]
Japan	1.116	1.134	1.131	1.248
New Zealand[a]	1.245	1.121	1.245	1.121
Portugal	1.343	1.172	1.462	1.175
Spain	1.034	1.117	1.173	1.227
Switzerland	1.193	1.295	1.241	1.501
Turkey	1.196	1.024	1.256	1.012
United States	1.155	0.999	1.244	1.051
Average	1.188	1.083	1.227	1.128
Average, excluding Canada and Iceland[c]	1.167	1.114	1.211	1.165

Sources: (1) Organization for Economic Cooperation and Development, *National Accounts: Detailed Tables, Vol. II, 1964–1981* (Paris: OECD, n.d.); and (2) Organization for Economic Cooperation and Development, *Revenue Statistics of OECD Member Countries: 1965–76* (Paris: OECD, n.d.), pp. 82–83.

Method: Table 1 of source (1) provided gross domestic product data in current prices. "Taxes" as shown above is the sum of "direct" and "indirect" taxes as given in Table 9 of source (1). "Taxes and social security" are the sum of "direct," "indirect," and "social security contributions" as given in Table 9 of source (1). In some instances, Table 9 of source (1) did not have complete information. However, Table 3, on p. 81 and Table 4 on p. 82 of source (2) have data on "total" tax revenue as a percentage of GDP" and "total tax revenue (excluding social security) as a percentage of GDP" for years 1965–1976. These per-

(Table 11-1. continued overleaf)

Notes to Table 11-1.   continued

centages were applied to GDP obtained from source (1) to complete the series when Table 9 of source (1) was incomplete. For each subperiod shown in Table 1 above, a least-squares annual compound growth rate was computed using the equation $y = ae^{bt}$, where y represents the estimated value for a given year t, a is the zero intercept, b is the annual growth rate and e is the natural log base. The annual growth rates shown above are the computed b coefficients.

[a] Australia and New Zealand have no social security taxes; they do have sizable social security benefits, however.

[b] Applicable only to 1972–1977 period.

[c] See text for explanations as to why this average is more relevant for comparisons.

Table 11-1 presents ratios for both total taxes excluding social security taxes, and total taxes including social security taxes for those countries that had social security taxes. Perhaps the dominant fiscal phenomenon of the past 25 years in industrialized or developed countries is the growth of social security systems and related entitlement programs. Aspects of this development will be discussed later. Meanwhile, some might argue that social security taxes are not taxes in a strict sense but, instead, a form of individual saving and insurance designed to implement an individual life-cycle saving program. Rather than try to resolve or to make implicit assumptions about this issue, Table 11-1 presents data treating both tax concepts.

What do the ratios shown in Table 11-1 indicate? First, the fact that most of the ratios exceed 1 says that the relative size of government (and taxes, both including and excluding social security) grew in both groups of countries, both before and after the imposition of VAT.[9] Second, some retardation in the relative growth rates of both tax categories has occurred in both groups of countries over time. Third, in most countries with social security taxes, social security taxes have grown more than have the aggregate of other taxes, in both VAT and non-VAT countries during the pre-VAT and post-VAT periods.

With respect to the assertion that a VAT increases the relative size of government, Table 11-1 indicates the following: After the imposition of VAT, the growth ratio of total taxes excluding social security taxes to GDP fell in 8 of the 12 VAT countries. It fell in 8 of the 12 non-VAT countries. In 9 of the VAT countries, the growth ratio of taxes including social security to GDP also fell during the latter period. It also fell in 7 of the 10 non-VAT countries that had social security taxes. Thus, by these measures there is essentially no differences between growth behavior of the size of the government sector in VAT and non-VAT countries. This suggests that other political and economic factors are determining the relative size of government.

In two of the non-VAT countries—Canada and Iceland—the ratio of taxes to GDP fell below 1 during the post-VAT period, suggesting a relative decline in the size of government. The main explanation for this behavior on Canada's part, however, appears to have been an increase in nontax government revenues, which were mainly mineral royalties. During the period 1972-1981, Canada's GDP grew 12.52 percent annually, and its total government revenues (including property earnings) grew 12.77 percent annually. If the latter figure were used, the 0.953 ratio shown in Table 11-1 would be 1.020. Thus, its government sector did not decline. Iceland's performance is unclear because tax data is only available for the 1972-1977 period.

GOVERNMENT SPENDING AND SAVING

An objection can be made that the Table 11-1 growth ratios take no account of government growth due to deficit spending.[10] Not to do so can indeed understate the relative size of government, as well as its relative growth. However, to the extent growing deficits do account for government growth, it seems the case for the "functional finance" model described at the beginning of this chapter is supported. What insight, if any, does government spending and saving behavior provide about this issue?

Table 11-2 presents data on government "disbursements" as an average percent of GDP for the years 1971-1973 and 1981-1983, for most of the countries treated in Table 11-1. In Table 11-2, "disbursements" are the sum of government consumption (including all defense spending), interest payments on debt, and transfer payments, including social security. (Not included is government capital formation, which for most of the period for most countries was either relatively small or, often, negative.) The third column of the table shows the change in the ratio of government disbursements to GDP as between these periods.

The table also shows the change in "government saving" as between these periods. Deficits are an increasingly prominent part of the fiscal landscape. However, during the early 1970s, at which time most of the European OECD countries adopted the VAT, most of the countries treated here ran surpluses on their current disbursement accounts.[11] Thus, for example, Belgium had an average annual government surplus of equal to 1 percent of its GDP during the 1971-1973 period. During 1981-1983, it had an annual deficit that averaged 8.3 percent of its GDP. Hence there was an adverse swing of 9.3 percentage points in Belgium's fiscal policy impact on capital formation. It can be argued that for an increase in the "share" that

Table 11-2.   Ratios of Government Disbursements to Gross Domestic Product for Countries with and without Value-Added Taxes, 1971-1973 and 1981-1983.

VAT Countries	Period 1971-73	Period 1981-83	Spending Change	Gov't. Saving	Taxation
Austria	33.1	44.4	11.1	-5.8	5.3
Belgium	35.9	52.9	17.0	-9.3	7.7
Denmark	37.6	56.9	19.3	-13.3	6.0
France	34.4	46.9	12.5	-3.6	8.9
Germany	35.1	44.5	9.4	-4.9	4.5
Ireland	34.3	52.9	18.6	-9.3	9.3
Italy	34.5	48.8	14.3	-3.5	10.8
Luxembourg	30.6	45.4	14.8	0.3	15.1
Netherlands[a]	43.9	55.4	11.5	-6.5	5.0
Norway	39.2	45.4	6.2	-1.6	4.6
Sweden	39.8	60.8	21.0	-10.7	10.3
United Kingdom	33.7	44.2	11.5	-5.0	6.5
Average	36.0	49.9	13.9	-6.1	7.8

Non-VAT Countries					
Australia	22.7	31.7	9.0	-3.4	5.6
Canada	32.8	41.4	8.6	-5.0	3.6
Finland	27.7	35.4	6.3	-5.4	0.9
Greece	22.0	36.8	14.8	-5.8	9.0
Iceland	25.4	27.8	2.4	-1.7	0.7
Japan	17.0	27.2	10.2	-4.5	5.7
New Zealand	n.a.				
Portugal[b]	19.7	37.8	18.1	-6.4	11.7
Spain	19.7	30.8	11.1	-0.3	10.8
Switzerland	22.7	29.9	7.2	-1.1	6.1
Turkey	n.a.				
United States	30.1	39.5	9.4	-3.4	6.0
Average	24.0	32.8	8.8	-3.7	5.1

Sources: Organization for Economic Cooperation and Development, *National Accounts: Detailed Tables, Vol. II, 1971-1983* (Paris: OECD, 1985), for all countries except Portugal; for Portugal, United Nations, *National Accounts, Statistics, Main Aggregates and Detailed Tables, 1982* (New York: UN, 1985).

n.a. = not available.

[a] 1972-1973, 1981-1982.

[b] 1972-1973, 1980-1981.

government is spending relative to GDP, some portion is accounted for by reduced government saving or increased deficits, and the remainder is financed by additional taxes. Table 11-2 provides such a perspective.

Table 11-2 indicates the following points. First, the VAT countries were bigger government spenders before or at the beginning of the introduction of VAT then were the non-VAT countries. Second, the relative size of government, as measured by disbursements, has increased noticeably more in the VAT countries than in the non-VAT ones, which supports the assertion that introduction of a VAT increases the size of government. However, the VAT countries also exhibited a larger adverse swing in government saving or deficits than did the non-VAT countries, which supports the claim that tax revenues do not constrain spending.

It is also evident from Table 11-2 (as in Table 11-1) that tax increases occurred in both VAT and non-VAT countries, as indicated by the last column, labeled "Difference," which is the increase in the government share of GDP not accounted for by the government saving.

The VAT countries had both a greater swing in net saving, or shift toward deficit spending, than did the non-VAT countries, as well as an increase in taxes. This latter behavior suggests that the tax structure of these countries be examined more closely.

Table 11-3 summarizes aspects of tax-structure changes. For the years 1971 and 1983, indirect taxes and social security taxes as a percentage of total taxes are shown for each country. (The difference between the sum of these and 100 percent is the share that direct taxes are of total tax revenue.) It should be mentioned that a VAT is classified as a so-called "indirect tax." In most of the VAT countries the VAT constitutes between one-half to two-thirds of total indirect tax revenues.

Table 11-3 indicates the following. First, in both VAT and non-VAT countries, indirect tax revenue as a share of total tax revenue has fallen, while the relative importance of direct and, especially, social security taxes has increased. In many of the VAT countries, the relative importance of indirect taxes (which includes the VAT) has fallen sharply (Austria, Belgium, France, Ireland, Italy are examples). Thus it appears that if a VAT induces additional spending and taxing, it does so by a process that encourages the relative growth of direct and social security taxes.

Second, it is noteworthy that non-VAT countries, both before and after the adoption of VAT by the VAT countries, had and continue to have a relatively heavier indirect tax burden than do the VAT countries. This evidence may be relevant to the claim that a VAT is "regressive." Even if it is, what is important for the distributional effects of tax policy is the overall impact of the tax systems on income distribution. During the period examined, it appears that the relative importance of income taxes, which are generally progressive, has increased.

Table 11-3.   Indirect Taxes and Social Security Taxes as a Percentage of Total Taxes, 1971 and 1983, for VAT and Non-VAT Countries.

	1971		*1983*	
VAT Countries	*Indirect*	*Social Security*	*Indirect*	*Social Security*
Austria	46.7	25.1	39.4	29.0
Belgium	36.1	30.6	27.7	29.8
Denmark	40.3	03.7	38.7	04.0
France	42.7	37.7	33.7	44.9
Germany	35.7	32.8	30.9	38.9
Ireland	57.2	13.4	44.6	20.1
Italy	39.2	40.2	27.1	35.2
Luxembourg	30.5	30.1	29.2[a]	31.2[a]
Netherlands[b]	29.6	37.9	24.8	42.3
Norway	41.7	26.1	35.5	24.7
Sweden	34.4	19.9	30.7	26.7
United Kingdom	42.6	14.2	42.4	18.0
Average	39.7	25.9	33.7	28.7
Non-VAT Countries				
Australia	42.6	—	46.0	—
Canada	42.7	08.6	38.1	13.0
Finland	41.6	14.7	39.8	12.9
Greece	57.4	26.9	49.5	32.5
Iceland	70.0	07.9	73.0	04.0
Japan	34.5	22.4	27.2	29.8
New Zealand	n.a.			
Portugal[c]	52.4	20.6	46.2	29.5
Spain (1982)	40.1	39.2	39.2	45.9
Switzerland	28.2	23.5	22.5	30.6
Turkey	n.a.			
United States	35.1	17.3	29.7	23.8
Average	44.5	20.1	37.9	24.6

Source: Same as Table 11-2.

n.a. = not available.

[a]1980.

[b]1970 and 1982.

[c]1970 and 1981.

Third, it is evident from Table 11-3 (as it is from Table 11-1) that social security taxes have grown significantly in both VAT and non-VAT countries. This development, of course, is in line with the growth of social security and related entitlement programs in virtually all countries which may be partly financed by sources other than social security taxes.

CONCLUSIONS

The idea that introduction of a new tax, and a VAT in particular, increases the ratio of total taxation to total economic activity is not supported by recent experience of the OECD countries. As indicated by Table 11-1, the ratio of total taxes to GDP increased in both VAT and non-VAT countries during the period since the VAT was in place in most of the VAT countries. During this period, the relative importance of indirect taxes to total taxes fell in both VAT and non-VAT countries, and indirect taxes continued to be relatively less important in the VAT-country revenue systems than they were and continue to be in the non-VAT countries. This behavior lends support to the idea claimed by VAT advocates during the 1960s that a VAT was motivated to rationalize existing indirect tax systems and, especially, to eliminate "turnover" taxes with their troublesome adverse effects on production efficiency. It also suggests that a VAT—even though it might be regressive by itself—need not lead to a more regressive tax system. Other elements of the tax and fiscal system can be and are simultaneously changed and, often, in ways that may offset the effects of a single instrument.

During the VAT period, however, total government spending, including entitlements and resource-using programs, increased significantly in both VAT and non-VAT countries. Moreover, this increase was greater in the VAT than in the non-VAT countries. In both groups of countries, there was a significant reduction in "government saving," either in the form of increased deficits, reduced surpluses, or an elimination of surpluses and a shift to deficit spending. Again, VAT countries exhibited a sharper shift toward deficits (or reduced surpluses) than did the non-VAT countries. Simultaneously, tax financing in both sets of countries shifted more toward social security and income taxes, again to a greater extent in VAT countries than in non-VAT countries.

This observed behavior does not support the simple idea that introduction of a VAT increases either the ratio of total taxes to total income, or total government spending as a share of total spending, the ratio of indirect to direct taxes, or any other interesting fiscal policy behavioral relationship. About the only thing that stands out is that VAT countries appear to have been big government spenders before the advent of VAT, and they have continued to behave that way, in part by increased reliance on deficit spending. And to the extent they have increased taxes, like everybody else they have adopted a tax program that places more reliance on direct and social security taxes.

Conversely, the behavior of these countries—both VAT and non-VAT—seems consistent with the functional finance model. Specifically, there appears to be no observable connection between government spending and taxing. At most, there might be some relationships, with a sizable lag, between social security programs and social security tax revenues in some countries. But even here the historical record is ambiguous: For many years, the U.S. Treasury enjoyed cash surpluses due to social security taxes exceeding benefits while many people complained about modest deficits in the administrative budget.

It should be recognized that the subject of this chapter presents a problem of deciding what, exactly, is the relevant question. A case can be made that there are several questions that can be asked, and it may not be possible to answer each of them.[12] The question initially posed is: Does imposition of a VAT increase the relative size of government? In terms of a theory (and model) of government and public finance, the maintained hypothesis is that the answer is yes. This assertion or hypothesis is the opposite of what the functional finance model indicates, namely, that government spending and taxing are not functionally related. Unfortunately, the theory implicit in the idea that a tax increase causes a spending increase is not well developed or, for that matter, even articulated.

Meanwhile, I shall assert that the experience of VAT and non-VAT countries examined here does not refute the functional finance model. Hence, the old-fashioned idea that a tax increase is one way to reduce a deficit remains useful practical advice for citizens and policymakers.

NOTES

1. In all countries adopting a VAT, export rebates and imposition of the VAT on imports has been a feature of the system. The rationale for this practice has been the idea that a VAT increases the prices of domestic goods relative to imports, and that something must be done to restore the pre-tax parity. Many advocates further like the idea of the export rebate because it resembles an export subsidy which may help mitigate balance of payment problems. But all of this concern is misplaced in a setting of flexible exchange rates.

2. Charles E. McLure, "Value-Added Tax: Has the Time Come?" in Charls E. Walker and Mark A. Bloomfield, eds., *New Directions in Federal Tax Policy for the 1980s* (Cambridge, Mass.: Ballinger, 1983), p. 199. See also Henry J. Aaron, ed., *The Value-Added Tax: Lessons from Europe* (Washington, D.C., The Brookings Institution, 1981), pp. 16, 59, for another example of this view.

3. Abba Lerner, *The Economics of Control* (New York: Macmillan, 1944), ch. 24.

4. This is not the main nor is it even a necessary part of the "supply-side" concept. Rather, it asserts that lower tax rates change incentives in such a way as to increase greatly the supply of factor services available in the market. However, a case can nevertheless be made that most "supply-siders," as policy advocates, oppose increasing taxes in order to reduce deficits.

5. This issue centers on the extent to which an increment of debt might be a money substitute instead of a substitute for other assets, like long-term corporate bonds or equities. This has been a major bone of contention between "Monetarists" and "Keynesians."

6. Robert Barro, "Are Government Bonds 'Net Wealth'?" *Journal of Political Economy 82* (November 1974): 1095-1117.

7. The International Monetary Fund in its *Government Finance Statistics* in addition provides much detailed data on government spending by function.

8. This section draws upon my "Value-Added Taxes and the Size of Government: Some Evidence," *The National Tax Journal 38* (December 1985): 547-552.

9. The relative size of government need not necessarily grow in proportion to the rate at which tax revenue increase. The government could run budgetary surpluses and retire outstanding debt. However, over the period with which we are concerned, this behavior was not evident. See below for further discussion.

10. See Chamber of Commerce of the United States, "Does the Value Added Tax Contribute to Increased Government Spending and Taxation?" *Backgrounders, No. 13*, Washington, D.C. (May 8, 1986): 1-2.

11. These were Japan, Australia, Austria, Belgium, Denmark, Finland, France, West Germany, Greece, Iceland, Ireland, Luxembourg, Norway, Spain, Sweden, Switzerland, and the United Kingdom. During the 1981-1983 period, Japan, Australia, Finland, West Germany, Norway, and Switzerland had surpluses.

12. One way of posing the question is to ask: What would have been the size of government in the VAT countries in the absence of VAT? To answer this question requires a model (and a theory for that model) in which the concept of a VAT is one of the independent variables. Unfortunately, no such theory and model exists.

Discussants:

THE RELATIONSHIP OF TAX REVENUES TO GOVERNMENT SPENDING

Bruce K. MacLaury

In Chapter 11 J. A. Stockfisch presents a very useful analysis of European nations' experience with the value-added tax (VAT). I have personally learned a great deal from reading his chapter and, frankly, I have no fundamental quarrel with the kinds of conclusions that he draws from his analysis of those data.

Nevertheless, I think that kind of an analysis misses some important points that ought to be taken into account when considering a consumption tax. If anything, Stockfisch takes too rational and sophisticated an approach, one that does not, in my view, take account of political realities. Now, when I say political realities, I realize that I am trespassing on the comments of the next respondent, Representative Dick Schulze, so I will tread carefully.

As Dr. Stockfisch emphasized at the end of his chapter, he was trying to answer a very specific question, but there are other ways of looking at that question. Indeed, in a footnote, he raises one of those other ways. He asks specifically, what would have been the size of governments in the VAT countries in the absence of a VAT? He then goes on to dismiss that particular way of looking at the question, because he says that there is no economic theory or model that will allow an economist to provide an answer to that hypothetical question.

And yet, I think that by dismissing that kind of a question, we are not accounting for a good deal of a practical nature as to how the VAT might work in practice in the United States today. It is, in fact, the very kind of question that we need to ask. Don't we need to supplement our economic analyses with some intuition, or counterintuitive suppositions, about how a VAT would work today?

Specifically, I think we ought to reject either end of the extremes in this context. Let me say what I think those extremes are. The first is that tax revenues and government expenditures are determined completely independently, one from the other. In fact, Dr. Stockfish said he believes that government spending is not constrained by a lack of revenues, because there is a central bank to pick up the pieces.

I guess that is where he and I most fundamentally differ. I think that there is good evidence that there is a constraint on expenditures arising out of the absence of tax revenues. I do not know how else to interpret, for example, the Congressional Budget Office and congressional budget process that was instituted in 1974 in an effort to give the Congress a handle on matching up tax revenues with expenditures. That was the whole purpose in giving Congress an overview of how the government finances what the Congress appropriates.

Second, it seems to me that the whole environment of 1985–1986, the environment of Gramm-Rudman-Hollings, is predicated upon the fact that there is, and must be, a linkage between expenditures on the one hand and revenues on the other. Although I agree with Jack Stockfisch that the major reason for the passage of the supply-side tax cuts in 1981 was to reduce marginal rates, to create greater incentives, to get government off the taxpayer's back. Nevertheless, it seems to me that as soon as one says, "Get government off our back," one is identifying the hidden, or not so hidden, agenda of the Reagan administration: to starve the Congress for revenues so that they will spend their time worrying about how to decrease government expenditures.

In that sense, I think the political evidence of the past few years says that there must be a connection between revenues on the one hand and expenditures on the other.

The other extreme view, which I also would reject, is the notion that there is any tight—and I emphasize the word "tight"—linkage in any particular time period between revenues, on the one hand, and expenditures on the other. If there had been any sort of a tight linkage, we would not find ourselves facing the problem of large deficits which we do today. It seems to me that politicians do, indeed, tend to increase expenditures until they can no longer justify doing so and have to face the political music of raising the taxes to pay for them.

And I think that this is the evidence that Dr. Stockfisch puts before us in terms of the Organization for Economic Cooperation and Development: There were major pressures to increase social expenditures in many European countries. It was true in the United States as well, and it was only the absence of revenues that, in some sense, called a halt to that process.

If we accept this kind of basic political proposition and the related fact that deficits do matter, we also have to accept the proposition that relatively "painless" sources of revenue, and powerful ones, such as a VAT, will indeed allow government expenditures to grow faster or remain higher than they would in the absence of that revenue.

Now, this does not mean, I hasten to say, that increased tax revenues will all go to finance higher spending and none to the reduction of deficits. Especially in today's circumstances in the United States, reducing the deficit has taken on such a high priority, politically as well as in economic terms, that any tax increase, whether a VAT or some other, will in fact go partly (I hope substantially) toward reducing deficits rather than simply blowing up expenditures once again.

I am convinced that we must raise revenues as part of the solution to reducing deficits. I am also convinced that these additional revenues will allow us to maintain defense and nondefense expenditures at higher levels than in the absence of those new revenues. Whether that means larger government is debatable. I would argue so myself, and I think we shouldn't blink at that. I agree with Jack Stockfisch that the answer we give depends very much on how we put the question.

A different set of issues is raised when we consider what kind of taxes to increase. It is an undeniable fact that a small percentage increase in sales taxes raises large amounts of revenue. We have heard that time and again. I think sales tax increases are a very powerful revenue-raising tool, especially starting at low marginal rates. Likewise, in the form of a business expenditures tax, the tax is partly hidden from the consumer and, again, more powerful.

Thus, like a powerful and to some extent painless drug, the value-added tax is a powerful revenue raiser and is effective in that sense. But it is also dangerous, at least when it is initially introduced. It is too easy.

The fact of the matter is that a revenue source can do either great good or great harm, and that depends entirely upon the circumstances. It is difficult, therefore, to make general propositions about whether we should or should not introduce a VAT, because it may give us "too much" government.

A CONGRESSIONAL VIEW

Dick Schulze

The American system of separation of powers between spending and taxation supports J.A. Stockfisch's functional finance theory, that there is little functional relationship between taxing and spending.

I realize that this can be argued either way, but if you look at Congress today, you can make the argument very succinctly. All you have to do is look at our current budget deficit, the arrangement of the Appropriations and the Ways and Means Committee, and what we have gone through since the imposition of the Congressional Budget Act. Then all I need to do is pose just one question: Has the budget process been successful since that time? I think we all would have to answer with a resounding "no." The idea was to get the budget under control, and obviously we have not done that.

Gross domestic product (GDP) statistics show that the size of government in both VAT and non-VAT countries has grown significantly and somewhat proportionately. Social Security and entitlement programs account for a great deal of this growth.

After imposition of the VAT, the growth ratio of total taxes to GDP fell in the majority of both VAT and non-VAT countries. Also, VAT countries were bigger spenders before the imposition of the VAT, and this may have encouraged greater use of government dissaving or deficit financing. This again supports the functional finance theory. Thus, government growth in VAT countries is attributable more to deficit financing than to imposition of a VAT.

In terms of the relationship of indirect taxes and social security, both VAT and non-VAT countries experienced a decline in the importance of indirect taxes relative to social security and to direct taxes. If VATs induce more spending, it seems to me they do so by encouraging increased direct or social security taxes, rather than being the vehicle themselves for increased spending. The study also shows that non-VAT countries do have a heavier *indirect* tax burden than VAT countries.

Dr. Stockfisch rightly concludes that the relationship between the imposition of a VAT and the growth of government is not necessarily supported by economic data.

In the United States the imposition of some form of consumption tax could be merged with a balanced budget-tax limitation constitutional amendment, or imposed as a Business Alternative Minimum Tax, such as I proposed, introduced, and offered as an amendment to the 1986 Tax Reform Act. Either one of these approaches would address the "money machine" aspect of a consumption tax.

Let's look for a minute at the overall picture. In Chapter 2 Dan Rostenkowski, chairman of the House Committee on Ways and Means, presents a very bold and firm position of being opposed to any consumption tax. Inasmuch as I admire the chairman and what he was able to accomplish over the past couple of years (although I don't agree with all of it), I think he could take no other position. If he did, he would be saying, in effect, that what he has accomplished was wrong.

I believe there are two important factors in determining the political future of a consumption tax. One is the competitive aspects of international trade, and the other is the impact of the newly enacted alternative minimum tax on small, emerging companies as well as more mature industries that are undergoing somewhat radical competitive changes. When the consequences of this burdensome, and even onerous alternative minimum tax becomes apparent, there will be a cry for a new type of tax. At that time, it may be that the imposition of a VAT to replace an alternative minimum tax would be considered.

In terms of the trade aspects, it seems to me that the executive branch has been hanging their hats on exchange rates as the solution to these tremendous trade deficits. Having been on the House Trade Subcommittee for 10 years, it is my view that certainly the exchange rates are part of it, but obviously, from the figures, it is not the entire solution. Exchange rates are important, but so is comparative advantage, and so are taxes of all kinds, excise, sales taxes and tariffs, income taxes and direct and indirect taxes, and so is the degree of government support in the overall picture of trade.

What we have got to do is sit down and decide what America's role will be in the international trade market at the turn of the century between 2000 and 2010 and how U.S. tax structure dovetails with what we envision for our country. I am afraid we did not do that in the passage of, or the working on, the 1986 Tax Reform Act.

Can a VAT be progressive? Yes. Can it be increase-resistant? Yes. But the answer is political.

For any consumption tax, in my opinion, there are four goals— goals that we strove for when we drafted the Business Alternative Minimum Tax Amendment. One is to provide for simplicity of administration; another is to impose it as a border tax, as a mechanism similar to our international competitors; third is to address the ability to pay, or the regressive-progressive arguments; and the fourth is to limit the so-called money machine aspects of a consumption tax.

※ *Chapter 12*

On the Incidence of
Consumption Taxes

David F. Bradford

Tax debates are usually plagued by ignorance, and the debate about consumption taxes is no exception. Participants often mean different things by the term *consumption tax*. Even when they mean the same thing, they often fail to understand the different ways that same thing may be implemented. When the discussion turns to who will bear the tax, the critically important details of how consumption tax rules might be introduced is typically overlooked. Thus, confusion about exactly what is under consideration is added to the already very difficult problem of determining the incidence of even a well-defined tax structure. The purpose of this chapter is to lay out the incidence issues in a nontechnical manner.

To illustrate the complexity of the subject, consider the case of introducing the Accelerated Cost Recovery System (ACRS) to the income tax system in 1981. By shortening the period over which the cost of newly constructed equipment and structures could be deducted from a company's revenues in calculating income subject to tax, ACRS reduced the tax liabilities of businesses. Most people probably regarded this step as regressive, that is, as relatively favoring the well-to-do. People liked the new policy who (a) thought the tax system was too progressive to begin with or (b) thought the stimulus to economic prosperity would buy general benefits that offset the distributional change.

However, economic analysis suggests a surprising twist to the story.[1] Increasing the depreciation allowances on newly constructed capital makes new assets cheaper than old. Since new and old assets must command the same prices, the introduction of ACRS presumably imposed a windfall loss on owners of existing assets, that is, on the wealthy, particularly compared with the alternative of lower rates of tax. Conversely, the sort of changes now in train, lengthening depreciation lives and lowering tax rates, may be expected to generate windfall gains for owners of existing assets, in contrast to the conventional view that these changes increase the burden on wealth owners.

I shall return to these ideas below. Before that, though, we must deal with matters of definition and of specifying the assumptions underlying the incidence analysis.

WHAT ARE CONSUMPTION TAXES?

Although the term *consumption tax* is widely used, there is very little uniformity of view about exactly what is meant by it. Most people seem to have in mind a tax like the sales taxes familiar in the states' fiscal armories. Followers of tax policy would add to the list value-added taxes (VATs) of the sort widely employed in other countries, along with the business transfer taxes (BTTs) that have been under discussion here and in Canada. The real aficionados recognize the possibility of a consumption tax that looks much like the existing income tax, variously referred to as a cash flow income tax or consumed income tax.[2]

I associate two properties with taxes based on consumption. Property 1 may seem obvious, namely, that a consumption tax relates tax liabilities to a measure of a household's or individual's consumption. This contrasts with the theoretical idea of an income tax, which relates liabilities to a measure of the algebraic *sum* of a household's consumption and saving during a year (since saving may be negative, income may be either larger or smaller than consumption). A tax on consumption might be levied at a flat rate or at graduated rates. It might be based on an annual aggregate of a household's consumption, or it might be based on a discounted flow of such expenditures.

Property 2 of a consumption tax is derived from the idea that consumption tax burdens should not be influenced by the level of saving. In other words, the reward to saving obtained by the saver should be equal to the payoff society obtains by investing the saved amount. Thus, a second defining characteristic of a consumption tax is equality between the "before-tax" and "after-tax" rates of return on saving.

Both of these properties are often but not always present in taxes commonly thought of as consumption taxes. Thus, a flat-rate tax on some annual measure of consumption will also imply a zero tax on the normal return to saving. However, a graduated-rate tax on an annual measure of consumption will generally not do so (because amounts set aside in a time of low consumption, and hence low marginal tax rate, may pay off in a future period of high consumption, and hence high marginal tax rate). Furthermore, some taxes (such as a tax on consumer purchases of gasoline) that do not affect the return to saving and are often thought of as consumption taxes do not attempt anything like a comprehensive measurement of consumption.

The X-Tax as Typical Consumption Tax

Rather than picking any one of the existing possible consumption taxes to analyze here, I would like to emphasize the range of institutional arrangements that would constitute introduction of a broad-based consumption tax. To draw attention to the elements that link and distinguish the various possibilities, I shall describe here a hypothetical consumption tax, which I call the X-Tax. In addition to having properties that might make it interesting as an actual policy option, the X-Tax provides a convenient framework for analysis.

The Basic Mechanics Explained. The X-Tax can be viewed as a variant of a value-added tax (VAT) with adjustment for vertical distribution; it is also a close relative of the Simple Flat Tax that has been promoted by Robert Hall and Alvin Rabushka.[3] The basic X-Tax is a *system* with two components: a business tax (paid by all businesses, whether corporate, proprietorship, or partnership) and a compensation tax (paid by all who receive compensation for services as employees or the equivalent). All businesses pay tax—to be specific, let us say at a rate of 7 percent—on a base consisting of the receipt from sales of all types (including sales out of inventory or sales of other existing assets) less the outlays for purchases from other businesses and less payments to workers, whether for current, past, or future services. All workers pay tax on the amount received from businesses (or payments of the same character from nontaxpaying entities such as governments). Payments from more than one employer are added together. The resulting total is taxed at graduated rates, with an exempt amount and marginal rates of, say, 3, 5, and 7 percent on successively higher levels of compensation. No other receipts of the workers (such as interest or dividends) are included in the compensation tax base. The top rate of compensation tax is the same as the single flat rate of business tax.

The X-Tax would be administered in conjunction with the existing income tax; virtually all of the information required is either used in

Table 12-1. The X-Tax Illustrated in a Simple Economy.

Basic X-Tax (Employee pay deducted)

Firm A

Receipts from sales	100,000
less	
Purchases from firm B	20,000
Salary to worker 1	15,000
Salary to worker 2	35,000
Business tax base	30,000
Tax (@ 7%)	2,100
Profits after tax	27,900

Firm B

Receipts from sales	80,000
less	
Salary to worker 3	75,000
Business tax base	5,000
Tax (@ 7%)	350
Profits after tax	4,650
Total business tax	2,450

Worker 1

Salary		15,000
Tax		
7% of amount over 50,000 and less than	50,000	0
5% of amount over 25,000 and less than	25,000	0
3% of amount over 10,000 and less than	10,000	
	25,000	150
Total tax		150
Disposable income		14,850

Alternative X-Tax (Earned income credit)

Firm A

Receipts from sales	100,000
less	
Purchases from firm B	20,000
Salary to worker 1	13,950
Salary to worker 2	32,550
Business tax base	80,000
Tax (@ 7%)	5,600
Profits after tax	27,900

Firm B

Receipts from sales	80,000
less	
Salary to worker 3	69,750
Business tax base	80,000
Tax (@ 7%)	5,600
Profits after tax	4,650
Total business tax	11,200

Worker 1

Salary		13,950
Tax credit		
7.53% of amount below	9,300	700
4.30% of amount over	9,300	
and less than	23,250	200
2.15% of amount over	23,250	
and less than	46,500	0
Total credit		900
Disposable income		14,850

Worker 2

Salary		35,000
Tax		
7% of amount over	50,000	0
5% of amount over	25,000	
and less than	50,000	500
3% of amount over	10,000	
and less than	25,000	450
Total tax		950
Disposable income		*34,050*

Worker 3

Salary		75,000
Tax		
7% of amount over	50,000	1,750
5% of amount over	25,000	
and less than	50,000	1,250
3% of amount over	10,000	
and less than	25,000	450
Total tax		3,450
Disposable income		*71,550*
Total compensation tax		4,550
Total of compensation and business tax		*7,000*

Worker 2

Salary		32,550
Tax credit		
7.53% of amount below	9,300	700
4.30% of amount over	9,300	
and less than	23,250	600
2.15% of amount over	23,250	
and less than	46,500	200
Total credit		1,500
Disposable income		*34,050*

Worker 3

Salary		69,750
Tax credit		
7.53% of amount below	9,300	700
4.30% of amount over	9,300	
and less than	23,250	600
2.15% of amount over	23,250	
and less than	46,500	500
Total credit		1,800
Disposable income		*71,550*
Total credit		4,200
Total business tax less credit		*7,000*

the existing tax or is necessarily required by the taxpayer to derived information used on the existing tax return. The left-hand panel of Table 12-1 describes the operation of the X-Tax in a simple two-firm, three-worker economy. The table indicates how, under the assumed schedule of rates, profits are taxed at a flat 7 percent and worker compensation is taxed at graduated rates ranging from 0 percent for the first $10,000 to 7 percent on amounts exceeding $50,000.

Policy Choices in Consumption Taxes. The X-Tax is a consumption tax. To see why this is so in both senses I have described above, it will help to back up and consider an X-Tax in which the compensation tax component is not on a graduated rate basis, but instead is assessed at the same 7 percent rate applicable to business "income." Such a tax would be exactly the same as one levied only on businesses but with no deduction at the business level for payments to employees. Because all transactions among businesses are netted out (what one business includes as a receipt, the paying business deducts as a business expense), the result would be a flat tax on sales to non-businesses.

We can see, therefore, that the X-Tax amounts to an annual tax on the aggregate of a household's purchases from firms, combined with a graduated relief from that tax based on the year's earnings from employment. The X-Tax is thus a combination of a consumption tax in the first sense with a subsidy to employment for relatively low earners. Furthermore, because businesses immediately deduct the cost of their purchases on capital account, the rate of return received by the investor is the same before and after tax. In effect, the government is a full partner in the investment, sharing, via the deduction, in 7 percent of all costs and, via the tax on receipts, in 7 percent of all returns. The X-Tax is thus also a consumption tax in the second sense mentioned above.

It may be asked, however, whether the aggregate of sales to household is what we *really* mean by consumption. As I have emphasized elsewhere, there is no scientific answer to this question.[4] What we mean by consumption in this context (as in the income tax context: income is the sum of consumption and saving) is necessarily a policy choice, made to effect the discriminations among taxpayers that we deem desirable as a matter of equity in sharing the aggregate tax burden.

There are many policy issues hidden in the question of how consumption ought to be defined for tax purposes, and the simple system described above adopts implicit positions on many debatable points (for example, the taxation of such institutions as universities).

To pursue all of these points would take us too far afield, and many of the particulars are not critical to the subject at hand. However, three issues, the treatment of consumer durables, inheritances, and transfer payments merit mention.

In including all sales of newly constructed consumer durables, a category within which I include owner-occuped housing, the aggregate of sales to households clearly diverges from consumption as we usually use the term. We would not normally include in a household's annual consumption the amount paid for a new house in a given year. Instead, we would impute to the owner-occupied house a flow of services over time. The X-Tax applies what has come to be called the "tax prepayment" approach to these outlays.[5] In effect, the tax paid on the acquisition of a newly constructed house or automobile constitutes payment in advance of the expected present value of taxes that would otherwise be collected over time on the flow of services if they were actually measured. This characteristic of the X-Tax provides an administratively simple solution to the problem of applying the same rate of tax to housing services as to other forms of consumption.

The X-Tax ignores inheritances and bequests. It may be described as taxing amounts inherited when they are consumed. This characteristic is a contentious property of many consumption taxes. One way to think about the matter is to ask whether amounts given away should be regarded as consumed by the donor. If so, bequests and other gifts would need to be added to the X-Tax base, presumably by levying a flat 7 percent tax on them.[6]

Not only does the X-Tax ignore private transfers (gifts and bequests), it ignores public transfers as well (such as unemployment compensation and welfare benefits). There is nothing that says such transfers could not be included in the compensation tax schedule. More probably, policymakers would be concerned not about the undertaxation of transfers but about their overtaxation. Intuitively, imposition of a VAT might be thought of as imposing a burden on transfer recipients. However, since both sides of the transfer—giver and receiver—are affected alike, they can presumably adjust. In the case of public transfers, this means holding benefits constant in real terms as the price level may vary under the influence of the tax. It is in this sense that the critical element of a correction for vertical distributional effects in the tax system is with respect to labor earnings. Private transfers will take care of themselves, and public transfers are subject to explicit public policy choice.

Finally, a word is in order on the distinction between a consumption tax and a tax on labor earnings, sometimes called a wage tax. If we think of the way people acquire claims to goods as divided into payments for working (labor earnings) and payments for providing capital services (capital income), then the observation that the X-Tax, like most consumption taxes, has the effect of eliminating the difference between the yield on investment and the reward to the saver makes it natural to describe it as a tax on earnings. In the formal sense just described (putting aside public and private transfers as other sources of claims to goods) the characterization is surely correct. However, it may also be misleading in conjuring up a tax imposed only on the ordinary wage-earner. In fact, the X-Tax would apply to such unconventional sources as new technological inventions, discovery of new mineral deposits, increased rental value of urban land, and many other types of increase in market value we not normally have in mind when we describe the world as divided into labor earning a wage, w, and capital earning a return, r.

The economics literature makes a second distinction between a wage tax and a consumption tax which has nothing to do with the question just discussed.[7] This difference turns out to hinge critically and nonobviously on the manner in which a consumption-type tax is *introduced.* Intuitively, a wage tax is levied on payments to labor, whereas a consumption tax is one levied on the purchases of consumption goods by the household, whether the source of funds is labor earnings or yield from capital. We know, though, that the two taxes, which sound very different, once in place have the same effect on the household's options over time. That is, the household's budget constraint over time makes the two types of tax into the same thing. Since ownership of capital is obtained by saving out of labor earnings, the household that must pay a flat 25 percent of its earnings in tax will face the same opportunities as does the household that pays no tax on its earnings, but a flat 25 percent tax on outlays for consumption (the outlays understood as including the tax itself).

In spite of this equivalence via the budget constraint, there is a useful distinction that we can associate with the labels "consumption" tax and "wage" or "earnings" tax as they are employed in the technical economics literature. That distinction is a matter of transition—that is, a matter of the way the new budget constraint is introduced. A wage tax can be said to result when the return flow from capital existing at the time of introduction of the tax is exempted from tax (to simplify, this discussion assumes there is no existing tax); a consumption tax can be said to result when the return flow from capital existing at the time of introduction is included in the tax base. It is probably fair to say that most taxes of the consumption type that are discussed in the policy literature would also be called consumption taxes in the theoretical economics literature. The transition rules by which a consumption tax is introduced are of critical importance, because the incidence in the course of transition to the new policy can differ greatly between two taxes that amount to the same thing once in place.

An Alternative Way to Offset Regressivity. Equivalences and near-equivalences abound in the world of consumption taxes and distinctions without a difference in economic terms may be very important in political terms. An illustration is the following equivalent to the X-Tax, a system that apparently levies much higher taxes on business and includes much more liberal treatment of workers: Instead of allowing businesses to deduct their payments to workers under the X-Tax, oblige them to pay a flat tax of 7 percent on the entire amount of the difference between their receipts from sales and their purchases from other businesses. Instead of the tax on compensation, provide workers an earned income credit of 7.53 percent (for the lowest earners), with the credit reduced to 4.30 percent on earnings in excess of the level at which the 3 percent compensation tax bracket was reached under the original plan, to 2.15 percent on earnings in the next bracket, and with no credit at the margin for earnings in the top bracket of the original compensation tax. (The odd percentages result from the necessity to base credits on what amounts to before-tax earnings.) This-tax-plus-credit system is exactly equivalent to the original X-Tax combination of business and compensation taxes, but it looks very different. The second panel of Table 12–1 puts the earned-income credit system side by side with the basic X-Tax, illustrating the way in which the two systems produce the same outcome for both workers and owners of firms.

Relationship of Well-known Alternatives to the X-Tax

Value-Added Tax

Subtraction versus Invoice Method. In introducing the X-Tax I described it as a variant of a value-added tax. More precisely, it is a variant of what we would normally call a value-added tax of the consumption type (because capital outlays are immediately expensed) administered by the subtraction method, coupled with an employment subsidy to modify the distributional effects of the flat-rate tax. The more familiar European style VATs differ from the hypothetical X-Tax in many details, including importantly the method of administration. To emphasize the connection with the familiar income tax and the potential for simplified administration through being piggybacked on the income tax, the firm's base under the X-Tax is calculated simply by adding together all sales and subtracting all purchases from other firms. (Payments to employees are treated differently under the two alternative approaches.) The European VATs employ the so-called invoice method, whereby the firm claims a rebate on purchases from other firms not on the basis of amounts paid to those firms but on the basis of VAT identified on the purchase invoices.[8] If a single rate of tax is employed, the invoice and subtraction methods are evidently equivalent, so the economic analyses of the flat-rate VAT and the X-Tax (putting to one side the graduated earnings offset) will also be identical.

The invoice method facilitates levying different tax rates on different commodities. In theory, one could also employ different rates of tax in the subtraction method as well (just as one could oblige firms to include different fractions of the receipts from sales of specific commodities and subtract different fractions of the purchases from other firms in calculating income subject to tax). Our interest, however, is in incidence and not administration. I shall comment below on the effect on the incidence effects of differentially taxing various commodities. As far as terminology is concerned, once multiple rates and exclusions become part of the system, the tax ceases to be a consumption tax in the first sense I described, namely, one based on a concept of annual consumption (it might be described as a multiple set of such taxes), although it typically continues to be a consumption tax in the second sense, in preserving the equality between the yield on investment with the rate of return earned by savers.

Origin versus Destination Basis. The description of the X-Tax implies that the firm will be taxed on the proceeds of all sales and may deduct all purchases from other firms. Since either the sale or purchase transactions might be with foreign residents or firms, the X-Tax would be regarded as on an origin basis. It would, however, be perfectly feasible to specify that sales to foreigners would be excluded from tax and purchases from foreigners disallowed as deductions. That would place the X-Tax on the destination basis common to most VATs. Despite the great political importance attached to the distinction, there is little reason to expect there to be much economic difference.[9] Consequently, the incidence analysis of the basic X-Tax will apply to a VAT on a destination basis.

Business Transfer Tax. Various versions of business transfer tax have been under consideration recently in the United States, and a

BTT is under active discussion in Canada.[10] The term generally refers to a VAT administered by the subtraction method, in other words, a very close relative of the X-Tax. Indeed, the X-Tax can be described as a BTT with employment subsidy. A BTT is normally conceived of on a destination basis.

Some versions of BTT differ from the X-Tax in drawing the line around the taxpaying firms more narrowly, stopping at the wholesale stage, for instance. The significance of such characteristics for incidence is probably minor.

Retail Sales. A retail sales tax differs from the business tax component of the X-Tax in being administered only at the point of sale to the public. The two taxes would be identical in economic effect if the definition of firms and final sales subject to tax were the same. In practice, it seems that retail sales taxes often exclude professional services and new housing construction. Also, just as a typical VAT applies lower rates for commodities believed to be particularly important in the budgets of poor people, such commodities may be exempt from retail sales tax.

Others. A broad-based consumption tax can be thought of as composed of a series of separate taxes on the various individual commodities or services embodied in the relevant consumption concept. We have noted that a VAT or retail sales tax may provide for lower or zero rates on particular commodities or services. It is obviously a small step to any arbitrary collection of excise taxes on particular commodities.

A specific commodity tax that is frequently mentioned as a revenue source is one on energy, sometimes more narrowly targeted at imported petroleum. To the extent these taxes are organized so as to impinge only on final sales to consumers, they fall within the general class of consumption taxes, and the analysis is a simple subset of the cases just described. If producer uses of energy are included, these taxes pose more complicated issues of incidence (and efficiency) analysis, issues that go beyond the scope of this survey.

STEADY-STATE INCIDENCE EFFECTS

Preliminaries: Basic Ideas of Incidence

Nominal versus Effective. Incidence analysis concerns the real burden of taxes. For this purpose, the person or institution that sends the check to the Treasury is of little or no relevance. Just as, in the familiar textbook analysis of a commodity tax, it matters not whether the tax is levied on the buyer or seller side of the market, it is of no economic importance whether taxes are nominally paid by individuals or firms. The two versions of the X-Tax, economically identical in spite of dramatically different nominal incidence, provide a good illustration. However, there may be very different political feelings about economically identical taxes. Those who would choose a form of tax because it is "hidden" and apparently fools the public and those who look for taxes that are most obvious to the public, and therefore resisted, agree that form, as well as substance according to the usual models of incidence, matters. If they are right, the usual models of incidence may be wrong. Apparently equivalent taxes may have different real effects. My further remarks reflect the economist's usual skepticism on this point, but one should recognize the alternative possibilities. (For an exploration of the issue in the context of labor supply, see Harvey Rosen's "Tax Illusion and the Labor Supply of Married Women."[11]

Differential Incidence.   In the example of the incidence of introducing ACRS, discussed at the beginning of this chapter, there was an implicit assumption that the reduced tax receipts due to shortening depreciation lives were made up in increased income tax rates. Actually, the receipts were made up through increased issue of debt. Because the government must operate on a budget constraint over time, it is not possible to change one tax without changing the deficit or spending or another tax. Just which other instrument is varied will have a bearing on the incidence of burdens.

Among the more likely uses of a consumption tax in the present situation is to reduce the outstanding government debt. Ideally, we would like to analyze the incidence of the policy option "consumption-tax cum reduced deficits" relative to the option "no reduced deficits." However, since I have very little to say about the incidence of deficit financing, I shall take as the base case here the assumption that the consumption tax revenue will be used to finance a wasteful increase in government expenditure. Obviously, I do not regard this as an interesting policy, but it can be taken as a convenient standard against which to compare alternatives.

Lifetime Perspective.   A more fundamental matter in incidence analysis is the choice of time perspective. Most readily available information about the distribution of tax burdens does something like attempt to allocate to existing individuals the equivalent of a current year's installment on their tax burdens. Treasury data showing tax burdens on households classified by current year's income are the standard fare of workaday incidence analysis.

Data of this kind are often less than satisfactory for two reasons. First, they frequently incorporate over-simple conceptions of incidence. For example, tables purporting to show the beneficiaries of tax expenditures typically equate reduced payments to the Treasury with reduced tax burdens (thus committing the fallacy just mentioned). Second, even where greater attention is given to matters of economic modeling of incidence,[12] an annual "snapshot" may give a misleading impression of both the tax burdens and the economic positions of households. Tax burdens may be misrepresented because of the difficulty of taking into account currently such phenomena as the income taxes payable at the time of retirement on savings set aside in a tax-sheltered account. Economic position may be misrepresented because of the life-cycle relationship among earnings, return to savings, transfer payments, and age. Thus, for example, those whose income is currently low include a preponderance of the young (just embarking on their career of earnings) and the old (in their retirement years). But the same person is once young, once middle-aged, and once old, and presumably some measure that takes into account this fact is needed for incidence analysis. This issue is of particular importance in the context of analysis of consumption taxes, a point to which I shall return shortly.

Transition Incidence. It is desirable not only to take a long view about the incidence of a tax in place but also to recognize the important incidence effects of the introduction of a tax, sometimes called "transition incidence." Actually, a full description of a tax policy includes not only the rates and base but also the time path and conditions with which the rate and base are introduced. Although we tend to take up transition incidence as a separate phenomenon because the analysis is otherwise simply too complex, it would be preferable to conceive of tax policy in terms of variation in the time paths of instruments such as rates and deductions. A stronger tradition of thinking in dynamic terms would perhaps lead us to pay more attention than we customarily do, for example, to the difference in investment incentives generated by a permanent and an on-again-off-again investment credit.[13]

In any case, the phenomenon of transition incidence is important, as may be illustrated by reference to the wage tax versus consumption tax distinction. A wage tax and a consumption tax, as distinguished earlier in this chapter, have the same steady-state properties. However, introduction of a consumption tax imposes a windfall loss on owners of capital (on average, the older generations), whereas introduction of a wage tax bestows a windfall gain on them. Intuitively, the consumption tax applies to the accumulated capital, and in a sense confiscates a fraction of it. The wage tax instead imposes the burden only on those in the earning phase of the life-cycle. Exactly this phenomenon is referred to in the opening section of this chapter.

Vertical Distributional Effects

In this section I focus on steady-state comparisons, to the neglect of wealth redistributions that may take place upon transition.

Probably most interest centers on the vertical distribution of consumption tax burdens. In this connection, the contrast between the "snapshot" and the long-run or lifetime perspective is of particular importance, as is the related question of how we classify people according to level of economic well-being. A proportional tax on a broad-based measure of consumption will be regressive measured against a single year's income. That is, the ratio of consumption tax to income will be a declining function of the amount of income.

The picture changes if the standard of well-being is lifetime resources, understood to be the discounted value of a person's labor earnings and transfers received. If individuals are uniform in the ratio of bequests they leave to lifetime resources, a proportional consumption tax will also be in the same proportion to lifetime resources for all households. Although we know remarkably little about the bequest behavior of U.S. families,[14] it is likely that the well-to-do bequeath on average a larger fraction of lifetime resources than do poorly endowed families. In that sense, a flat consumption tax will also be regressive in some degree when measured against lifetime resources, although not when measured against the resources of the sequence of individuals in a bequest chain. Davies, St-Hillaire, and Whalley who explored these issues in the context of a simulation model based on Canadian data, found surprisingly little increase in the ratio of bequests to lifetime resources with increasing resources.[15] Their study also supports the intuitive expectation that lifetime incidence calculations indicate more progressivity of the tax system as a whole than do annual snapshots, and the calculations are much less sensitive to variations in the assumptions made about the incidence of the major taxes.

The vertical distribution can also be affected by selectively reducing the rate of tax applicable to commodities making up a relatively large portion of the expenditures of the poor. However, since virtually no broad category of consumption is wholly absent from their expenditures, there are distinct limits to what can be done to modify the vertical distribution through these means. Davies, again referring to Canadian data, found that the usual sorts of special rates (on food, clothing, and shelter) do rather little to change the vertical distribution of burdens, with an exemption for clothing actually reducing progressivity because it forms a larger fraction of the budgets of the rich than of the poor.[16] By contrast, the application of graduated rates to a consumption base or to an earnings base, as in the X-Tax, permits wide latitude to vary the vertical distribution of burdens.

Horizontal Distributional Effects

All taxes discriminate among individuals with different characteristics. For example, an earnings or income tax imposes a larger burden on individuals with high earning power or a taste for working long hours than would a uniform lump-sum tax. A consumption tax shares this property of an income tax.

Taste for Saving. The most obvious way in which a consumption tax differs from an income tax is in the variation of burdens among people with different tastes or necessities to save. In the context of the assumption that people with the same lifetime resources as defined above have access to the same consumption possibilities ("perfect capital markets"), a consumption tax that satisfies the second property (no tax on savings) is neutral among equally endowed individuals. By contrast, an income tax places a relatively heavy burden on those who save, or rather on those whose lifetime resources are paid to them relatively early and on those whose tastes favor later consumption.

Taste for Goods. In much the same way, consumption taxes that differ in their inclusion of different commodities create differences in burdens among individuals according to their taste for the goods that are relatively heavily taxed. A nonsmoker, I find the burden of the tax on tobacco quite bearable, but I would welcome relief from the tax on wine.

Specialized Production Factors. The discussion thus far has stressed the commodity consumption side of the story. But people differ in their ownership of productive factors as well. Anyone owning resources with specialized application to particular commodities will naturally suffer relatively heavily from taxes on those commodities. The taxation of energy, involving significant amounts of rent obtained from ownership of resources of little value in alternative uses, is a particular case in point.

TRANSITIONAL INCIDENCE

Age/Generation Differences: The Case of Directly Owned Capital

Differences in ownership of specialized resources is of particular importance in connection with the short-run transition, when careers and other long-lived commitments are difficult to change. In the long run, resources of talent and labor supply are quite flexible in their uses, and capital can be directed to a variety of applications. However, the length of the adjustment period is doubtless very long in some cases and in the short run human, intellectual, and physical capital are fixed, and transition incidence is a significant phenomenon.

The most-studied such effect is the tendency, mentioned above, of the introduction of rules that favor new capital over old to induce a loss in value of existing assets. In the simplest case, with highly durable capital and no costs of adjusting the level of the capital stock, introduction of a consumption tax at some flat fractional rate effectively expropriates the same fraction of the existing capital stock. (This accounts for the finding in several studies that introduction of a flat-rate consumption tax leads to higher long-run living standards than does introduction of a flat-rate wage tax. The wealth expropriated by the consumption tax is used to finance lower tax rates and higher consumption for future generations.[17] This effect is moderated if adjustment costs give existing capital owners an advantage in exploiting the newly profitable investment opportunities.

Because it imposes an implicit windfall tax on wealth, introducing a consumption tax also has intergenerational incidence effects. It is usual to model the economy as though the older generation owns the existing stock of capital, planning to sell it to the younger generations to finance retirement consumption. To the extent this model is accurate, the transition effect of introducing a consumption tax results in a redistribution from the old to the young and future generations.

Portfolio Differences. However, the story is complicated by the availability of financial assets. It is quite possible for the young to own the real assets, having issued debt to the old. In this case, introducing a consumption tax will not affect the consumption of the old; the young will bear the cost.

One may think that owners of debt will bear the consumption tax by virtue of price inflation that its introduction will induce. However, this confuses two things: the effect of the tax and the determinants of the terms of borrowing and lending. If appropriate inflationary expectations are built into the terms of the loan, creditors will not lose from introduction of the tax. To put the matter more simply, if the lending is carried out in real purchasing power terms (indexed bonds would be the obvious mode), lenders will be unaffected by the introduction of the tax.

Specialized Production Factors

Finally, we should note that the differential effect on owners of specialized resources applies in particular to the introduction of different rates of tax on different commodities. In an elegant extension of general equilibrium modeling techniques, Goulder and Summers have put plausible quantitative dimensions on the differential impact on the value of firms in broad industry categories of introducing a variety of tax alternatives.[18] Their figures show substantial differences in capital value changes across sectors, with considerable sensitivity to the degree to which the policy change is anticipated in capital markets.

CONCLUDING COMMENT

This chapter has three themes: First, there are several quite different methods of implementing a consumption tax. Economically these approaches are very similar, if not identical, in their effects, but they appear very different to many of those involved in the policy debate. Once the connection among the different methods is understood (for example, the two forms of the illustrative X-Tax discussed in the chapter), it becomes clear how policy decisions in one (for example, the treatment of owner-occupied housing) translate into the same decisions in the others. Analysis suggests that some politically contentious choices such as that between an origin and a destination basis for a value-added tax may be of little economic significance. Similarly, some hopes raised by consumption taxes, such as the expectation of dealing with the underground economy, are not supported by economics. Second, because they are so similar economically, in their flat-rate form all of these taxes spread the burden of taxation similarly, namely, in proportion to a household's discounted lifetime consumption. The most commonly employed approach to introducing progressivity to these taxes, namely, exemption of purchases of particular commodities or services from tax, is very limited in its power to alter the vertical distribution of burdens. However, alternative methods are available to introduce any degree of progressivity desired by policymakers. Third, although the various consumption taxes are similar in their long-run incidence, they may differ significantly in "transition incidence," the effective taxation of wealth implied by their introduction. Intuitively, we can think of a choice between taxing or not taxing consumption funded out of past saving. Some care is required, however, to determine the transition incidence of a particular tax, and such matters as the choice of financial portfolio by a household (between stocks and bonds, for example) may make a critical difference.

Policy positions on the various forms of consumption tax are often based on inadequate models of incidence, and public discussion suffers from confusion about the alternative approaches that might be taken to taxation based on consumption. A greater appreciation in the policy debate of the basic similarity of the alternative approaches to taxation based on consumption would improve the chances of avoiding complex rules that ill serve the objectives they are introduced to achieve.

NOTES

1. See, for example, the following references: Alan J. Auerbach, "Corporate Taxation in the U.S." *Brookings Papers on Economic Activity* (Washington, D.C.: The Brookings Institution, 1983), p. 2. Alan J. Auerbach and James R. Hines, "Tax Reform, Investment, and the Value of the Firm," National Bureau of Economic Research Working Paper No. 1803, Cambridge, Mass., Jan. 1986. Alan J. Auerbach and Lawrence Kotlikoff, "Investment versus Savings Incentives: The Size of the Bang for the Buck and the Potential for Self-Financing Tax Cuts," in Laurence H. Meyer, ed., *The Economic Consequences of Government Deficits* (Boston: Kluwer-Nijhoff, 1983), pp. 123–149. J. Alan Auerbach and Lawrence Kotlikoff, *Dynamic Fiscal Policy* (New York: Cambridge University Press, forthcoming).

2. See, for example, the following references: Henry J. Aaron and Harvey Galper, "A Tax on Consumption, Gifts, and Bequests and Other Strategies for Tax Reform," *Options for Tax Reform* (Washington, D.C.: The Brookings Institution, 1984), pp. 106–146. David F. Bradford, *Untangling the Income Tax* (Cambridge, Mass.: Harvard University Press, April 1986). David F. Bradford and the U.S. Treasury Tax Policy Staff, *Blueprints for Basic Tax Reform*, 2nd ed., reg. (Washington, D.C.: Tax Analysts, 1984; originally published by U.S. Treasury, 1977). Nicholas Kaldor, *An Expenditure Tax* (London: Allen and Unwin, 1955; Westport, Conn.: Greenwood Press, 1978). U.S. General Accounting Office, "Tax Policy, Choosing Among Consumption Taxes," Staff Study, August 20, 1986. U.S. Treasury Department, *Tax Reform for Fairness, Simplicity, and Economic Growth*: Vol. 1, *Overview*; Vol. 2, *General Explanation of the*

Treasury Department Proposals; Vol. 3, *Value-Added Tax* (Washington, D.C.: U.S. Government Printing Office, November 1984).

3. Robert E. Hall and Alvin Rabushka, *Low Tax, Simple Tax, Flat Tax* (New York: McGraw-Hill, 1983) and *The Flat Tax* (Stanford, Calif.: Hoover Institution Press, 1985).

4. Bradford, *Untangling the Income Tax.*

5. Bradford et al., *Blueprints for Basic Tax Reform.*

6. For more extended discussion of this issue, see ibid., esp. ch. 8.

7. See, for example, Auerbach and Kotlikoff, "Investment versus Savings Incentives," and *Dynamic Fiscal Policy*, as well as James B. Davies and France St-Hillaire, "Reforming Capital Income Taxation in Canada: Efficiency and Distributional Effects of Alternative Options," mimeo, Department of Economics, University of Western Ontario, London, Canada, 1986.

8. For a good discussion see Henry Aaron, ed., *The Value Added Tax: Lessons from Europe* (Washington, D.C.: The Brookings Institution, 1981), or Charles E. McLure, Jr., *The Value-Added Tax: Key to Deficit Reduction?* (Washington, D.C.: American Enterprise Institute, 1987).

9. See, for example, Bradford, *Untangling the Income Tax*, pp. 328-329, and Gene M. Grossman, "Border Tax Adjustments: Do They Distort Trade?" *Journal of International Economics 10* (1980): 117-128.

10. James B. Davies, "Manufacturers' Sales Tax, Value-Added Tax, and Effective Tax Incidence," Canadian Tax Foundation, Thirty-Seventh Tax Conference, Toronto, 1986.

11. Harvey S. Rosen, "Tax Illusion and the Labor Supply of Married Women," *Review of Economics and Statistics 57-2* (May 1976): 167-172.

12. As, for example, in Joseph E. Pechman, *Federal Tax Policy*, 4th ed. (Washington, D.C.: The Brookings Institution, 1983) and *Who Paid the Taxes, 1966-85?* (Washington, D.C.: The Brookings Institution, 1985), and in Joseph E. Pechman and Benjamin A. Okner, *Who Bears the Tax Burden?* (Washington, D.C.: The Brookings Institution, 1974).

13. See Auerbach and Hines, "Tax Reform and the Value of the Firm," and David F. Bradford and Charles Stuart, "Issues in the Measurement and Interpretation of Effective Tax Rates," National Bureau of Economic Research Working Paper No. 1975, Cambridge, Mass., July 1986.

14. Bradford et al., *Blueprints for Basic Tax Reform*, pp. 169-173.

15. James B. Davies, France St-Hillaire, and John Whalley, "Some Calculations of Lifetime Tax Incidence," *American Economic Review 74* (September 1984): 633-69.

16. Davies, "Manufacturers' Sales Tax, Value-Added Tax, and Effective Tax Incidence."

17. See Auerbach and Kotlikoff, "Investment versus Savings Incentives," and especially *Dynamic Fiscal Policy*.

18. Lawrence H. Goulder and Lawrence H. Summers, "Tax Policy, Asset Prices, and Growth: A General Equilibrium Analysis," National Bureau of Economic Research Summer Institute Paper, Cambridge, Mass., July 1986.

Discussants:

A CONGRESSIONAL RESPONSE

Bill Gradison

Incidence is an especially appropriate subject for economists, and there are none better to discuss this than David Bradford (Chapter 12) and Charles McLure and Joseph Pechman (the following Discussants). But if war is not just for the generals, tax incidence is not just for the economists—or maybe I should put it the other way around. If war is for the generals, the impact of taxation is for the generalists, like members of Congress, because we are, after all, the ones who are called upon to vote on these issues and to stake our careers on whether we go the right way. We are in the unusual situation of being subject to premature and involuntary retirement every two years. That is a little bit unusual in American corporate and academic life, and it does affect our behavior.

There are at least three types of consumption tax policy alternatives which we might discuss: a consumed income tax as a replacement for the present income tax; some kind of sales, excise, or value-added tax as an addition to the present income tax; and finally, a tax such as a sales or value-added tax as a replacement for the present income tax system.

David Bradford has eased our analytical burden by focusing on a consumption tax as an additional tax, not as a replacement for the present income tax. That is probably that just as well, after what Congress has been through in revising the tax code—that is, deciding to reform it, not replace it. (I might digress and say that the House Ways and Means Committee had the benefit of a weekend long retreat with, among other participants, Joe Pechman and David Bradford, in which we disucssed many of these broad alternatives before the committee decided to turn its focus to the income tax itself.)

The Bradford chapter reveals one of the best-kept secrets of students of tax policy: Consumption taxes can provide whatever degree of progressivity is comfortable. Since desired tax incidence, like beauty, is in the eye of the beholder, this ability to produce the results we want through income taxes or consumption taxes should open up great opportunities for those of us who believe additional revenues are needed and are not too picky about the label on the package.

The trouble with the notion that we can achieve the incidence we seek, is that tax incidence does not always follow predicted patterns. Even in the final stages of rewriting the income tax laws, with a well-advertised shift of the tax burden from individuals to businesses of $120 billion over a five- or six-year period, the debate had already begun over the true impact this shift will have.

Certainly, those businesses and industries which can pass on the added tax will do so. To the extent this burden is shifted, the difference in incidence decreases between income and consumption taxes. If incidence is uncertain from a tax we have had on the books for years, caution and modesty should certainly mark our attempts to anticipate the incidence of a new tax, such as national consumption tax.

David Bradford has done an excellent job in dealing with some of the central objections to some of his earlier proposals in this field. In particular, the heavy burden placed on the young, such as students with consumption expenditures but little income, and the elderly, who often use their previously taxed savings to permit consumption at levels above their current income, is addressed.

Dr. Bradford's wage tax is clearly a step toward dealing more fairly with these groups. The Bradford thesis, as I understand it, that a consumption tax may be not only as fair as, but actually fairer than an income tax, is certainly not accepted among politicians, who have been schooled in the ability-to-pay idea. I personally find it impossible to argue against the notion that enjoyment of goods and services—that is, consumption—is as fair a tax base as income, which may be saved or given away rather than consumed. Indeed, the public seems more receptive toward sales-type taxation than added income taxes if additional federal revenues are needed.

Here, as I see it, the public is ahead of the politicians, most of whom say that consumption taxes are regressive and therefore they are bad and must not be enacted. This seems to be the prevailing political wisdom of the day.

One feature of national tax policy we can count on is unpredictability. That goes without saying after major changes in 1981, 1982, 1984, and again in 1986. The Ways and Means Committee is not going to hang out a "Gone fishing" sign for the next five or ten years. There is already talk of revising the Tax Reform Act of 1986. This rather fluid tax-writing process could open up opportunities to give consumption taxes the consideration they deserve.

The move toward a flat-rate income tax—with 80 percent of taxpayers in the 15 percent tax rate bracket—makes proportional taxes more acceptable than would be true with steeper income tax rates. Of course, this is nothing new. Joseph Pechman's earlier work shows very clearly that the income tax system has a high degree of proportionality, in sharp contrast to the fiction of progressivity. The new law brings reality and perception closer together on that central issue. Consumption taxes can be structured to achieve desirable incidence through exemptions and multiple rate schedules, providing fairness if we are willing to do so, at the expense of much greater complexity.

We are unlikely to have any major tax increase under the Reagan administration—that seems like a safe statement. Therefore, there is time to explore incidence problems that must be dealt with as a political matter.

Undesirable effects of consumption taxes can be offset by changes in the income tax laws, such as increasing the earned income tax credit or the standard deduction. In other words, many, perhaps most, of the political problems related to incidence can be fixed, and should be, if consumption taxation is seriously considered.

The topic is incidence. However, I do want to indicate that I consider complexity and compliance to be very serious issues. Dr. Bradford's chapter, in my view, understates the complexity problem and, as for compliance, European experience shows that there are just as many opportunities for evasion of consumption taxes as income taxes. Recent Ways and Means Committee hearings, in fact, disclose that this is true in this country, as well, with regard to the federal gasoline excise tax, which one would think would be one of the easiest consumption taxes to enforce without major opportunities for fun and games through evasion.

Finally, on the subject of incidence, there is no perfect tax, including the income tax. Therefore, diversified tax structure and a diversified tax base, make sense. And, amazingly, that is just the direction we have been moving in, with major sources as different in their incidence as income taxes, which are used at the federal and state and to a lesser extent the local level; payroll taxes, which finance Social Security, Medicare, and unemployment compensation (very similar, if not identical to the wage tax that Dr. Bradford was talking about); sales taxes, which are in broad use at the state and local level; and property taxes, which are used today primarily by school boards and local governments.

With regard to the income tax, the public is sending signals that the federal government is relying excessively on income taxation. That is one reason that it has been possible to get as far as we have with so-called income tax reform. On a subject this important, when the public talks, we should listen.

THE OPTIMAL CONSUMPTION TAX
FOR THE UNITED STATES

Charles E. McLure, Jr.

It is not clear whether the United States should shift to greater reliance on consumption taxes, be it via an indirect tax such as the value-added tax (VAT) or a more direct tax such as the X-Tax proposed by David Bradford. But certainly we should be thinking seriously about the question.

The debate on the proper role of consumption taxes raises many subsidiary issues, including administration and compliance, effects on saving and capital formation, issues of intergovernmental fiscal relations, and the regressivity (incidence) of consumption taxes. Since Dr. Bradford has provided a masterful exposition of the incidence issue, I want to comment on a few other topics that arise in the debate on whether the United States should adopt a tax on consumption, as well as directly on the incidence issue.[1] Since George Will, in Chapter 6 has already addressed some of these issues, many of my comments are brief.

The Tax Mix

First, why are we considering a consumption tax? Many economists and business representatives argue that it would be good to use revenues from a tax on consumption to replace part (or all) of the income tax. Dr. Bradford refers to the neutrality of a consumption tax toward the saving/consumption choice, and other economists talk about increasing capital formation. Of course, the neutrality issue is not as simple as it appears at first glance; it depends on the tax rates that would be necessary under a consumption tax, relative to those under an income tax, and on relationships between present consumption, future consumption, and work effort, parameters about which knowledge is woefully deficient.

On the more practical issue of whether a change in the tax mix would increase saving and capital formation my comment is somewhat different. Frankly, it seems to me that basing the choice between income and consumption taxation on postulated effects on private saving is to focus on secondary effects, as long as the federal government is borrowing $200 billion per year. Stated differently, if the federal government would quit borrowing that $200 billion per year, we might have an adequate level of national saving, regardless of our tax mix. In any case, if we think the national savings rate is too low, we should use the direct remedy of deficit reduction, rather than the substantially weaker indirect technique of changing the tax mix.

The strongest arguments for a consumption-based personal tax is its relative simplicity. We showed definitely in Treasury I just how difficult it would be to implement a reasonably pure tax on real economic income. The really tough issues of inflation adjustment and time value problems do not exist under a tax on consumption. Even so, I do not think that we are likely to substitute a consumption-based tax such as the X-Tax for the income tax anytime soon or that we are likely to replace part of the income tax with a value-added tax or some other kind of general sales tax in a revenue-neutral swap. We might use some of the revenues from a VAT for that purpose, but basically I think we are—and should be—talking about using some form of sales tax to raise total revenues and reduce the federal budget deficit.

The Need for Increased Revenue

That raises a more fundamental question: Why impose a sales tax instead of cutting federal spending? My own view is that we are not likely to eliminate the deficit or even reduce it to manageable proportions, simply by cutting spending. The president does not want to cut military spending, Social Security seems to be sacrosanct, and I presume we will continue to meet the obligation to pay interest on the national debt. There is not enough spending outside those three areas to make a sizable contribution to deficit reduction, even if we were to cut remaining programs further than is likely or sensible.

Nor do I think we can grow our way out of the deficit. If anything, the short-term outlook seems to be for economic weakness, rather than strength. Though I believe strongly that fundamental tax reform could have contributed significantly to greater productivity, only the most optimistic supply-side advocate of tax reform could believe that the Tax Reform Act of 1986 will lead to such a large increase in productivity and growth that the deficit will be reduced substantially. Finally, I am concerned about the long-run prospects for reappearance of inflation; if that occurs, interest on the national debt could increase dramatically and swell the budget deficit.

Having said that I think we should be thinking about a federal sales tax, let me reemphasize my concern about the "money machine" problem. Though I do not have a well-articulated political theory to explain why, I do believe that government spending in the United States will be higher if we enact a federal sales tax than if we do not. While I continue to worry about the money machine, I have come to fear the consequences of continuing to run large federal budget deficits more than those of the money machine.

I might note, as an aside, that the evidence presented in Chapter 11 by J.A. Stockfisch to refute the money machine argument is not really dispositive. He argues that the relative rates of growth of government spending in member Organization for Economic Cooperation and Development countries that adopted a VAT could not be distinguished from those in countries that did not adopt a VAT. This test provides no insight into the money machine argument. After all, every country in his sample that adopted a value-added tax already had some form of national sales tax; in other words, they replaced one form of money machine with another, albeit a better one. Examining experience in those countries tells us nothing about what would happen if a country that had no national sales tax were to adopt one.

Why a General Sales Tax?

Despite what Ways and Means Chairman Rostenskowski says in Chapter 2, I do not think that we are likely to increase the income tax very soon in order to make substantial inroads into the deficit. Given the attention that has been paid to reducing individual and corporate tax rates, I would guess that those rates will remain chipped in stone for at least a few years. If anyone thinks they can raise revenue by broadening the tax base, I wish them luck; we just tried base broadening in a revenue-neutral context, with notable lack of success.

I also do not favor using either increased excise taxes or energy taxes for deficit reduction. My objection to increases in excise taxes goes well beyond their well-known regressivity. I believe that taxes on motor fuels should be based primarily on the best available estimates of highway user charges, rather than on revenue needs; imposing taxes higher than required to cover marginal costs of highway use discourages this form of transportation and discriminates against the consumption of transportation-intensive products. In the case of taxes on alcoholic beverages and tobacco products, the argument is somewhat different. I would argue that these taxes are more appropriately left to the states. In all these cases excises involve substantial horizontal inequities between those who happen to consume above average amounts of the taxed products and those who do not. Finally, let me add that I have substantial sympathy for the notion of disallowing business deductions for the expenses of advertising alcoholic beverages and tobacco products or imposing a separate excise on such advertising.

When you consider energy taxes, the room for mischief is almost unlimited. As you proceed from motor fuel taxes to taxes on energy from all sources, to taxes on only oil and gas, and finally to oil import fees, matters get progressively worse. In the extreme case of oil import fees, production decisions are substantially distorted, an incentive is provided to "drain America first" and thereby increase future dependence on imported oil, and income is redistributed in favor of one of the wealthiest segments of American society.

Problem Areas

Federal consideration of a value-added tax has long been opposed by governors, mayors, and other representative of state and local governments, who note that the sales tax field has historically been the fiscal preserve of state and local governments. This opposition to "federal preemption" has typically been based more on gut reaction than on clear analysis of the problem. I have recently attempted to describe in just what sense enactment of a federal sales tax would limit the fiscal sovereignty of state and local governments; much of the answer involves the need to avoid hopelessly complex overlapping of inconsistent state and federal sales tax regimes.[2] I would point out in passing, for those who have not yet noticed, that the 1986 act involves, in a sense, de facto federal preemption of the sales tax base by eliminating itemized deductions for state and local sales taxes. Frankly I think that was a mistake; It would have been better to eliminate some fraction of itemized deductions for all state and local taxes.

The second crucial problem in the taxation of consumption is that of regressivity. As in volume 3 of Treasury I, David Bradford mentions various methods of dealing with regressivity. First, food can be exempted (or zero rated), but that is a very blunt, inefficient, and complex way of going about reducing regressivity. After all, most food is consumed by the nonpoor, and the average propensity to consume food does not vary greatly across income classes.

A second approach is to increase transfer payments. But there are many poor people who do not receive transfer payments. For them the regressivity of a value-added tax would be quite real.

Third, it would be possible to adopt a system of refundable income tax credits (perhaps patterned after the earned income tax credit, but presumably available to all the poor), a family assistance plan, or a negative income tax. But that seems to me to represent a very fundamental decision about social welfare policy that should be decided on its own merits, and not simply as an afterthought in the debate on the national sales tax.

This leads to the fourth method of avoiding regressivity, what in Treasury I we called the personal-exemption value-added tax. It is based on the Hall-Rabushka flat-tax proposal and, with slight modification, is incorporated in the Bradford X-Tax. I believe that this is an extremely imaginative approach and may be the most promising way of dealing with the regressivity issue. But I would offer several caveats. First, the X-Tax resembles very closely a subtraction method VAT. As such, it would be highly vulnerable to lobbying efforts. (See also A Pitfall to Avoid, below.)

Second, it is unrealistic to believe that the compensation tax component of the X-Tax would be comprehensive. More likely, many of the same exclusions, exemptions, deductions, and credits we now have under the income tax would appear. If so, rates would be higher, and economic neutrality, equity, and simplicity would suffer.

Third, altogether too little attention has been paid to taxation of international transactions in most discussions of proposals such as the Hall-Rabushka flat tax and the X-Tax.[3] This is in marked contrast to discussions of the traditional VAT, where international aspects have generally been overemphasized.

I take it as given that U.S. firms would want to see border tax adjustments (BTAs—export rebates and compensating import taxes) allowed for either of these taxes, as for European VATs. There is no doubt that an ordinary credit-method VAT would be acceptable within the rules of the General Agreement on Tariffs and Trade (GATT). Moreover, a credit-method tax combined with a separate system of family allowances or a negative income tax would almost certainly also be acceptable.

Combining a credit-method value-added tax with a separate earned income tax credit probably would be acceptable, but this is not certain. Because they explicitly combine personal exemptions with a subtraction-method VAT, the GATT treatment of both a Hall-Rabushka flat tax and the X-Tax appears to be rather iffy. Most obviously, these taxes appear to be direct taxes, for which border tax adjustments are not allowed, rather than indirect taxes, for which they are allowed. Even if they were characterized as indirect taxes, the outcome is not clear; we would be saying that we would like to make export rebates for taxes that have not been paid, and we would like to collect compensating import taxes that would not have been paid if we produced the same thing in this country. Confronted with this proposition, our trading partners might think us a bit daffy, and would probably say so. But limiting BTAs to taxes actually paid would be the source of considerable controversy and complexity.

Finally, I would second the contention of Milka Casanegra that introducing a value-added tax would cause considerable administration and compliance costs (see Discussants following Chapter 13). In this regard the situation is quite different from what existed in Europe, where converting cascade turnover taxes to credit-method VATs was relatively simple and probably caused little net change in costs of administration and compliance. The substantial costs of implementing a VAT suggest that it would not be advisable to follow such a source unless it was intended to raise a substantial amount of revenue—say, at least $60 billion and more likely $100 billion.

A Pitfall to Avoid

I want to emphasize strongly that *if* the United States considers a value-added tax, we should be very careful not to impose it in the wrong way. In particular, the subtraction method or business transfer tax approach would lead to tremendous problems. Under the subtraction method the incentives for gaining preferential treatment of pre-retail stages is far greater than under a credit-method tax. And yet the administrative and economic costs of differential rates is also far greater: accurate border tax adjustments cannot be achieved, it is difficult to relieve capital goods of precisely the amount of tax otherwise incorporated in prices, and pre-retail differentials cause substantially greater distortion of production and consumption choices than under a credit-method VAT.[4] If we want to have a value-added tax, we should adopt a European-style VAT implemented using the credit method. After all, it is no accident that all of the roughly 40 countries in the world that have VATs use this approach, rather than the subtraction method underlying the business transfer tax.

Of course, the X-Tax approach advocated by David Bradford is based on the subtraction method. This causes me some concern, for I believe in general that the X-Tax approach may have some possibilities and is worthy of further consideration.

These brief remarks should indicate the nature of some of the complex issues involved in deciding whether the United States should shift toward greater reliance on consumption-based taxes. Issues of incidence and means of reducing regressivity are important, but not unique.

NOTES

1. These remarks draw heavily on arguments developed in greater detail in Charles E. McLure, Jr., *The Value-Added Tax: Key to Deficit Reduction?* (Washington, D.C.: American Enterprise Institute, 1987).

2. On this topic, see Charles E. McLure, Jr., "State and Federal Implications of a Federal Value Added Tax," Academy for State and Local Government, Washington, 1986, as well as ibid., ch. 9.

3. This argument is developed more fully in Charles E. McLure, Jr. and George N. Carlson, "Pros and Cons of Alternative Approaches to the Taxation of Consumption," in the *Proceedings of the 77th Annual Conference, 1984.* National Tax Association—Tax Institute of America, Columbus, Ohio, 1985, pp. 147-54.

4. The defects of the subtraction method or the business transfer tax technique of imposing a VAT are examined in detail in McLure, *The Value Added Tax*, esp. chs. 6 and 8.

A CONSUMPTION TAX IS NOT DESIRABLE FOR THE UNITED STATES

Joseph A. Pechman

Relation between Income and Consumption Taxation

David Bradford's discussion of the similarities and differences between the consumption tax and the income tax, in Chapter 12, is important. What he has to say on this subject is not well known even among economists, let alone among policymakers and the public at large.

Briefly, Bradford tells us that in a world in which the life-cycle hypothesis holds—that is, everybody consumes his or her income during a lifetime—a general consumption tax is the same as an equal tax on wages. An important difference arises, however, if the life-cycle hypothesis does not hold. In this case, there is an equivalence between a consumption tax and a wage tax only if bequests and gifts are subject to tax under the consumption tax and inheritances and gifts received are subject to tax under the wage tax. This is why Henry Aaron and Harvey Galper call their cash flow tax, which would tax bequests and gifts, a "lifetime income tax" and not a consumption tax.[1]

I am puzzled why most advocates of the consumption tax approach are either silent about the treatment of bequests and gifts or actually oppose their inclusion in the consumption tax base.

Clearly, this omission would greatly reduce the progressivity (measured with respect to income) even of a graduated consumption tax or convert it to a regressive tax at least in the top part of the income distribution where consumption is much less than earnings. Under the circumstances, I wish proponents of the consumption tax would be explicit about their views on the taxation of wealth transfers.

But even if wealth transfers are included in the consumption tax base, it is not obvious that the consumption tax is superior to an income tax. The answer to this question hinges on whether the lifetime perspective is suitable as a basis for personal taxation.

Most economists would automatically support taxation on a lifetime basis, yet the case is by no means airtight. Richard Goode recently addressed this question in an article that has, unfortunately, been overlooked by public finance analysts and policymakers.[2] He points out, first, that many households lack foresight and that imperfections in the capital market prevent optimization of consumption over a person's life cycle. Robert E. Hall and Peter Diamond and Jerry Hausman have estimated that a sizable minority of households for one reason or another fail to behave the way the life cycle model says they should.[3] In practice, therefore, ability to pay taxes depends on income (that is, consumption plus accretions to wealth) over much shorter periods than a lifetime. Second, the higher rates imposed to finance a war or to combat inflation are intended to apply to people with unusually large income during such periods. Taxing consumption alone or averaging of incomes over a lifetime undermines the effectiveness of income taxation for such purposes. Third, most people would be puzzled by a tax that imposes the heaviest burdens on families precisely when they consume the most (the young and the old) and the lightest burdens on those who are able to save (the middle-aged). Fourth, the advocates of a lifetime perspective have neglected the technical problems that would occur when marriages were dissolved by divorce or death.

I conclude that consumption taxation is inferior to income taxation even if gifts and bequests are included in the consumption tax base. One way to avoid these disadvantages would be to include accretions to wealth in the consumption tax base once every five or ten years. What I am suggesting is that the Aaron-Galper tax would be tolerable if it were applied to much shorter periods than a lifetime. This marriage between the consumption and income tax approaches would appeal to me, but consumption tax proponents certainly do not have such a system in mind. Even if they did, I doubt that it could be sold to the Congress or to the public.

Consumption Taxation as a Supplement to an Income Tax

I gather that many of the consumption tax proponents are now concentrating on the use of such a tax as a supplement to the income tax rather than as a substitute for it. Bradford, for example, has now modified his X-Tax so that it will have a peak rate of 7 percent rather than 25 or 30 percent, which would be needed to replace the income tax.

Bradford quite rightly points out that his X-Tax is the same as a value-added tax with a vanishing personal exemption. In fact, Charls Walker and others have proposed the enactment of a value-added tax with a tax credit for low-income recipients. This type of tax would have the same distributional effects as Bradford's X-Tax.

I am delighted to see that at least some consumption tax advocates have learned that they must do something about the regressivity of the consumption tax if they are to carry the day. I have two points to make about this particular modification of the traditional consumption tax. First, introducing an exemption or a tax credit makes the resulting consumption tax progressive only up to the point where the exemption or credit vanishes. Thereafter, the tax resumes its regressive profile. The point where the exemption or credit disappears depends, of course, on the size of the allowance and the tax rate. In the typical case, they would disappear at incomes between $15,000 and $30,000. I cannot understand why anybody would want to enact a new tax that would impose the heaviest burden in this income range and progressively lighter burdens above it.

Second, Bradford's X-Tax and Walker's value-added tax with a credit illustrate the weakness of the case for a consumption tax in the context of U.S. tax policy. In effect, they are recommending a tax that would exempt low-income people. We already have such a tax in our tax system—it is the income tax. I see no reason for introducing an elaborate new tax when the income tax would fill the bill. In fact, the income tax would do it more effectively, because it is progressive with respect to income throughout the income scale rather than only in the bottom brackets.

Obviously, the proponents of a consumption tax are after much bigger game. Thus far, they have not been able to persuade any administration (Republican or Democratic), the Congress, or the public that a consumption tax should be substituted for an income tax. Their strategy is to start modestly, say, with a consumption or value-added tax of 5–7 percent, and then gradually to build up the rates while reducing the income tax. Proponents of progressive taxation should not be fooled and should remain alert to prevent this strategy from succeeding.

NOTES

1. See their excellent book, *Assessing Tax Reform* (Washington, D.C.: The Brookings Institution, 1985).

2. See his "Long-term Averaging of Income for Tax Purposes," In Henry J. Aaron and Michael J. Boskin, eds., *The Economics of Taxation* (Washington, D.C.: The Brookings Institution, 1980), pp. 159–178.

3. Robert E. Hall, "Stochastic Implications of the Life Cycle-Personal Income Hypothesis: Theory and Evidence," *Journal of Political Economy 86* (No. 6 December 1978): 971–988; and P.A. Diamond and J.A. Hausman, "Individual Retirement and Saving Behavior," *Journal of Public Economics 23* ((1–2) February-March 1984): 891–914.

✳ *Chapter 13*

A Federal Consumption Tax: Design and Administrative Issues

George N. Carlson

To its supporters, a federal consumption tax offers promise of alleviating three troublesome economic problems facing the U.S. economy: the federal budget deficit, inadequate capital formation, and unsatisfactory international competitiveness. In the eyes of some fiscal observers, the additional revenues generated by a broad-based federal consumption tax, when combined with realistic and necessary expenditure cuts, would produce an acceptable political compromise that would place the economy on a glide path toward substantially reducing the federal deficit, which reached a record high of $220 billion in fiscal 1986. Even if the budget deficit is reduced to the $170 billion figure predicted by the administration for fiscal 1987, those concerned about the deficit contend that it would still be too high. Progress in reducing the federal deficit, the argument goes, would enable the United States to generate more savings of its own and to rely less heavily on foreign savings to finance its demands for capital formation. This would reinforce recent efforts by policy officials to reduce the foreign exchange value of the dollar and further improve the international competitive position of U.S. business. If done with a consumption tax, the argument concludes, the anti-savings and anti-capital formation bias of an income tax would be avoided.

The strongest case for a federal consumption tax rests on these grounds, and other chapters discuss the important issues of capital formation and international competitiveness. This chapter considers the design and administrative issues that would arise if a federal consumption tax were adopted. These considerations point in favor of either a retail sales tax or an invoice-type value-added tax, with a modest preference for the latter because of its relative ease in avoiding the taxation of capital equipment and other business purchases.

In reaching this conclusion, alternative methods of calculating VAT liability (addition, subtraction, and credit) are discussed and evaluated. This discussion is confined to a consumption type VAT; the income and gross product versions are not considered. In light of recent U.S. Senate interest in a manufacturers' sales tax to finance an expanded Superfund program, the chapter reviews why sub-retail sales taxes fail the basic tests of a consumption tax and should not become part of the federal fiscal arsenal. The relative merits of a value-added tax and retail sales tax are discussed, as are the design and administrative issues relating to zero rating, exemptions, multiple rates and the underground economy. Where appropriate, relevant European experience is discussed, as a guide both to choosing a workable form of consumption tax and to alleviating some of the likely problems of administering the tax.

A federal value-added tax would not be easy to administer nor would it be self-enforcing. European experience has shown that successful implementation of a VAT must be preceded by an extensive education program. Once adopted, its successful operation requires the continual attention of experts trained in VAT administration. This is not to say that the tax would create insuperable administrative problems. In a highly developed, interrelated, and complex economy like the United States, it is probably unrealistic to expect any broad-based tax to be simple. Especially after the Tax Reform Act of 1986, no one would seriously contend that the federal income tax is not complex. Thus, to denigrate a value-added tax for its complexity may be to hold it to a standard of performance that even the income tax is not required to meet.

This chapter does not consider or evaluate an expenditure or "consumed-income" tax. Notwithstanding discussions in the U.S. Treasury's 1977 *Blueprints*, the report of the Meade Commission in England, and Professor Lodin's study for Sweden, virtually no country has practical experience with such a tax. Thus, it could not be implemented in the United States without a prolonged period of additional study and analysis. This is one of the primary considerations that prompted the U.S. Treasury Department not to consider a consumed income tax in its 1984 tax reform proposals. Moreover, in light of the recent overhaul of the federal income tax system under the banner of tax reform, it is doubtful that Congress would have the appetite to make the additional modifications necessary to transform the income tax into a consumed income tax.

VALUE-ADDED TAX: DESCRIPTION

Each stage or link in the production and distribution process is subject to taxation under a VAT. *Value added* is normally defined as sales less purchases. Consider a typical manufacturing operation, in which a firm purchases raw materials from its suppliers and produces a product by manufacturing, processing, or otherwise "adding value" to the materials it has purchased. If sales are $100, and if purchases for business use are $60, then value added is $40. With a VAT rate of 10 percent, the firm's tax liability would be 10 percent of $40 or $4.

A firm's value added is a measure of its economic contribution to the value of the product or service it helps to produce or provide. The retail price of a product or service is equal to the total of the values added through all of the various production and distribution stages, including the retail stage. Thus, a VAT, imposed at a uniform rate on all stages of production and distribution, including the retail level, would collect the same amount of revenue as would a retail sales tax imposed at that same rate. Given these assumptions, a 10 percent VAT is equivalent to a 10 percent retail sales tax. The only difference is an administrative one, tax is collected sequentially and in stages under a VAT and entirely at the retail level under a retail sales tax.

Calculation of VAT Liability

Though the invoice or credit method of determining VAT liability is widely used in Europe, tax liability can also be calculated by either the addition or subtraction methods. (The Business Transfer Tax proposed by Senator William Roth relies on the subtraction method.) These alternatives are illustrated in Table 13-1, which is adapted from the U.S. Treasury Department's 1984 tax reform study.

Table 13-1 illustrates a production process consisting of a manufacturer, wholesaler, and retailer. Though the manufacturer buys $100 in supplies, the seller(s) of those supplies is excluded from the example in the table. The tax rate is 10 percent.

Under the subtraction approach, illustrated in the top panel of Table 13-1, VAT liability is simply equal to sales less purchases. For

Table 13-1. Comparison of Three Methods of Calculating Liability for a 10 Percent Value-Added Tax.

	Stage of Production			
	Firm A Manufacturer	Firm B Wholesaler	Firm C Retailer	Total Economy
Subtraction Method				
Sales	$350	$850	$1,100	$2,300
Purchases	100	350	850	1,300
Value added (sales minus purchases)	250	500	250	1,000
VAT	25	50	25	100
Credit Method				
Sales	350	850	1,100	2,300
Tax on sales	35	85	110	230
Purchases	100	350	850	1,300
Tax on purchases	10	35	85	130
VAT (tax on sales less tax on purchases)	25	50	25	100
Addition Method				
Factor payments plus net profit				
Wages	150	300	200	650
Rent	50	100	20	170
Interest	25	75	20	120
Profit	25	25	10	60
Total	250	500	250	1,000
VAT	25	50	25	100

example, Firm B, the wholesaler, has sales of $850, purchases of $350, value added of $500 and a tax liability of $50 (10 percent of $500). The invoice or credit approach is shown in the middle panel of the table. In this case, Firm B (wholesaler) determines its tax liability by subtracting its tax paid on purchases (10 percent of $350, or $35) from the tax due on its sales (10 percent of $850, or $85). Thus, Firm B's liability is $50, or $85 less $35. Under the addition method, illustrated in the bottom panel of Table 13-1, the VAT base is calculated by adding the components of value added, wages ($300), rent ($100), interest ($75), and profit ($25). The 10 percent tax rate is then applied to Firm B's value added of $500, again resulting in a tax liability of $50. While a firm's tax liability is usually the same under the subtraction, credit, and addition methods, there are important differences with policy implications for the United States.

Evaluation.   While the fiscal goal should be a uniform tax applied to as broad a base of consumption as possible, a federal value-added tax will, inevitably, be met with suggestions for exemptions and multiple rates. Under any of these three methods, the tax on a product can be reduced by applying a lower tax rate at the retail level. But under the subtraction method, the total tax liability on the final retail sale of a product is also reduced by any exemptions or preferential rates applied at pre-retail stages. Referring again to Table 13-1, if Firm B is exempt from tax on its entire $500 of value added, then the total VAT on the retail sale of this product is reduced by $50, or Firm B's forgiven tax liability.

Since pre-retail exemptions and preferential rates reduce the total tax on a product under the subtraction method, firms and industries may be inclined to exert political pressure in search of special treatment. Under the credit method, in contrast, the tax on a product depends exclusively on the tax rate applied at the final or retail level. Referring again to Table 13-1, if no tax is imposed on either Firm A (manufacturer) or Firm B (wholesaler), the entire $110 in tax will be collected at the retail level because Firm C (retailer) will have no purchase tax to credit against its sales tax liability of $110. Due to this "catch-up" feature, requests for lower rates or exemptions may be less prevalent under the credit method than the subtraction method, at least prior to the retail level.

Since the tax on a final product depends exclusively on the tax rate applied at the final sale, the credit method, in contrast, to the subtraction method also permits the correct amount of tax to be rebated on exports and imposed on imports for border tax adjustment purposes. Indeed, this is the primary reason why the European Community adopted the credit-method VAT. With the credit method, the entire tax is relieved on exports simply by applying a rate of zero (hence known as zero rating) to export sales and allowing the exporter a full refund (or credit) for tax paid on purchases for business use. The purchase tax is shown as a separate item on the firm's purchase invoices.

But under the subtraction method, it does not suffice simply to apply a zero rate to export sales; that frees the exporter's margin from tax but does not eliminate the tax paid on the exporter's purchases. Calculation of the purchase tax is not difficult if all purchases have been taxed at the same rate. But if different rates and exemptions have been applied to earlier stages, it will not, absent an elaborate tracing procedure, be possible to know how much tax to refund on export sales. In this case, the refund is not simply equal to the pre-tax value of purchases multiplied by a single nominal tax rate. Because the subtraction method lacks the catch-up feature of the credit method, the purchase invoice does not show the full tax paid on those purchases. The invoice will show the tax on the value added by the purchaser, but not the tax paid on the purchaser's supplies.

With respect to imports, unless it is a final sale, it is not even necessary to impose tax under the credit method. The tax is merely collected on the first domestic sale through the absence of a credit. But under the subtraction method, unless domestic sales are all taxed at a uniform rate, it would not be possible to know the equivalent tax to impose on imports.

Thus, the credit method is preferable to the subtraction approach in that: (1) the tax base is less vulnerable to erosion from exemptions and special rates at pre-retail levels, and (2) it permits precise border tax adjustments, even if all transactions are not subject to tax at a uniform rate. While uniform taxation of consumption expenditures comports with the objectives of economic neutrality and administrative feasibility, both European and state experience in the United States demonstrate that a uniform rate may be politically unacceptable. (New Zealand, in a noteworthy departure, introduced a value-added tax on October 1, 1986 at a single 10 percent rate.) If departures from base and rate uniformity are unavoidable, the credit method is preferable to the subtraction method in accommodating those differences. For example, if it is necessary to eliminate the tax on certain commodities, the credit method allows this to be done entirely at the retail level by applying a rate of zero on the sale and allowing a full refund for tax paid on purchases. With the subtraction method, it would not be possible to relieve all of the tax on a product with an adjustment only at the retail level.

Admittedly, the most difficult problems with the subtraction method, particularly those of freeing exports and other goods from the tax, arise in the context of exemptions and multiple rates. While the subtraction method probably would be subject to base erosion through political pressure, there may be a balancing factor to consider. Precisely because multiple rates greatly complicate the operation of a subtraction VAT, perhaps the subtraction method would be successful in resisting pleas for multiple rates and exemptions. That is, an awareness by policymakers that multiple rates and exemptions create insuperable problems may serve to make the subtraction method less susceptible to political tampering.

Both the credit and subtraction methods contain a pro-enforcement characteristic in that businesses have an incentive to ensure that their purchases are properly invoiced by their supplies. This is because the business buyer receives a credit for tax paid on purchases (invoice method) or a deduction for the purchases themselves (subtraction method). "There is a measure of self-policing [under the credit method] in that (except at the retail stage) evasion by suppliers through understating tax collected is counteracted by the purchasers' interest in ensuring that all tax paid is recorded. Similarly, evasion by purchasers in overstating tax paid runs counter to the interests of suppliers."[1] This incentive for accurate invoices does not, however, mean that either the subtraction or the credit method tax is self-enforcing. Even if the tax is correctly stated on an invoice, this is not an iron-clad assurance that the tax was paid to the fiscal authorities. Thus, tax administrators will still need to check the relationship between a firm's sales and purchases to determine if it is "reasonable." This is similar to the analysis that must be made for retail sales tax purposes.

The addition method of determining tax liability is more suited to an income-type VAT. This is because the profit element used in calculating value added would normally include an allowance for depreciation but not the expensing of capital goods. Using the addition method to determine tax liability for a consumption tax would require a firm to recalculate its profits by adding depreciation allowances back in and then subtracting or expensing capital purchases. Because the depreciation and capital purchases associated with foreign-produced goods would be unknown, this would be particularly difficult for imports, again complicating the correct border tax adjustment.

SALES TAX ALTERNATIVES

A consumption tax should satisfy the following criteria:

1. Tax all consumption expenditures at a uniform rate.
2. Avoid taxing capital expenditures or other purchases for business use.

The first requirement means that tax liability should be uniform with respect to consumption expenditures. Otherwise, consumer satisfaction will be reduced as individuals receive signals from the tax system to consume less of heavily taxed items and more of less heavily taxed or exempt items. One exception to this requirement is the so-called sumptuary taxes on alcohol and tobacco which are deliberately designed to discourage consumption of commodities perceived to have social costs, the increased occurrence of alcoholism and diseases associated with smoking. This first criterion requires uniform taxation with respect to an individual's consumption expenditures. It does not require uniformity among individuals in that it would permit a progressive expenditure tax.

The second criterion requires that the tax be confined to consumption expenditures. If business purchases are taxed as part of the tax base, the tax will be a nonuniform percentage of consumption expenditures, depending upon how important the taxed business purchases are in a product's overall costs of production. Moreover, if machinery and other capital goods are taxed, business will have an incentive to substitute labor for capital. Production methods will be distorted and altered by the tax. The taxation of business purchases will encourage firms to integrate vertically to avoid the tax.

A sales tax accomplishes these objectives by taxing expenditures or the use of income, rather than income itself with a deduction for saving. On the basis of the above criteria, a retail sales tax or retail VAT would qualify as a consumption tax. Because they include business purchases and capital equipment in the tax base, neither a manufacturers' or wholesale sales tax qualifies as a consumption tax. They are taxes on sales but not taxes exclusively on consumption. Some consumer expenditures, notably on services, are beyond the reach of the typical manufacturers' or wholesale level sales tax, and some business purchases are taxed.

Value-Added Tax. A broad-based VAT imposed at a single rate would constitute a uniform percentage of consumption expenditures, or at least of consumer expenditures on taxable items. Special rates, perhaps dictated by the necessity of taxing some goods more heavily (alcohol, gasoline, or tobacco) and others not at all (food) could be accommodated within a VAT structure. Thus, any departures from uniform taxation of consumer spending would be the result of explicit policy decisions to depart from a uniform tax rate.

Business purchases can be excluded from the scope of a value-added tax. Under the subtraction approach, all business purchases, including capital equipment, would be allowed as an immediate deduction or expense in determining tax liability. With the credit approach, the tax paid on those business purchases would be deductible from the tax due on sales. In either case, this would eliminate all business purchases, including capital equipment, from being taxed separately as part of the tax base. The goods and services produced by capital equipment are, of course, subject to tax. The deduction or credit for capital purchases does not treat capital more favorably than labor. It simply avoids taxing capital twice, once on the purchase of the asset and again on its return. Under either the subtraction or credit method, capital is deductible only because its purchase has already been taxed. By excluding capital equipment from taxation, a consumption-type VAT is neutral between choice of production methods, favoring neither labor nor capital.

Retail Sales Tax. Though state experience with the retail sales tax indicates that the goal of taxing all consumption expenditures may not be realized, this is not an inherent defect of the tax. While food, clothing, and medicine are often exempt from retail sales taxation, this is by design, to lessen the tax burden on "necessities." Indeed, experience with the VAT in Europe shows a similar pattern of exemptions and preferential rates aimed at achieving social or distributional objectives.

Based on state experience, a retail sales tax may not be as successful as a VAT in avoiding the taxation of capital goods and business purchases. Perhaps as much as 20 percent of state sales tax revenue is derived from taxing producers' goods.[2] Though two methods are used to exempt taxation of business purchases, they do not succeed in eliminating all business purchases from retail sales taxation.

First, registered firms are allowed to make purchases for resale on a tax-free basis. The buyer provides the seller with an exemption certificate indicating the purchases are for resale. The right to buy tax-free with an exemption certificate, however, is normally limited either to items to be resold or to items that become physical ingredients or component parts of goods destined for resale. Other purchases, such as fuel, machinery, and equipment are usually not covered by the resale exemption provision. They are exempt from tax only if covered by a specific statutory exemption. The combined effect of the resale and statutory exemptions is to free most but not all business purchases from retail sales taxation. Compared to a value-added tax, "freeing producer goods from tax may be slightly more difficult under a retail tax."[3] Under a VAT, of course, business purchases are automatically freed of tax, either through the credit of tax or immediate deduction of purchase price. Based on the U.S. Treasury's 20 percent estimate, a significant portion of the retail sales tax is collected from business purchases and, thus, distorts consumer buying habits and production methods, as well as being included in export prices.

Under either a retail sales tax or VAT, revenue officials are faced with the problem of ensuring that exempt business purchases are not diverted to taxable consumption. With a VAT tax this can occur if a firm takes a credit for the tax paid on an item purchased for personal, nonbusiness use or claims a deduction in the case of a subtraction

VAT. The same problem arises under a retail sales tax if items are purchased on a tax-free basis for business use but are diverted to personal consumption. In either case, tax administrators must analyze the relationship between the firm's purchases and its sales to determine if business purchases are being consumed on a tax-free basis.

Compared to a VAT, a retail sales tax may involve fewer taxpayers, but the difference is not dramatic. This is because a retail sales tax applies to any firm making a retail sale, not just retailers. Both manufacturers and wholesalers make retail sales. Moreover, even firms that do not make retail sales must be checked to ensure that their exempt purchases are for business uses. The 1984 Treasury study concluded that there would be about 10 percent fewer taxpayers with a retail sales tax than with a VAT.

Some tax experts believe that evasion is more likely with a retail sales tax, especially at high rates of tax. The basis for this assertion is a belief that it may be difficult to collect large amounts of tax at a single stage. In light of successful state experience with the retail sales tax, it is doubtful that this criticism is applicable to the United States.

Manufacturers and Other Pre-retail Taxes. In developing countries, sales taxes confined to the manufacturers or wholesale level are popular because they apply to a smaller number of taxpayers (then a retail tax) and because recordkeeping at the retail level is poor. Neither of these reasons applies to the United States, where the feasibility of retail sales taxes has been amply demonstrated at the state level. Pre-retail taxes, because they do not tax consumer spending uniformly and because they impose tax on business purchases, should not be considered candidates for a federal consumption tax.

A pre-retail tax would not constitute a uniform percentage of consumer expenditures, even of spending on taxable items. Many services provided to consumers, such as laundry and cleaning, personal care, and repair work are provided only at the retail level. They would be excluded entirely from the scope of a manufacturers or wholesale tax. Since many services are excluded from the tax base, the tax imposed on taxable goods would have to be higher in order to raise a given amount of revenue. The net effect would be to discriminate in favor of those individuals purchasing tax-exempt services and against those with strong preferences for taxable goods.

Another source of unintended distortion is that wholesale and retail margins differ widely among kinds and categories of goods. A pre-retail tax would impose the heaviest burden on those goods with the smallest trade margins, or most of their value added before the tax point and the lightest tax on those commodities with the largest trade margins, or where most of the value is added after the manufacturers or wholesale level. To the degree that "luxury" goods have relatively high wholesale-retail margins, they would bear a lower tax rate than other goods. These differences in tax burdens are not the result of any policy decision to modify the tax on certain commodities for distributional reasons. They simply are a consequence of the fact that trade margins vary sharply among goods and industries.

In addition to failing to tax consumer spending uniformly, a pre-retail tax creates production distortions by taxing capital goods and other business purchases and by favoring or disfavoring certain production channels. Though it may be possible to exempt machinery and other capital equipment from a pre-retail tax, it is often taxed. Nearly one-half of the revenue from the Canadian manufacturers' sales tax is from business purchases of intermediate inputs and capital goods.[4]

Taxation of producers' goods has a number of undesirable consequences. It creates production distortions by encouraging the substitution of labor for the taxed business purchases. Consumption neutrality is harmed because the taxed purchases will not be a uniform percentage of final goods prices. Though sales taxes can normally be rebated on exports, the portion of the tax on business purchases will be borne by exports as a hidden, nonrebatable tax.

The diversity of distribution channels among businesses also gives rise to production distortions under either a manufacturers' or wholesale tax. With respect to a manufacturers' tax, for example, all manufacturers do not sell exclusively to wholesalers and all imports are not purchased by wholesalers. Thus, manufacturers selling directly to retailers (and engaged in some wholesaling functions) are discriminated against. To minimize tax liability, firms have an incentive to transfer distribution activity past the point of tax liability. With a manufacturers' tax, for example, firms may transfer advertising, packaging, and assembly activity beyond the manufacturing function. With a wholesale tax, retailers will seek to reduce their tax liability by buying direct from the manufacturer (backward integration). With either tax, imports are tax favored if they incur fewer distribution costs (advertising, warranty, credit) than their domestic counterparts. This is the case with the Canadian manufacturers' tax. "Because the trade level at which imports are taxed is often lower than the level of domestic manufacturers, there is an inherent bias in the tax in favor of imports. This bias became so pronounced in the automobile, cosmetics, health goods, and pre-recorded video cassettes industries that the level of tax was shifted to the wholesale level for imports and domestically produced goods alike.[5]

Compared to a tax that includes the retail level, pre-retail taxes pose unique administrative problems and complexities for fiscal authorities. Manufacturers selling directly to retailers will petition the tax authorities for discounts so that their tax liability is more closely based on a manufacturer's sales price. With a wholesale tax, the manufacturer's price to the retailer may be increased, or subject to "uplift" to more closely correspond to a wholesale price. "In order to create fairness in the tax base . . . there is a complex notional valuation system . . . to determine the value for tax, rather than a reliance on actual selling prices."[6]

Thus, pre-retail taxes are unsatisfactory because the variations in tax liability on consumer products are unintended and perhaps unknown, production channels and methods are distorted, and the tax includes capital as well as consumption goods.

EXEMPTIONS AND ZERO OR PREFERENTIAL RATES

Any proposal for a federal consumption tax is likely to be criticized on distributional grounds for adding a regressive element to the federal tax structure. A tax is regressive if the tax burden, as a percentage of income, is higher for low-income individuals and families than for those with higher incomes. A number of responses can be made to this criticism. Even if a progressive federal tax structure is desired, this does not mean that every tax must be progressive on its own. The individual income tax, with multiple rates, personal exemptions, and an earned income credit can be used to achieve whatever progressivity is desired in the federal system. A consumption tax may be regressive with respect to current income but not when measured against so-called permanent or lifetime income. This is because individuals and families may maintain their current level of consumption even if income fluctuates because of unexpected losses or gains. Thus, on an annual basis, consumption may not be proportional to current income. But viewed from a lifetime perspective, consumption is more likely to be proportional with respect to income. This would make a consumption tax proportional, not regressive with respect to income when measured on a permanent or lifetime basis.

In spite of these qualifications, attempts would undoubtedly be made to modify the distributional effects of a federal retail sales or value-added tax with exemptions and special rates. If policymakers decide that the distributional impact of the tax must be adjusted, they should resist the temptation to do so through the rate structure. Nonuniform rates distort consumer choices, create administrative difficulties, require higher rates on fully taxable commodities to raise the same amount of revenue, and are not a cost-effective way of alleviating the regressive aspects of the tax.

A food exemption, for example is undoubtedly motivated by a desire to free "necessities" from taxation. But a blanket food exemption would encourage high-income groups to increase their purchases of expensive gourmet food items. State and European experience shows that attempts to prevent this by more clearly defining exempt purchases result in a complex and administratively unwieldy tax system that purports to distinguish between biscuits and cookies, fruit juice and soft drinks, nonprepared and carry-out food, and other exempt and taxable items. The rationale for some decisions is often unclear. In the Netherlands, "expensive meat is taxed at 4 percent but expensive fish at 18 percent. Prepared meals are taxed at the lower rate, but pancakes, fish and chips, and salads bear the normal rate unless they are consumed in hotels or restaurants, where they are taxed like all other foods at 4 percent. Obviously, these examples do not make for an internally consistent value-added tax."[7] Lower rates and exemptions are expensive in terms of forgone revenues since they apply to all individuals and families, not just those with low incomes. In the United States, individual states forfeit 15 to 20 percent of their potential sales tax revenue from allowing food to be exempt.

A more cost-effective way of alleviating the burden of a retail sales or value-added tax on low-income groups is to provide a refundable credit or reimbursement for tax paid on an essential or minimum level of consumption. The current poverty level of income for a family of four is about $12,000. If 75 percent of consumer expenditures are subject to taxation (even a broad-based tax is unlikely to include housing, foreign travel, and religious and welfare activities), this family would qualify for a refundable credit of $900 ($12,000 × .75 × .10), assuming the tax rate is 10 percent. According to the U.S. Treasury's 1984 study, this alternative alleviates nearly as much of the burden of the tax on low-income groups as not taxing a wide array of necessities and at about one-fourth the cost.

This is not to suggest that the reimbursement approach is problem-free. The refund must be delivered to qualifying individuals and families. A major objective of the Tax Reform Act of 1986 was to remove poor people from the tax rolls by increasing the personal exemption and standard deduction. In 1988, for example, the personal exemption will be $1,950 and the standard deduction for a married couple will be $5,000. Thus, a family of four with poverty-level income of about $12,000 would have no income tax liability. Though this family may be eligible for the earned income credit (administered through the income tax), it may be preferable to administer the VAT reimbursement separately, rather than through the income tax. This would require the design and establishment of a vehicle to make the reimbursement and the associated bureaucracy to administer it. The amount of the payment would have to be specified. Should it, for example, exceed income? How should income be defined? Should it include tax-exempt income, such as Social Security payments? How would the reimbursement vary with family size? Because the objective is to provide relief at lower income levels, the reimbursement should phase out as income exceeds poverty-level amounts. Otherwise, it becomes unnecessarily expensive. Care must be taken, however, to ensure that the phase-out does not produce an unacceptably high marginal tax rate.

While a broad-based tax is desirable, some consumer expenditures, such as on housing, education, and medical care probably would be beyond the reach of even a broad-based consumption tax. Exports also would be sold on a tax-free basis. Thus, the question of exemptions and preferential rates cannot be entirely avoided. With a retail sales tax, the tax is eliminated by exempting the retail sale. To the extent that producers' goods are subject to taxation under a retail sales tax, some tax would still remain on the exempt good or service.

Because a value-added tax is collected in stages, the question arises as to whether the tax on only one stage or all stages of production and distribution should be eliminated from the product. With a credit-method VAT, two alternatives are available: exemption or zero rating. If a commodity or service is exempt, no tax is charged on the sale, but no credit is available for tax paid on purchases. Tax is eliminated only on the exempt stage. Zero rating is equivalent to exemption under a retail sales tax. All of the tax on the zero-rated good or service is removed. This is accomplished by taxing the sale at a zero rate and allowing a full refund or credit for tax paid on purchases related to the sale of the zero-rated item.

Whether exemption or zero rating is more desirable depends on the policy objective. An exempt firm is, in effect, treated like a final consumer, paying tax on its purchases and receiving no credit or refund for that tax. An exempt firm is outside the system, it need not register. Exemption is desirable for those entities which the government does not wish to register nor to eliminate all of the tax from their product or service. Farmers, small service establishments, sidewalk vendors, and religious and welfare organizations are possible candidates. Firms with business customers, however, may prefer not to be exempt. This is because customers of exempt establishments will bear the tax imposed on the exempt firm's taxable purchases but will not be allowed a credit or refund for that tax. Generally speaking, exemption is attractive if a firm sells to final consumers but not if it sells to businesses.

Zero rating is the proper choice if the objective is to eliminate the tax entirely on a good or service. Export sales are one example. Housing may be another, though one alternative is to treat housing as an exempt activity with no tax charged on the sale of a house but no allowance for tax paid on purchases of materials and supplies. In the export case, the firm would charge a rate of zero on its foreign sales and receive a credit for all tax paid on purchases related to those sales. Unlike the case of a retail sales tax that includes some producers' goods, this method would eliminate all of the tax on export sales.

Fiscal authorities should avoid creating a situation where a firm makes both exempt and taxable sales. This could arise, for example, if a bank were treated as exempt on its consumer lending activity but as taxable on its service fees. This would require the bank to apportion the tax paid on purchases between exempt (not creditable) and taxable (creditable) activities. This presents administrative difficulties both for businesses and tax authorities, particularly regarding purchases of capital equipment and the need to forecast the relative degree of use of the equipment between exempt and taxable activities.

With a subtraction VAT, the opportunity to zero rate a product or service does not exist. Thus, it is more difficult than with the invoice approach to entirely eliminate the tax on a produce or service. Export sales, for example, cannot be freed of tax by only exempting the exporter's margin. There must also be a mechanism for eliminating the tax paid on purchases related to the export sales. If all purchases have been subject to tax and at a uniform rate, the tax paid on purchases can be estimated by multiplying the pre-tax value of purchases by the correct tax rate. This does not work, however, if all purchases have not been taxed or if there is more than one rate of tax. If there are any gaps in coverage or differences in rates, the amount to be refunded to the exporter could only be approximated. This could lead to disputes with U.S. trade partners as to whether the border tax adjustments were excessive. In a subtraction regime, precise export adjustments could be achieved only by exempting all stages in the production and distribution process. This, however, would require prior knowledge that a particular item was destined for the export market. Thus, the subtraction method may not be capable of achieving full and accurate elimination of the tax on exports or any other sales where the goal is complete removal of the tax on the product.

UNDERGROUND ECONOMY

A value-added tax may be successful in penetrating the underground economy, which consists of informal activity (small service operations and casual sales) not reported for income tax purposes and illegal activities (gambling and narcotics). Even if no VAT is charged on the output or sales of these activities, tax will be collected on the purchases associated with these activities, provided a credit is not improperly claimed for the purchase tax.

The underground economy accounts for only about 15 percent of the income "tax gap" estimated by the Internal Revenue Service. The tax gap is defined as the difference between the income tax (individual plus corporate) which is owed and the amount voluntarily paid. Much of the tax gap is attributable to unreported income from partnership activity, interest, and dividends. To the degree that tax gap income is spent on taxable items, it would be subject to either a federal retail sales or VAT, even though it escapes the reach of the income tax. Consider an individual, A, who makes consumption purchases out of income that he does not report for income tax purposes. A's purchases are income to individual B, who reports the income and pays tax on it. In this case, individual B is paying income tax, but A is not. If A's purchases from B are now subject to a value-added tax, A will at least be paying tax on the use of his income. The problem of avoiding income tax, however, remains.

This ability of a consumption tax to penetrate the underground economy, however, needs to be tempered by the realization that neither a retail sales or VAT is fraud-proof. Either tax can be evaded if a seller successfully understates its sales for reporting purposes. The Europeans are familiar with situations in which small shopkeepers or providers of services will charge a lower price for a cash sale if the customer does not require a receipt or invoice. "Contractors to private householders are tempted to say, 'Pay me in cash and I will deduct VAT.'"[8] Finally, the lower income tax rates under the pending U.S. tax reform legislation may make incursions into the underground economy by reducing the benefits of tax evasion or avoidance. A study of the United Kingdom's experience with the value-added tax indicates that high compliance costs may prompt smaller firms to seek relief by entering the underground economy. "Another possible effect of the differential burden of compliance may be to push the proprietors of small firms toward tax evasion and the black economy."[9]

EUROPEAN ADOPTION AND EXPERIENCE

European experience with the value-added tax provides useful lessons for the United States, both with regard to the type of tax and its implementation. France adopted a wholesale VAT in 1955 as a substitute for the cascade turnover tax. The formation of the European Economic Community (EEC) in 1957 provided the impetus for more widespread adoption of the tax. The objective of the EEC was economic union, or creating a single integrated market where goods, services, people, and capital could move freely. When the community was established in 1957, each of the member states, apart from France (Belgium, West Germany, Italy, the Netherlands, and Luxembourg) imposed cascade turnover taxes. With this type of levy, a tax is imposed on each transaction, or each time a good or service is sold as it moves through the production and distribution process. Naturally, this type of tax encourages vertical integration to minimize the total tax imposed on a product. Of special importance to realizing the EEC's goal of economic integration, the total tax on a product can only be approximated because it depends on the number of separate (and hence taxable) links in the production and distribution process. Because the total tax on a product cannot be known with certainty, it is impossible to equalize the tax burdens on goods crossing national boundaries.

Under international trading rules and agreements, sales and other taxes on products, also known as indirect taxes, can be imposed on imports and rebated on exports. The effect of these border tax adjustments is to equalize the taxes on products where they are consumed. Because of uncertainty as to the amount of cascade tax on a product, accurate border tax adjustments were impossible. With respect to goods crossing national borders, export rebates and compensating import taxes had to be estimated. The Europeans recognized that inexact border adjustments "could be used for protection purposes, a situation clearly inconsistent with the aim of creating a common market."[10] This prompted the founders of the EEC to require that member countries substitute VAT for the cascade turnover tax. Subsequently, the VAT was adopted by Denmark (1967), West Germany (1968), the Netherlands (1968), Luxembourg (1970), Belgium (1971), Ireland (1972), and Italy and the United Kingdom (1973).

The EEC Directives required member countries to adopt a consumption VAT with tax liability calculated under the credit method. The invoice or credit method was chosen, rather than the subtraction approach, because of a recognition that it would permit exact border tax adjustments, even if the rates and coverage differed among countries. The invoice-type VAT was the only type of value-added tax seen as consistent with the objective of economic union.

While economic integration with Europe is not a U.S. policy objective, accurate border tax adjustments are important. For nearly two decades, discussions have periodically arisen in the United States as to whether the federal tax structure should rely more heavily on consumption or sales taxation. This discussion is motivated in part by a belief that the United States would benefit from an improvement in its trade balance if it adopted a federal sales or value-added tax. Notwithstanding this perception, it is far from clear that the United States would gain a trade advantage from increased reliance on sales or value-added taxation. Moreover, the decision to adopt a federal consumption tax should be based on much more than the expected trade effects. But if the United States adopts a sales or value-added tax, it should avoid getting involved in international disputes over the size of the allowable border tax adjustments. From this standpoint, an invoice VAT would be the most desirable alternative.

With the exception of Denmark, none of the European VATs is limited to a single positive rate. (In all countries, exports are always taxed at a zero rate.) While the multiple rates in the European system are aimed at lessening the burden of the tax on the poor, they have well-established drawbacks. Administrative problems arise in drawing borderline distinctions between items subject to tax at a higher and lower rate. "Liability borderlines were frequently cited as a difficulty in the construction sector, where construction and alterations are zero-rated, but repairs and maintenance are standard rated."[11] If some goods are taxed at a reduced or zero rate, the rate must be higher on those goods taxed at the standard rate to raise a given amount of revenue. Multiple rates also increase administrative costs. "The cost of administration of a VAT rises sharply with complexity. Everyone we spoke to in Europe recommended that the base be kept as comprehensive as possible and that we (Canada) stick to a single rate."[12] Viewed from this perspective, European fiscal authorities have concluded that the benefits of multiple rates are not worth the costs.

> The central technical lesson of European experience is that multiple rates can be used to eliminate the regressivity of the value-added tax, but that the penalties in administrative complexity, increased compliance costs, and distortions in consumption decisions have been high and probably unjustified. Most conference participants agreed . . . that it would be preferable to use other taxes and transfer payments to alleviate the undesirable distributional consequences generated by a value-added tax imposed at uniform rates.[13]

Even in the European countries where the VAT replaced a cascade turnover tax (Belgium, West Germany, Italy, Luxembourg, and the Netherlands), and thus had experience with multistage sales taxes, the government needed to embark on an extensive campaign to educate business on the new tax system. West Germany's cascade tax, for example, was one of the most comprehensive in Europe. Very few taxpayers were subject to the new VAT that were not subject to the prior cascade tax. Still, the German government conducted a 12-month education program before the VAT become effective.

For the United States, the experience of the United Kingdom may be more relevant. The United Kingdom had no broad-based national sales tax. The VAT replaced the selective employment tax and the purchase tax, a limited wholesale sales tax. To educate consumers and businesses, the U.K. Customs and Excise Department publicized the new tax in seminars, newspapers, television, radio, and pamphlets for a two-year period. The 1984 Treasury Department study concluded that the Internal Revenue Service would need 18 months lead time, after enactment, before it could begin to administer a VAT.[14]

CONCLUSION

The design and administrative issues associated with a federal consumption tax point in favor of either a retail sales tax or an invoice-type value-added tax, with a modest preference for the latter because of its superiority in avoiding the taxation of capital equipment and other business purchases, a must under a consumption tax. Though VAT liability can be calculated by either the invoice, subtraction, or addition methods, the invoice (or credit) alternative has important policy and practical advantages. Compared to the subtraction method, it would be less susceptible to political pressure for exemptions and the attendant base erosion. The addition method is not appropriate for a consumption tax because the profit component of value added would normally allow for depreciation but not the expensing of capital. In comparison to the other two approaches, tax can be eliminated on exports and other goods more easily and with greater accuracy under the invoice method. Both the subtraction and credit approaches have pro-enforcement characteristics, but neither are self-enforcing.

An acceptable consumption tax should tax all consumption expenditures uniformly and should avoid taxing capital expenditures or other purchases for business use. Otherwise, consumer spending decisions will be distorted and capital will be taxed more heavily than labor, as it is under the income tax. On the basis of these requirements, a retail sales and retail level VAT are the only sales taxes that qualify as a consumption tax. Pre-retail sales taxes on manufacturers or wholesalers are not acceptable consumption taxes.

Any proposal for a federal consumption tax is likely to be criticized on distributional grounds as being regressive. A progressive federal tax structure, however, does not require every tax to be progressive on its own. The income tax provides policymakers with sufficient flexibility to achieve whatever progressivity is desired in the federal tax system. If political considerations dictate that the distributional impact of the tax must be adjusted, the temptation to use exemptions and rate differentials should be resisted. A refundable credit would avoid the economic and administrative costs inherent in the use of multiple rates.

A value-added tax must be successful in penetrating the underground economy. Even if no tax is collected on the informal economic activity itself, it will be collected on purchases associated with those activities. A VAT may also reduce the tax gap, estimated by the Internal Revenue Service at about $100 billion, by taxing tax-gap income when it is consumed.

European experience reaffirms the conclusion that an invoice VAT would be the most desirable consumption tax for the United States. That experience also shows that economic and administrative costs are minimized by a broad-based tax imposed at a single rate. After enactment, it may take as long as 18 months before a VAT could be made operational in the United States.

NOTES

1. Henry Aaron, *The Value-Added Tax: Lessons from Europe* (Washington, D.C.: The Brookings Institution, 1981), pp. 3-4.

2. *Tax Reform for Fairness, Simplicity, and Economic Growth*, Vol. 3: *Value-Added Tax* (Washington, D.C.: U.S. Treasury Department, Office of Tax Analysis, 1984), p. 32.

3. Sijbren Cnossen, "Sales Taxation in OECD Member Countries," *Bulletin*, International Bureau of Fiscal Documentation (1983): 159.

4. S. Malcolm Gillis, "Federal Sales Taxation: A Survey of Six Decades of Experience, Critiques, and Reform Proposals," *Canadian Tax Journal* (January-February 1985): 78.

5. C.D. Weyman, "Pros and Cons of the Value-Added Tax," Eastern Regional Association of Sales Tax Administrators, unpublished conference paper, 1985, p. 8.

6. Ibid., p. 8.

7. Aaron, *Value-Added Tax*, p. 47.

8. Cedric Sanford, Michael Godwin, Peter Hardwick, and Ian Butterworth, *Costs and Benefits of VAT* (London: Heinemann Educational Books, 1981), p. 152.

9. Ibid., p. 151.
10. Cnossen, "Sales Taxation in OECD Member Countries," p. 154.
11. Sanford, *Costs and Benefits of VAT*, p. 67.
12. Weyman, "Pros and Cons of the Value-Added Tax," p. 16.
13. Aaron, *Value-Added Tax*, p. 16.
14. U.S. Treasury, *Value-Added Tax*, p. 124.

ADDITIONAL BIBLIOGRAPHY

Aaron, Henry J., and Harvey Galper, "A Tax on Consumption, Gifts, and Bequests and Other Strategies for Tax Reform," *Options for Tax Reform* (Washington, D.C.: The Brookings Institution, 1984), pp. 106–146.

Bradford, David F., *Blueprints for Basic Tax Reform*, 2nd ed., rev. (Arlington, Va.: Tax Analysts, 1984).

Carlson, George N., *Value-Added Tax: European Experience and Lessons for the United States* (Washington, D.C.: U.S. Treasury Department, 1981).

Lodin, Sven-Olof, *Progressive Expenditure Tax—An Alternative?*, Report of Government Commission on Taxation (Stockholm: LiberForlog, 1978).

Meade, James E., *The Structure and Reform of Direct Taxation*, Institute for Fiscal Studies (London: George Allen and Unwin, 1978).

U.S. Department of the Treasury, *Blueprints for Basic Tax Reform* (Washington, D.C.: U.S. Treasury Office for Tax Analysis, 1977).

_____. *Tax Reform for Fairness, Simplicity and Economic Growth*, Volume 1: *Overview* (Washington, D.C.: U.S. Treasury Office for Tax Analysis, 1984).

Discussants:

THE ADMINISTRABILITY OF A VALUE-ADDED TAX

J. Gregory Ballentine

There is a common conclusion about value-added taxes that I think is very much overstated; that conclusion is that VATs are much simpler than other taxes. This may be true of many very pure VAT systems, it may be true of David Bradford's X-Tax, but it is not true of the kind of realistic tax that we would face as a result of the political process.

There are two contexts in which we might get a value-added tax. The first is the substitution of a VAT for some part of the income tax, and the second is the introduction of a VAT or some kind of retail sales tax as an additional tax to deal with the deficit.

I will start with the substitution context. The value-added tax we must consider is a *populist* consumption tax (as pointed out by Ways and Means Chairman Dan Rostenkowski in Chapter 2). If any VAT is going to be considered seriously in Congress, it will be a populist kind of tax. A populist bill requires business tax increases and individual tax cuts skewed to lower income groups.

We may be able to avoid populist tax bills when we cut taxes in general, as occurred in 1981. The cuts were not intended to redistribute income; they were across the board. Further, the 1981 legislation did not have to raise corporate taxes to finance rate cuts, because it was designed to lose revenue.

Since 1981, however, we have either raised taxes, as in 1982 and 1984, or had revenue-neutral reform. In this setting, the political process requires that you raise taxes on business so that it can be said that people do not pay the tax increases. Further, as shown by the Tax Reform Act of 1986, whatever individual tax cuts there are have to go to particular income groups. That is the populist context for a value-added tax.

Thus, I believe that, if a value-added tax is substituted for other taxes, on balance there will have to be an increase in corporate income taxes and a reduction in personal income taxes. This will allow the Treasury distribution tables to show the overall tax change as a tax cut for people. If this is the case, it is hard to argue that we will get any greater administrative simplicity out of that switch. Further, to get more of a perceived tax cut down at the bottom end, the value-added tax will have a lot of exemptions: including food, health care, and maybe rental property.

These exemptions are not a minor matter. Exemptions cause complexity. One good example, which I believe occurred in France, was a long and extensive debate over whether or not Head and Shoulders anti-dandruff shampoo was a medicine or a cosmetic. That may seem minor at this point, but the Internal Revenue Service is going to have to write regulations dealing with such issues and businesspeople will have to learn the regulations. Further, people will have to check to see that the correct product is taxed as a cosmetic.

Another example of the kind of line drawing that has to be done concerns food. Usually an exemption is given for food, but it is only for food eaten off premises. In such a case, what is McDonald's, and what happens if a McDonald's does not have tables and booths in the area where food is sold but puts them somewhere else, thus letting people eat outside the restaurant? Is that food off premises, which is exempt, or is it food that really is consumed on premises? You can imagine a setting in which rather nice restaurants become simply kitchens with affiliated dining rooms where customers eat "off premises."

All these are examples of necessary line drawing. Such examples are the reason why the general experience in Europe, where countries have exempted many products, has been that the VAT is not a simple tax.

The alternative to exemptions that has been suggested (by George Carlson in Chapter 13) is to provide some kind of mechanism by which you give a refund through some other system. That would be a nightmare. Too many analysts have been all too casual in describing what is involved in such rebates.

Giving the refund back through the income tax system would cause two problems to arise. First, a large share of the elderly simply do not file taxes under current law, and even fewer would do so under the new law. Yet the political process, if it is a populist tax bill, is going to want to give a refund to those elderly. That means registering those elderly and requiring them to file forms.

Second, one of the major elements of the most recent populist tax legislation, the Tax Act of 1986, that is attracting a lot of attention is the removal of approximately six million low-income persons from the income tax rolls. Is the new VAT going to put them back on the income tax rolls so they can file a return, in order to get the refund for the VAT taxes? If so, not only will the six million go back on the roles, but so will many others exempt under current law.

This problem is quite messy. Even David Bradford's solution in his X-Tax will not be simple. What Bradford describes is a system in which you give a rebate based on somebody's wages, with no apparent need to file a return. But our political system will want to base the rebate on the family's income, and how many dependents they have, not just on the level of one person's wages. In that setting, you cannot provide a given dollar rebate to a taxpayer because the person has received $15,000 in wages, without knowing whether or not he or she is single or married and whether his or her spouse works. For example, are two persons with $15,000 in wages going to get the same wage rebate if one is single and the other has two kids and a spouse who works and earns $85,000 a year, or $50,000, or $10,000? All those characteristics are going to determine the kind of rebate the system is going to give to offset the regressivity of the value-added tax. The resulting rebate system will require filing returns and will not be simple.

Further, think of what kind of a money loser this could be if we go into a recession. The danger is that some in Congress will argue that, because of the recession, we ought to rebate a little more VAT to give a big kick to the economy. Even without a recession, the rebate system provides a new checkwriting program in the federal government. That system, like all of the others, runs the danger of growing and taking on a life of its own.

Consider now the context of using the VAT as an additional tax. All the same problems still arise. We still would have a populist tax bill of some sort. That means various changes, exemptions, and rebates in order to make the VAT appear to be progressive. Further, in this setting, the VAT would be a new tax, so there are no gains in simplicity. If the VAT is simply a new tax, all that results is added complexity.

If there is a need to raise $75 to $100 billion, maybe the VAT is the least complex choice. However, the assumption that the political system will perceive a great need for revenues, and that there may be a bandwagon for a VAT to bail us out of a politically unacceptable deficit is, I think, incorrect. Charles McLure (see Chapter 12 Discussants) stated the usual structure of the logic behind this assumption: Congress will not cut domestic spending, the president will not agree to a cut in defense spending, and therefore we are going to have to raise revenues. Logically, that sounds good. In fact, however, it is misleading.

The defense build-up is over. As a result, the Congressional Budget Office (CBO), using economic growth rates about the same as the average of the postwar era, including recessions and recoveries, has forecast the deficit going down to about $70 billion in 1991 under current policies.

The key to these lower deficit estimates is the end to the defense build-up. Defense budget authority in 1985 was $295 billion. In 1986 it was $286 billion. In 1987 it will be about $290. The forecast of $200 billion deficits as far as the eye can see, or the old CBO forecast of deficits rising to $300 billion are no longer relevant. Those forecasts assumed *real* defense budget authority growth of at least 5 percent.

We are simply not in that exploding $300 billion deficit setting anymore. It is going to take a few months for this change in deficit forecasts to sink in, but next summer we are going to have experienced a year with significantly lower deficits than 1986, and we will be looking at deficits going down in the future. I do not think that is the context in which Congress is going to consider a $75 billion tax bill, particularly given the administration's reluctance.

Thus, it seems to me, we should expect much less political pressure to raise revenues. (I do not mean that it would not be good for the economy to raise taxes so as to lower the deficit even more: it would be very good to do so. I only mean that declining deficits will reduce the political will to raise taxes.) I doubt that, in this setting, Congress is going to move to an entirely new tax system.

One final issue is the underground economy. It is not clear to me that the VAT has a great deal of benefit with respect to the underground economy. One common mistake is to conclude that a VAT does not have the underground economy problems that an income tax has because, when somebody works in the underground economy and gets income and does not pay income taxes on it, nonetheless, a VAT is paid when that person spends their income on taxed products.

The same point applies under an income tax. If I get income and do not report it under the income tax and then buy something, that purchase of mine generates income for somebody else and they pay income taxes on it. My activity is part of the underground economy and is untaxed. The same loss will exist under a value-added tax. But in both cases, VAT and income tax, my use of my untaxed income gives rise to taxes.

Overall, I think there are sound economic reasons to adopt a pure consumption tax and maybe even to adopt the impure ones we would likely get. I do not, however, see that the administrative simplicity is a great argument for a VAT.

PROBLEMS IN ADMINISTERING A CONSUMPTION TAX

Milka Casanegra de Jantscher

George Carlson reaches two basic conclusions in Chapter 13. First, sales taxes that do not reach the retail stage fail the essential tests of a consumption tax because they do not tax consumer spending uniformly. Such taxes exlude services, which are available only at the retail level. In addition, pre-retail sales taxes create unintended distortions, since they impose the heaviest burden on goods with the smallest wholesale and retail margins. Carlson's second basic conclusion is that a value-added tax is modestly preferable to a retail sales tax on the grounds that capital purchases can be more easily excluded from taxation under a VAT.

While I agree with both conclusions, there are in my view other and much stronger administrative reasons for preferring a VAT to a retail sales tax. I shall explain some of these below. I shall also discuss some of the administrative requirements for implementing a VAT that have not been dealt with by Carlson.

Background

Two circumstances will necessarily exert great influence on any decision regarding the enactment of a national sales tax. First, the U.S. federal government has had no experience administering a broad-based sales tax. In all industrial countries that have a VAT, the taxing jurisdiction that administers the tax had some prior experience with a broad-based sales tax before the VAT was enacted. In some instances the previous sales tax did not reach the retail stage, but it usually covered at least manufacturers and wholesalers.

The second circumstance that distinguishes the case of the United States from that of other industrial countries (except Canada) is the existence of a state revenue system that relies heavily on retail sales taxes. How to coordinate a federal sales tax with the retail sales taxes of the states may be the greatest technical and political challenge faced by those who favor a national sales tax. The coexistence of two sales taxes levied on different bases, with different rates and exemptions, would seriously complicate tax administration and increase

The views expressed here are those of the author and should not be attributed to the International Monetary Fund.

taxpayers' compliance costs. In particular, the compliance cost of sales taxes is greater at the retail level, particularly among medium-sized and small retailers.

If a national sales tax is to be implemented successfully, state and federal revenue requirements must be reconciled. Several alternative solutions can be envisaged. First, the notion of having two separate sales taxes—one at the federal and the other at the state level—could be abandoned and only one sales tax, at the national level, would be levied. A portion of the revenue collected could then be assigned to the states. A similar solution is used in another large industrialized country with important state revenue needs, the Federal Republic of Germany. Administration of the single tax could, in principle, be assigned either to the federal or the state governments. Another solution could entail some form of state piggybacking on the federal sales tax. Whatever the solution, a major consideration should be its administrative feasibility.

Administrative Arguments Against a National Retail Sales Tax

It is true, as Carlson points out, that the feasibility of retail sales taxes has been demonstrated in the United States at the state level. However, there are two important reasons for the success of the states in implementing retail sales taxes. Current retail sales tax rates are relatively low and many states do not extend the tax to services, or they tax very few services.

In 1985 rates of the state retail sales taxes ranged from 3 to 7.5 percent, with the median rate equal to 4.6 percent. Additional local sales taxes at lower rates are applicable in some jurisdictions, but in no case do the combined state and local taxes exceed 9 percent. Experience elsewhere has shown that moderate sales tax rates are easier to enforce than high rates, particularly at the retail stage. But in order to raise revenue equal to the yield of current state sales taxes plus the contemplated yield of a national sales tax, a much higher rate would have to prevail. The current administrative experience with retail taxes imposed at low to moderate rates, therefore, may not be relevant when discussing a proposed national sales tax.

In addition to the moderate rates that currently prevail, sales tax administration is facilitated in many states by the exclusion of services from the tax base. In 1985, 25 states in America either did not levy a sales tax on services or taxed only a few services. It is a well-known fact that except for services provided by a few large suppliers, such as public utilities, it is much easier to enforce sales taxation on goods than on services. Typically, goods pass through several stages of production and distribution before they reach the retail stage, so there is a chain of information available from suppliers that is highly useful for auditing retailers. Services by their nature usually offer much less information from pre-retail stages.

How well a retail sales tax with a broad coverage of goods and services could be enforced by the states is questionable. Such a broad-based tax would require that not only services be taxed but also other major items such as food, which is exempt in 29 states. Until such a tax exists in a majority of states, it is not appropriate to suggest that a broad-based federal retail tax is administratively feasible in the United States simply because individual states are successfully administering their retail sales taxes.

Most tax administrators of both developed and developing countries agree that it is more difficult to enforce sales taxes at the retail stage than at any other stage of production or distribution. That is why most countries, both developed and developing, have opted for sales taxes other than a retail sales tax in spite of the theoretical advantages of the latter. A VAT that covers all stages of production and distribution has the same neutral and nondistorting characteristics of a retail sales tax but is a more secure source of revenue because it relies only partly on collections at the retail level, where noncompliance tends to be greater.

Administrative Requirements of a VAT

The successful implementation of a VAT depends in large measure on whether the country has had previous experience with general sales taxes, the nature of the taxes that the VAT would replace, the lead-in time, and how the VAT is structured in terms of rates, exemptions, and treatment of small taxpayers. In the interests of easier administration, a single rate is highly desirable. Exemptions complicate VAT administration because the distinction between what is exempt and what is taxed is often tenuous or arbitrary. Zero rating, which requires the granting of refunds and therefore burdens the administration, has wisely been limited to exports by most countries. A variety of method for dealing with small taxpayers is in use, but all methods present technical and practical problems.

The main issues of VAT administration concern identifying taxpayers, processing returns, controlling collections, making refunds, auditing taxpayers, and levying penalties. Before a VAT is enacted, authorities must decide what organization will administer the tax, how many staff will be needed, how they will be organized, and what training they will require, and how much computer capacity must be added for processing returns and payments. Countries that have introduced a VAT successfully have also mounted extensive publicity and educational campaigns.

Suppose we assume that the VAT would be a national tax in the United States, administered by the federal government. Then the Internal Revenue Service would be the logical agency to administer the tax. There are many advantages to be gained by closely integrating VAT and income tax administration. Such integration allows for better planning and coordination of enforcement efforts for both VAT and income taxes and facilitates the efficient use of information relating to a given taxpayer, his suppliers, and his customers. These considerations have led most countries that impose a VAT to entrust its administration to the department that is in charge of income taxes, although in a few instances (Denmark, Israel, and the United Kingdom) it is the Customs Department that administers the VAT.

What would the administration of a VAT entail for the IRS? Before answering this question I would like to comment briefly on the current operations of the IRS. The basic task of this organization is the administration of income taxes. Other duties include the administration of estate and gift taxes and excises, but these occupy only a small fraction of the organization's resources. Of the gross receipts of the IRS, about 70 percent are taxes withheld by employers. The remaining revenues are collected directly from the taxpayer.

It is well known that withholding is the most effective system for collecting taxes. As a former Commissioner of Internal Revenue once said of withholding, "The U.S. tax system is based on voluntary compliance, but compliance is best when it is least voluntary." Because of the importance of withholding within the federal tax system, it has been possible to maintain an adequate overall compliance level in spite of the fact that audit coverage has decreased substantially during the past few years. In 1985 the IRS examined only 1.34 percent of all income, estate, and gift tax returns filed. Another 0.79 percent were verified or corrected through correspondence from service centers. From the figures one can appreciate that (leaving aside withholding) the federal tax system is truly based on *voluntary* compliance. But, as we also know, studies in recent years show that compliance—particularly among individual proprietorships and the self-employed—has been declining.

How does this situation compare with the task of administering a VAT?

First, in a VAT there is no such thing as withholding. The entire amounts that are due to the government must be paid by the registered taxpayers voluntarily at the end of each taxable period. The only point at which VAT is more easily collected by a mechanism similar to withholding is at the import stage—that is, by Customs. In several industrial countries the amounts of VAT collected on imports are substantial. In such countries as Belgium and France, for example, the amounts of VAT collected on imports are equal to more than 30 percent of VAT collections. Because of the characteristics of the U.S. economy, it is probable that the proportion of VAT collected at Customs would be lower. This means that the one easy handle for VAT collection would be available only to a limited extent in the United States.

Collection of VAT due on domestic transactions requires the cooperation of traders, who must be willing to turn over to the government the amounts they have collected on their sales. This brings up the self-policing features of VAT, about which much has been said since the introduction of the tax in Europe. In theory, VAT ought to be a self-enforcing tax, because traders should be motivated to demand invoices from their suppliers in order to deduct the taxes they pay on their inputs from the tax they collect on their sales. In practice, however, the self-enforcing feature of VAT has some limitations. Buyers and sellers may collude to understate prices or to omit invoices; invoices may be falsified; fraudulent claims may be submitted for VAT refunds (particularly on exports); these are some of the schemes used by taxpayers to evade VAT. In response to these schemes, countries with VATs maintain quite a high level of VAT audit coverage in order to ensure compliance. Audits of 10 or 15 percent of registered taxpayers each year are not uncommon in European countries. Many of these audits are performed at the taxpayers' premises. Although computers are useful for selecting taxpayers for audit when their gross sales or their input credits depart from standard norms, computerized cross-checking of information provided by buyers and sellers has proved less helpful than originally expected. European countries still rely heavily on physical controls of inventories and goods in transit to police the VAT.

Carlson does not deal in Chapter 13 with the resources that would be needed to administer a national consumption tax. The only estimates available are those that appear in the 1984 Treasury Department Report to the President on Tax Reform. In this report, it is estimated that the administration of a VAT would require about one tax official per thousand registered taxpayers and that an audit coverage of 2.2 percent of all registered taxpayers per year would be sufficient. These figures are much lower than those in other industrial countries, where ratios of 150 to 250 registered taxpayers per tax official are common, and audit coverage of 10 to 15 percent is maintained.

If a VAT is to be seriously considered for the United States, a realistic estimate of the resources needed to administer it is crucial. It is not a simple tax, particularly for an organization like the IRS with no experience in administering a broad-based sales tax. The notion that computers can substitute for physical controls and field audits must be dispelled. To prepare for introducing the VAT, skilled personnel will also be needed to explain to taxpayers what their obligations will be under the new tax. No quantity of printed material can replace well-trained staff who can answer taxpayers' queries and ensure compliance.

Perhaps the main lesson that the United States can learn from countries that impose a VAT is that an appropriate administration is critical to the success of the tax. But in order to achieve good compliance the complexities of administering the tax should not be underestimated, and adequate resources should be given to the organization responsible for administering it.

LESSONS FROM THE EUROPEAN VAT EXPERIENCE

Edwin S. Cohen

At the Treasury Department in the late spring of 1970 Charls Walker informed me to my surprise that the secretary and he were sending me to Europe on a whirlwind three-week tour of six different countries to study the European experience with the value-added tax (VAT). A decade later George Carlson was sent to Europe on a similar mission, and he wrote an excellent report that was published by the Treasury in October 1980, which I shall refer to as Carlson I. Then in November 1984 he was the principal author of Volume 3 of the Treasury Department's proposals for tax reform; Volume 3 was the result of a detailed study by both the Treasury and Internal Revenue Service of problems associated with the value-added tax and how they might be solved. That volume I shall call Carlson II and it is "must" reading for all those considering the VAT. And Carlson III, Chapter 13 of this book, is in essence a summary and restatement of Carlson I and II.

When I was sent abroad in 1970 I was instructed to interview a wide cross-section of Europeans—not merely government personnel, whether elected or civil servants, but also their counterparts in the opposition shadow governments; and I was told to obtain the views of heads of businesses, sales and financial personnel, economists, lawyers, accountants, journalists, professors, taxi drivers, and bartenders. I took my instructions to heart: I sampled VAT 69 with the best bartenders in Europe.

In between bartenders I managed to fit meetings with some 150 to 200 people to discuss their views and experiences with the value-added tax. I found particularly instructive my sessions with M. de la Martiniere, the head of the French tax system, who told me that fittingly he was the grandson of a pirate; and with my counterpart in the Italian Ministry of Finance, Signor Machiavelli. They had mastered the art of keeping taxpayers sullen but not mutinous.

Wherever I went in Europe the number 1 point made to me was that as an administrative matter the VAT tax worked far more easily if there were a single rate of tax on all goods and services. This was emphasized to me not only by tax administrators but also by business-people. The president of a Parisian department store described to me the difficulties of training and supervising personnel to apply four different rates of VAT to the merchandise sold in his large store. The head of a large French grocery store almost wept as he described the delays stemming from the struggles of his employees to choose the applicable rate. Carlson I notes the trouble the Irish have in distinguishing between bread and nonbread; they are instructed that "the zero rate normally applies, therefore, to loaves, turnovers, pan loaves, soda bread, brown bread, vienna rolls, french sticks, bread rolls, some fruit loaves, bread scones, etc. [However,] confectionary, cakes, barm bracks, biscuits, cream crackers, wafers, crisp breads, etc. are liable at the low rate." (p. 56)

Indeed, the Danes, who were the only ones in Europe to have a single-rate VAT, pointed with considerable pride to their VAT return, which was printed on a postcard with only three entries, one for tax on sales, one for tax on purchases and one for the net amount due. Each month, as I recall, taxpayers took their filled out postcard to the post office and paid to the post office the tax due. I suppose it would be a close call as to whether we should use our post office or the IRS Philadelphia Service Center.

Obviously multiple rates have been used by most countries as a political means of alleviating the regressive effect of a single rate VAT. I pressed the Danes on this point. They responded that taken as a whole they had the most progressive economic structure in the world, and they were not concerned that one feature of that structure, the value-added tax, was by itself regressive. That regressivity they felt was overcome by the combination of other taxes and government provided benefits. They noted that the VAT was not as regressive as liquor and tobacco taxes.

I concluded from my discussions abroad that a VAT in the United States would be far simpler as an administrative matter if we held to a single rate and we resisted the political temptation of multiple rates. To eliminate the regressive effect, we could use a refundable income tax credit in an amount that would reflect the VAT paid on a specified amount of purchases consistent with the poverty level.

It was also abundantly clear to me that, even with a single rate of value-added tax, there are a series of administrative problems with respect to specific matters that are difficult to solve. Among these problem areas are banking and financial transactions, insurance, the sale and leasing of land and buildings, and the treatment of nonprofit organizations and state and local governments. I concluded that there were no clear-cut solutions in these areas and that by and large the Europeans meet this challenge simply by muddling through. But let us not snicker; think how in our income tax law we muddle through the intricacies of the foreign tax credit, or industrial development bonds, or percentage depletion.

I was somewhat surprised to learn from Carlson II that the IRS estimated it would take 18 months following the enactment of a VAT for the Service to gear up to administer it. If we were to adopt such a tax I would have thought that much of the work could be done while the bill was wending its way through the Congress. I do not underestimate the magnitude of the administrative problem, but the blueprint outlined in Carlson II is the most detailed I have seen and should expedite the work.

Finally, I would call attention to a most serious problem with the introduction of a value-added tax in the United States, and that involves overcoming the opposition of the governors and mayors and other state and local officials. After I had made two sweeps of Europe in the summer of 1970 and the administration was weighing the possibilities, the governors happened to hold one of their periodic conferences in Washington. The Treasury thought it might be useful to inform the governors that a federal VAT was under consideration and make sure their feathers were not ruffled.

We invited several governors to lunch at the Treasury while they were meeting in Washington, anticipating that the secretary and the under secretary would bring up the matter after lunch was concluded. As the entree was cleared and dessert was about to be served, Governor Dale Bumpers, of Arkansas, now Senator Bumpers, rose and thanked the secretary for the nice luncheon; but, he added, in case the secretary had in mind mentioning a federal value-added tax, he wanted the secretary to know that the governors were inalterably and irrevocably opposed to any such tax at the federal level and would not even discuss the possibility, since sales taxes were the exclusive province of the states and localities.

And that was that. Governor Bumpers' emphatic statement marked the end of the Treasury's consideration of the VAT in the early 1970s. George Carlson's studies in 1980 and again in 1984 have thus far met a similar fate. It is difficult for a VAT student to keep his chin up. My experience in 1970 leads me to urge that the governors and mayors must be converted before there is a serious possibility of our adopting a VAT.

COMMENTS FROM A LEGISLATOR

Ronnie G. Flippo

I agree with Senator Durenberger when he says that Congress seldom legislates except in a crisis, but I think it is constructive to have some debate about these things and have a better understanding about them before that crisis develops so we would know which way to go and how to proceed. I am particularly interested in the value-added tax. I know the theoretical appeal of the VAT stems from its economic efficiency, but looking at all of the countries that have a VAT, we see that economic efficiency has been undermined without the complexity being lessened in any way. So I think VAT's economic efficiency is at the price of complexity. The administration of the VAT is probably its weakest point.

The only serious proposals in regard to the value-added tax have been based on the credit method, comparing that to some type of national sales tax. Maybe we ought to have another study, since House Ways and Means Chairman Dan Rostenkowski has said that the way to address the possible need for additional revenues was to increase the income tax rates of the present U.S. tax code (see Chapter 2). Perhaps a study comparing the various factors involved with an increase in income tax rates to the value-added credit approach and to the national sales tax might give us a better view of the alternatives.

When a VAT under the credit approach is compared with a national sales tax on administrative cost, the national sales tax has the advantage. In terms of the time required to implement a new tax, it has been said that the shortest amount of time needed to begin collecting a national value-added tax would probably be about 18 months. However, we already have in place many of the administrative programs connected with a national sales tax. So the national sales tax would have an advantage in that regard as well.

When it comes to avoiding the double taxation of intermediate goods and services, a VAT appears to have an advantage over a national sales tax. Because better records would be required under value-added taxation, enforcement would probably be better than for a national sales tax. The VAT would be a broader tax with a better maximum tax yield.

One of the areas that has been debated, though, is invisibility. I have heard both the value-added tax and the national sales tax called invisible. I have some experience with the sales tax in the Alabama legislature. When I was in the Alabama Senate we passed a sales tax increase, and I didn't find that tax very invisible. As a matter of fact, everyone I met on the street pointed out to me that as long as we increased income taxes, they only had to worry about it once a year, but when I increased the sales tax, every time they went to the store they thought of me. And that does not make you feel politically secure.

As an entirely new tax system, either the VAT or the national sales tax may have a lot to recommend it. But as a supplemental tax, the complexity may not be worth the revenue.

Overall concerns about savings and investment and the relative cost of capital to American firms dictate that we need to look to some other way, perhaps toward the further integration of the individual and corporate taxes, to find some other relief. The thing that really strikes me is that any new system that would require you to spend some $700 million to hire some 20,000 new IRS agents, to audit some 5 million to 10 million—or however many firms would be included—requires some further examination and explanation before I could convince the people I represent that it would be a right way to go.

But I do believe that unless we debate these issues and the concerns that face us, we will never resolve our problems. Many people take it as a given that the federal budget deficit must be resolved tomorrow. If I read my history correctly, we have had a deficit in every year since World War II except one. The most popular president in many, many years has doubled the federal debt (or has been the president when it has doubled). I have great concerns about the deficit, but I don't think it has reached the voter out there yet. We may have a crisis that draws the voter's attention, but it may be awhile getting there.

In the meantime, I think we ought to continue to look at alternatives and any improvements, especially toward the further integration of the individual and corporate tax.

✳ *Chapter 14*

Addressing Issues of the Regressivity of a Consumption Tax

Thomas E. Vasquez

The two-year effort to reform the U.S. federal tax structure culminated in the Tax Reform Act of 1986, the outcome of which will be a major change in the U.S. income tax system, with substantial reductions in marginal tax rates and a significant broadening of the tax base. During the course of the two-year debate, the single focus was on the reform of our current individual and corporation income taxes. No serious consideration was given to the enactment of a new consumption tax as a possible substitution for or addition to our existing revenue system. The failure to consider a consumption tax should neither dissuade supporters of consumption taxes nor encourage their opponents from recognizing their revenue potential. Indeed, with each new report from the Office of Management and Budget (OMB) and the Congressional Budget Office (CBO) on the future budget outlook, it seems more and more likely that tax increases in some form will be part of the equation for closing the large and persistent fiscal gap. Revenue neutrality may ultimately have to give way to fiscal necessity. The Herculean effort to reform the federal income tax system and reduce marginal tax rates is not the last word on tax policy. The next effort, however, must focus on exploring additional revenue sources, which will require an even greater demonstration of political will.

In this context, some form of a consumption tax could emerge as a mechanism for raising revenue and contributing to closing the fiscal gap. Consumption taxes are generally perceived to be regressive, with a disproportionate amount of the tax borne by low-income taxpayers. Indeed, the distributional impact has been the Achilles' heel of previous consumption tax proposals. It is the issue around which the most heated debate can be anticipated in the future. A full understanding of these distributional effects will be critical to an informed public policy discussion. The purpose of this chapter is to discuss the conceptual issues involved in measuring the distributional effects of a consumption tax and to quantify the effects of alternative consumption taxes.

CONCEPTUAL ISSUES

There are four major issues related to the measurement of the incidence of a consumption tax that are addressed in this part of the chapter. These are (1) the appropriate economic unit for the analysis; (2) the measurement of well-being; (3) the incidence of the tax; and (4) the time frame of analysis. Although these issues are inter-related in many ways, each is discussed separately in the discussion below.

The Appropriate Economic Unit

Until recently, policymakers have relied on distributional analyses that use tax returns as the economic unit. There are several problems inherent in this use. First, the analysis is limited to those individuals who file a tax return. This excludes about 12 percent of the adult population. Second, tax filing units are an artifact of the current tax system and do not provide a meaningful measure of the relevant economic unit's ability to pay. Indeed, no other government agency uses tax returns as the appropriate economic unit for analysis; instead, households or families are generally used. In recognition of the problems associated with using tax returns as the economic unit, the Treasury Department's 1984 tax reform proposal, *Tax Reform for Fairness, Simplicity and Economic Growth*, used the family as the basis for measuring the distribution of the tax burden.

Nearly all analysts agree that the family is the best economic unit for assessing the distributional effects of taxes. Families live together, combine income, and share expenses. In cases where dependents have incomes and pay taxes, it is appropriate that their income and taxes be combined with the incomes and taxes of those who support them in measuring the distribution of tax burden. In this report, the family is used as the economic unit for making estimates of the impact of the consumption tax.

Table 14-1. Percentage Distribution of Adjusted Gross Income (AGI), 1986 Levels (%).

AGI Class ($1,000s)	Tax Unit Definition			Family Unit Definition
	Tax Filers	Nonfilers	Total	
0-10	4.58%	82.56%	5.04%	2.69%
10-20	14.39	11.39	14.37	11.04
20-30	16.87	2.62	16.78	16.04
30-50	31.67	0.41	31.48	33.32
50-100	21.06	3.02	20.95	24.58
100-200	5.93	0.00	5.89	6.61
> 200	5.51	0.00	5.48	5.71
Total	100.0%	100.0%	100.0%	100.0%

Table 14-1 shows the significance of nonfilers and the choice of tax unit in assessing distributional issues. The table shows that the income distribution is more heavily concentrated at low-income levels under the tax unit definition than under the family definition.

Measurement of Well-Being

The distributional consequences of tax proposals have often been estimated using an incomplete measure of income, because of lack of availability of data for a broader based definition of income. The Treasury and the Joint Committee on Taxation have until recently used adjusted gross income (AGI) in this analysis. The exclusion of income, whether it be income from government transfer payments, fringe benefit income related to employment, or excluded investment income such as tax-exempt interest or corporate profits, can seriously distort estimates of the distribution of tax burden.

A broad-based definition of income was used by Treasury in the distribution analyses that it presented in its November 1984 tax reform proposal, and estimates developed by the Policy Economics Group are based on a comparable definition. This allows the annual incidence estimates, given the inherent limitations due to time perspective, to reflect more accurately the degree of regressivity or progressivity of the tax being analyzed. Table 14-2 shows the adjustments to adjusted gross income that are made by the Policy Economics Group to arrive at this broad-based income measure.

The distributional effects of the use of the two alternative income measures is highlighted in Table 14-3, which shows the distribution of consumption expenditures by both AGI income class and the broad-based definitions of income. The results show that the use of the narrower definition would tend to overstate the impact of a consumption tax on low-income families.

Table 14-2.   Adjustments to Adjusted Gross Income Used in the Distributional Analysis of the Consumption Tax.

Adjusted gross income (AGI)

plus   Excluded capital gains (except corporate stock)
IRA and Keogh contributions
Two-earner deduction
All other statutory adjustments

Employer contributions for
  Pensions
  Health insurance
  Life insurance
  Profit sharing
  Other

Fringe benefits

Military benefits

Transfer payments
  Unemployment Compensation
  Workers' Compensation
  Aid to Families with Dependent Children (AFDC)
  Supplemental Security Income (SSI)
  Veterans Compensation
  Social Security and Railroad Retirement
  Food Stamps

Earnings on pension funds and life insurance plans (including earnings on IRA and Keogh plans)

Tax-exempt interest
Net rent on owner-occupied housing

less   Taxable pension income

plus   Economic depreciation rather than tax depreciation
Economic depletion rather than tax depletion
Corporate income

equals: Broad-based family income

Table 14-3.   Percentage Distribution of Consumption When Classified by AGI and Broad-Based Income (*1986 Levels*).

Broad-Based Family Income Class ($1,000s)[a]	Classified by AGI	Classified by Broad-Based Income	
		Including Corporate Profits	*Excluding Corporate Profits*
0–10	15.98%	7.23%	7.71%
10–20	15.84	13.05	13.68
20–30	16.69	14.16	14.95
30–50	28.20	27.35	28.26
50–100	17.48	27.94	26.64
100–200	3.68	6.73	5.67
> 200	2.14	3.52	3.10
Total	100.0%	100.0%	100.0%

[a] The components of broad-based family income are shown in Table 14–2.

The Incidence of the Tax

There is a large body of economic literature on the subject of the incidence, or ultimate resting place, of tax burdens. Indeed, this literature is enriched by Chapter 12 of this book, by David Bradford. While there is some agreement on the theoretical structure for measuring incidence, the complexities and data problems faced when actually measuring incidence precludes agreement. In spite of these problems, until recent years the general conclusion from this body of literature as it relates to the incidence of consumption-based taxes was that such taxes are borne by consumers.

To the extent that this is true, it follows that consumption-based taxes are regressive when measured at any given point in time because savings rates are higher at high income levels than at low income levels. Indeed, one study estimates that about three-fourths of household saving is concentrated in the top 10 percent of the income distribution.[1]

In recent years, the conclusion that consumption-based taxes are borne by consumers has become increasingly challenged. A major factor underlying this challenge is that a substantial part (about 10 percent) of consumption is financed by government transfer payments, many of which are indexed to the consumer price index or a related price index. As a result, tax-induced increases in the price level do not affect consumers who finance their purchases from indexed transfer payments. Since consumption is financed by transfer payments and factor income, to the extent that transfer payments are fully indexed and therefore held harmless from the tax, the tax is borne by factor incomes.

To the extent that a consumption-based tax is, in fact, borne by factors of income, the issue then is which factors. It could be argued that such a tax would be likely to rest on labor income, not capital income, if capital expenditures are exempt from the tax base, as they usually are for consumption taxes, and the rate of return on capital is not affected. If this were true, the tax burden could be expected to increase as a share of income at the lower income levels, to be essentially proportional at middle income levels covering a large percentage of the population, and to decline as a share of income at high income levels.

The distributional impact of a consumption tax under the two alternative incidence assumptions—that it is borne by consumers or by labor income—is illustrated in Table 14-4, which shows the distribution of consumption and labor income by broad-based family income. The table shows that consumption is much more heavily concentrated at low income levels than labor income.

Table 14-4. Percentage Distribution of Consumption and Labor Income, 1986 Levels (%).

Broad-Based Family Income ($1,000s)	Consumption	Labor Income
0-10	7.23%	0.97%
10-20	13.05	5.94
20-30	14.16	12.03
30-50	27.35	30.94
50-100	27.94	37.52
100-200	6.73	8.71
> 200	3.52	3.89
Total	100.0%	100.0%

Time Frame of Analysis

Most presentations of the distributional impact of tax burdens, including those by the Treasury Department and the Joint Committee on Taxation, are based on a one-year time frame. Most economists would argue that lifetime incidence calculations are preferable for economic analysis. However, data limitations and political reality have precluded the use of lifetime calculations.

The issue is not whether one year is a good representation of the well-being of the tax unit. This is a problem whether analyzing income taxes or consumption taxes, but it is highlighted when comparing the distributional impact of an income tax with a consumption tax.

The reason that a one-year time frame is especially critical when comparing income and consumption taxes is because consumption expenditures are less volatile than income. This relationship has two facets. First, the *life-cycle* hypothesis states that individuals tend to borrow heavily in their early years to finance consumption and then to save in their peak earning years to finance consumption in retirement. During their lifetime, then, individuals tend to try to smooth their level of consumption. Second, individuals face periods of unemployment, both voluntary and involuntary but fully expect to be full-time employees in the near future. During these periods of unemployment, individuals try to maintain their standard of living and consumption levels by dissaving. While this second effect is over a shorter time period than the life-cycle effect, the result is the same: consumption does not vary as much as income.

The current income tax system taxes the income received during the year. Thus, tax liability follows the pattern of income. This necessarily means that individuals with annual income that is temporarily low will have a relative tax increase under a consumption tax.

If the analysis were conducted over a two- or three-year period, however, the tax liability might not be very different under a consumption or an income tax.

Studies that have analyzed the distributional impact of taxes over the lifetime of a taxpayer have arrived at substantially different conclusions from those that have analyzed the impact for a single year. The most recent article on lifetime incidence calculations produced two conclusions that are highly important to the analysis of the distributional impact of a consumption tax.[2]

First, lifetime estimates of tax burden distribution are significantly less affected by the assumptions about tax incidence than annual estimates. This implies that the issue of tax incidence described above is less critical to the distributional estimates when the lifetime measure of income and tax burdens is used.

Second, the variation in consumption-to-income ratios is substantially smaller for lifetime calculations than for annual calculations, a result that is consistent with numerous other studies on the life-cycle of savings and consumption. The implication of this result is that the lifetime measure of the distributional impact of consumption-based taxes is substantially less regressive than the annual measure.

Table 14-5 shows estimated distributional effects of sales and excise taxes under both annual and lifetime incidence assumptions. Although the estimates were based on tax and income data for Canada, comparable estimates for the United States could be expected to produce similar distributional results. The annual and lifetime distributional effects are shown to be strikingly difrerent, with the annual estimates showing much greater regressivity of consumption taxes than the lifetime estimates, which are only mildly regressive.

Table 14-5. Sales and Excise Average Tax Rates of Canadian Households by Decile (%).

Decile	Annual Incidence	Lifetime Incidence
1	27.2%	15.0%
2	20.3	14.3
3	15.8	14.1
4	14.6	13.9
5	14.0	13.8
6	13.4	13.5
7	13.5	13.6
8	13.2	13.3
9	12.8	13.2
10	8.5	12.4

Source: James Davies, France St-Hilaire, and John Whalley, "Some Calculations of Lifetime Tax Incidence," *American Economic Review* (September 1984): 643.

It is important to note that while the use of either a current or a lifetime measure is critical to the comparison of income and consumption taxes, it is of less importance to the measurement of alternative income tax schemes. Under a personal income tax, a taxpayer with temporarily low income will pay commensurately low taxes and a taxpayer with temporarily high income will pay commensurately high taxes. In effect, annual data on both income and the income tax that is paid on that income, are transitory measures. As a result, there is a comparable matching of the income and tax liability.

In sharp contrast, consumption is linked much more closely to permanent income than to transitory income. Thus, in years when income is unusually low, the ratio of consumption to income will be high, and vice versa. Measures of consumption taxes relative to income at any point in time are therefore significantly biased, because consumption is linked to a permanent level of income, whereas income is measured on a transitory basis. It is this mismatching of a permanent measure of tax with a transitory measure of income that so greatly biases estimates of distributional effects of consumption taxes.

Data limitations restrict severely the options available to analysts in addressing the measurement bias that accompanies the use of annual data. Since lifetime income and consumption data are not available, proxy measures must be considered. This chapter suggests two such measures.

First, consumption taxes could be measured relative to consumption rather than income. In the context of the previous discussion, this would match a permanent measure of tax with a proxy for a permanent measure of income, thereby avoiding the mismatch described above. If a consumption tax were levied on all consumption goods, the tax would be shown to be proportional over all consumption (permanent income) classes. If consumption items that are purchased disproportionately by low-income families, such as food, are excluded from the tax base, the consumption tax would be modestly progressive.

Alternatively, the burden of consumption taxes could be measured relative to income, but the analysis could be disaggregated among taxpayers of different age groups. Since a large part of the variation in consumption/income ratios is related to the life-cycle of the family, the disaggregation into age groups would remove a significant part of this variation.

The lifetime incidence argument is an important one and one that should be introduced into the debate on a consumption tax because the annual and lifetime incidence measurements are so greatly different. Nevertheless, it can be expected that estimates of the annual distributional impact will dominate the debate because of the data limitations related to developing lifetime tax incidence estimates. Certainly, any estimates prepared by Treasury or the Joint Committee on Taxation will reflect annual incidence estimates. Accordingly, much of the debate on distributional impacts of a consumption tax will necessarily focus on annual incidence estimates.

Offsets to Gross Tax Impact

Traditional measures of distributional impact show the effects of consumption taxes on taxpayers without recognizing the impact of the tax on beneficiaries of government transfer payments. Indeed, this distinction lies at the heart of some researchers' conclusions that at least part of consumption taxes is borne by factor incomes rather than consumption.

It can be demonstrated that income derived from indexed government benefit programs is not affected by the imposition of a consumption-based tax. (This demonstration ignores the potential impact of lags between price increases and benefit increases.) If the tax is passed forward as higher prices, the purchasing power of transfer income is left unchanged because cost-of-living increases compensate for the increase in tax burdens. Alternatively, if the overall price level remains unchanged, and other prices decline in response to the imposition of the consumption-based tax, the beneficiaries are again left unchanged by the imposition of the tax.

Any measure of the distributional impact of the tax that assumes that the tax is distributed according to the pattern of consumption should show an offset for increases in transfer payments that would accompany the imposition of the tax. Since transfer income is heavily concentrated in the lower end of the income distribution, this offset substantially reduces the measured regressivity of the tax.

Conclusions

Each of the preceding points indicates significant ways in which traditional estimates of the distributional impact of consumption-based taxes may be biased toward overstating the regressivity of these taxes. Data limitations may preclude addressing all of these issues in distributional analyses that are prepared for the future debate on the impact of a consumption tax, particularly the annual versus lifetime incidence issue, but it is important that those who are participating in the policy debate on tax issues recognize the importance of these issues.

ALTERNATIVE STRUCTURES OF A CONSUMPTION TAX THAT WOULD AFFECT THE TAX BURDEN DISTRIBUTION

There are essentially three different ways in which the distribution of a consumption tax can be altered. One is to modify the tax base by excluding certain items for which low-income consumers have a high spending propensity, such as food, shelter, and health care. A second is to provide some form of credit against tax liability that is linked to estimates of consumption taxes paid. A third way is through increased transfer payments. Each of these alternatives is discussed below. The discussion assumes the traditional view that a consumption-based tax is passed forward to consumers and that regressivity is measured at a point in time rather than over the lifetime of the taxpayer.

Modifications to the Consumption Tax Base

Strong arguments based on economic efficiency can generally be made for making the tax base for a consumption tax as broad as is feasible. If some goods are subject to a tax and others are not, the market pricing system is distorted in favor of the untaxed goods. The greater the tax, the greater the distortion. The exclusion of some goods from the tax base can also lead to significant administrative problems. In the case of food, for example, explicit definitions of what constitutes food must be developed and administered as a specific tax exemption.

Invariably, in the development or reform of any tax system, trade-offs must be made between equity and economic efficiency. States have addressed this issue in the development of sales tax structures with widely varying results. While many states include the full range of retail sales, many others exclude certain types of food and other goods and services from the tax base.

The good that is most commonly suggested for exclusion from the tax base to address equity concerns is food consumed at home. As Table 14-6 shows, food consumed at home represents a much higher share of low-income budgets than of high-income budgets. For families in the lowest income quintile, food at home comprises more than 17 percent of total consumption; for families in the highest quintile, the corresponding figure is only 11 percent. Thus, a decision to eliminate food at home from the consumption tax base would reduce the tax burden of low-income consumers by 17 percent as compared to only 11 percent for high-income consumers.

Table 14-6. Distribution of Basic Necessities Expenditures (*Percentage of Total Consumption*).

Quintile	Food at Home	Shelter	Health Care	Total
Lowest 20%	17.1%	29.9%	12.2%	59.2%
Second 20%	15.7	29.6	12.3	57.5
Third 20%	14.5	27.3	11.6	53.4
Fourth 20%	13.8	26.0	11.6	51.4
Highest 20%	11.0	27.5	11.2	49.6

Health care expenditures are a smaller share of total consumer expenditures than food at home, but the share of total expenditures declines slightly as income rises. For consumers in the lowest two income quintiles, health expenditures comprise 12 percent of consumption whereas for the highest income level it is 11 percent.

Consumer expenditures for owner-occupied and rental shelter also decline as a share of total expenditures as income rises, but again the decline is less marked than for food. For consumers in the lowest income quintile, these shelter expenditures comprise nearly 30 percent of total consumption expenditures; for the highest income quintile they are 27.5 percent. Housing expenditures are generally excluded from the tax base of a consumption tax because of the administrative difficulties associated with taxing the imputed rental value of owner-occupied housing. The regressivity of a consumption-based tax can clearly be reduced by excluding basic necessities from the tax base. Relative to a base that taxes all consumption, a tax that excludes food at home, shelter, and health care expenditures would reduce the tax burden of taxpayers in the lowest 20 percent of the income distribution by nearly 60 percent; the corresponding reduction for taxpayers in the highest 20 percent of the income distribution would be about 50 percent.

Table 14-7 presents estimates of the distribution of alternative consumption-based taxes, where the basic necessities are excluded from the tax base individually and in the aggregate. The distributional results are presented both using a broad-based income concept and total consumption as classifiers of ability to pay. The broad-based income classifier is the measure most likely to be used by Treasury and the Joint Committee on Taxation, but as described earlier in this chapter, the consumption classifier has merit as a better measure of permanent income.

Tax Credits

An alternative to narrowing the base of a consumption-based tax to alter its distributional impact is some form of accompanying tax

Table 14-7. Percentage Distribution of Alternative Consumption-Based Taxes, 1986 Income Levels (%).

Income Class ($1,000s)	Broad-Based Consumption Tax	Consumption Tax Excluding:				Total Tax Burden
		Food at Home	Shelter	Health Care Expenditures	All Basic Necessities	
I. Distribution using broad-based family income						
0–10	7.23%	6.85%	6.90%	7.17%	5.93%	0.59%
10–20	13.05	12.69	12.70	12.94	11.65	4.18
20–30	14.16	13.94	14.20	14.15	13.80	9.35
30–50	27.35	27.21	27.97	27.36	28.04	24.36
50–100	27.94	28.32	28.28	28.01	29.27	36.89
100–200	6.73	7.08	6.57	6.76	7.18	12.10
> 200	3.52	3.90	3.36	3.60	4.12	12.53
Total	100.0%	100.0%	100.0%	100.0%	100.0%	100.0%
II. Distribution using consumption as classifier						
0–10	2.36%	2.22%	2.12%	2.44%	1.89%	1.25%
10–20	18.22	17.64	17.64	18.30	16.41	13.81
20–30	27.17	26.73	27.44	26.95	26.40	23.42
30–50	35.62	35.82	36.21	35.40	36.47	35.91
50–100	13.28	13.86	13.31	13.43	14.65	17.48
100–200	2.21	2.45	2.11	2.24	2.57	5.07
> 200	1.15	1.28	1.18	1.23	1.60	3.05
Total	100.0%	100.0%	100.0%	100.0%	100.0%	100.0%

credit. Three alternative credit mechanisms are discussed below: a payroll tax credit, an earned income tax credit, and a refundable credit linked to some measure of income.

It should be noted that all three of these mechanisms, by virtue of being linked to the income tax system, suffer from similar shortcomings. First, they do not address the cash flow problem facing the taxpayers. The tax benefits would accrue generally at the end of the year, while the consumption tax is being paid currently. Second, the benefits are limited to individuals that file tax returns.

The Payroll Tax Credit

The payroll tax credit was proposed in the original proposal for a business transfer tax introduced by Senator William Roth. Under conventional incidence assumptions, the payroll tax is borne by labor, and since the tax applies only to a base amount of earnings beyond which no tax is levied, the tax is generally regarded as regressive. Accordingly, reducing this tax through a credit mechanism would reduce the tax of low-income wage earners by a greater percentage amount than of high-income wage earners.

A major problem with the payroll tax credit is that it does not provide any benefit to low-income individuals who use nonwage income for consumption expenditures. To the extent that these individuals use transfer payments that are indexed to the cost of living, there is no problem, since these transfers will be adjusted for any price increases that occur in response to the tax.

However, to the extent that individuals finance their consumption with income that is not adjusted for tax-induced price increases, they would be adversely affected by the tax. This group would include individuals receiving nonindexed transfer payments and capital income. Most transfer payment programs, including Social Security, railroad retirement, federal employee retirement, SSI, and federal food and nutrition programs, are indexed to the cost of living. The only sizable programs that are not fully indexed are unemployment benefits, AFDC, benefits for disabled coal miners (which are linked to federal pay raises), and retirement benefits of former state and local government employees.

Although capital income is heavily concentrated at high income levels, it is also a high proportion of income at low income levels, largely because of the concentration of retirees at low income levels. For these individuals, for whom some adjustment of tax burdens may be desired on equity grounds, the payroll tax credit, therefore, would not be an effective mechanism.

The Earned Income Tax Credit

The earned income credit could be liberalized in response to the imposition of a consumption tax to provide relief for low income families. Under pre-1986 law, families eligible for the credit are allowed a refundable credit against income tax equal to 11 percent of the first $5,000 of earned income, for a maximum credit of $550. The credit is phased out between incomes of $6,500 and $11,000. The Tax Reform Act of 1986 liberalizes this credit, increasing both the rate and the income level at which the credit would begin to phase out.

The existence of the earned income tax credit makes it a potential vehicle for providing relief to low-income families from a consumption tax. The percentage of the credit could be increased or the rate at which the credit phases out could be modified.

It was estimated that over five million families would claim the earned income tax credit for 1986. If it is assumed that all income of such families is consumed and that a broad-based consumption tax is imposed that taxes all consumption, then a family with $6,500 in income would bear a $130 tax increase from a 2 percent consumption tax. This could be offset by increasing the earned income tax credit by 2 percentage points. To the extent that the tax base is less than comprehensive, the percentage increase in the earned income tax credit necessary to offset the consumption tax would be less than 2 percent.

Use of the earned income tax credit mechanism, however, suffers from the same problem as the payroll tax credit mechanism as a means of reducing the consumption tax burden for low-income taxpayers: it does not compensate low-income families who consume out of nonwage income. Also, since the credit applies only to families filing joint returns who claim a dependency exemption, surviving spouses, or heads of household claiming a dependency exemption, this credit affects a much narrower segment of the population than the payroll tax credit.

The fact that the earned income credit applies only to low-income families and individuals means that it is much more effectively targeted for low-income individuals than the payroll tax credit, which would be available to all families with wage income, regardless of the level of income. The more effective targeting means that more can be done for low-income families at a lower net federal revenue cost than with the broader payroll tax credit mechanism. The degree to which this is a virtue, of course, depends upon the overall goals of the redistribution program.

A Broad-Based Refundable Credit

As an alternative to the earned income tax credit, which applies only to earned income of eligible individuals, a broader based refundable credit could be developed, potentially as an addition to or substitution for the earned income credit. This credit could apply to more than just earned incomes and address one of the potential concerns about both the payroll tax credit and the earned income credit.

The broad-based refundable credit has considerable appeal, because the base to which the credit applies can be tailored as desired and because the income levels to which the credit applies can be designed to target funds to the desired income levels. If the goal of the redistribution program is to protect low-income individuals and families, this credit is a potentially very effective mechanism for achieving this goal. It is worth noting that five states currently use a refundable income tax credit to offset regressivity of sales taxes.

The major argument against a broad-based refundable credit is that it could increase significantly the workload of Internal Revenue Service by increasing substantially the number of returns that must be processed in order for individuals to receive their tax refund. The Policy Economics Group estimates that in 1986 there will be 24 million nonfilers. The number of nonfilers that would be eligible for a refundable credit would depend upon the income base that is adopted for calculating the credit but the increase could be large.

Under the extreme assumption that all nonfilers found it beneficial to file returns to get a refund, the number of returns filed would increase by about 25 percent. The IRS budget for processing and reviewing tax returns is about $3.5 billion in fiscal year 1986. Even assuming economies of scale in the processing of additional returns, which may not be warranted given the difficulties that IRS incurred in handling last year's returns, the required increase in the IRS budget would be substantial.

Tax Credit: Conclusions and Estimates

Any measure that is designed to reduce the regressivity of a consumption-based tax will reduce the net revenue gain from that tax. If the goal of the effort to reduce regressivity is to protect low-income families, some form of refundable credit appears to be the most effective mechanism. Because such a credit can be targeted to the low-income population, the federal revenue loss will be much less than under mechanisms such as the payroll tax credit or modifications to the tax base, both of which would reduce the taxes of virtually all taxpayers. Also, the refundable credit appears much more

Table 14-8. Percentage Distribution of Alternative Credits, 1986 Income Levels (%).

Broad-Based Family Income ($1,000s)	Payroll Tax Credit	Earned Income Tax Credit	Broad-Based Credit
0–10	1.46%	17.60%	26.83%
10–20	8.03	52.80	45.82
20–30	14.90	17.08	14.61
30–50	35.51	9.57	9.23
50–100	33.24	2.59	3.11
100–200	5.10	0.36	0.39
> 200	1.76	0.01	0.01
Total	100.0%	100.0%	100.0%

desirable than modifications to the tax base, such as eliminating food at home, because it does not produce the significant change in relative prices and the economic distortions that accompany that mechanism.

Table 14-8 shows the percentage distribution of (1) a 1 percent payroll tax credit, (2) a 1 percentage point increase in the earned income credit, and (3) a broad-based credit that is patterned after the earned income credit but that includes transfer payments as well as earned income. While these alternatives do not yield equal revenue, the percentage distribution estimates highlight the degree to which each mechanism is effective in targeting money to lower income taxpayers. The actual size of the credit could be tailored to the revenues made available to reduce the regressivity of the consumption-based tax.

Aggregate Distribution of the Tax Burden

While the distribution of each major revenue source is of great importance to policymakers, it is the distributional impact of the overall tax system that is of paramount importance. If the distributional impact of the overall tax system is in accord with policymakers' goals, it matters little whether that distributional impact is met with, say, two moderately progressive taxes, or one highly progressive tax and one regressive tax. Hence we shift focus here from a consumption-based tax to the overall tax system.

Table 14-9 shows the distribution of the federal tax system under pre-1986 law and under the Tax Reform Act of 1986. The distribution reflects the three major revenue sources of the federal government; the individual income tax; the corporation income tax; and the payroll tax. (The corporation income tax is distributed according to corporate equity and the payroll tax is distributed according to labor

Table 14-9. Aggregate Distribution of the Federal Tax Burden, 1986 Income Levels (%).

Broad-Based Family Income ($1,000s)	Current Law	Tax Reform Act of 1986
0-10	0.59%	0.57%
10-20	4.18	3.98
20-30	9.35	9.25
30-50	24.36	24.25
50-100	36.89	37.31
100-200	12.10	12.35
> 200	12.53	12.28
Total	100.0%	100.0%

income.) The results show that the overall distribution of taxes is not greatly affected by tax reform. Families with incomes of less than $30,000 and with incomes of greater than $200,000 experience reductions in tax burdens, while taxpayers with incomes between $30,000 and $200,000 experience increases.

If a consumption-based tax were enacted as part of an effort to close the fiscal gap, these distributional estimates would be modified somewhat. The degree to which they would be modified would depend upon (1) the absolute dollar size of the new tax and (2) its specific structure. Using the distribution under the Tax Reform Act as a base, Table 14-10 shows how the overall distribution would be affected under a $50 billion and $100 billion consumption-based tax (1986 income levels); for each revenue-raising alternative, two alternative tax bases are shown, one of which covers all consumption and one of which excludes food away from home, medical expenses, and shelter costs.

NOTES

1. France St-Hilaire and John Whalley, "A Microconsistent Equilibrium Data Set for Canada for Use in Tax Policy Analysis," *Review of Income and Wealth* (June 1983): 175-204.

2. James Davies, France St-Hilaire, and John Whalley, "Some Calculations of Lifetime Tax Incidence," *American Economic Review* (September 1984): 633-649.

Table 14–10.   Aggregate Distribution of the Federal Tax Burden with a Consumption-Based Tax, 1986 Income Levels (%).

Broad-Based Family Income	Total Tax Burden under Tax Reform Act	Total Tax Burden with			
		$50 Billion Consumption Tax		$100 Billion Consumption Tax	
		All Consumption	Excluding Basic Necessities	All Consumption	Excluding Basic Necessities
0–10	0.57%	1.02%	0.93%	1.40%	1.24%
10–20	3.98	4.58	4.49	5.11	4.94
20–30	9.25	9.58	9.56	9.87	9.82
30–50	24.25	24.45	24.50	24.63	24.72
50–100	37.31	36.69	36.78	36.14	36.31
100–200	12.35	11.98	12.01	11.65	11.71
> 200	12.28	11.70	11.74	11.19	11.26
Total	100.0%	100.0%	100.0%	100.0%	100.0%

Discussants:

CONSUMPTION TAXES ARE NOT REGRESSIVE

Ernest S. Christian, Jr.

My analysis may seem somewhat heretical compared to others in this book. Thomas Vasquez has done an excellent job in illustrating what is admittedly the traditional view of the burden of a so-called consumption tax—namely, that such a tax is fundamentally a tax on consumption that shows up in higher consumer prices and is, therefore, basically to be distributed in accordance with family-unit consumption levels. Ergo, so the mythology goes, such a tax is inherently regressive. Nevertheless, Dr. Vasquez points out that the traditional view has increasingly been challenged in recent years. In Chapter 14, he himself at one point correctly refers to a "consumption tax" as a tax on output, although he would apparently incorrectly allocate the entire burden to the output of labor instead of correctly allocating it proportionately to the output of labor and the output of capital.

I challenge the traditional view. I go even further. I challenge some of the basic implications and false assumptions traditionally associated with the topic we are presently discussing. First, we ought to be careful not inadvertently to perpetuate the idea that we are really talking about a tax *on* consumption as popularly understood. The mere use of the term *consumption tax* has unfortunate political connotations. Too often, it is of little utility to point out that the term means nothing more than some form of tax that allows a deduction for savings. Such a tax is distinguished from our present income tax primarily by the fact that our present income tax allows only limited deductions for savings. If Congress amended the present income tax to allow unlimited deductions for savings, the present income tax would be a "consumption tax" as that term is correctly used.

Second, we should *not* perpetuate the idea that there is some particular "regressivity" problem associated with any and every form of so-called consumption tax. Why should such a tax carry a burden of proof not imposed on other taxes? I am tempted to suggest an amendment to the Civil Rights Act to preclude, in the case of taxes, discrimination based on nomenclature or mechanical operation. Whenever I hear the allegation of regressivity, I always ask, "Compared to what?"

Third, we should *not* risk further confusing ourselves and others by implying that there is some broad generic category of consumption taxes all of which are the same and about which very many useful generalizations can be made.

We need to be specific about which form of consumption tax we are talking about. We also need to keep in mind that we now have, and probably will continue to have, a two-tier tax system. A consumption tax imposed on corporations may be quite another thing from a consumption tax for individuals. From the perspective of regressivity, we must also keep in mind that we already have income taxes, excise taxes, and payroll taxes. The question is, in part, whether some particular form of consumption tax is going to be substituted for one or more of these existing taxes.

Getting Down to Specifics—Query, Wherein Lies the Regressivity?

For this purpose, let us *not* use as our example a national sales tax, which tends to make the regressivity issue more difficult to understand. For much the same reason, let us also set aside the European-style invoice and credit VAT, the fascinating mechanics of which are probably the source of most of the wrong-headed thinking about so-called consumption taxes that presently exists in the United States.

Instead, let us think about some form of tax substantially similar to the Business Transfer Tax (BTT) introduced as S. 1102 by Senator William Roth in the 99th Congress. The BTT provides the most readily understandable framework for analysis of the regressivity question. As a practical matter, the BTT is also the most likely form of so-called consumption tax to be considered for enactment in the United States.

The BTT is a subtraction-method VAT, which will produce the same arithmetic result as the European-style VAT if you want to go through all that mechanical folderol.[1] The BTT is an annual tax imposed at the corporate level. In that respect, it is similar to the corporate income tax. The primary difference is that the BTT uses a value-added base and is, thus, proportionately a tax on the output of labor and the output of capital. The corporate income tax is primarily a tax on the output of capital. That difference is critical in other respects, but insofar as regressivity is concerned, it is hard to see how a $100 annual corporate tax called a BTT could have any more or less effect on consumer prices than a $100 annual corporate tax called an income tax. Remember, the supposed regressivity arises from the assumption that a tax imposed at the business level on value added will be passed on to consumers in the form of higher prices.

If, in the terms of the assigned topic, there is a "regressivity issue" with the BTT, why is not there precisely the same "regressivity issue" with the corporate income tax? Solely insofar as concerns regressivity from a pass-on in the price of consumer goods, there simply is *no* difference between a tax on output measured by income, and a comparably constructed tax on output measured by value added.

For example, would the regressivity issue with the BTT disappear if we merely made a few amendments to the corporate income tax and still called it an income tax? Purists might quibble, but the BTT's value-added base—essentially the net of receipts minus purchases—probably more accords with most people's commonsense definition of "income" than does the definition of income under the corporate income tax.

Further, for the sake of argument, let us assume that Dr. Vasquez is correct in distributing the tax to family units essentially on the basis of consumption expenditures, assuming a pass-on price effect. Why, then, did not the Congress and the Treasury distribute in the same way to the same family units, the $120 billion corporate income tax increase in the Tax Reform Act of 1986? They clearly did not. On the other hand, the Congress and the Treasury have made much of the "politically good" income class distribution of the individual income tax cuts proposed and essentially shaped the Tax Reform Act around the rubric of taking six million poor off the tax rolls, providing larger tax cuts for low- and middle-income families, and smaller tax cuts for the rich. This is not to say that the Congress and Treasury were right, and Dr. Vasquez is wrong. Rather, the fact simply is that had the Congress and the Treasury distributed their $120 billion corporate tax increase in accordance with family-unit consumption levels, their "politically good" income class distribution would have been destroyed. The poor would not have been taken off the "tax rolls," and lower and middle income families would not have the larger tax cuts. In fact, those families would probably have a tax increase under the Tax Reform Act of 1986.

If it strikes you that there is something funny going on here, then I have made my point. Either *both* the BTT and the corporate income tax should be distributed by income class, essentially in accordance with family-unit consumption patterns, or neither should be.

The Real Incidence Of The BTT and the Real Regressivity Issue: A Problem Readily Solved

The BTT is proportionately a tax on the output of labor and the output of capital.[2] Because, under the BTT, the corporation does not deduct the cost of direct labor purchased, the output of labor is taxed to the extent reflected in the firm's value added, but taxed only once. Because interest and dividend payments also are not deducted, the output value of capital services is also taxed, but taxed only once. The cost of machinery and equipment purchased from a third party is deducted, but only in order that its value not be taxed more than once—having in mind that the value of the machinery and equipment has already been included in the taxable base of the firm from which it was purchased. This simple little explanation is probably the least understood aspect of the BTT and its first cousin, the European-style VAT.

Now to regressivity. If there is any particular regressivity in the BTT, it is because the BTT is in part a tax on the output of labor similar to the payroll tax, both of which presumably reduce the return to labor. Some suggest that labor income tends to be concentrated in the low- and middle-income classes—hence, possible regressivity.

The cure for that potential regressivity is simple. Partially repeal the existing payroll tax or allow all or part of the BTT as a credit against the employer's share of the payroll tax.

Conclusion

My concluding exhortation is as you might expect. Beware the traditional wisdom! With so-called consumption taxes, all is not necessarily as it would appear. There are reasons, primarily related to international trade, to consider seriously enactment of a BTT or some other similar type of VAT in the United States. It will, however, be difficult for any serious consideration to occur unless and until we get beyond the political shibboleths, mythology and, in some cases, outright self-delusion traditionally associated with so-called consumption taxes.

NOTES

1. Thus, as a general proposition, all comments made herein with respect to a BTT are equally applicable to the European-style invoice and credit VAT.

2. There is necessarily substantial overlap between the discussions of the incidence of consumption taxes, following Chapter 12, and discussions of regressivity following Chapter 14. To the extent of that overlap, this discussion was prepared without the opportunity to review any of the discussions of incidence and, therefore, stands on its own with apologies for any redundancy.

THE POLITICAL DYNAMICS

Robert T. Matsui

From a substantive point of view I think a consumption (or value-added) tax or an excise tax makes very good sense. If you look at the possible ways to raise substantial revenues in the late 1980s, under the Tax Reform Act of 1986, you will find there will be very few options. A value-added or a consumption-type tax would be one way to be able to do that quickly without a lot of interest groups lobbying the Ways and Means Committee, Finance Committee, and various members of Congress on the floor of the Senate and the House of Representatives.

Tax policy has to be totally integrated into macroeconomic policy. It makes a lot of sense. Our pre-1986 tax code, although we moved away from it, did to a certain degree encourage consumption. It was not a code based on savings incentives. And a consumption-type tax, such as a Business Transfer Tax, in spite of what Ernest Christian suggests, would tend to dampen consumption somewhat.

And you couple that with the provisions of the Tax Reform Act of 1986, that is, the elimination of deductions for sales tax and the consumer interest, along with the fact that we retained the Individual Retirement Account (IRA) for those who make $40,000 and less, which allows the broad spectrum of the middle class to continue IRAs, then you see we are moving toward increasing the incentive to save and decreasing the incentive to consume. The low tax rates of the Tax Reform Act of 1986 should motivate Japan and our Western allies to reexamine their own tax systems. Perhaps they will then realize that we can deal with the trade balance somewhat by discouraging consumption and increasing savings in our country while our Japanese and European counterparts simultaneously increase consumption and decrease saving.

Income distribution, may not really be a problem from a substantive point of view. In fact, combining the exemptions of food, shelter, medical expenses, and perhaps education expenses, along with a refundable credit could even bring an element of progressivity to a consumption-based tax.

For example, a large refundable credit could be given to those in the lower income groups; the amount of the credit would decrease as income increased so that persons or families with a high level of income would be denied completely the refundable credit. In fact, this system can be used to redistribute some of the benefits of the consumption tax. And so the issue of regressivity is not a major issue from a substantive point of view.

The issue of progressivity and regressivity is of course, a major political problem and crucial to any decision regarding a consumption tax. In Chapter 2 House Ways and Means Committee Chairman Dan Rostenkowski talked about the issue of fairness as one major component of opposition to such a tax. And when you think of the phrase, "consumption tax" you think of it almost in the same terms of a corporate minimum tax.

In 1985 a resolution came up from the floor of the House of Representatives instructing the Ways and Means Committee to include a strong corporate minimum tax in the tax reform bill. As much as members on the committee tried to explain that we have to be very careful about a corporate minimum tax, that it isn't a catch-all or solve-all answer to the problem that some companies are avoiding their obligation to pay taxes, the resolution passed overwhelmingly. It was almost a stampede. And the same attitude will occur with respect to the perception that a consumption tax is a regressive tax. Frankly, it is quite possible that policymakers will not be able to overcome the perception that it is a regressive tax. That perception may be so firmly embedded as to be immutable.

Individual tax rates under the Tax Reform Act of 1986 will be 15 percent and 28 percent in 1988. If asked to impose a consumption tax, many members in both the House and the Senate would say that it would just compound the regressive aspects of the two-tiered rate structure. That major obstacle will have to be overcome, because many members in the Senate will attempt to increase the rates to restore the perception of progressivity in the tax system.

The original purpose of the recent tax reform was to make the system of taxation in the United States fairer and simpler. Eventually the purpose became to give the broad middle class a tax cut. That is the way that tax reform was sold, nationally and in our home districts, mainly because there has not been a great outcry for tax reform on the basis of simplicity and fairness.

Now, we have all calculated what the middle class is going to get under the Tax Reform Act of 1986. They are going to get some money back but not a lot of dollars. And as a result of that, in 1988, when members of the broad middle class begin paying their income taxes, they are going to be very unhappy. In fact, because of the delay phasing in those rate reductions, many people in the middle class will have a tax increase. And so people are going to be very offended and are going to say to their representatives in Congress, "You know, you sold us [on tax reform] on the basis that I was going to get a tax cut, and I was willing to give up my deductions and credits for that, but now I'm finding that my taxes have gone up and you misled me."

As you know, Washington doesn't have a good reputation for truth and honesty anyway, and this will compound that problem. To talk about a consumption tax on top of that will, in my opinion, create utter chaos out there in the grassroots.

One of the golden rules of the Ways and Means Committee is that if a group or an individual or a segment of society is to be taxed, it is better that they don't know about it. But, let me tell you, everybody is going to know about a consumption tax; it will get wide play, because obviously it is a new form of taxation. Many people whom we will have taken off the tax rolls, who will not have to file a return, *will* have to file a return to obtain refunds of a consumption tax and they are going to complain. They are going to complain a lot. So everybody will know about this form of taxation.

Obviously, state and local government will be very unhappy with this tax because as we are cutting back on the appropriations of state and local governments and cutting back on the entitlements to individuals. Therefore, state and local governments will have to pick up some of the slack. There is no question about it. And as a result of that, they will want to use a value-added, consumption, excise, or sales tax to get revenue to pay for these programs that we are cutting back at the federal level. The budget process would probably be an impediment to a consumption-type tax. In the spring of every year we must pass a budget resolution before the Ways and Means Committee or the Appropriations Committee pass their particular bills. To have a $50 billion tax increase in a budget resolution would be almost impossible to pass off the floor of the U.S. Senate because the conservatives will say "no" and the liberals will be suspicious because they expect it to be a regressive tax. It would be very difficult to get 218 votes off the floor of the House even before we could begin deliberating and discussing the whole issue of a consumption tax.

Now where do we go in view of that? It seems obvious, in light of what Rudolph Penner (Chapter 4) and others say in this book that a tax increase will be needed. Obviously, if there is a recession, any kind of revenue increase will be very difficult, especially a consumption tax that would raise a considerable sum of revenues.

If there is a tax increase during a recession, I envision it more like the kind of tax increase we had in 1982, which was a combination of a lot of hits on various segments of the economy and different industries. It is unlikely to be a big tax, because that could dampen the economy even further in the middle of a recession. We will also have to get over President Reagan's resistance to any kind of tax increase itself.

If in fact the economy holds to a 2–2.5 percent rate of growth until 1988, if in fact the deficit looms large (the CBO numbers are probably not accurate even though Congress uses them in the best of faith), the deficit at the end of this fiscal year will be $230 billion instead of the $170 billion it was projected to be. This is not because anyone juggled the numbers. It is just because there is so much uncertainty in the economy, both internationally and domestically.

But assuming that our deficits are large and we are not in a recession and we realize that a major significant tax increase is necessary and we don't want to cut entitlements or cut the defense budget further, I do see a rate increase and, at the same time, I do see the possibility of a consumption tax in spite of all these problems. But it is going to take time to educate the public. It is better to educate the public than the politicians, because the public will be the key to whether the politicians act on a consumption tax or not. Even if we the elected policymakers are convinced that such a tax is not regressive, that it is a commonsense type of tax, we are still going to go back home to face reelection every two or six years. So, if the perception back home is that it is an unfair, regressive tax, I can tell you that you will not get the lawmakers to pass such a tax.

✳️ *Chapter 15*

The Liberal Case for a Value-Added Tax

Robert Kuttner

From the perspective of the American Council for Capital Formation, a value-added tax (VAT) must seem a revenue-raiser preferable to other likely alternatives on the political horizon, such as an additional top bracket on the personal income tax or further curtailment of business preferences and increases in net corporate taxation. In the final round of tax reform, despite the supposed triumph of supply-side economics, Congress discovered a politically compelling variation of Russell Long's famous "Don't tax you, don't tax me, tax that fellow behind the tree." Congress cut individual taxes by raising corporate taxes, and all the $600 suits in Washington were no match for the plain electoral appeal of lower, simpler personal taxes. The fellow behind the tree was business.

As a political scientist, my own hunch is that businesses, as corporate taxpayers, did not resist this reform as fiercely as they might have, because most business leaders, as individual taxpayers, stood to benefit. This is a variation on the familiar contention that "corporations don't pay taxes; people do." In this case, people stood to gain, even if corporations stood to lose.

But when the tax increase does come, it is likely that investors, or corporations, or the wealthy, or all three, could feel the pinch. So business is prudent to fear that the next round of tax reform could well take the form of still higher taxes on capital, and to consider alternatives such as a VAT.

In this respect, I am a strange bedfellow. From my perspective, a VAT has other attractions. I would not mind at all if we restored effective corporate tax rates to their pre-1981 level; I would also like to see the 1987 top personal rate of 38.5 percent made permanent, because I think the principle of progressivity was excessively sacrificed in the 1986 tax reform legislation. Before the 1986 reform, affluent Americans could minimize their effective tax burden by means of a variety of convoluted shelters, many of them economically illogical. Now they can minimize their effective tax load far more straightforwardly.

Tax reform in 1986 was one giant step for efficiency but only a small step for equity. So I consider that while substantial, and even surprising progress has been made in reforming taxes, the job is not complete. Where I depart from many of my liberal friends is in viewing a value-added tax as a necessary part of that reform agenda.

ATTRACTIONS OF A VAT

A VAT is necessary, first, because conservatives are right that excessive marginal income tax rates are dangerous. As a matter of economics, a supply-sider might define an excessive marginal rate as 35 percent and I might define it as 65 percent, but we can both agree on the principle. However, where conservatives would emphasize the negative economic effects of high marginal rates, I would worry more about their impact on the political economy of taxation. What liberals ignored, to their peril, is that excessive marginal rates become politically catastrophic, particularly when marginal rates above 30 percent began reaching well down into the working middle class. By ignoring the effects of bracket creep, liberals seeded a tax revolt, and they deserved it. Now that we have traded base broadening for lower rates, it is reasonable to explore other revenue-raising measures. To have added new taxes to an unreformed income tax would have been unconscionable.

One sometimes hears the argument that a VAT is unwise because a VAT is an indirect, hidden tax. In this view, taxes should be as visible and as painful as possible, in order to reduce the public's willingness to tax itself. Moreover, it is also argued that a tax is a tax, and that if the tax wedge is what discourages productive investment, then what counts is the tax burden as a whole and not the form of the tax. But apart from ultimately unresolvable speculations about how high the total tax load must be before serious disincentive effects set in, this view flies in the face of long-standing tax theory, which recognizes the desirability of a diversified tax base. At the state and local level, we have long taxed income, property, and sales. If we attempted to load all of that tax burden onto a single source, it would distort business and consumption decisions, and it would exaggerate the perceived tax burden.

A VAT, as part of a three-legged tax stool, neatly dilutes the problem of high, visibly painful tax rates. Conservatives are not only right about marginal tax rates; they are also right to worry some about a VAT, because a VAT is indeed a terrific revenue raiser, and it usefully deprives conservatives of their best argument against high taxes—the supposed effect of taxation on incentive at the margin. I conceive of a VAT as a way for society to finance much of its social overhead—the various functions that society should provide in common, such as education, health, and other services which we ought to enjoy as citizens rather than consumers. It does not trouble me that a VAT is not highly redistributive on the revenue side of the ledger, because the services that it can help underwrite are redistributive in their incidence, and conducive to social solidarity.

The Europeans have won public tolerance of a larger, more effective public sector, in large part because they finance their social sector substantially with a VAT. If the modern state chooses to spend a substantial fraction of its national income collectively—whether that fraction is one-third as in the United States, or two-thirds as in Sweden—it is simply not practical to finance the bulk of that spending by means of very high marginal tax rates on personal income. Either the political outcry will be so great that the public will demand and get loopholes, which will defeat the principle of progressivity and inflict high marginal rates on the middle class, or an increasing fraction of economic activity will go underground. In the United States, the cycle of higher rates and bigger loopholes finally played itself out, and was reversed. At last we have a fairly broad tax base, and fairly low income tax rates. Now it is time to repair the rest of our system of public finance.

REBUILDING A PUBLIC SECTOR

A VAT probably offers the most plausible fiscal strategy for rebuilding a viable public sector, at a time when the huge deficit seems to preclude any additional public spending. The federal deficit must be, and will be, reduced. There are only two ways to cut the deficit—higher taxes or reduced spending. I happen to think that military spending ought to be cut, but even deep cuts in arms outlays will not, by themselves, reduce the deficit to a sustainable level of 2 or even 3 percent of gross national product.

I would not like to see domestic spending cut further. On the contrary, a good case can be made for substantial increases in some categories of spending, such as universal health insurance, education and retraining, and rebuilding of public infrastructure. A VAT is a sufficiently powerful revenue raiser that it can finance both a reduction in the deficit and an increase in spending.

REGRESSIVITY?

Most of my American liberal friends reject a VAT out of hand, because they learned somewhere back in Economics 101 that "consumption taxes are regressive." There are several rejoinders to that assumption. It is indeed true that a flat, universal consumption tax is regressive, for the well-known reason that the poor spend more of their total income than the rich. But there are several ways of counteracting that effect, which can make a VAT, on balance, moderately progressive.

One approach, which the Europeans have used with mixed success, is to tax different goods and services at differential rates. The European Common Market nations raised about $146 billion from VAT collections in 1984, or about 17 percent of their total revenues. For Europe as a whole, the typical VAT rate averages about 15-20 percent, but with the exception of Denmark, which exempts some commodities but taxes all others at a uniform rate, the pattern has been to tax different goods and services at different rates. In Italy, where there have been as many as nine separate VAT categories, the rate ranges from 2 percent on food to 38 percent on certain luxury items. Holland taxes food, public transportation, and medicine at 4 percent, and other consumption items at 18 percent. As a result, most studies have shown that the European VAT, in practice, tends to be mildly progressive with respect to consumption, but proportional or mildly regressive with respect to income.[1]

Another difficulty with taxing different products at different rates is that it further complicates a tax whose main liability is its basic complexity; and besides, the attempt to distinguish luxury spending from necessity spending by broad category of purchase is often misleading. Food, for example, is considered a necessity; most states exempt food from the sales tax, or tax it at a lower rate. However, spend a Saturday morning in Georgetown, and you will perceive that a great deal of food spending is luxury spending of a mouth-watering order. There is no practical way of taxing pâté and exempting Spam.

It is far more effective, if you desire a progressive VAT, to define a baseline income level at which all consumption is assumed to go for a minimally decent standard of living—say 110 percent of the poverty level. It is possible to "zero rate" all purchases, simply by refunding the VAT paid on that amount of necessities consumption. Under this approach, all domestically consumed goods and services would be subject to value-added tax, with medical care and education as the only major exempt categories. This would produce a taxable base of about $1.8 trillion, and gross tax receipts of $180 billion.

If there is universal VAT of 10 percent, and $12,000 is the floor income for a family of four, then a household with $12,000 income would simply receive an annual rebate of $1,200, paid, say, quarterly. At this level of household income, all of consumption would therefore be tax-free.

There would be a minor administrative problem of making sure that extremely poor people, a disproportionate fraction of whom lead disorganized and chaotic lives, would receive the tax rebate; otherwise, the very poorest among us would be the only ones paying a tax on food. This challenge is not unlike the challenge of making sure that food stamps are available to all who may need them. A small fraction of intended beneficiaries is likely to "fall between the cracks." The food stamp take-up rate is estimated at between 60 and 65 percent of eligible persons. The take-up rate of the federal earned income tax credit is substantially better.

As a better analogue to a progressive VAT, evidence from New Mexico, which uses a refundable tax credit to offset the regressive aspects of the state property and sales taxes, suggests that the vast majority of people who qualify for the tax credit in fact apply for it.

The New Mexico approach is probably the closest current U.S. counterpart of the proposed progressive VAT. The program, which is now in its fourteenth year, offers a refundable tax credit intended to offset the regressive aspects of other state taxes. Its top cash benefit is currently $375 a year, and the program costs the state upward of $12 million annually, or nearly 1 percent of state general revenues. According to New Mexico Assistant Secretary of Revenue James O'Neill, the program is extremely well known, and few people fail to apply for it. Last year, there were over 100,000 applications for refunds from people who would not otherwise have filed a state income tax.

The New Mexico comprehensive tax rebate program is restricted to moderate-income families. Under the proposed progressive VAT, middle-class families would also receive the same rebate, to give them the same tax-free consumption of their first $12,000 of purchases. The rebate would phase out for very well-to-do families, beginning at $100,000, to offset the tendency of the VAT to become extremely regressive at very high income levels, where most income is not consumed. That combination of total rebates for low-income households, partial rebates for most households, and a total income limit of, say, $100,000 to qualify for the rebate, could convert the VAT into an effectively progressive tax, for all but the wealthiest 2 or 3 percent of the income distribution.

ILLUSTRATION

Consider, for example, three families. The first family has an income of $20,000, and no savings. With a necessities credit of $12,000, only $8,000 of their expenditures would be taxed. Their tax would be $800 (10 percent of $8,000), and their effective tax rate as a fraction of all consumption would be 4 percent. The second family has an income of $60,000, and savings of $10,000. They would pay tax on consumption of $38,000 (the $50,000 that is consumed minus the $12,000 necessities credit, for a total tax of $3,800, and an effective tax rate of 6.33 percent. The third family, with income of $500,000, and consumption of $250,000, would pay a tax of 10 percent of $250,000, or $25,000. Expressed as a fraction of consumption, the tax rate is the full nominal rate of 10 percent. However, because of the family's substantial capacity to save, the VAT taxes only 5 percent of their income, so their tax rate is lower than that paid by the $60,000 income family.

For very high income families, the incidence of the VAT does indeed turn regressive, when the tax is expressed as a fraction of income. This, of course, can be remedied by enacting the VAT as part of a package that would include a top income tax bracket on families with incomes of over $100,000 a year. Here it is important to emphasize that a VAT should not be seen in isolation but as part of the overall tax system. If the VAT is an efficient revenue raiser but does propose regressivity problems at very high incomes, that need not be addressed by hobbling the VAT but can be solved with an income tax surcharge.

VAT VERSUS PROGRESSIVE EXPENDITURE TAX

In this respect, a VAT is far more acceptable than the other frequently advocated form of consumption tax—the "progressive expenditure tax," or "cash flow consumption tax," in which all income not consumed is exempted from taxation, and the rest taxed according to a graduated rate structure. An expenditure tax is usually advocated as a substitute for an income tax, while a VAT presumes that the income tax is retained as a tax on income. Since very wealthy people consume a substantially lower fraction of their income, there is no feasible means of making an expenditure tax effectively progressive without imposing very steep marginal rates. In fact, assuming that a person with $1 million per year of income saves half of that income, marginal rates of over 100 percent would be needed to make a cash-flow consumption tax even moderately progressive with respect to income. Since that is obviously not feasible, any such consumption tax must either abandon the principle of taxation according to ability to pay, or alternatively treat progressivity as a lifetime income question and therefore require confiscatory (and politically inconceivable) rates of taxation on estates and gifts. Such a tax would also present a thicket of transitional difficulties and complications involving international capital flows and harmonization with the tax systems of other nations.

A tax system that combines a VAT with a conventional income tax and exempts necessities consumption through refunds, solves these problems while retaining both relatively low marginal rates and the implicit savings incentives of consumption taxation. Although it is sometimes criticized as administratively complex, a VAT is marvel of simplicity compared to expenditure taxation.

Moreover, when one evaluates the regressivity of a tax, it is not enough to consider that tax in isolation. One must ask the question of the old "How's-your-wife" joke: Compared to what? A VAT, measured against some idealized, steeply progressive income tax, is not very progressive. But compared to the tax system as a whole that currently exists, it is not bad. If half of the proceeds from a VAT were used to replace a major portion of Social Security payroll taxes, or to finance Medicare, the net effect would be highly progressive, because almost any conceivable form of VAT is less regressive than the current payroll tax.

ALTERNATIVE USES OF A VAT

I would prefer a VAT that exempted only medical care, education, and certain public services like transportation. This would produce a taxable base of approximately $1,800 billion. A 10 percent VAT applied to that base would raise gross revenues of $180 billion, minus about $60 billion in rebates, or net new revenue of $120 billion.[2] This would have to be phased in over several years, to mitigate the inflationary impact on prices, and the simultaneously deflationary fiscal effect. The inflationary impact, of course, would be a one-time increase in the price level. If this were phased in over five years, it would add only two points to the consumer price index, minus the items not taxed.

The additional revenue could be used partly for deficit reduction, partly for new domestic spending, and partly to buy out a portion of the payroll tax. If $40 billion of the proceeds were used to reduce the payroll tax, the employee portion of the tax could be cut by about 30 percent. This could be done, progressively, by exempting the first $100 per week of earnings from the payroll tax, which would substantially improve the progressivity of the payroll tax as a whole. This is consistent with the original design of the Social Security system, which called for a portion of the system to be financed from general revenue.

I would prefer to see the remaining $80 billion in estimated new revenue divided between deficit reduction and new nondefense public spending. Others, undoubtedly, will argue that a share of the new revenue should go to carve out new tax preferences for capital formation. Still others will argue that the entire amount should go for deficit reduction, until the deficit is brought down to sustainable levels.

The debate is a useful one, and the decision, of course, will be the subject of intense political contention. But for someone who believes in a role for affirmative government, it is painfully clear that no such role will be enhanced until the deficit is substantially reduced by means of revenue increases.

VATs, SAVINGS, AND TAX REFORM

Unlike many of my liberal friends, I do believe that the United States suffers from a deficient savings rate. Consumption taxation can ameliorate that. But at the same time it is necessary to deal with other aspects of the tax code that continue to discourage savings. The 1986 provision eliminating the tax deductibility of most consumer interest is a big step in the right direction. The big remaining loophole is the tax treatment of housing, which continues to encourage people to overconsume housing and to use their home equity as a substitute for financial savings. One study of savings in different industrial nations, by the Organization for Economic Cooperation and Development found that "housing savings" in the United States, serves as a surrogate for household financial assets.[3]

By allowing tax deductibility of home equity loans and thereby inducing banks to market such loans, this remaining preference could actually stimulate consumer debt by introducing homeowners who had never considered equity loans to this potential line of substantial tax-favored credit. Needless to say, this remaining loophole is also regressive, since the homeowner who uses home equity to collateralize a tax-deductible automobile loan, on average, is in a higher income bracket than the renter who must pay interest on his automobile loan in after-tax dollars.

Although the nearly unlimited mortgage interest deduction is relatively less valuable in a reformed tax system with lower marginal rates, it is also relatively more valuable because there are now fewer other available ways to shelter income. As part of the next round of reform and the shift to consumption taxation to promote savings, the mortgage interest deduction should be capped, at the mortgage interest on an average-priced house (which is a variation on British tax policy). An alternative would restrict the deductibility of mortgage interest to the 15 percent tax rate (which is the approach taken in Sweden). Either approach would make the incidence of the mortgage interest deduction less regressive, and also raise additional revenues, for deficit reduction. It makes little sense to add a VAT with one hand, ostensibly to stimulate financial savings, while the other hand continues to beckon scarce capital into tax-sheltered housing. If we are serious about repealing the consumption bias in the tax code, reform must extend to housing. We can do that in a progressive way by retaining the tax favoritism for moderately priced housing.

POLITICAL CONSIDERATIONS

Liberals dislike a VAT, in part because the acceptance of a VAT seems to signal a further retreat from the principle of progressive income taxation. When I have advocated a progressive VAT, other liberals have responded that my brand of VAT, though technically feasible, is politically improbable. If I can find the votes for an acceptably progressive VAT, why don't I just use them to reform the income tax? Conversely, if there are not the votes for a truly progressive income tax, where will the votes be for a progressive VAT?

I think that analysis misreads the political reality. In the 1986 tax reform, there was a grand liberal-conservative compromise. Liberals got something they have pursued in vain since 1969: they broadened the base of taxation and eliminated many tax preferences that were both contrary to equity and contrary to efficiency. Conservatives got substantially lower tax rates. On balance, I think the 1986 legislation was a real gain for the liberal view and for economic efficiency. Who would have dreamed, in year 8 of the supply-side revolution and year 6 of the Reagan presidency, that corporate taxes would be raised substantially, that capital gains would come to be treated as ordinary income, and that most of the shelters added in the 1981 legislation in the name of capital formation would be restricted or eliminated? Yet the 1986 legislation, most conservatives would agree, promises a real gain for economic efficiency.

By the same token, a VAT could be a grand liberal-conservative entente. One can, and should, debate the fine details. As I have suggested, it is entirely feasible to design a VAT that is itself progressive at nearly all income levels, and to offset its regressivity at very high income levels, by other means. With that sort of VAT, conservatives would get a real incentive for financial savings, and a deflection of the impending tax increase away from business. Liberals would get the wherewithal to restore and expand public services, without stimulating a new taxpayer revolt, and without having to accept a regressive form of consumption tax. The public would get a form of tax that did not depress the incentive to increase earnings or savings, as well as the means to restore public services and reduce the crippling deficit.

As tax policy goes, that is a pretty good bargain.

NOTES

1. See Henry J. Aaron, *The VAT: Lessons from Europe* (Washington, D.C.: The Brookings Institution, 1981), and George N. Carlson, *Value-Added Tax, European Experience and Lessons for the United States* (Washington, D.C.: U.S. Treasury Office of Tax Analysis, 1980).

2. George Carlson's 1980 U.S. Treasury Office of Tax Analysis study, *Value Added Tax, European Experience and Lessons for the United States* estimated that a refundable credit based on a necessities expenditure of $2,000 per person would cost the Treasury an aggregate refund of $4.4 billion for each 1 percent of value added tax. I am proposing a more generous refund of about $3,000 per person. Thus, with a 10 percent VAT, the total rebate would be about $66 billion, less $5-6 billion saved from the phase-out for upper income households and from failures to apply for the rebate.

3. Peter Sturm and Derek Blades, "International Differences and Trend Changes in Savings Ratios," OECD, Paris, 1981.

 *Chapter 16*

A Political Strategy for a Consumption Tax

Kevin P. Phillips

The title of the preceding chapter, by Robert Kuttner, is "The Liberal Case for a Value-Added Tax." I am not going to offer the conservative case for a VAT, because I think we can be a good bit more ecumenical than that. But we have gotten off to a good start in that I suppose I will overlap what Bob Kuttner had to say by 50 or 60 percent. The differences are significant, but our overlap does suggest a framework.

Today's circumstances are leading toward a climate in which a viable consumption tax package can be put together. Public opinion is not necessarily hostile to the notion of a consumption tax, and could become amenable. Even the political climate could move in that same direction. The economic case, I think, is really very, very substantial.

House Ways and Means Committee Chairman Dan Rostenkowski and President Reagan are obviously, by their own statements, major obstacles to this type of legislative development (for the near term, at least). On the other hand, it is hard to take very seriously Dan Rostenkowski's comments about the Tax Reform Act of 1986 creating a level playing field. It does not. And what is more, the U.S. electorate did not seem to be any more enthusiastic, if I read the opinion polls correctly, than were the chief financial officers of U.S. multinational corporations. This is not a tax reform for the ages. Nor is it a glory train for its political architects. Finally, if it has some negative economic consequences, or if it just happens to tie in to a bad part of the business cycle, even its chief proponents could wind up looking at some alternative approaches and bail-out; and that could change the political climate.

Three circumstances ought to come together to give a lot of push to the idea of a consumption tax. The first, obviously, is the deficit. Dr. Rudolph Penner's (Chapter 4) discussion of the current services budget and the likelihood of the deficit declining to $100 billion or so by 1991 obviously was not the version in which Congressional Budget Office (CBO) assumes that there will be some kind of economic downturn between 1987 and 1991. If a downturn comes, according to that version, the current services forecast stays up in the $220–$280 billion range.

If you go back and look at the mis-estimates by Office of Management and Budget (OMB) and CBO since the mid-1970s, comparing the ultimate deficit with their earlier numbers in the budget resolutions and so forth, you see some appalling divergences. The most appalling came after the 1981 tax cut, when the revenue estimates just turned over and sank. Now, if we have anything resembling the same ability of the official forecasters, who, to the best of my knowledge, have never predicted one postwar recession (that is, never in the official data), in the event of an economic downturn, then the deficit and the need to have a high revenue raiser are really going to come front and center. This will be especially necessary if we are looking at $200 billion deficits in 1988 or 1989.

Will the Tax Reform Act of 1986 add to the deficit? There is a very good chance that it will aggravate things by fiscal 1988, particularly if the tax overhaul helps bring a recession that then damages the deficit reduction mechanism, invoking Gramm-Rudman suspension. I won't dwell on it, but we can come up with a 1 in 4 or 1 in 5 scenario that is a horror story, and a 1 in 3 that is just pretty unnerving.

The last ingredient in the way in which these forces may be converging to mandate consideration of the consumption-tax type of revenue approach is the trade crisis, which has been so underwhelmingly anticipated and handled by the Treasury Department, the White House, and the rest. They clearly have not been much good at forecasting, and their strategizing has not been too impressive either. There has been too much talk of "Morning Again in America" and too little recognition of the twilight in the trade statistics.

It is true that tax policy is not a solution for trade problems, but it is a partial corrective. And it is also probable at this point that currency alignments and trade law negotiations by themselves will not be able to bear more than a certain percentage of the corrective burden. There would be benefit in a tax system that moved toward taxing consumption more and capital formation less. There would be great benefit in reducing the deficit to take away pressure for higher interest rates and holding up the dollar. With less of a deficit and with rates easing, any dollar decline would be safer. Finally, and also important, there would be the border-neutral aspect of a consumption tax, the ability to rebate against exports and tax imports.

When Chairman Rostenkowski, I'm told, was asked about tax policy and trade, he said, "Well we've got the Democratic import surcharge." That, of course, is not exactly the most sophisticated way to approach fiscal remedies for trade policies.

In contrast, a consumption tax (especially some version of a business transfer tax (BTT) which is adjustable in terms of its foreign impact, its trade impact, by the extent of a FICA rebate or something like that) would yield better and safer leverage on the trade deficit.

So there are three pro-consumption tax dimensions: (1) budget deficit pressures, (2) the weakness of the 1986 tax reform and the possible need for new revenues to offset some revenue-losing changes in the tax code, and (3) the trade issue. It seems to me that convergence is really very substantial.

We probably will not be able to state the case definitively in 1987; we might be able to start doing so in 1988. That suggests something of the time frame. In Chapter 5, Canada's Finance Minister Michael H. Wilson explains how Canada is considering a BTT or a VAT, partially for border-neutral, trade-related reasons. There is some interest on the part of the Japanese; the electronics industries there is worried that the other East Asian countries that have trade-oriented tax systems are beginning to give them a problem. All of this can create a force that begins to affect the United States as soon as some of the people responsible for U.S. policy figure out that you can't do it all by realigning the dollar against the yen and the deutschmark and the franc and so forth.

Public opinion on a consumption tax is a highly relevant question. If you take the economic reasons behind such a step, the deficit question, the question of revenue alternatives to an income tax increase, and the trade question, you find that, lo and behold, the great American public, which is often so much smarter than the politicians and what George Wallace used to call the "pointed heads," is already giving it some thought.

Let me list the reasons the public sees for considering this type of tax. Basic support for a consumption tax, albeit described in different ways, does not go above 20 or 30 percent. That many people will pick it out of a list of revenue options. Linkage to reducing the deficit adds some strength.

Support rises to 35 or 40 percent with a reference to taxing imports, especially taxing imports as do Western European countries with VATs. The basic idea of taxing imports by itself, brings 60–70 percent support if it is a reasonably framed question.

Then there is the idea of using a sales tax, or some other consumption tax to avoid an income tax increase. A 50–55 percent majority prefers that option. So this starts to be a framework for public support. The idea of a consumption tax does not elicit across-the-board rejection. Not at all. There is not enthusiasm, but given the level of public awareness of the basic problems, the indications that the public will respond on these issues exist.

The business community is obviously fairly supportive. A joint poll of corporate government relations executives by *Business & Public Affairs Fortnightly* and the Public Affairs Council in spring 1986 surveyed their attitudes toward a consumption tax. Twenty-eight percent showed open support of a consumption tax and 42 percent said business ought to get a dialogue going. So we have about two-thirds either backing the idea or wanting a dialogue. If the dialogue develops around issues on which the public is sensitive and if the public shows interest in a consumption tax or at least tolerance of it, that dialogue will be a very useful thing. I think it will start changing politicians' opinions and intensifying public interest.

I first started looking at the 1986 tax reform process from the standpoint of public opinion, and whether it could bring a political realignment. There is a real question whether it is actually going to bring any real political benefits to the people who pushed it. It is fascinating to look at the emerging public opinion profile.

A Gallup-*Newsweek* poll in fall 1986 showed only 40–34 percent support of the 1986 Tax Reform Bill; 52 percent thought it was done too hastily. *U.S. News & World Report* asked people to choose between the tax code existing before passage of the 1986 legislation—the alleged zenith of unfairness—and the new "reform." Fifty percent chose the earlier tax code, and just 38 percent opted for the Packwood-Rostenkowski handiwork. Consumer pollster Albert Sindlinger in Pennsylvania ran questions on the tax reform bill; he told *Barron's* in September 1986 that it was a dud. He was more blunt in his own publications, writing, "It's poison for the politicians who are pushing it, because it's contributing to a confidence decline. Stock owners think it's going to penalize business, non-stock owners are worried about jobs and falling income." So the history of the Tax Reform Act of 1986 has not yet been written.

But the question is, What climate is it going to create in the near future? Are we going to be looking at a climate in which the Democrats are screaming, as Rostenkowski hinted, "Raise the rates, raise the rates?" Is the public going to be screaming for more progressivity? Well, I suppose it is possible. And if they are screaming, it complicates the idea of a consumption tax, even as it makes it even more important for the business community.

Now, let me look at the strategy very quickly, at what I think has to be knit together. First, the consumption tax must raise a fair amount of money. The public is not going to be interested in more confusing peripheral change; it must have some real dynamic. As to what it can do, it ought to reduce the deficit, restore some incentives in the tax code—that is the business side, whether investment tax credits, capital gains differential, whatever, changes in that dimension.

I think Robert Kuttner is absolutely right when he said that a consumption tax can be used to change the burden of the Federal Insurance Contributions Act (FICA), to keep it from going up and possibly to roll it back. Incidentally, Labor Secretary Bill Brock discussed just that issue before the Joint Economic Committee of Congress in summer 1986. He did not endorse it outright, but he said, "We've got to do something to spread the burden of taking care of the elderly, and a consumption tax could be a way to pick up part of the FICA burden." I'll come back later to the usefulness of interrelating FICA and a consumption tax from the standpoint of gathering support.

Obviously, a consumption tax must lend itself to the trade issue by being border-neutral—which is to say, it has to tax imports and rebate against exports, as do European value-added taxes. That means a VAT or a BTT. Forget a federal sales tax; that could be an interim measure, but it does not lend itself to border neutrality under the General Agreement on Tariffs and Trade. Maybe somebody could think of a way to solve that problem, but from what I have seen, it seems best to be thinking of more obviously usable consumption tax measures.

To come back to the FICA trade-off and the idea of centrist coalition building: Some of the things that you want to do with a consumption tax are deficit reduction, improvement of the tax code with some incentives, and avoidance of income tax rate increases if revenue demands intensify. But using it for deficit reduction also has some linkage to not cutting domestic programs. I wouldn't flat out say, "Let's restore the Great Society," and Bob Kuttner didn't say that either. But on the other hand, a consumption tax would take some of the pressure off domestic program cuts. That would be a plus for liberals and a minus for conservatives.

So the new tax should raise big money, and it must be a VAT or a BTT for trade reasons. It must be big money from the FICA standpoint, too. First, it should pick up part of the FICA burden, which provides a big boost by creating support among organized labor and the young. It also should get rid of part of the regressivity argument, because partial substitution for FICA or substitution for a FICA increase means taking away a regressive tax and substituting something that is broader based.

In a BTT, the level at which it is rebated against FICA can be used to vary the effect the tax has on domestic versus foreign industry. Senator Bob Packwood, in an interview with *U.S. News & World Report* in November 1985, actually discussed the potential usefulness of a consumption tax with a heavy FICA rebatability aspect that would weigh 80 or 85 percent on foreign corporations. Obviously the more you maximize rebatability in the United States, the larger the percentage of the burden borne by imports. That is a little too raw, but the FICA tie-in has a lot of flexibility in that way.

As for regressivity, I think Ernest Christian's argument that the BTT essentially avoids that problem is quite an important one. A business transfer tax that does not apply at the retail level is not going to offend the consumers very much. It sidesteps the tough arguments and its image is easier to sell. A VAT, by contrast, is applied at the consumer level, generating the tougher regressivity argument and the political problem of the partial dislocation of state sales taxes. A BTT would not really do that.

CONCLUSIONS

There is a way to knit together these three ingredients and maneuver the substance and content to relate to public opinion best. A BTT is probably better than a VAT, and the refundability administrative problems underscore it. We are not likely to see any real debate until 1988 when pressures will converge and Chairman Rostenkowski and President Reagan will be heading off for retirement. At that point the political climate becomes more conducive.

But before we get a discussion going in time for the 1988 elections, we need serious backstage discussions in Washington. I think every interest group concerned, every business organization, every lobby, ought to start internal dialogues on this, ought to start seeing what works, and what does not. Let's get it out on the table. Let's get the public's reaction, the politicians' reaction, before some last-minute situation develops where everybody is running around like a chicken with its head cut off, wondering, "Gee, what is this? What's it going to be?"

The time to act is before the crisis is at hand, and the time to start thinking about it is now.

Discussant:

THE POLITICAL CONTEXT

Stephen E. Bell

It has been true for two centuries in this country that it is always easier to cut taxes than it is to cut spending. We really have proved that true in the last five or six years. That is the context in which I think any strategy ought to be developed.

Robert Kuttner says in Chapter 15 that we can develop a value-added tax (VAT) that in fact solves the progressivity problem, at least as far as it is perceived politically. I don't think most Americans in Oshkosh, Wisconsin, and Albuquerque, New Mexico, care much about progressivity; they don't think they would get an even break from *any* kind of tax code.

Kevin Phillips says in Chapter 16 that there is a strategy that can be put together by tying this kind of VAT or a business transfer tax (and I agree absolutely with what he said concerning a BTT) to other things that the United States may want. America may want to be more, shall we say, aggressive in its trade policy. And it would be nice if we had a policy with which to be aggressive.

I come to the political context of a consumption tax from a somewhat more cynical point of view, given all the scar tissue I accumulated trying to cut public spending while I worked on the Senate Budget Committee. We in Congress have not cut spending very well. We managed, during 1985 and 1986, to cut defense. And, for the first time probably in two decades, an American Congress will preside over two consecutive years, not of flat defense growth, but of declining defense growth. So we have taken care of defense; the effects will start showing up by 1990.

About 80 percent of the budget is for things over which we have fought for the last 25 years: Social Security, Medicare, disability insurance, payment on the interest of public debt, and, of course,

This discussant refers to Chapters 15 and 16.

defense. That short little list of government services is almost 80 percent of the budget.

We have managed to just about freeze the remainder of the budget. To a conservative, that may be a little bit shortsighted; to a liberal, it may be a little bit of a nightmare. To me, a pragmatist, it is stupid.

We are mortgaging the future for the present. We are now encouraging consumption, whether it is Social Security, or other kinds of entitlements, or price supports for farmers.

How does a consumption tax fit in with what I perceive to be a change in American attitude? I think we are getting beyond a simple Marxist kind of determinism where we think that our economic statistics reflect the true measure of a country. I think we are moving in a new direction. We saw farmer-to-farmer aid during the drought of 1986. We see a tremendous concern about drugs. We see a very interesting kind of development in Texas where student athletes are being told, "If you don't pass, you can't play football." I'm from Texas and I can tell you that is a radical proposition.

I have a feeling something else is emerging in the second half of the 1980s. America is going to make a decision whether it wants to be known as a rich country or a good country. The only explanation I have for why Mario Cuomo continued to do well in polls of the Democratic party (while he was considering whether to run for president) is that he says, "I believe something. I may be wrong, I may be arrogant, but I believe something. And I think we ought to do A, B, and C."

A pragmatist will agree to a BTT, for two reasons. First, we need to start spending money in this country in those areas where it is most intelligent and most prudent—that is, in the areas that have been neglected since 1980. I already know this from firsthand experience.

I have already tried to solve the Social Security problem politically, so we raised taxes for it; we did not do anything else. I have already tried to make some really fundamental changes like means-testing Medicare, another great idea that went exactly one step backward. I think the decisions about these entitlement programs probably have been made, at least for the rest of this decade. If we want to continue to fulfill those commitments, and if the politicians want to be able to go home and say to their constituents, "I'm doing something to make America a good and strong country again," then they are going to have to have some way to pay for it.

If Rudolph Penner is right and deficits are going to get better as the Congressional Budget Office (CBO) baseline projections are telling us (see Chapter 4), then I think consumption tax is dead. And if he is wrong and the economy goes to hell in a handbasket, then I think consumption tax is dead. It seems that I have set up a situation where it's either dead or it's dead.

But, in fact, I think that is not the only outcome. If we get away from the notion that it is only the economic viability of America and all these funny numbers that are coming out every month from the Commerce Department that dictate everything, maybe we will find a way to have a consumption tax. To persuade voters to support a BTT, they must be told, "If you want to invest in education, if you want to invest in agriculture, if you want to repair what is obviously a decaying infrastructure in this country, then you are going to want to pay for it." It is obvious no one will want to cut any more in the 73 to 80 percent of the budget I described earlier.

I think a BTT is a possibility if members of Congress tell their constituents, "Yes, we are going to raise taxes through a business transfer tax, but we are going to use those taxes both to reduce the debt and to make this a better country," however you want to define that.

Regressivity is a nice thing for economists to talk about, it is an interesting thing, and it is an important thing, probably. I don't know how progressive or regressive the tax system is now and some very, very bright people (much brighter than I will ever be) have told me exactly opposite things over the last two or three years.

If U.S. policymakers tell the American public, "We are going to be able to go to Boise, Idaho, and repair that dam if we have a little bit more money," or "We are going to be able to construct and launch a fourth Orbiter, if we had the money," and "We may be able to crack down on drugs, if we have the money, and here is a way to raise the money that won't hurt poor families to any great degree," then I think you can put together a strategy that will sell. And that seems to me the only way to put it together.

If you just talk about who in this country is going to get the benefit from a tax cut, when none of us knows, or is this good only for rich Americans, it continues that some old war that we have fought since the 1960s. Then, I certainly would agree we are fighting the last war, and a BTT will lose. Just making sure our tanks are in working order, making sure the Maginot Line is in working order, that we have a lot of mustard gas masks is wrong, because I don't think that is the war we are going to fight any more. We are seeing a new America emerge. Maybe it's the maturing of the "Me Generation," but, I think we are going to want more social services. And I say, as a pragmatist, "How do we pay for it?" I don't think we will continue to borrow and borrow. I think a strategy would incorporate the following:

1. Satisfy the notion of progressivity through a business transfer tax or value-added tax.

2. Very important is to take the notion of our trade competitiveness, and say, "We can solve that or at least set the stage for beginning to solve that with a BTT."

3. Just as important is to promise that we will do the things that most Americans want us to do. We'll start investing money in those areas where we have not been investing. And who knows, we may even get the gumption to make some changes in some of the broad-based income support programs in this country in which we have not had the courage to make changes before.

It seems to me a simple strategy like that can win and may be the only strategy that can win. Certainly, trying to fight on the basis of "The deficit is this; tax as a proportion of GNP is that," as we've done for so many years now would seem to guarantee the same old result. So I don't think Ways and Means Chairman Rostenkowski is right that we ought to soak the rich and corporations and increase marginal taxation. I notice that no other country in the world seems to be going in that direction. I suspect the American people don't think he is right. If we know where the voters are, I suspect over time we may be able to get the votes needed to support change.

There is only one way to get the votes. We need to appeal to this emerging notion of Americans helping Americans; Americans investing in things they care about, in the basics like education and highways. It is obvious we are not going to cut spending anymore. So, as I have said for all these years with no good result really, we need to figure out how we are going to raise taxes. The BTT seems the best way.

✳

Index

About the Editors

Charls E. Walker is voluntary chairman of the American Council for Capital Formation and its education and research affiliate, the American Council for Capital Formation Center for Policy Research. Dr. Walker is the chairman of Charls E. Walker Associates, Inc., a Washington-based consulting firm. He served as deputy secretary of the Treasury from 1968 to 1972 and assistant and principal adviser to the secretary of the Treasury from 1959 to 1961. He holds the Alexander Hamilton Award, the highest honor granted by the Treasury Department. Dr. Walker is co-editor of *New Directions in Federal Tax Policy for the 1980s* (Cambridge, Mass.: Ballinger Publishing Company, 1983), the collection of papers prepared for a conference sponsored by the American Council for Capital Formation Center for Policy Research.

Mark A. Bloomfield is president of the American Council for Capital Formation and its education and research affiliate, the American Council for Capital Formation Center for Policy Research. Mr. Bloomfield served as secretary of President-elect Reagan's Task Force on Tax Policy for the first Reagan administration. Mr. Bloomfield lectures and writes on tax policy, economics, and politics. He is the co-editor of *New Directions in Federal Tax Policy for the 1980s* (Cambridge, Mass.: Ballinger Publishing Company, 1983), and a contributor to *The Value-Added Tax: Key to Deficit Reduction?* (Washington, D.C.: American Enterprise Institute, 1987).

The American Council for Capital Formation Center for Policy Research (CPR) was established in 1977 as the research and education affiliate of the advocacy-oriented American Council for Capital Formation. The CPR's mandate is to promote an understanding by the public, policymakers, and opinion shapers of the importance of capital formation to the economy. To achieve its objective, the CPR sponsors original research on the determinants of savings, investment, and economic growth; underwrites conferences and seminars on tax, budget, and international competitiveness issues; and assists in the development of alternative economic policies conducive to economic growth. In September 1986, the American Council for Capital Formation Center for Policy Research sponsored a conference; *The Consumption Tax; A Better Alternative?* is a collection of the papers prepared for the symposium.

The American Council for Capital Formation Center for Policy Research is a Washington, D.C.-based nonprofit tax-exempt organization under section 501(3)(c) of the Internal Revenue Code. It is funded by tax deductible contributions from corporations, trade associations, foundations, and individuals.

✳

List of Participants

Henry J. Aaron is a senior fellow at the Brookings Institution and professor of economics at the University of Maryland. Dr. Aaron served as assistant secretary (planning and evaluation) of the Department of Health, Education, and Welfare from 1977 to 1978. He was a senior staff economist for the Council of Economic Advisers from 1966 to 1967. He contributed to *New Directions in Federal Tax Policy for the 1980s*.

Harvey E. Bale, Jr. is the assistant U.S. trade representative for trade policy and analysis. He has served in several positions in the Office of the U.S. Trade Representative for the past 10 years, including assistant U.S. trade representative for international investment policy, U.S. trade representative chief economist, and deputy assistant U.S. trade representative for policy development.

J. Gregory Ballentine is a principal and national director for tax analysis at the accounting firm of Peat, Marwick, Mitchell & Company. Dr. Ballentine served as deputy assistant secretary (tax analysis) of the Treasury Department from 1981 to 1983. He was associate director (economic policy) at the U.S. Office of Management and Budget from 1983 to 1984. He contributed to *New Directions in Federal Tax Policy for the 1980s*. He is a member of the board of directors of the American Council for Capital Formation Center for Policy Research.

Max Baucus (D-MT) serves on the Senate Finance Committee, the Senate Environment and Public Works Committee, and the Senate Small Business Committee. Senator Baucus is a leading congressional spokesman on international competitiveness; in testimony before the International Trade Commission in 1986, he said, "We've argued about who gets which tax break, without considering the impact tax reform will have on the overall competitiveness of the American economy." After two terms in the U.S. House of Representatives, Senator Baucus is now serving his second term representing the state of Montana.

Stephen E. Bell is a vice president and manager of the Washington, D.C. office of Salomon Brothers Inc., the New York investment banking firm. Mr. Bell opened the Washington office in March of 1986. He served as chief of staff of the Senate Committee on Budget under Chairman Pete V. Domenici from 1981 to 1986. Mr. Bell also served as a staff member of the Senate Committee on Budget and as the news secretary and executive assistant on Senator Domenici's personal staff from 1972 to 1979.

David F. Bradford is a professor of economics and public affairs and also the associate dean of the Woodrow Wilson School of Public and International Affairs at Princeton University. Dr. Bradford served as deputy assistant secretary (tax analysis) of the Treasury Department from 1975 to 1976. He received the U.S. Treasury Department Exceptional Service Award in 1976. Dr. Bradford is a research associate and the director of research in taxation of the National Bureau of Economic Research and an associate editor of the *Journal of Public Economics*. He contributed to *New Directions in Federal Tax Policy for the 1980s*.

George N. Carlson is director, economics of taxation, in the Office of Federal Tax Services at Arthur Andersen and Company. Dr. Carlson served as director, Office of Tax Analysis, of the Treasury Department from 1984 to 1986.

Milka Casanegra de Jantscher is chief of the tax administration division in the fiscal affairs department of the International Monetary Fund. Mrs. Casanegra de Jantscher served as assistant commissioner for planning and research in the Internal Revenue Service of Chile from 1966 to 1972. She has also been a consultant to the United Nations and the Inter-American Development Bank.

Ernest S. Christian, Jr. is a partner in the Washington law firm of Patton, Boggs & Blow. Mr. Christian served as deputy assistant secretary (tax policy) and tax legislative counsel of the Treasury Department during the Ford Administration. He is a member of the board of directors of the American Council for Capital Formation and the American Council for Capital Formation Center for Policy Research.

Edwin S. Cohen is a partner in the Washington law firm of Covington & Burling. Mr. Cohen is also the Joseph M. Hartfield Professor of Law at the University of Virginia. He served as under secretary of the Treasury Department from 1972 to 1973 and assistant secretary (tax policy) of the Treasury Department from 1969 to 1972. He contributed to *New Directions in Federal Tax Policy for the 1980s.*

Dave Durenberger (R-MN) is a member of the Senate Finance Committee and chairman of its Health Subcommittee. Senator Durenberger is chairman of the Senate Select Committee on Intelligence. He serves on the Senate Committee on Governmental Affairs and the Senate Committee on Environment and Public Works. Senator Durenberger is also a member of the National Republican Senatorial Committee. The *Washington Post* called Senator Durenberger one of "the best-informed and most independent-minded players in the Washington policy game." He is serving his second term representing the state of Minnesota.

Ronnie G. Flippo (D-AL) is a member of the House Ways and Means Committee and its Select Revenue and Oversight Subcommittees. Representative Flippo is also a certified public accountant. He is the first member from Alabama to serve on the Ways and Means Committee in nearly 70 years. Representative Flippo is serving his fifth term representing Alabama's fifth district. The district includes the seven northernmost counties.

Henry H. Fowler served as secretary of the Treasury under President Johnson. Mr. Fowler is co-chairman of the Committee on the Present Danger, the Committee to Fight Inflation, the Bretton Woods Committee, and the Fowler-McCracken Commission. He was a general partner of Goldman Sachs and Company from 1969 to 1980 and was chairman of Goldman Sachs International Corporation from 1969 to 1984. During Mr. Fowler's distinguished career in public service he also served as under secretary of the Treasury from 1961 to 1964 in several defense-related government positions during the Korean War, and as economic adviser to the U.S. Mission for Economic Affairs in London during World War II.

Bill Gradison (R-OH) is a member of the House Budget and House Ways and Means Committees. Political columnist David Broder said that Representative Gradison "has inherited from retired Rep. Barber B. Conable Jr. (R-NY) the role of spokesman for orthodox conservatism on the Budget and Ways and Means Committees." He is serving his sixth term in Congress and represents the second district of Ohio. The district includes the east side of Cincinnati and its eastern Hamilton County suburbs.

Gary Hufbauer is the Marcus Wallenberg Professor of International Financial Diplomacy in the School of Foreign Service and Department of Economics at Georgetown University. At the Treasury Department, Dr. Hufbauer served as deputy assistant secretary (international trade and investment policy) from 1977 to 1980 and director of the International Tax Staff from 1974 to 1976. He contributed to *New Directions in Federal Tax Policy for the 1980s*.

Robert Kuttner is the economics correspondent of the *New Republic* and one of four contributing columnists to *Business Week's* "Economic Watch." He frequently writes for other publications, including the *Atlantic Monthly*, the *Boston Globe*, *Dissent*, the *Harvard Business Review*, *Mother Jones*, the *Washington Journalism Review*, and the *Washington Post*. Mr. Kuttner has received the Jack London Award for labor journalism. His most recent book, *The Economic Illusion*, which challenges the view that economic growth must come at the expense of economic equity, was nominated for a National Critics Circle Award.

Bruce K. MacLaury is the president of the Brookings Institution. Dr. MacLaury is a member of the board of trustees of the Joint Council on Economic Education and the Committee for Economic Development. He is a director of the Dayton Hudson Corporation, American Express Bank, Ltd., and the Salzburg Seminar. Dr. MacLaury served as deputy undersecretary (monetary affairs) of the Treasury Department from 1969 to 1971 and president of the Federal Reserve Bank of Minneapolis from 1971 to 1977.

John H. Makin is the director of fiscal policy studies at the American Enterprise Institute. He is on leave from the University of Washington, where he is professor of economics. A former consultant to the International Monetary Fund, the U.S. Treasury Department, and the Federal Reserve System, Dr. Makin's most recent book is *The Global Debt Crisis: America's Growing Involvement.* He is also a frequent contributor to *Business Week,* the *New York Times,* the *Wall Street Journal,* and the *Washington Post.*

Robert T. Matsui (D-CA) is a member of the House Ways and Means Committee and its Select Revenue Measures and Public Assistance and Unemployment Subcommittees. Representative Matsui is also a member of the House Select Committee on Narcotics Abuse and Control. Characterized as a "sober-minded legislator" by *Congressional Quarterly,* he is serving his fourth term in Congress and represents the third district of California. The district includes the state Capitol, downtown Sacramento, and its affluent suburbs.

Charles E. McLure, Jr. is a senior fellow at the Hoover Institution at Stanford University. He served as deputy assistant secretary (tax analysis) of the Treasury Department from 1983 to 1985. While in that position Dr. McLure had primary responsibility for the development of "Treasury I," the report to President Reagan on fundamental tax reform. He is author of a new book, *The Value Added Tax: Key to Deficit Reduction?* and contributed to *New Directions in Federal Tax Policy for the 1980s.*

Charles W. Parry is the chairman of the board and chief executive officer of the Aluminum Company of America (Alcoa). He also is a director of Alcoa. Mr. Parry is a director of several corporations and trustee of various civic and educational organizations. He has served as chairman of the Aluminum Association; director of the First Interstate Bancorp and Nalco Chemical Company; and trustee of the American Enterprise Institute, the Conference Board, and the Tax Foundation. Mr. Parry has also been active in the Brookings Council, the Business Committee for the Arts, and the Business Roundtable. His service to community and educational organizations includes trusteeship of Carnegie-Mellon University and Carlow College and presidency of the Pittsburgh Opera.

Joseph A. Pechman is a senior fellow in economic studies at the Brookings Institution. Dr. Pechman was director of the economic studies program at the Brookings Institution from 1962 to 1983. He served as an economist with the Committee for Economic Development from 1956 to 1960 and with the Council of Economic Advisers from 1954 to 1956. Dr. Pechman has published numerous books and articles on the federal tax system, income distribution, Social Security, and welfare reform.

Rudolph G. Penner is the director of the Congressional Budget Office. Dr. Penner was director of fiscal policy studies and a resident scholar at the American Enterprise Institute for Public Policy Research from 1977 to 1983. He has also served as assistant director (economic policy) of the Office of Management and Budget, deputy assistant secretary (economic affairs) of the Department of Housing and Urban Development, and a senior staff economist to the Council of Economic Advisers during the Nixon and Ford administrations.

Kevin P. Phillips is the president of the American Political Research Corporation and editor-publisher of the *American Political Report* and *Business and Public Affairs Fortnightly*. Mr. Phillips is a contributing columnist for the *Christian Science Monitor*; a regular contributor to the *Los Angeles Times, New York Times*, and *Washington Post*; a member of the political strategists' panel of the *Wall Street Journal*; a commentator for National Public Radio and CBS Network Radio; and an elections commentator for CBS Television News. In 1968 he served as chief political and voting patterns analyst for the Republican presidential campaign.

Joel L. Prakken is the vice president and director of model development of Laurence H. Meyer and Associates, an economic forecasting firm. In 1965 and 1986, Dr. Prakken testified frequently before congressional committees on the economic impact of the various tax reform proposals. He also teaches at Washington University in St. Louis.

Dan Rostenkowski (D-IL) is the chairman of the House Committee on Ways and Means. Chairman Rostenkowski is one of the principal architects of the Tax Reform Act of 1986. The *Wall Street Journal*, describing his leadership on the House-passed tax reform bill, said, "with a political acumen admired by even his detractors, he shaped a package and built a coalition to back it that, against all odds, became an irresistible force in the House." After passage of what was the most comprehensive tax bill ever, Chairman Rostenkowski was named "the most effective legislative leader in Congress" by 79 percent of House and Senate staffers polled. Chairman Rostenkowski is serving his 14th term in Congress representing the eighth district of Illinois. The district includes the northwest side of Chicago and nearby suburbs.

Dick Schulze (R-PA) is a member of the House Ways and Means Committee and its Oversight and Trade Subcommittees. Representative Schulze is a leading congressional proponent of a business transfer tax. He is the chairman of the Republican Study Committee, the largest ad hoc group of Republicans in the House of Representatives. Representative Schulze is serving his sixth term in Congress representing the fifth district of Pennsylvania. The district includes part of Chester, Delaware, and Montgomery counties in the southeastern corner of the state.

John B. Shoven is a professor of economics at Stanford University. Dr. Shoven has served as a consultant to the Council of Economic Advisers, World Bank, Board of Governors of the Federal Reserve, and Departments of Labor and the Treasury. He is a senior adviser to the Brookings Institution and associate editor of *Public Finance Quarterly* and the *Journal of Public Economics.* Dr. Shoven is also a member of the board of directors of the American Council for Capital Formation Center for Policy Research.

J.A. Stockfisch is a senior economist for the Rand Corporation. Dr. Stockfisch served as deputy assistant secretary (tax analysis) and director of the Office of Tax Analysis of the Treasury Department from 1961 to 1963. He has taught at Virginia Polytechnic Institute, the University of California at Los Angeles, and the University of Wisconsin.

Lawrence H. Summers is a professor of economics at Harvard University. Dr. Summers served as a domestic policy economist at the Council of Economic Advisers from 1982 to 1983. He is a research associate for the National Bureau of Economic Research, a member of the Brookings Panel on Economic Activity and serves on the National Science Foundation Economics Panel. Dr. Summers contributed to *New Directions in Federal Tax Policy for the 1980s.* He is a member of the board of directors of the American Council for Capital Formation Center for Policy Research.

Thomas E. Vasquez is the president of Policy Economics Group, a Washington, D.C. economic forecasting firm. In the Office of Tax Analysis of the Treasury Department Dr. Vasquez served as the deputy director from 1981 to 1983, the assistant director from 1977 to 1981, and a fiscal economist from 1972 to 1976.

George F. Will is an author, columnist, and commentator. Mr. Will writes a syndicated column for the *Washington Post*, that now appears in over 460 newspapers. He won a Pulitzer Prize for commentary in 1977. Mr. Will was a regular panelist on "Agronsky and Company" from 1977 to 1984. In 1981 he became a founding member of the panel of ABC's "This Week with David Brinkley." Since 1984 he has been an occasional editorial commentator for ABC's "World News Tonight."

Michael H. Wilson is the minister of finance for Canada. Mr. Wilson was first elected to Canada's House of Commons in 1979 and was appointed minister of state for international trade in the same year. He was reelected in 1980 and subsequently served as the Progressive Conservative Party spokesman for a number of portfolios including industry, trade and commerce; energy; finance; and regional industrial expansion. Mr. Wilson was executive vice president of Dominion Securities, a Canadian investment firm, prior to his election to Parliament.